SACRED
VIOLENCE

SACRED VIOLENCE

THE EUROPEAN CRUSADES TO THE MIDDLE EAST, 1095–1396

JILL N. CLASTER

UTP

University of Toronto Press

Copyright © 2009 Jill N. Claster

www.utphighereducation.com

LIBRARY AND ARCHIVES CANADA CATALOGUING IN PUBLICATION

Claster, Jill N.
Sacred violence : the European crusades to the Middle East, 1095–1396 / Jill N. Claster.
Includes bibliographical references and index.

ISBN 978-1-4426-0058-4 (bound). — ISBN 978-1-4426-0060-7 (pbk.)

1. Crusades. 2. Jerusalem — History — Latin Kingdom, 1099–1244. I. Title.

D157.C53 2009   909.07   C2009-904756-X

We welcome comments and suggestions regarding any aspect of our publications — please feel free to
contact us at news@utphighereducation.com or visit our internet site at www.utphighereducation.com.

North America
5201 Dufferin Street
Toronto, Ontario, Canada, M3H 5T8

2250 Military Road
Tonawanda, New York, USA, 14150
ORDERS PHONE: 1-800-565-9523
ORDERS FAX: 1-800-221-9985
ORDERS EMAIL: utpbooks@utpress.utoronto.ca

UK, Ireland, and continental Europe
NBN International
Estover Road, Plymouth, PL6 7PY, UK
TEL: 44 (0) 1752 202301
FAX ORDER LINE: 44 (0) 1752 202333
enquiries@nbninternational.com

The University of Toronto Press acknowledges the financial support for its publishing activities of the
Government of Canada through the Book Publishing Industry Development Program (BPIDP).

Designed by Daiva Villa, Chris Rowat Design.

Printed in Canada

For my husband, Will, who shared this journey.
And, as always, in memory of my beloved daughter
Elizabeth.

Contents

Illustrations

Black-and-white photographs

Color plates

Maps

Acknowledgments

The inspiration for *Sacred Violence* came from my students in The History of the Crusades and Their Legacy, a freshman honors seminar at New York University that I began teaching in 2003. The thoughtful questions they asked, the areas they craved to know more about, and their unwavering enthusiasm for the subject helped me, unbeknown to them, shape this book. As I wrote, I had these students always in mind. Although I remember with affection each and every one of them, regrettably, they are far too many to name here. My heartfelt thank-you to all of them. They will know who they are.

I am immensely blessed that two wonderful friends gave generously and lovingly of their time and expertise to read — many times to reread — every page of the manuscript at every stage: Marilyn Nissenson, author and editor par excellence, and acclaimed medievalist and Chaucer scholar Robert R. Raymo, Professor Emeritus of Medieval English Literature at New York University. Their astute, educated, and thoughtful suggestions, always gently given, and their unwavering faith in this project have, quite simply, made all the difference. There are not words adequate to express my gratitude to them. Sadly Robert Raymo died on July 16, 2009. This book, like my life, has been enhanced by his friendship and his support. He will be greatly missed.

I have always believed that special people do special things, and the people who provided much-needed and valuable help along the way have reaffirmed my faith. I am happy to thank them and to acknowledge them here. Professor Kathryn Ann Smith of the NYU Fine Arts Department took precious time from her own writing to lend her expertise in medieval manuscript illumination to the project. Her vast knowledge was always cheerfully shared. My book has benefited from the unique intelligence of my longtime dear friend and colleague F. E. Peters, Professor Emeritus of Middle Eastern and Islamic Studies at NYU. His sound advice was imparted with his usual acumen and humor.

I had the good fortune to have worked with numerous gifted graduate students, many now close friends. Among them is Paulina Koryakin, whose talent for organization and knowledge of the subject were invaluable as I planned the book. She stayed by my side throughout the work, and I am deeply grateful for her support. Wendy Schor-Haim offered important insights and comments as I formulated my ideas for the book, and Katherine Allen Smith, Assistant Professor of History at the University of Puget Sound, offered excellent advice based on her own teaching experience.

I am grateful to the three New York University students who helped find the illustrations for the book: Julie Elizabeth Kantor, Julie Beth Goldstein, and Malcolm St. Clair. These individuals made this work seem like fun, and indeed they made it so for me.

Several other people had a hand in the preparation of the book, and it gives me great pleasure to thank them publicly here. Michael Goodman took on the unenviable task of helping me check and correct all the footnotes, and did it with enthusiasm as well as talent; Paul Sager helped with the infinite details of the final preparation of the manuscript with care, patience, and good humor.

Mical Moser, the former History Editor at Broadview Press, brought me into the project and shepherded me through the proposal and the original outline. It was a joy to work with her, even for a short time, and I am happy to express my gratitude to her.

My editor at the University of Toronto Press, Natalie Fingerhut, is also a joy to work with. Natalie has been sympathetic, responsive to all my queries, and understanding of the vicissitudes of life as well as the vicissitudes of writing. Her unflagging support is only one of the many gifts she has given me. Michael Harrison, vice-president of the Higher Education division, delighted me with his ready replies to my questions and his willingness to say yes to them. The indispensable task of shepherding the manuscript through the final stages to its completion was handled by production coordinator Beate Schwirtlich. Beate approached the task with expertise, grace, and infinite patience with both the process and the author. On all counts I am deeply grateful to her. It is owing to them that I have developed a deep affection for Canadians and for Canada.

I take this opportunity to express my appreciation to my beloved friends in Jerusalem, the late Professor Moshe Barasch, a great art historian and a man of many gifts, among them the gift of friendship. He and his wife, Berta, introduced me to Jerusalem and shared with me their love for the Holy City. Their daughter, Emanuela Barasch-Rubinstein, scholar and author, is a valued and supportive colleague and a dear friend with whom I have shared many conversations about the business of writing.

And last, but never least, my husband, Millard Midonick, affectionately called Will, has been infinitely patient and generous-spirited about all the time I have spent in my study. From first to last he has been, as always, lovingly in my corner.

Author's Note

In the interests of simplifying the text, I have chosen to refer to the Middle East as simply the East throughout the book. When the Far East enters the history, this is made clear.

The Arabic names and words, with a few exceptions, are presented in their familiar anglicized form and without diacritical marks. Terms that may be unfamiliar are explained or translated the first time they are used in the text.

The Selected Bibliography and Suggestions for Further Reading are arranged as follows: the Bibliography at the end of the book includes the general histories of the crusades and the primary sources in English translation. Books and articles that are recommended for specific topics within each part of the book are in the Suggestions for Further Reading sections at the end of each Part and at the end of the Epilogue.

Almost all the manuscript illuminations and other artwork in the book were produced during the period the book covers, or very soon thereafter. They were chosen to illustrate how the story was perceived by contemporaries, or near contemporaries, of the events. In many cases these graphic depictions are truly worth a thousand words.

Prologue

There is not a more dangerous tendency in history than that of representing the past as if it were a rational whole and dictated by clearly defined interests.
   —J. Huizinga, *The Waning of the Middle Ages*

In the early winter of 1095, Pope Urban II addressed an assembly of churchmen and nobles standing in an open field in the town of Clermont, France. The pope spoke to them of the capture of Jerusalem by the Turks in 1071; he spoke passionately about the Turkish desecration of Christian churches and holy places in the Holy Land and the horrific Turkish massacres of Christians. Above all the pope spoke of the urgency to reclaim Jerusalem. When he finished, the assembly, with one voice, cried, "Deus vult! Deus vult!" ("God wills it! God wills it!"). In the beautiful words of the eighteenth-century historian Edward Gibbon, "a nerve was touched of exquisite feeling; and the sensation vibrated to the heart of Europe."[1]

In the months that followed the pope's appeal, group after group of nobles, knights, priests, monks, women, children, the aged and infirm, rich and poor set out for the Holy Land to reclaim Jerusalem and the sites sacred to Christianity. Urban had inaugurated the first in the long series of Christian holy wars we call the crusades.

The astonishing, unanticipated result of the First Crusade was the foundation of a Christian kingdom in the Holy Land known as the Latin Kingdom, or, more simply, Outremer, "the land across the sea." Outremer endured, against great odds and against all probability, for two hundred years.

This is a book about the history of the crusades, the warfare during the Middle Ages between Christians and Muslims for control of the most embattled city and the most desired lands in the Middle East. This is a book about the Latin Kingdom, the heroism and failings of its defenders, and the disasters the Christians suffered that culminated in its bitter end. It is the history of

---

[1] Edward Gibbon, *The Decline and Fall of the Roman Empire*, vol. III (New York: The Modern Library, 1983) 417.

how—and why—the movement we call the crusades came about, the impact of the crusades on the eastern Mediterranean and on Europe, and the legacy left to us by the crusading era.

Beginnings and endings are often difficult for historians to determine. One period of history, like time itself, flows into the next, and the demarcations between them are not usually clear-cut. For the history of the crusades, however, the beginning is unmistakable; it is the inauguration of the First Crusade by Pope Urban II in 1095.

Until recently the traditional date for ending the history of the crusades was 1291, the year the last remnants of the Latin Kingdom were permanently lost to the Christians. In the past several decades there has been an outpouring of scholarship on the crusading era, challenging many traditional views that have been held since the nineteenth century. Current research is reconsidering the length of time the ideology of crusading lasted; no firm consensus has yet been achieved.

The date I have chosen for ending this history extends the story to 1396, the year of a crusade fought at Nicopolis, on the lower Danube River, the first major battle the Europeans fought against the Ottoman Turks, and an overwhelming disaster for the Christian forces. The battle of Nicopolis was a turning point in the relations between Christians and Muslims, and it marks the beginning of a new era. From Nicopolis until the Turks were turned back the second and final time from the gates of Vienna in 1683, Europe was on the defensive against the Muslim Turkish onslaught. Jerusalem and the Holy Land were neglected in the centuries that followed Nicopolis, and the circumstances and character of the later so-called crusades dramatically changed.

A contemporary school of historians has enlarged the boundaries of crusading to include the wars against the pagan Slavic peoples and the Muslims in Spain, as well as wars fought against heretics and the Christian enemies of the Roman Church. Mindful of this research, I include these wars in this history, and a discussion of how central or how tangential they were to the ideology of crusading.

Throughout the period covered by this book, despite the nearly constant warfare, Christians, Muslims, and Jews lived cheek by jowl with one another in the Middle East and came to know each other, with varying results. The interrelationships among the religious and social groups are a characteristic feature of the crusade period, and the book will present the reader with an understanding of these relationships, how the ideas each group held of the other came to be, how the Christian perception of the "terrible Turk," and the Muslim perceptions of the Christians took root and flourished. The book will explore the position of the Jews in Europe and the Middle East and how they were affected by the shifting power struggles in the Holy Land. The story of the Byzantine Empire and its role in the tangle of relationships that influenced—and was influenced by—the strategic and commercial value of the great city of Constantinople is also part of the narrative.

When the first crusaders journeyed east they went as pilgrims to the Holy Land; they understood themselves to be pilgrims—some armed and some not—but nonetheless all pilgrims. Pilgrimage was an integral part of the religious life in Europe from the early Christian centuries. To journey to pray at a saint's shrine was, at first, an act of simple piety. Over time other reasons were added for going on pilgrimage; for many it was a form of penance, usually imposed by a priest, undertaken as a way to seek forgiveness for sin; for some it was the path to martyrdom.

The sense of sinfulness hung heavily over Christians in the late eleventh and the twelfth centuries, and an uncertainty that was palpable about whether they deserved salvation at the end of life. In the harsh and unpredictable world of medieval Europe, the assurance of a peaceful eternity was greatly desired. For penitents, the more difficult the pilgrimage, the more hazardous the journey, the greater the distance, the more the pilgrim could hope that he was fulfilling his penance and would one day enter the Heavenly Kingdom. Of all the distant holy places, Jerusalem was paramount.

For the armed pilgrim to Jerusalem, the first step was to make a vow, usually before a priest. Afterward the crusader affixed a cloth cross onto his garments as the outward sign of his vow to go to the Holy Land. The crusader was then granted privileges that could be bestowed only by the pope. The most important of these was the remission of sins for those going off to reclaim Jerusalem, the freedom from the punishment in purgatory that would, under other circumstances, await the guilty.

From the beginning Christianity had within it a strong pacifist strain—Christ had after all said, "[W]homsoever shall smite thee on thy right cheek, turn to him the other also" and "love your enemies, bless them that curse you, do good to them that hate you" (Matt. 5.39, 44). However, violence was always present, and in the late fourth and early fifth centuries, St. Augustine defined for many centuries to come the terms of a "just war," the conditions under which it was permissible for Christians to wage war. A "just war" necessitated a legitimate purpose; this included the recovery of property that had been wrongfully seized and the defense of one's home and country against an enemy. The war to recover Jerusalem, to right the wrong that it was believed had been done to Christianity, thus became a "just war" and morally defensible. Nonetheless, many churchmen and theologians held fast to the belief that warfare, whatever the purpose, was un-Christian and in direct opposition to Christ's teachings of brotherly love and forbearance.

In the decades before the First Crusade a remarkable transformation in the ideology of warfare was brought about by the papacy. This was the sanctification of wars fought on behalf of Christendom as not only "just" but spiritually beneficial. Knights accustomed to fighting against one another instead became soldiers of Christ, going off to battle wearing the sign of the cross, secure in the knowledge that their warfare in defense of their religion would bring them spiritual rewards. The holy war, the war fought in the cause of religion, was thus implanted in Western thought and is, for good or ill, a lasting legacy from the crusader period. For medieval Christians it was a noble ideal, for what greater good could come to a man than to win redemption by fighting for God and His Son? Yet, it harbors within it that religious zeal which, easily unleashed, can turn into cruelty against anyone seen as an enemy of the true faith. It was only a step away from persecution of the "other" — we need only reflect on the phenomenon of pogroms of the twentieth century to understand.

The crusades thus had three intertwined aspects: pilgrimage, penance, and holy war. These three elements made up the crusade in its most idealistic form; we shall follow how they evolved in the course of the crusading era.

The book will follow as well the idea of the holy war in Islam, the meanings and uses of the ideology of the *jihad*. It was, and is, a term with two distinct meanings. On the one hand, *jihad* (the word means "struggle" or "strive") is an inner struggle (the "greater *jihad*") to achieve a good Muslim life, to live virtuously according to the teachings of Islam. It is a word that also means the outward struggle (the "lesser *jihad*") to preserve Islam from its enemies. Although the lesser *jihad* did not necessarily presuppose an aggressive act of war rather than a defensive one, the early Muslim armies and even the Prophet himself made use of the ideology of *jihad* in their campaigns against their enemies. And it was used that way during the crusades, to rally the Muslims against the Christian invaders and reclaim the Holy Land.

The crusades have a special resonance for us now, living as we are through a most grievous time in history. "Crusade" has become a battle cry for the American war against terror, and "*jihad*" has entered our vocabulary as a pejorative for the Islamic movements in the Middle East. Once again, the presenting cause is religion. But there is, of course, a larger context and a multiplicity of motivations for the people fighting in the area. So it was at the time of the crusades. Not all the wars were religious or holy wars, but religion was more often than not invoked; it became part of the rhetoric in both cultures, and the ideas that characterized Christian holy war and Islamic *jihad* became fixed.

From the moment the First Crusade was preached, the writers who heard the pope's speech and the many chroniclers who accompanied the crusades knew they were witnesses to momentous events. The urge to record the events, to describe the heroes and the villains, the violence and the piety, the strange places and even stranger people, produced many remarkable books. The same is true for the Byzantine historians and for the Muslim writers whose understanding of the invaders from the West was quite different from that of the Western chroniclers. These sources will be quoted throughout the book to add life and flavor to the story and to illuminate the divergent ways in which these writers represented the wars and the peoples fighting them. Few subjects demonstrate as vividly as does the writing about the crusades — in the Middle Ages and now — how much the ground on which one stands is responsible for the way the subject is understood. It is a history lumbered with prejudice.

The underlying theme of this book is the quest for Jerusalem and the belief that Jerusalem was, and remained, central to the ideology of crusading, even after the Holy City was lost to the Christians, and even though crusades were preached in other parts of the world. Jerusalem is the chief protagonist in this history. The book begins, therefore, with the spiritual importance of Jerusalem, how and why the holy sites were then — as now — so central to the religious beliefs of Jews, Christians, and Muslims, and why so many thousands of people, for many hundreds of years, have willingly given up their lives to possess the Holy City.

So now, as an early chronicler of the First Crusade wrote, "I must turn my pen to history: so that those who have not heard of them may learn about the deeds of those who made the journey to Jerusalem, what happened to them, how great was the enterprise."[2]

---

[2] Fulcher of Chartres, *A History of the Expedition to Jerusalem, 1095–1127*, trans. Martha E. McGinty (Philadelphia: U of Pennsylvania P, 1941) 21.

Part One

1.1 Photograph of Jerusalem.

CHAPTER ONE

Jerusalem and the Eastern Mediterranean before the Crusades

And now, behold, I go bound in the spirit unto Jerusalem, not knowing the things
that shall befall me there.
— Acts 22.22

The goal of the First Crusade was to wrest Jerusalem from the Muslims, who had held it since the seventh century. According to the Christian view, Jerusalem had been, and should surely be again, a Christian city. "Under Jesus Christ, our Leader," Pope Urban II told the men about to take the cross, "may you struggle for your Jerusalem, in Christian battle-line . . . and may you deem it a beautiful thing to die for Christ in that city in which he died for us."[1]

The walled city of Jerusalem is small, only two and a half miles (four kilometers) in circumference, and its geography has little to commend it. Jerusalem has never been on a trade route, has never been a center of industry, and, until late in the nineteenth century, the way from the sea to Jerusalem, up into the Judaean hills, was perilous. Yet, despite its inauspicious setting, Jerusalem from early in its history was a magnet for invaders.

The City of Three Faiths

At the beginning of the first millennium BCE, the Israelites began their conquest of the city. In the following centuries Jerusalem suffered wars and invasions

---

[1] Balderic of Dol, quoted in S.J. Allen and Emilie Amt, eds., *The Crusades: A Reader* (Peterborough, ON: Broadview Press, 2003) 44.

and was held captive by several foreign powers—the Babylonians, the Persians, Greek dynasties from Egypt and Syria, the Romans, the Byzantine Christian Greeks, briefly again the Persians, and then, also briefly, the Byzantines once more. In the seventh century, Jerusalem was taken by the Muslim Arabs.

Although the conquests, the cultural footprints, the changes in fortune are all significant and part of the richness of Jerusalem, it is the spiritual life of the city that has secured its special, pre-eminent place in the world. The intense emotions aroused by Jerusalem are rooted in its religious history.

Long before the crusades, Jerusalem had become, as it is today, a cherished place—part dreamlike, part real—on a spiritual landscape treasured by Jews, Christians, and Muslims alike. Within its walls are enshrined the religious sites sacred to the three monotheistic religions, sites imbued with holiness and freighted with history. For all three religions the name *Jerusalem* evokes a sacred past and the promise of a sacred future. How this came to be shaped the city the crusaders found when they arrived.

A. The Israelites Come to Jerusalem: The Hebrew Tradition

The Jews were the first to claim Jerusalem as their holy city. In the second millennium, the Israelites followed their patriarch, Abraham, from their home in Ur, near the southern end of the Euphrates River, in what is today Iraq, to wander westward across the Fertile Crescent until they reached the land of Canaan. According to the Book of Genesis, where the story of their migration is told, God appeared to Abraham, first called Abram, in a place called Haran, saying, "Get thee out of thy country ... unto the land that I will show thee. And I will make of thee a great nation and I will bless thee and make thy name great" (Gen.12.1–2). When Abram asked God what He would give him, "the Lord made a covenant with Abram, saying, unto thy seed I have given this land, from the river of Egypt to the great river, to the river Euphrates" (Gen. 15.18). And Abraham and the Israelites went to Canaan and settled there.

Abraham's descendants and some of their followers left Canaan and went to Egypt, where they were at first welcomed but later taken captive and kept as slaves until, circa 1225 BCE, they were led out of Egypt by Moses. As the Israelites made their way back to Canaan across the Sinai Desert, Moses was called to Mount Sinai by God and given the laws that contained God's rules for the religious lives of the Israelites and His covenant with them. Then Moses, with God to guide him, led the Israelites to the border of the land God had promised for Israel.

The Israelites conquered and gradually settled the land, and their society grew and flourished. Soon after 1000 BCE, King David chose Jerusalem as the capital for his kingdom and brought to it the Ark of the Covenant, the sign and symbol of Israel's compact with God. David was succeeded by his son, Solomon, who built a temple of astonishing size and beauty to serve as the "House of God" and to enclose the Jews' most sacred relics, the Ark of the Covenant with the tablets of the laws God had given to Moses. Solomon chose to build his temple on Mount Moriah because it was there that God had tested Abraham's faith by commanding Abraham to offer his son Isaac as a burnt offering to Him. When God saw that Abraham was prepared to sacrifice his son for his faith, He stopped Abraham. "And Abraham called the name of that place ... 'the mount where the Lord is seen'" (Gen. 23.14).

Solomon's Temple was made of the cedars of Lebanon, cypress, and olive wood, and limestone with ivory-paneled doors, all beautifully carved and ornamented. Within the temple sanctuary Solomon built the Holy of Holies, the chamber where the Ark was placed. "[He] overlaid the house within with pure gold; and he drew chains of gold across the wall before the Sanctuary; and he overlaid it with gold. And the whole house he overlaid with gold" (I Kings 6.21). The temple became the holiest of the Jewish holy places. Over time, the most important rituals could be celebrated only in the temple in Jerusalem, and every Jew was obliged to come to Jerusalem to celebrate the holy festivals of Passover, Shavuoth (or Weeks), and Sukkoth. For all Jews everywhere Solomon's Temple became the one place where God was most surely present. From Solomon's reign on, the political capital and the religious center of Judaism were inextricably joined.

In 587 BCE, after a siege of eighteen months, the Babylonians destroyed Jerusalem; Solomon's Temple was burned to the ground, and a significant portion of the Jewish population was forcibly deported to Babylon. During the time of this first exile the Psalmist wrote the words that have resonated throughout Jewish history, have become part of Jewish liturgy, and are lodged in Jewish consciousness: "If I forget thee, O Jerusalem, let my right hand forget her cunning. If I do not remember thee, let my tongue cleave to the roof of my mouth; if I prefer not Jerusalem above my chief joy" (Ps. 137.5–6).

When the Jews were allowed to return to Jerusalem (in 525 BCE) they built a small temple where Solomon's had stood, a structure so lacking in grandeur that no one bothered to describe it. Not all Jews chose to return; some who lived outside Jerusalem migrated to Syria, Egypt, and other parts of the East, beginning the diaspora, or dispersion, of the Jews. From the end of this first exile on, Jerusalem was part of a larger province, called Judaea, ruled first by Persians, then by Greeks, and then by the Romans.

In 20 BCE, King Herod, a Roman appointee whose rule was conditional on his loyalty to the Romans, began work on the great shrine known as the Second Temple. So huge and so lavish was this edifice that it took fifty years to complete and was one of the great marvels of antiquity, certainly the crowning glory of Herod's ambitious and much-despised reign.

In the course of the Roman expansion throughout the Mediterranean world, begun in the second century BCE, to protect their growing possessions in the Middle East, the Roman general Pompey annexed Syria to the empire in 63 BCE, a move that inevitably brought the Romans into direct contact with the Jewish communities and the leadership in Jerusalem. The decision to make Judaea a client-kingdom, which brought Herod to power, was confirmed by the first emperor of Rome, Caesar Augustus. The difficulties that arose following Herod's death (in 4 BCE) were complicated by serious civil unrest within Jerusalem and the growing intransigence of the Romans in their dealings with the Jewish community. On both sides there were grievances and misunderstandings.

The Jewish wars of rebellion against the Romans began in 66. Four years later, in 70, Roman legions led by the Roman emperor's son Titus, after a brutal siege, stormed Jerusalem, razed the city to the ground, and burned the Second Temple. Only the massive platform that helped support the temple remained standing; its western wall, traditionally known to Jews as the Western Wall (sometimes now referred to as the Wailing Wall), has remained the holiest of the Jewish holy shrines, the visible reminder of the sanctity of Solomon's Temple. Early in the second century, in the wake of another insurrection, the Romans banished the Jews from Jerusalem, and the city, which was once the center of Jewish pilgrimage, became a city of furtive visits for Jews who came, as best they could, to worship "on the mount where the Lord was seen."

B. The Christian Holy City

For Christians, the identification of Jerusalem as their holy city came in the fourth century. The places where Christ preached in Jerusalem, where he spent his last hours before the trial, and the sites of the Crucifixion and Resurrection were known to Christians from the traditions passed down from generation to generation and from the Gospels, which paint a vivid and memorable picture of the places where the final scenes in Christ's life and Passion were enacted. Nevertheless, during the first three hundred years of Christianity, Jerusalem did not have the resonance for Christians that it would take on after Christianity was legalized by the Edict of Toleration in 311 and in the centuries following the Emperor Constantine's reign. Although it seems likely that Constantine did not formally convert to Christianity until he was on his deathbed (in 337), he favored Christians in his empire and was in every way generous to them. The emperor ordered the Governor of Judaea and the Bishop of Jerusalem to identify the sites associated with Jesus, and he spent lavishly from state funds and his own wealth to build basilicas and shrines to enclose them.

Constantine, with his mother, Helena—a Christian convert who was eventually canonized—established the sites described in the Gospels as centers of Christian worship and pilgrimage: Bethlehem; Nazareth, where Joseph brought the holy family after they left Egypt; the Galilee, along whose shores Jesus preached and performed miracles of healing; the River Jordan, where he was baptized; and, foremost among them, Jerusalem.

Constantine's most impressive achievement in Jerusalem was the Church of the Holy Sepulchre, built to enclose the tomb of Jesus. Although Christ's tomb had been covered over and lost to view in the centuries since his death, the memory of the site had been kept alive. When Constantine ordered the tomb to be uncovered and the rock surrounding it to be cut away, he sent the Bishop of Jerusalem a letter instructing him to erect over it a church "such that all the fairest structures in every city may be surpassed by it"[2] And then, his biographer wrote, he built a basilica "which looked towards the rising sun ... a truly extraordinary work, reared to an immense height, and of great extent in both length and breadth. Slabs of variegated marble lined the inside of the building, and the appearance of the walls outside exhibited a spectacle of surpassing beauty."[3]

Helena undertook the arduous journey to Palestine when she was seventy-three years old in order to locate the places hallowed by Christ's life and death. She visited Bethlehem and built the Church of the Nativity to enshrine Christ's birthplace; in Jerusalem she built several churches within and outside the city walls. The most famous discovery attributed to her was finding the True Cross on which Christ had been crucified and died. Helena put the pieces of the cross in a silver case and had a church built to house them.

Thus a change of immense importance for Christians was created by Constantine and Helena. As early as 333, Christian pilgrims began to make their way to Jerusalem and Palestine to reenact at the actual sites the events of Jesus' sufferings, death, and resurrection. Palestine became a Christian Holy Land, and the primacy of Jerusalem as the most sacred of Christian cities was asserted, the Church of the Holy Sepulchre its most precious adornment.

C. Jerusalem in the Islamic Tradition

Islam was the final monotheistic religion to establish its connections to Jerusalem. The Prophet Muhammad was born in Mecca, in the Arabian Peninsula, circa 570. In his early years he was involved in the life of the caravan city as a businessman, he married and had children. It was his custom in the month of Ramadan to retreat from Mecca to nearby Mount Hira to fast and pray. According to Muslim tradition, while on his retreat in the year 610, Muhammad received his first revelation from God, transmitted to him by the

---

[2]   Eusebius, *Life of Constantine*, trans. John H. Bernard, 1896 (New York: AMS Press, 1971) 5.

[3]   Eusebius 7.

angel Gabriel. He began to preach publicly in 612 and continued until his death in 632. Each revelation was preserved and repeated and later transcribed to become a chapter, called a *sura*, in the book of God's revelations we know as the Quran.

Muhammad did not believe that he was starting a new religion. He believed that he was restoring the pristine form of the religion that God had first revealed to Abraham. In his understanding of history, the Jews and the Christians had, over time, deviated from the true path of God's revelations. Muhammad believed himself to be a prophet in the tradition of the great biblical prophets — among them Moses and Jesus, whom the Muslims regard as a prophet, rather than the Son of God — who had appeared to chastise the people who had strayed from God's original revelation and exhort them to return to right-eousness. Muhammad also believed, and in Islam it is accepted, that he was called by God to be the last of the messengers, the so-called Seal of the Prophets.

The Muslim associations with Jerusalem were in the first instance biblical. In the uncompromising monotheism that Muhammad preached, and in his understanding of the covenant God made with Abraham, Muhammad and his followers became Abraham's rightful spiritual heirs. In the Jewish tradition, the son whom God called upon Abraham to sacrifice was Isaac. In Islam Abraham was called upon to sacrifice Ishmael, the son borne by Hagar, the handmaiden to Abraham's wife, Sarah. And God said to Abraham, "And also of the son of the bondwoman will I make a nation, because he is thy seed" (Gen. 21.13). In the Muslim interpretation of the narrative, it was therefore through Ishmael and his descendants that God's promise would be fulfilled. Mount Moriah, the scene of Abraham's near sacrifice, was thus integrated into Islam.

In the early days of Islam, Muhammad had called upon his followers to pray facing toward Jerusalem. Although the *qibla*, or the direction of prayer, was subsequently changed by the Prophet so that Muslims faced, as they do still, toward Mecca, the first choice of Jerusalem underscores Muhammad's under-standing of the significance for Islam of the Holy City, which came to be known simply as *al-Quds*, the Holy.

The most famous and singular Muslim connection with Jerusalem is the story told in the Quran (17.1) of Muhammad's Night Journey — the tradition according to which the angel Gabriel carried Muhammad from one holy shrine, the "Sacred Mosque" located in Mecca, to a "distant shrine." From this "distant shrine" Muhammad was lifted to heaven and then returned.[4] In the generation following Muhammad's death the "distant shrine" was believed to be located in Jerusalem.

---

[4] For a full discussion of the "distant shrine," see the excellent book by F.E. Peters, *The Distant Shrine: The Islamic Centuries in Jerusalem* (New York: AMS Press, 1993).

Jerusalem Under the Muslims

During his lifetime Muhammad won many converts and extended his dominion over the Arab tribes as the political leader of a Muslim state. Immediately
following his death, in 632, the Muslim Arabs began their astonishing expansion; in only a few decades they had conquered Syria, Persia, Palestine, Egypt,
and North Africa. Jerusalem was not a primary objective of this advance, but
it was on the Muslim line of march, and in 638 an army led by the second
caliph, Umar, captured Jerusalem in a negotiated capitulation. The population
surrendered to Umar, and there is no record of destruction. From that time
until the crusaders came in 1099 Jerusalem was a Muslim city.

Umar ordered the first mosque to be built in Jerusalem, and he chose a site
on the Temple Mount. The Mount was deserted when the Muslims arrived;
its principal use was as a repository for garbage, and Umar and his followers
had to crawl through dung to reach the Herodian platform. Umar's mosque,
on the southern end of Herod's platform, came to be called al-Aqsa, "the distant," in memory of the Night Journey. Though large enough to hold three
thousand worshippers, the mosque was not an impressive building, but it was
a beginning. During the seventh century, the whole of the Temple Mount
was transformed into Muslim sacred space, called the *Haram al-Sharif*, or the
Noble Sanctuary, and late in the seventh century work was begun on the two
structures that rise so majestically over the Holy City, the new Dome of the
Rock and the newly expanded al-Aqsa Mosque.

On the Temple Mount the Muslims found an enormous rock, variously
identified as the foundation stone of Solomon's Temple, the foundation stone
of the world, and, most significantly for Muslims, the rock from which
Muhammad was lifted to heaven on his Night Journey. Over this outcropping
the Dome of the Rock was erected. The description written by a Muslim at
the beginning of the tenth century is the earliest one we possess: "In the
middle of the *Haram* area is a platform measuring 450 feet [137 meters] in
length, 60 feet [18 meters] across, and at its height is $13\frac{1}{2}$ feet [4 meters]. It
has six flights of stairways leading up to the Dome of the Rock. The Dome
rises in the middle of this platform.... In the Dome every night they light
300 lamps. It has four gates roofed over, and at each gate are four doors, and
over each gate is a portico of marble.... The [building of the] Dome is covered with white marble and its roof with red gold. In its walls and high in the
drum are fifty-six openings, glazed with glass of various hues."[5] And another
visitor wrote, "At the dawn, when the light of the sun first strikes on the
Cupola, and the Drum catches the rays; then is this edifice a marvelous sight

---

[5] Ibn al-Faqih, quoted in F.E. Peters, *Jerusalem* (Princeton, NJ: Princeton UP, 1985) 213–14.

to behold, and one such that in all Islam I have never seen its equal; neither have I heard tell of aught built in pagan times that could rival in grace this Dome of the Rock."[6]

Although damaged and repaired at least five times in the course of several centuries, the Dome as it stands today is in its essential plan and many of its details the same as the original.

The rebuilt al-Aqsa Mosque at the southern end of the *Haram* was meant to rival in size and splendor the Church of the Holy Sepulchre. Begun soon after the Dome of the Rock was completed, the mosque was finished at the beginning of the eighth century. Narrow colonnades ran along one side of the *Haram,* and an enormous atrium with fountains and plants and trees led to the covered area, large enough to hold five thousand worshippers. Originally the gates of the mosque were covered in gold and silver, but in 746, the mosque suffered damage in one of the many earthquakes that plagued Jerusalem and the caliph ordered the gold and silver to be removed. Later in the century the mosque was repaired "and the edifice rose firmer and more substantial than ever it had been in former times. The more ancient portion remained, even like a beauty spot, in the midst of the new."[7]

In its architecture and demography Jerusalem became a Muslim city, but it did not become the Muslim capital in the East. Jerusalem was incorporated into the new Muslim province of Syria, governed from Damascus, and under the local control of the Muslim subdistrict headquarted in Ramla, which became a prosperous and elegantly adorned city.

After the Muslim conquest the largely Christian population was permitted to remain in Jerusalem and Jews were welcomed to return. This was in keeping with the special position of Jews and Christians under Islamic law. The two People of the Book, as they are known, whose Scriptures preceded Muhammad's revelations, were protected minorities. Their place in Islam's social hierarchy was third, following the Arab Muslims and the non-Arab converts. The Jews and Christians were subject to taxes greater than those paid by Muslims; in exchange they were permitted to practice their religions, though not publicly; maintain an economic life; and establish their own schools and cultural centers.

The Early Expansion of Islam

Within a hundred years of their explosion out of Arabia, Muslim armies had conquered a vast empire that extended eastward as far as India and China. From

---

6   Mukaddasi, *Description of Syria, Including Palestine,* trans. Guy Le Strange, 1896 (New York: AMS Press, 1971) 46.

7   Mukaddasi 41.

North Africa the Muslims had crossed the Strait of Gibraltar to conquer Spain, although a few small Christian communities survived in the north. This stunning westward advance was stopped when the Muslim armies crossed the Pyrenees into France and were turned back in 732, according to Carolingian tradition, by Charlemagne's ancestor, Charles Martel.

During the late seventh and early eighth centuries, the Muslims besieged Constantinople mercilessly, throwing against it the full weight of their armies and the navy they had built for the express purpose of capturing the grand city, but Constantinople held firm and the Arab advance was halted. Nevertheless, before the end of the tenth century, Muslims were in control of Sicily, part of southern Italy, the Balearic Islands, Sardinia, Corsica, and Crete, in addition to North Africa and most of Spain. The Mediterranean, once a Roman sea, was dominated by Muslims.

The factionalism, the feuds, and the civil wars within Islam, which would prove a boon to the crusaders, had surfaced in the generations following Muhammad's death. The central issue was the question of the succession, the understanding of who should succeed Muhammad as leader of the Muslim church-state, called the *umma*, and how the caliphate, or leadership, should be passed down from generation to generation. In Islam, the community and how

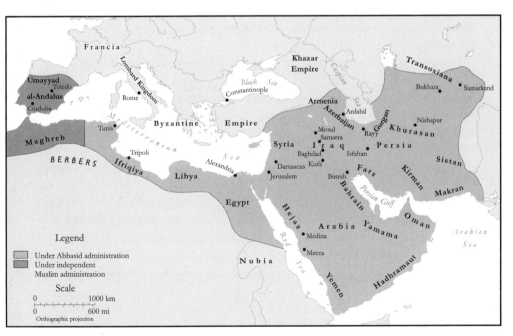

Map 1.1 Islamic World, ca. 800.

it should be governed, and religious belief and how it should be construed, are, at least in theory, inseparable.

In the time of uncertainty after the Prophet died, the Meccans closest to Muhammad and among his earliest converts came forward to take control. The first caliph—or successor—who stepped forward was Abu Bakr, whose brief reign was marked by the pacification of Arabia and who ordered the first major campaigns out of Arabia. He was followed by Umar, another of the Prophet's companions, a great military commander and the real architect of the Muslim state. His successor was Uthman, an unfortunately weak leader who was assassinated in 656. It was during the caliphate of the fourth successor, Ali, that the split between the Sunni and Shiite Muslims that endures to this day became manifest, although it had been festering since Muhammad's death.

Ali was Muhammad's cousin and son-in-law, and he and his followers believed that the divinely designated succession, which was bestowed on Ali by God Himself, should only be transmitted through the male line of his and the Prophet's family. In this view the first three caliphs had no legitimate claim to rule. The party of Ali, the *Shia*, whom we know as Shiites, originated in opposition to the Muslims we know as the Sunnis. The Sunnis are the majority in Islam who believe that they adhere to the exemplary practice (the custom, or *sunna*) of Muhammad and his early followers, including the election of the first caliphs, the "Rightly Guided Caliphs" as they are called. The Sunnis believe that they practice their religion in accordance with the *sunna* of the Prophet and that their beliefs should be the standard for all Muslims.

To the Sunni-Shiite schism was added other sectarian groups, and underlying these religious differences was the fact of Arab tribalism and competitiveness, which fueled the civil wars that broke out during Ali's reign. In 661, he was murdered, and the caliphate passed to the Sunni Umayyad clan, who established their capital at Damascus and ruled until they were overthrown in 750. Their place was taken by the Abbasids, who built the beautiful new city of Baghdad as their capital and who managed, despite many encroachments on their authority, to maintain a tenuous hold on the caliphate. It was an Abbasid caliph who was nominally in power when the crusaders came East.

The Abbasid claim to sovereignty over the entire Muslim Empire was challenged from within in the tenth century by rival caliphates in Egypt and Spain. An extreme form of Shiism, the Ismaili Shiite sect,[8] became firmly entrenched in North Africa and in 909 the Ismailis had founded their own

---

[8]   The Ismailis have had a continuous and significant history within Islam. For their origins and medieval history, see Farhad Daftary, *Ismailis in Medieval Muslim Societies* (London and New York: I. B. Taurus Publishers, 2005) and by the same author, *A Short History of the Ismailis* (Princeton, NJ: Markus Weiner Publishers, 1998).

caliphate, calling it the Fatimid Caliphate, named for Ali's wife and Muhammad's daughter, Fatima. During the last half of the tenth century, the Fatimids won control of Egypt and declared Egypt an independent caliphate. The Fatimids governed from Cairo and refused to recognize the Sunni Abbasids as Muhammad's legitimate successors. Early in the same century the caliphate at Cordova in Spain also declared its independence from the Abbasids and went its separate way. These internal rifts in no way changed the essential fact that at the turn of the millennium the expansion of Islam had altered the map of the Mediterranean world.

Byzantium and the West

Meanwhile the gulf between the Christian Latin West and the Christian Greek Empire on the eastern shores of the Mediterranean, called the Byzantine Empire, had, by the late tenth century, filled almost to overflowing with mis-understandings, disputes, and prejudice.

Among the issues that created the hostility between Byzantium and the West, three emerge as the most vexing: the rival claims to the Roman impe-rial title, the divergent paths followed by Christianity in the East and West, and the language difference that fed the growing cultural differences. By the fifth century, Greek had been forgotten in the West; in the East, where mili-tary Latin had long since disappeared, Greek remained the living language of the empire. The inability to communicate and the disdain the Greeks and Latins had for each other's language and culture exacerbated the first two problems.

The invasions and crises that afflicted the Roman Empire in the third century had made it necessary to strengthen imperial rule, particularly in the vulnerable provinces in the eastern Mediterranean. Emperor Constantine's choice of a location was brilliant. He chose the site of an ancient Greek settlement named Byzantium; the new city, renamed Constantinople in the emperor's honor, was dedicated in 330. Protected by the Black Sea and the Aegean, sheltered by straits that made entry into the harbor nearly impossible, and protected by massive, well-fortified walls on the landward side, Constantinople survived for over a thousand years all attempts to raze the walls and destroy the empire.

Constantine's purpose was to preserve the unity of the eastern and western Mediterranean of the early Roman Empire. With hindsight it is easy to see that the die had been cast. By Constantine's lifetime the integrity of the empire had become too fragile to maintain, and the divergent histories of Europe and Byzantium made reconciliation too difficult to achieve.

When the Roman provinces in the West were lost to invading Germanic tribes in the fourth and fifth centuries, the one remaining emperor was in Constantinople, and he claimed the exclusive right to be called "emperor of the Romans." The first challenge to his title and authority was made by the Frankish King Charlemagne in 800, when he was crowned Roman emperor by the pope. To add insult to injury, the emperors in the West insisted on calling the Byzantine emperors "emperors of the Greeks," thus, figuratively at least, reducing their authority to the Greek-speaking East.

In the late tenth century another German king who had taken the imperial title, Otto I, tried to establish a friendly relationship with the Byzantine emperor—an enterprise doomed almost from the start. His ambassador, Liudprand of Cremona, went twice to Constantinople on Otto's behalf; the first time the visit was cordial, but the second time Liudprand was mistreated and during his stay the issue of the title emerged full-blown. The Byzantine emperor made plain how furious the Greeks were with the Western emperors: "Do you want a greater scandal than that he [the German king] should call himself Emperor and claim for himself provinces belonging to our Empire? Both these things are intolerable; and if both are insupportable, that especially is not to be borne, nay, not to be heard of, that he calls himself Emperor."[9] This usurpation of the imperial title rankled in Constantinople for as long as the Byzantines remained in power, and the mutual distrust between the Greeks and Latins hovered over the entire crusading era with sometimes vicious consequences.

As the churches in the East and West evolved during the early Christian centuries, they grew further and further apart. In the West, by the fifth century, the primacy of the bishop of Rome in matters of dogma and liturgical practice was growing. The language used in the church was Latin, still the lingua franca of Europe, and Latin would remain until late in the twentieth century the only language acceptable in the Western church.

In the East, as Christianity spread, Christ's message was transmitted in a variety of vernacular languages used in the provinces. This was the recognition that there existed national languages and—to use modern terminology—a national consciousness in the ancient parts of the empire. From the linguistic differences grew differences in the liturgy and practice and often in theology as well. So there arose, among others, a Coptic Church in Egypt, a Syriac Church in Syria, an Armenian Church, a Jacobite Church, and Nestorian and Monophysite Churches, all of which had been declared heretical by church councils but had nonetheless survived. Each church had its own archbishop or patriarch. Of the patriarchs, the most eminent was the Greek patriarch at Constantinople, given his pride of place by his special relationship to the emperor and the imperial government. To Latin Christians the many

---

[9] Liudprand of Cremona, *The Embassy to Constantinople and Other Writings*, ed. John J. Norwich, trans. F. A. Wright (London: J. M. Dent; Rutland, VT: Charles E. Tuttle Co., 1993) 188.

houses in the mansion of Eastern Christianity were dismaying and bewildering.

Nonetheless, despite strained relations between Byzantium and the West and despite political tensions within Islam that threatened to erupt, at the turn of the millennium the Byzantine Empire entered a period of renewed prosperity and great artistic and literary flowering. Trade across the Mediterranean was beginning, and Italian traders from Venice and Genoa, from Pisa and Amalfi carried woolen cloth, arms and armor, and slaves from Europe to the flourishing markets in Constantinople and returned with luxuries for wealthy laymen and for the church—spices, silks, carpets, jewelry, and gold chalices. And pilgrims in ever-increasing numbers made their way to the Holy Land.

Pilgrimage to Jerusalem

At certain times of the year Jerusalem was so overrun by visitors that, as one Christian pilgrim complained, "crowds of various nations stay in that hospitable city for some days, while the very great number of their camels and horses and asses, not to speak of mules and oxen for their varied baggage, strews the streets of the city here and there with the abominations of their excrements: the smell of which brings no ordinary nuisance to the citizens and even makes walking difficult."[10]

Still the pilgrims came. Jews, Christians, and Muslims came from all corners of Europe and the Byzantine Empire, from as far away as Russia, from Persia and Syria and Egypt, from the Arabian Peninsula, and even from Scandinavia. The wealthy came and so did the poor and uneducated. A letter of introduction for a poor Russian Jew wishing to make the pilgrimage, written in the eleventh century by a member of the Jewish community in Salonika, asked for help from other Jewish communities along his way. "Please help him to reach his goal by the proper route, with the support of reliable men, from town to town, from island to island. For he knows neither Hebrew nor Greek nor Arabic but only Russian, the language of his homeland."[11]

Although the spiritual benefits of the Jerusalem pilgrimage were different for each religious group, they all shared the belief that holiness was located in a specific place and the desire to be in the presence of the holy.

To the Jews, the Temple Mount and the Western Wall served as visible reminders of God's covenant with Abraham and Israel. In memory of the destruction of Solomon's Temple, the Jews who visited the Temple Mount recited the prayers for the dead and wept to remember the past. No special

---

[10] *The Pilgrimage of Arculfus in the Holy Land*, trans. Rev. James R. Macpherson, London: Palestine Pilgrims' Text Society, 1885 (New York: AMS Press, 1971) 3–4.

[11] Franz Kobler, ed., *A Treasury of Jewish Letters*, vol. 1 (Philadelphia: The Jewish Publication Society of America, 1953) 143.

1.2 Pilgrims to Jerusalem and Santiago. Twelfth-century sculpture on the tympanum of the Church of St. Lazare at Autun, France. The cross on the pilgrim denotes the journey to Jerusalem, the seashell signifies the pilgrimage to Santiago da Campostela, and the third figure has usually been identified as a crusader.

spiritual merit attached to Jews who made the pilgrimage, no reward or expiation of sin, only the personal spiritual gratification that came from praying in the most sacred place in the land God had promised for Israel.

For Christians pilgrimage was a devotional act that brought valuable spiritual rewards: pilgrimage could expiate sin, and a voyage to the Holy City was often undertaken as an act of penance; a person who died on pilgrimage was assured the blessings of heaven, and the hardship of the travel itself brought spiritual benefit. The veneration of saints and their relics and, above all, sharing in the liturgies and praying at the sites that marked Christ's life, death, and Resurrection, all were essential to the Jerusalem pilgrimage. But however central to their spiritual well-being, pilgrimage was not a requirement for all Christians, as the pilgrimage — or *hajj* — was for Muslims.

Before the coming of Islam, the Arab tribes had made a yearly pilgrimage to Mecca to worship at the great stone house called the Kaaba and to trade in the town. When the Arabs were converted to Islam, the Kaaba was absorbed into the new religion; indeed the Quran explicitly asserted (2:125–127) that Abraham and Ishmael had built the Kaaba and established the *hajj* as the central rite it remains to this day.

So pilgrimage was from the beginning one of the Five Pillars of Islam, as the basic obligations incumbent on Muslims are known: the exclusive worship of the One God; prayer five times daily; almsgiving; fasting and other forms of penance during the holy month of Ramadan; and, if at all possible, undertaking the *hajj* to Mecca at least once in a lifetime. Some Muslims, unable to travel to the Arabian Peninsula, made the *hajj* to Jerusalem instead.

The focus in Jerusalem for Muslims was the Noble Sanctuary, Herod's original Temple platform, and prayer at the proscribed times in the al-Aqsa mosque and pious visits to the shrines that eventually dotted the *Haram*. According to one pilgrim in the mid-eleventh century, as many as twenty thousand Muslims — likely an exaggeration — came to Jerusalem during the sacred times. In addition to praying, they came to celebrate their sons' circumcisions.

The difficulty in ascribing benefits to the Muslim pilgrimage to Jerusalem was that city's place in the hierarchy of holy places after Mecca and Medina. After the crusaders took Jerusalem from the Muslims, the propaganda that stirred the Muslims to regain the Holy City ultimately assigned ever greater merits to the Jerusalem pilgrimage.

The eleventh century was also the great age for Christian and Jewish pilgrimage to the Holy Land, although when the century opened it seemed unlikely that they would be able to come again. In 1004 the Muslim ruler of Egypt, the Shiite caliph al-Hakim, for reasons best known only to himself, began persecuting Christians and Jews living under his rule, confiscating and destroying church property and synagogues. In 1009 he ordered the Church of the Holy Sepulchre to be demolished. That act was the most flagrant declaration of anti-Christian policy ever enunciated in the Holy Land, and the destruction of the holiest of Christian churches was by far the most incendiary abuse of al-Hakim's power. In 1020 the persecutions ended as suddenly as they had begun, and a year later al-Hakim literally disappeared. Lacking a rational explanation for the caliph's behavior, the general opinion is that he was quite mad.

Visitors who witnessed the total and frenzied destruction of the Church of the Holy Sepulchre could not believe that it would ever be rebuilt. Yet in

1030 a Byzantine emperor took responsibility for restoring the church, and the work was completed in 1048. It was not the same as Constantine's church because his huge basilica was never rebuilt, but the rotunda over the tomb was restored, and the Byzantines spared no expense in the gold and mosaics that were placed in the interior. By all accounts it was beautiful again.

Once more Christians and Jews traveled to Jerusalem. The largest Christian pilgrimage, which is considered to have had some seven thousand pilgrims when it began, came from Germany in 1064–1065. Against the good advice of the Byzantines, the Germans journeyed overland through Muslim territory to reach Jerusalem and encountered much hostility. Providing food and shelter for a contingent as huge as the German pilgrimage created many difficulties for the native populations, as one can easily imagine. Pilgrims suffered the indignities of travelers the world over—theft, trouble with customs officials, even some physical skirmishes. All along the pilgrim routes hospices were built expressly for pilgrims—in Europe, in Constantinople, and along the Syrian-Palestinian coast, and of course in Jerusalem itself. On the whole, the pilgrimage routes were well guarded, and pilgrimage, though hazardous, was not a life-threatening enterprise.

The Shifting Balance of Power in the East

By the mid-eleventh century the eastern Mediterranean world had begun to change in ominous ways. Although there were inklings of the approaching danger from the East early in the century, the threat posed by the Seljuk Turks to the Muslims and Greeks had not been fully appreciated by either of them. They had simply not seen the disaster that was coming.

The nomadic and semi-nomadic Turkish peoples from the steppes of central Asia had been sending raiding parties and mercenary soldiers westward for decades. Eventually these warrior nomads were converted to Sunni Islam and were employed as his new praetorian guard by the Abbasid caliph to fight against his Shiite enemies in Cairo and help maintain him in power. The Turks, having tasted power, became greedy for more as they recognized the impotence of the Abbasid caliphate and the weakness of Persia.

After many notable conquests, particularly in Persia, in 1055 the leader of the Turkish forces, Tughrul Bey, was welcomed into Baghdad with his army by the caliph and given the title of sultan (the word means "power") and the authority to preserve the caliph's position. Their positions were in fact reversed; the Turks now had the upper hand, and the floodgates of aggression were opened.

In 1064, led by the sultan Alp Arslan, who would later become well known to the crusaders, the Turks began their invasion of the important Byzantine province of Armenia. The account written in the twelfth century by the

Armenian historian Matthew of Edessa conveys the terrors instilled by the Turks: "Alp Arslan, the brother [and successor] of the [late Turkish] sultan Tughrul, rose up and went forth like a torrential stream; with a tremendous number of troops he marched forth and arrived in Armenia like a cloud filled with murky darkness, bringing with him much destruction and bloodshed."[12] In less than a decade Armenia was conquered for Islam. The Turks then advanced into Asia Minor, the heartland of Byzantine territory, vital for providing grain and manpower for the empire.

The decisive blow to Byzantium was delivered at the battle of Manzikert in 1071. It was for Christian contemporaries a dismal story. The Turks captured Manzikert; the Greek forces, led by the Emperor Romanus IV Diogenes, regained the city; then, when the sultan offered to make a peace treaty, Diogenes refused and, as Matthew of Edessa wrote, "he became more bellicose than ever"[13] and determined to destroy the Turkish army in the field. Instead the imperial forces were destroyed. The Byzantine soldiers were either slaughtered or taken captive, and the emperor himself was taken prisoner. In addition to the severe economic, military, and political consequences attendant on the loss of most of Asia Minor, the Byzantine army had behaved badly, many soldiers and their officers turning tail and running, and the emperor had made some serious strategic mistakes. All in all Manzikert was a devastating event for the Greeks. In the aftermath the Turks established their capital at Nicaea, across the narrow straits from imperial Constantinople.

The captured Byzantine emperor was released by the sultan, but not before his enemies at home had taken the opportunity to set another emperor on the throne at Constantinople. So the defeat at Manzikert set in motion civil war in the empire.

In the same year, the Byzantines suffered another crushing defeat, this one in the West at the hands of Normans (or Northmen) who had come to Europe as invaders and then, early in the tenth century, settled the rich land in western France that bears their name. Raiders from Normandy had been making steady inroads into Byzantine territory in southern Italy, and the month before Manzikert they annihilated the Byzantine army at the port city of Bari in southern Italy. Sicily had been lost to the Greeks when the Muslims conquered it in the eighth century, and the island would soon succumb to the Normans. The conquest of Bari marked the effective end of Byzantine rule in Italy and the central Mediterranean and a new stage in the evolution of hostility between the Greek emperors and the Latinized Normans.

---

[12] "Armenia and the Crusades: The Chronicle of Matthew of Edessa," trans. A.E. Dostourian, in S.J. Allen and Emilie Amt, *The Crusades: A Reader* (Peterborough, ON: Broadview Press, 2003) 32.

[13] Allen and Amt 33.

The instability that resulted from the grievous loss of Asia Minor, the loss of southern Italy, and the political uprisings in Constantinople brought to a close Byzantium's short-lived golden age.

Until the Turkish advances in the decades leading up to 1076, Egypt under the Fatimids was the most formidable power and the wealthiest country in the East. Jewels, spices, and raw materials from India; gold and ivory from the Sudan; luxuries from the Far East; goods from North Africa, Italy, and Sicily came into Egypt; and duties and taxes flowed into the Egyptian treasury. Since ancient times Egypt had been the granary for the Mediterranean, and grain was still an important export in the medieval period, along with sugar, glass, metalwork, and paper produced in Egypt. Alexandria became the major port and the great emporium for the trade that crisscrossed the eastern Mediterranean. With their vast income, the Fatimids built Cairo into a splendid capital city, which the crusaders insisted on calling Babylon, after the Roman fortress of that name that once stood near the site. The Fatimids also built a fine navy, which assured Egypt's pivotal role in the eastern Mediterranean for centuries. This remained true even when Egypt suffered setbacks on land.

The enmity between the Abbasids and their Turkish armies as upholders of Sunni Islam and the Shiite Fatimids was fierce. Their incessant wars were fought out over control of Syria and the Syrian-Palestinian coast. At the height of their power, in the mid-eleventh century, the Fatimids ruled Sicily, North Africa, western Arabia, and large areas of Syria. They had seemed to be on the verge of defeating the Abbasids when the Turks thrust themselves into the mix and swept victoriously through Syria and down the Syrian-Palestinian coast. Although the Fatimids did not lose all their cities on the coast, they were considerably weakened, and in 1076 they lost Jerusalem to the Turks.

Even after the Sunni Turks captured Jerusalem, pilgrims were still able, although with difficulty, to enter the Holy City, but travel to reach it had become precarious. The Abbasid Empire was crumbling; the Sunni Turks and the Shiite Fatimids were fighting in Syria; and Arab and Bedouin tribes roamed the Palestinian coast, robbing and generally harassing travelers.

William of Tyre, by far the greatest and most responsible historian of the crusades, wrote a monumental and lively history in the late twelfth century. He was born in the East, possibly in Jerusalem, and he based his history on voluminous research, verbal reports, and his own intimate knowledge of the Holy Land. His description of the maltreatment accorded to pilgrims in the period following the Turkish conquest of Jerusalem therefore carries weight in assessing how perilous the situation actually was.

Thousands of pilgrims, according to William of Tyre, had risked life and limb on their travels to Jerusalem, and many had had their possessions stolen and had nothing left with which to pay the tribute demanded of all Christians and Jews before they could enter the city. "So it happened that more than a thousand pilgrims, who had gathered before the city ... died of hunger and nakedness. These people, whether living or dead, were an intolerable burden to the wretched citizens. Those pilgrims who paid the usual tribute and received permission to enter Jerusalem brought still greater responsibility upon the citizens. For there was danger, as they wandered about incautiously in their eagerness to visit the holy places, that they would be spit upon, or boxed on the ears, or, worst of all, be furtively smothered to death."[14] The good citizens followed these pilgrims, carefully watching to prevent any harm from coming to them.

Although dramatic reports were thus brought back to Europe describing the dangers of travel in the East, it is difficult to know where the truth lies and how much the reports influenced the papacy's decision to preach the crusade.

The Crusade Idea Emerges

The first pope to fix on the idea of a crusade was Gregory VII (1073–1085). Even before he became pope, Gregory had embarked on a program to increase papal power over the churches in Europe and to extend papal authority. At the same time Gregory had been keeping an eye on events in Spain, where the Christians were having some successes against the Muslims. Christian Spain in the north was divided into small kingdoms, and there was rivalry among the rulers and little united action against the Muslims in the south. In fact, the remarkable truth about life in Spain was how integrated into Muslim society the Jews and Christians were and how, side by side, they produced and shared a beautiful culture for centuries.

Despite the cultural harmony, the defining theme in Spanish history has been the *Reconquista*, the drive to reconquer the lands that had formerly been under Christian control. For a long time historians maintained that the *Reconquista* had the nature of a Christian holy war and therefore was a precursor of the First Crusade. However, historians of medieval Spain no longer agree that the idea of a holy war had taken root in Spain as early as the eleventh century. Whatever the final verdict, the Christian advances against the Muslims during the eleventh century are a chapter in a long and complicated story. The relevance to crusading in the East is the perspective from which Gregory VII viewed the Christian successes in Spain.

During the reigns of Ferdinand I (1037–1065) and his son Alfonso VI (1072–1109) of Léon-Castile, the Christians made serious inroads against the Muslims and conquered substantial territories in western and central Spain.

---

[14] William, Archbishop of Tyre, *A History of Deeds Done Beyond the Sea*, trans. and annotated E.A. Babcock and A.C. Krey, vol. 1 (New York: Columbia UP, 1943) 80.

In 1064, an army composed mainly of French knights crossed the Pyrenees to help their Spanish brethren. Though in the long run they were not successful, there is a sense in which the papacy and perhaps the knights themselves now began to think of the war in Spain as a Christian holy war.

When French knights prepared for a second expedition to Spain in 1073, Pope Gregory VII addressed a letter to the French barons in which, in his usual fashion, he made explicit the papacy's claim to sovereignty over the churches in Spain. "We are sure that it is no secret to you that the kingdom of Spain was from ancient times subject to St. Peter in full sovereignty [*proprii juris*], and up to the present time, though long inhabited by pagans, nevertheless, since the law of justice remains inviolate, it belongs of right to no mortal, but solely to the Apostolic See."[15]

Gregory then turned his attention to the East. He had received reports of the devastation that followed Manzikert, the perilous situation of Eastern Christians and the hardships suffered by Christian pilgrims. To Gregory the time seemed ripe for rapport with the eastern churches and the extension of his power over them. He sent several letters to the faithful in Europe urging them to defend the Christians in the East. In a letter to King Henry IV of Germany he wrote, "I would rather stake my life for these [the Eastern Christians] than reign over the whole earth and neglect them.... I am especially moved toward this undertaking because the Church of Constantinople ... is seeking the fellowship of the Apostolic See." Gregory claimed that as many as fifty thousand men were already preparing to respond to his summons "if they can have me for their leader and prelate, to take up arms against the enemies of God and to push forward even to the sepulcher of the Lord."[16]

The crusade Gregory hoped to lead did not happen. The pope spent his last years warring against Henry IV over the issue of papal sovereignty; he died in exile in the Norman kingdom in southern Italy in 1085.

The East on the Eve of the First Crusade

Meanwhile, at Constantinople, four years before Gregory's death, a young man, already highly regarded for his generalship although he was only twenty-four years old, ascended the Byzantine throne. Alexius I Comnenus (1081–1118) was a remarkable ruler. When he became emperor it seemed that everything that could possibly have gone wrong for Byzantium had gone wrong. The empire was beset on all sides by enemies and suffering from the loss of valuable territory and income, and it appeared unlikely that it could be salvaged.

---

[15] Pope Gregory VII, "To the Barons of France," *The Correspondence of Pope Gregory VII: Selected Letters from the Registrum*, trans. Ephraim Emerton, 1932 (New York: W. W. Norton & Co., 1960) 6.

[16] Pope Gregory VII, "To King Henry IV, 7 December 1074," *The Correspondence* 57.

Alexius's credentials were impeccable: the nephew of a former emperor and the adopted son of the widowed empress, he had married into an influential aristocratic family. He was also shrewd, resolute, devoted to the empire, and determined to restore what he could of its former greatness.

Not least of Alexius's problems was the threat from the Normans in Italy, who, perceiving the weaknesses of the empire, invaded Byzantine Durazzo on the eastern Mediterranean coast, intending to establish themselves on both sides of the Adriatic and possibly even invade Constantinople.

Alexius found an ally in Venice. The Venetians were concerned lest the Normans usurp their increasingly prosperous Mediterranean trade, and they were willing to support the emperor against the Normans — for a price. The price the Venetians extracted was in the long run a heavy one for Constantinople. Alexius granted the Venetians trading privileges in Constantinople and other Byzantine ports, which secured Venetian supremacy in the eastern trade. Nonetheless, the war with the Normans was another near disaster for Byzantium. The empire was saved in 1085 by an outbreak of cholera that took hundreds of Norman lives and eventually caused the death of the Norman leader, Robert Guiscard. The Normans retreated, although in their view they were only marking time until they resumed the war. So the antagonism between the emperor and the Normans was further exacerbated.

Over the centuries several theological disputes between the Eastern and Western churches had increased the distance between them, and there were long periods when there was an overt rupture, or schism, between the churches. Even the worst disputes were able to be resolved — save one. The heart of the matter, the sticking point, was the issue of papal supremacy. The power of the papacy was recognized in the West as supreme, but the papal claim to sovereignty over all Christendom was never accepted in the East. The quarrel, which had been bubbling up for centuries, reached a crisis in 1054, when the pope's representative in Constantinople and the patriarch each excommunicated the other. Partly this schism was caused by the obstinate personalities of the two men involved, but it revealed the explosive nature of the issue. Although dialogue between the churches has gone on intermittently for centuries, the schism of 1054 has so far remained intractable. At the time it occurred, this split did not seem irremediable, but after 1054 the relationship, if such it can even be called, between Byzantine emperors and popes steadily deteriorated. When Alexius ascended the throne in 1081 he was excommunicated by Pope Gregory VII.

It was against this background that the connections between the Byzantine emperor and the papacy were actually resumed. As a first step in restoring harmony, Pope Urban II, soon after his election in 1088, lifted the ban of excommunication. For his part Alexius permitted the Latin churches, closed since 1054, to function again in Constantinople. Then, in 1095, Alexius sent a delegation to a papal council held at Piacenza to ask for aid against the Turks. "There arrived at this council an embassy from the emperor of Constantinople which humbly beseeched our Lord, the Pope, and all the faithful of Christ to procure for him some help against the pagans for the defense of our holy church which the pagans had destroyed in his territories. The pagans had rendered themselves masters of his [Alexius's] territories as far as the walls of the city of Constantinople. Our Lord the Pope [Urban II], therefore, urged many to furnish this aid."[17]

Ever since the Turks had taken Asia Minor, which had been a major recruiting ground for troops, Alexius had been sorely in need of manpower. It was not unusual for him to hire mercenaries, including many from the West, and it is likely that "some help"—but not too much—from mercenaries was exactly what Alexius had in mind. From his vantage point, when he saw the crusaders massing before the walls of Constantinople in 1097, he had been sent a Trojan horse.

The year 1076 had been glorious for the Turks. The victory at Manzikert and the successes in Syria and along the Mediterranean coast were seminal events, even though the Seljuks had not succeeded in capturing all the Fatimid cities along the coast. In the 1080s, the major port cities of Acre and Tyre, lost at first to the Turks, were taken back by the Fatimids, who still controlled the sea.

Until 1092 Syria was ruled by one of its most impressive sultans, Malik-Shah. During his twenty-year rule he had been able to hamper the rivalries and warfare among the various Turkish tribes and, on the whole, maintain control over them. The difficulties were formidable. From time to time certain tribes would ally themselves with the Seljuks, but these alliances were often transitory at best. The fierce nomadic tribes of Turcomans had always been independent of the sultan and, of all the Turkish tribes, had caused the most serious destruction in Asia Minor in the decades before Manzikert. In the chaos that followed their rampage through Asia Minor, several Turkish leaders had taken advantage of the turmoil to set themselves up as autonomous rulers. Nonetheless, Malik-Shah had been able to hold in check the disunity that was always close to the surface in his empire.

In 1092 the great Malik-Shah died, and his relatives immediately went to war for control of the Seljuk throne in Isfahan, in Iran. The Turkish desire for independence surged up—also immediately—and the fragmentation of the empire was rapid. Two years later the last of the strong Egyptian caliphs died

17 Bernold, *Chronicon*, trans. Peter Charanis, in Kenneth Setton and Henry Winkler, *Great Problems in European History*, 2nd ed. (Englewood Cliffs, NJ: Prentice-Hall, 1966) 97.

after a fifty-eight-year rule. Although power was restored for a time in Egypt, the closing years of the eleventh century marked the beginning of serious political problems, economic troubles, and religious factionalism.

During the three years from 1092 until Pope Urban II delivered his famous speech in 1095, the political landscape in the East had thus changed its character once more. In the midst of this destructive internal strife, the Latin armies entered the East.

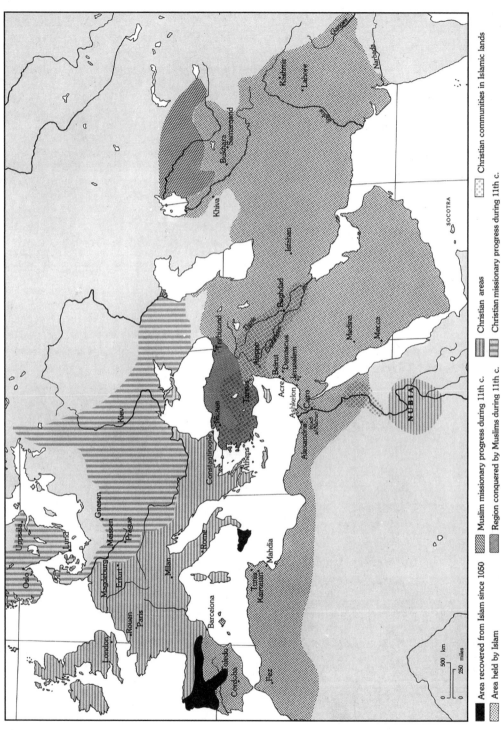

Map 1.2 Christianity and Islam on the eve of the First Crusade, 1096.

Area recovered from Islam since 1050   Muslim missionary progress during 11th c.   Christian areas   Christian communities in Islamic lands

Area held by Islam   Region conquered by Muslims during 11th c.   Christian missionary progress during 11th c.

CHAPTER 2

The Scene Is Set:
Western Europe before the
First Crusade

One cold day in late November 1095, on a plain outside the French town of Clermont (in the Auvergne), Pope Urban II addressed an assembly of some three hundred or more prelates and laymen and delivered one of the most compelling, eloquent, and persuasive speeches in European history. "From the confines of Jerusalem and the city of Constantinople," he began, "a horrible tale has gone forth ... namely that a race from the kingdom of the Persians, an accursed race, a race utterly alienated from God ... has invaded the lands of those Christians and depopulated them by the sword, pillage and fire; it has led away a part of the captives into its own country, and a part it has destroyed by cruel tortures; it has either entirely destroyed the churches of God or appropriated them for the rites of its own religion." Near the conclusion of his speech, Urban exhorted his listeners to "Enter upon the road to the Holy Sepulchre; wrest that land from the wicked race and subject it to yourselves.... When Pope Urban had said these and many similar things ..., he so influenced to one purpose the desires of all who were present that they cried out, 'God wills it! God wills it!'"[1] By the early summer of 1096, several oddly assorted, oddly linked together groups of fighting men and noncombatants began their hazardous journeys to Constantinople, where they all planned to meet, from there to march to Jerusalem. And so the First Crusade began.

The circumstances that set the First Crusade in motion have long been debated by historians of the crusading movement. It was once accepted wisdom that the impetus came from the Holy Land itself, in the particular

---

[1] Robert of Rheims, "The Jerusalem History," in August C. Krey, *The First Crusade: The Accounts of Eyewitnesses and Participants* (Gloucester, MA: Peter Smith, rpt. 1958) 30–32.

conditions in the last half of the eleventh century and the changes that, as we have seen, affected the Muslims and Eastern Christians alike. Current historical research, however, has augmented our knowledge of the complex forces in Europe in the decades before the crusades as well as the relationship between Europe and Middle East, and interpretations have changed. The weight of opinion now is that we must first look within Europe itself to understand the soil in which the crusades were germinated.

Renewal in Europe
In the centuries preceding the millennium, Europe had suffered wave after wave of invaders — Vikings from the north, Magyars from the east, and Muslims from the south. The destruction of land, property, and human lives was incalculable. The attempt by Charlemagne in the late eighth century to unify much of Europe under his strong leadership proved transitory; his empire was divided into three kingdoms in the first half of the ninth century, and the invasions left disorder and chaos in their wake. The invaders were finally repulsed, although some remained, as the Normans did, to settle permanently and become absorbed into European society. By the last half of the tenth century, Europe was finally unfettered to begin the long, arduous task of renewal. "It was as if the whole world," a medieval chronicler wrote, "were shaking itself free, shrugging off the burden of the past."[2]

It was on the land that the first tangible signs of improvement appeared. The effects of the invasions on Europe's land and agriculture had been uneven. The most grievous devastation had fallen on France, and the picture, particularly in the north, is of large areas that had lain fallow for generations, tracts of land so destroyed that they were unproductive, and a sparse population, its ranks decimated after centuries of warfare and starvation. Although no part of Europe had been immune from invasion, Germany and northern Italy were the least damaged and their economic recovery was therefore more rapid than that of other areas.

Despite the diverse rate of progress, more land was put under cultivation. The three-field system of crop rotation, developed earlier but not widely known, gradually spread throughout Europe. The heavy plow, which enabled farmers to turn over the rocky, clayey soil of northern Europe, and the use of oxen rather than horses as plow animals all increased the agricultural output, as did the work of land reclamation. Marshes were drained, forests were cleared, and the boundaries of arable land were extended. The result

---

[2] Rodulfus Glaber, *The Five Books of the Histories*, trans. John France and Paul Reynolds (Oxford: Clarendon Press, 1989) 117.

was greater cereal production, greater fertility, and, over time, new crops, such as legumes, which added protein to the diet and nitrogen to the soil.

As a consequence of the increased food supply, the population of Europe increased. Exact population figures are notably lacking for these centuries, but some estimates suggest the population increased from roughly 40 million in 1000 to as many as 48 million in 1100. The growth in population, although difficult to document precisely, was a demonstrable and seminal change in Europe. As fewer hands were needed to work the land, more people were freed to learn a skill, to become blacksmiths and harness makers and masons and craftsmen of all kinds. Villages expanded; local markets for the exchange of goods increased, and new towns were founded. With the greater prosperity came more movement of people and goods throughout Europe and a new momentum in long-distance trade.

Nevertheless, in this essentially agricultural society, life on the land remained tenuous; famine remained a constant part of rural life; the peasant settlements more usually than not remained isolated one from the other. And yet, however frightening it seemed at first, the world outside these small communities increasingly beckoned. The merchant, the pilgrim, the energetic and the hungry looking for work, the adventurer, the warrior—all these and more began to respond to the siren call of the outside world. A remarkable transformation began that would ultimately affect all aspects of European life. The eleventh century was characterized by an immeasurable amount of hard work, a new optimism, and the determination to bring order out of the disorder that had existed at the turn of the millennium.

The work of re-establishing effective governmental organizations was slow but steady throughout the eleventh century. In the course of the long invasions and the anarchic conditions that followed, effective ruling power had been greatly diminished at all levels. The growth and stability of political centers in France was evident first in the duchies and counties of western France, primarily in the great duchy of Normandy. The Normans, who were to play a crucial role in the crusades, had instituted a highly efficient governmental structure in their duchy before they began their extraordinary expansion into Sicily and southern Italy in the first half of the eleventh century, culminating in the conquest of England in 1066.

Although recognized in the French-speaking world as legitimate royalty, the French monarchs had to fight for several centuries to secure control of the land within the borders of their realm. The king's own holdings had been reduced to a small amount of territory, centered in Paris, known as the Île-de France, and even there his authority over the unruly and warlike barons was far from secure. Despite the formidable difficulties, the Capetian monarchs began in the eleventh century to develop their governmental institutions and a viable political structure.

The most imposing power in the eleventh century was that of the kings of Germany, who held the title of Holy Roman Emperor. The reputation of King Otto I of Germany as the greatest monarch in Europe had been secured when he defeated the Magyar invaders at the Battle of Lechfield (near Augsburg in Germany) in 955. In 961 he went to northern Italy, presumably to rescue the Lombard Queen Adelaide, whose kingdom was under attack. He stayed to marry Adelaide, thus becoming King of Lombardy; in 962, having subdued his enemies in Italy, Otto went to Rome, where he was crowned Roman emperor. Otto's assumption of the imperial crown, following the tradition set by Charlemagne, carried with it the title of Protector of the Holy See, a position that bound the emperors to the papacy and the church in ways that became a decidedly mixed blessing for the papacy. Control of northern Italy, which was a necessary condition for receiving the imperial crown, was, in the long run, a decidedly mixed blessing for the internal history of Germany. But that was in the future. All through the eleventh century the German monarchy seemed the strongest and most secure in Europe.

The sense that society was finally "shrugging off the burden of the past" was persuasive. In all areas of human endeavor there was new and luxuriant growth: in education, in literature, and in art, as well as in the ways that people began to think about themselves and the world they inhabited and its possibilities. This renewal came slowly. The dislocations caused by the many changes in the eleventh century increased the sense of insecurity and unease that people felt. Warfare had become an unavoidable part of life, and fighting and feuds between landowners caused havoc on the lands of the peasants and nobility alike. Alongside the signs of betterment was the undeniable fact that European society, at all levels, was violent, competitive, greedy, and restless. It was a world accustomed to brutality and cruelty.

The churches and monasteries had not been exempt from the devastation caused by the invasions. Unable to defend themselves, bishops, abbots, and parish priests turned, when they could, to local magnates for protection and were drawn into the feudal system, incurring secular obligations to the overlords who had protected them. Although there were occasionally able men on the papal throne in the ninth and tenth centuries, they were powerless to exert control over the churches in Europe. Discipline became lax, the clergy often married and had families, parish duties were frequently neglected, monastic communities lost members and fell away from the rules that had governed them. Overall the church had emerged from the invasions fragmented, subject to lay control, and sorely in need of revitalization and reform.

Religious Revival and Reform

The first manifestation of change was the revival of monastic life, which began on a small scale—indeed a tiny scale—in the monastery of Cluny in Burgundy, established by the Duke of Aquitaine in 910. This was quickly followed by the foundation of a monastery in Lower Lorraine, another at Gorze in Upper Lorraine, and yet another in England. Although different in certain particulars from one another, these monasteries had in common two overarching goals: the return to the purity of the apostolic life as it was lived in the early Christian centuries and the return to strict observance of the Rule of St. Benedict. From small beginnings in the first half of the tenth century, the monastic revival grew and expanded throughout Europe. Although the monasteries customarily derived support from lay patrons, and in Germany and England from royal patronage, the essential fact about this revival is that it was popular in the literal sense of the word. The monastic movement was part of, and a symptom of, the dynamic growth of popular piety in Europe that reached into all levels of society.

The outward expressions of this new religious vitality began to appear everywhere: in the remarkable growth of new monasteries, the small churches in every peasant community, and the large ones that dominated the towns— the "white mantle of churches," the chronicler called it—visible across Europe; in the shrines dedicated to saints that dotted the landscape; and in the pilgrims, unarmed, going to the holy sites, carrying only their purses and staffs. Religious and secular alike went to shrines and chapels to pray before the saints and their relics in the places where the saints were most present, in the hope of a miracle—of healing, of childbirth, of sight restored—above all to be touched by the sanctity of the holy place.

Over this popular religiosity there hovered the shadow and fear of the final reckoning, the day when Christ would return to judge whose soul would be saved and whose would be damned for eternity. Both guilt and punishment attached to the sinner, and only a priest, after hearing confession, could absolve the sinner of his guilt and assure him of salvation by giving him a penance. The desire to do penance was therefore very strong. For a minor offense the penance could be as little as reciting extra prayers or fasting; for major offenses, such as theft or homicide, the penance was often a pilgrimage. The more distant the holy place, the more hazardous the journey, the more assured the penitent could be of forgiveness. At the close of the eleventh century, at the time the First Crusade was preached, the nature of penance was equivocal; whether the penance, when fulfilled, would assure the penitent his place in the Kingdom of Heaven on the Day of Last Judgment was uncertain. The role of the papacy during the crusading era was pivotal in clarifying the ambiguities, as we shall see. Until then, the desire to be close to the spiritual purity of the monks, who represented the highest form of Christian life, and the belief in the efficacy of their prayers on behalf of penitents—indeed of all those hoping for the assurance of the Kingdom of Heaven—gave the monks a special role in European society.

The monasteries of Cluny and Gorze in particular became famous for their purity, discipline, and organization. The abbots of Cluny and Gorze were called on to reform existing monasteries or to found new ones, and the influence of these orders spread wide and far. The fame of Cluny has overshadowed the role played by other monasteries in the striking religious changes that came in the mid-eleventh and early twelfth centuries owing in large measure to Cluny's special relationship with the papacy. From its beginning Cluny was given the protection of the papacy and, with it, freedom from all other control, ecclesiastical and secular. The only authority to which Cluny was subjected was that of the papacy and, second to the papacy, the Abbot of the mother house of Cluny. In its freedom from secular control, recognizing only the supremacy of the pope, Cluny was a paradigm of what could be achieved. Basically, however, it was the deep religiosity of the monks—whatever their monastic affiliation—coupled with the growth of popular piety and the influence of a new reforming spirit that have relevance for the dramatic changes that transformed the papacy and Western Christendom in the last half of the eleventh century.

The foundation for one of the major problems confronting the papacy in the eleventh century was laid as far back as the Carolingian era. When Charlemagne's father, Pepin, was crowned King of the Franks in the late eighth century and the Carolingians were established as legitimate rulers, Pepin was anointed with holy oil and sanctified, first by the highest prelate in Germany and then by the pope himself. The coronation established Pepin and the Carolingians as theocratic monarchs in a tradition that harked back to the anointing of David in the Old Testament, who was the prototype of divinely appointed kingship. Charlemagne extended his understanding of his role as a divinely appointed monarch to mean that he had authority to rule over both religious and temporal life in his kingdom. Charlemagne envisioned a total Christian orientation of society under the leadership of the king. To that end he enacted laws governing the clergy, the laity, the church, and the monasteries; he appointed bishops, summoned church councils, and, insofar as was possible, imposed uniformity in the liturgy and all church ritual.

Papal history in the tenth and early eleventh centuries was, by any standard, dismal. The papal office had become a prize fought over by the noble families in Rome. When the opportunity arose—or was manufactured—the Holy Roman Emperors appointed their own nominees to the See of St. Peter. The power of the papacy had been so eroded over time that the popes had not been able to assert meaningful authority over Christendom for many centuries. In the atmosphere of spiritual revival in the eleventh century, the need for reform of the papal office and the spiritual quality of the men who held the office became acute.

The first of the so-called reforming popes, Leo IX (1048–1054) was elevated to the papal throne by the Roman emperor, Henry III. Both emperor and pope believed that reform was the equal responsibility of the two highest, divinely appointed powers in Christendom, that theirs was a bond established by God and could not—should not—be dissolved. Leo proved to be energetic and capable in the cause of reform, but always in this traditional mold. However, during his pontificate a much more radical program was being formulated by a group of churchmen he had brought to the papal court.

The fullest expression of the program came during the papacy of Gregory VII (1075–1082). He was a true revolutionary who desired the absolute freedom of the church from all secular control and the recognition of the supremacy of the pope over secular rulers. "[E]very Christian king," Gregory wrote in one of his many, many letters stating his position, "every Christian king when he approaches his end asks the aid of a priest as a miserable suppliant that he may escape the prison of hell.... But who, layman or priest, in his last moments has ever asked the help of any earthly king for the safety of his soul?"[3] Gregory was not a man to mince words.

Gregory envisioned a thoroughgoing reform of the church and Christian society emanating from Rome, and he dedicated his formidable intelligence and zeal to carrying out his mission. Gregory was, in the way of single-minded revolutionaries, intransigent. He had, however, the good judgment to call to the papal court to help him a Cluniac monk, born into a French noble family, well connected to the important French families, educated, experienced in both the world and the cloister, and a man of outstanding diplomatic skills, Odo of Lagery.

Odo was elected to the papacy as Urban II in 1088. He brought to the office his experience as a monk—he had entered Cluny in 1070—and his subsequent experience in church affairs, first as Cardinal Bishop of Ostia and then as Pope Gregory's legate, an appointment he held for three years, from 1082–1085. In that capacity the future pope traveled through Germany and France, placing in important dioceses, whenever a vacancy permitted, church officials who were faithful to the ideas of Gregorian reform. He held church councils and was involved firsthand in the troubled history of the papacy's attempts to extend its sovereign power over lay and religious alike. Pope

---

[3] Pope Gregory VII, "To Hermann of Metz, 15 March 1081," *The Correspondence* 171.

Gregory had made many enemies—not surprising, given his radical views of papal supremacy—particularly incurring the active hostility of the Holy Roman Emperor Henry IV, and was forced to spend his last years in exile from Rome.

Urban's path to the papacy was far from easy. The emperor, Henry IV, put his own candidate on the papal throne—the Archbishop of Ravenna, a man named Wibert, who immediately took control of Rome in 1084. Urban was elected in March 1088, but he could not gain entry into Rome for six years. During his enforced exile Urban traveled extensively through Germany and Italy as well as France. During those years, along with promoting church reform, Urban began to rally support for a military expedition to the eastern Mediterranean to aid the Byzantine emperor, Alexius I, who had asked the pope for help against the invading Seljuk Turks. In the spring of 1094, Urban was at last able to take up his permanent residence in Rome; in November of the following year he presided over the famous council held at Clermont.

Pope Urban II and the Council of Clermont

Urban called the council for the express purpose of continuing church reform and reinforcing the papal program. Much had been accomplished in the short time since the Gregorian reforms had been instituted: the upper ranks of the clergy were more securely under papal control than they had been for centuries, and the monasteries were becoming models of spiritual discipline and organization. Still, opposition remained within the church to the puritanical reforms Gregory had insisted on, and the fight to gain the freedom of the church from secular control was in its initial stages, the outcome far from certain.

Pope Urban was a visionary, a reformer, deeply spiritual, eloquent, and, when necessary, a remarkably good diplomat. He also had a deep understanding of the complex forces at work in his world. Urban was at the height of his powers when he presided over the council, which began on November 18, 1095. "In the plaintive voice of an aggrieved Church he expressed great lamentation, and held a long discourse with [the prelates] about the raging tempests of the world ... because faith was undermined. One after another, he beseechingly exhorted them all ... to try to restore the Holy Church, most unmercifully weakened by the wicked, to its former honorable status."[4] He castigated the bishops and abbots in the strongest language, enumerating all the sins the clergy had fallen heir to. "Set yourselves right before you do others," was the heart of his message. "If you wish to be friends of God, gladly

---

[4] Fulcher of Chartres, *Chronicle of the First Crusade*, trans. Martha E. McGinty (Philadelphia: U of Pennsylvania P, 1941) 12.

practice those things which you feel will please Him."[5] As to the Church itself, he told them to "[U]phold the Church in its own ranks altogether free from all secular power."[6]

For more than a century ecclesiastical officials along with some influential laymen had been struggling to curtail the violence and lawlessness in Europe. In 1041 the Church had enacted the Truce of God, which prohibited fighting every week from Wednesday evening until Monday morning. The purpose, in addition to the obvious cessation of brigandage of all kinds, was to protect the land worked by the peasants. Unfortunately, the truce had had only a limited effect; in different places and at different times during the eleventh century, new decrees were issued.[7] At Clermont Urban insisted that the truce be renewed. "In admonition, I entreat you to adhere to it most firmly in your own bishopric. But if anyone affected by avarice or pride breaks it of his own free will, let him be excommunicated by God's authority and by the decrees of this Holy Council."[8]

The Drama at Clermont

Then, on the next to last day of the council, on November 27, Urban delivered the great address for which he is so famous. Several versions of his speech have come down to us, all of them part of contemporary chronicles about the First Crusade, all of them written within fifteen — at most twenty — years following the capture of Jerusalem by the crusaders in 1099. Three chroniclers were present at Clermont and heard the speech. Their versions, however, differ depending on their own backgrounds, their education and experience, their political loyalties, and their interest in the language of rhetoric. For the modern student of these chronicles, the caveat is to remember that our insistence on accuracy was not yet fully formulated or valued. A number of themes are common to all the speeches, and, taken together, elucidate the pope's justifications for the First Crusade and the remarkable popular response his speech engendered. The story of the crusades, as we will see, played a significant role in the development of historical consciousness and writing, but that would come in the course of the twelfth century.

The pope had left nothing to chance, and the drama at Clermont had been skillfully planned. Urban had traveled for months before the council to meet with his countrymen in France especially, but in Italy as well, to gather their support. At a council he held in Piacenza, in March 1095, the pope had

---

5   Fulcher of Chartres, McGinty 14.
6   Fulcher of Chartres, McGinty 14.
7   See for example, the "Declaration of the Truce of God," in Allen and Amt 28–29.
8   Fulcher of Chartres, McGinty 15.

been approached by envoys sent by the Byzantine emperor Alexius I, who requested aid from the West against the punishing and successful onslaught of the Seljuk Turks. The situation of the Eastern Christians was perilous, and Alexius was without the resources to fight the Turks. The pope acceded to the emperor's request, promised that aid would be forthcoming, and encouraged his countrymen to go East. It is quite certain that Alexius expected only a contingent of knights who would come to Constantinople and, as had happened on earlier occasions, fight as mercenaries under imperial control. The crusading army that subsequently arrived was not at all what he had had in mind.

In addition to the prelates, many noblemen and knights had also come to Clermont in expectation of the pope's call for a war to the East. They were not disappointed. Their passion to go east was inflamed by the descriptions of the Turkish atrocities against the Eastern Christians. In all the versions of the pope's speech the descriptions are graphic, but especially so in Robert the Monk of Rheims's version. "[The Turks] circumcise the Christians and pour the blood from the circumcisions over the altars or in the baptismal fonts.... Some they kill in a horrible way by cutting open the abdomen, taking out a part of the entrails and tying them to a stake.... Some they use as targets for their arrows.... It is better to say nothing of their horrible treatment of women."[9] And there was more in that vein, calculated to arouse the assembly against the Turks.

The pope's essential goal was the restoration of Jerusalem to the Christian Church. It is the main theme common to all the versions we have of Urban's speech: "You should be moved especially by the holy grave of our Lord and Savior which is now held by unclean peoples, and by the holy places which are treated with dishonor and irreverently befouled with their uncleanness.... Set out on the road to the holy sepulcher; take the land from that wicked people and make it your own.... Jerusalem is the best of all lands [which] our Savior made illustrious by his birth, beautiful with his life, and sacred with his suffering.... This royal city [Jerusalem], is now held captive by her enemies, and made pagan by those who know not God. She asks and longs to be liberated and does not cease to beg you to come to her aid."[10]

The singularly striking feature of the call for this First Crusade was the juxtaposition of the virtue of waging war against God's enemies and the papal promise of the remission of sins for those who undertook to fight. The ideology of the Christian holy war had been developing through much of the eleventh century. During his papacy, Gregory VII had begun to use the term "militia Christi" — the soldiers of Christ — and to encourage, indeed strongly

---

[9] Robert the Monk, in Allen and Amt 41.
[10] Robert the Monk, in Allen and Amt 41–42.

encourage, the use of knights to fight in defense of the Church. The ideology of holy war was given its fullest expression by Urban II at Clermont.

The Church's endorsement of warfare in the service of God was a dramatic change in a religion that had, from the beginning, been a religion of peace. In the late fourth century the great theologian St. Augustine of Hippo, recognizing that the real world was not, after all, a peaceful place, formulated the doctrine of a Just War, enumerating the circumstances under which Christians were allowed to engage in warfare. The main thrust of the Church's policy during the eleventh century had been the attempts to curb the fighting within Europe, and this remained true in Urban's speech, although the context was new.

Urban's message was clear in all the versions of the speech. Give up fighting among yourselves to become instead soldiers of Christ and to rescue His holiest city. "Let those," he said, "who are accustomed to wage private wars wastefully even against Believers, go forth against the Infidels.... Now, let those, who until recently existed as plunderers, be soldiers of Christ...." The pope then took an unprecedented step, which goes far toward explaining the religious fervor for the expedition. "Remission of sins," the pope said, "will be granted for those going thither, if they end a shackled life either on land or in crossing the sea, or in struggling against the heathen. I, being vested with that gift from God, grant this to those who go."[11] In the memorable words recorded by Robert the Monk of Rheims, the pope said, "Set out on this journey and you will obtain the remission of your sins, and be sure of the incorruptible glory of the kingdom of heaven."[12]

Small wonder that with one voice those present cried out "Deus vult! Deus vult." "God wills it! God wills it." Those wishing to go then confessed their sins to a priest and took a vow pledging themselves to go on this holy pilgrimage to Jerusalem. As an outward sign of this pledge they placed the sign of the cross on their clothing—crosses woven of silk and gold or made of the cheapest cloth—worn on the front of their persons when they set out and placed on their backs when they returned home. "And so by embroidering the symbol [of the cross] on their clothing, in recognition of their faith, in the end they won the True Cross itself."[13]

The first person to come forward to take the vow was Adhemar of Monteil, Bishop of Le Puy, an ecclesiastic who had a reputation for spiritual purity and for his ability to interact with military men. The bishop had gone on a pilgrimage to Jerusalem some ten years before Clermont, so he was

---

[11] Fulcher of Chartres, McGinty 16.
[12] Robert of Rheims, in Allen and Amt 42.
[13] Fulcher of Chartres, McGinty 18.

more knowledgeable than most about conditions in the Holy Land. Urban accepted his vow and chose Adhemar to go to the Holy Land as his representative, formally called his legate, to lead the crusading armies in his stead. This decision was likely prearranged, since Urban had visited with the Bishop at Le Puy before the council met.

The crusade was in the nature of a pilgrimage, albeit a special kind of military pilgrimage; it was nonetheless at its core a pilgrimage, and the pope had to confront the thorny problem of who actually should be allowed or encouraged to join the crusade and who should not. He was quite explicit that old people, the infirm, the very young, women without the protection of husbands or brothers, and those untrained to fight should not go. Monks and priests were forbidden by the church to bear arms and could only go on the crusade if they had received permission from their superiors. Despite the best efforts of every pope and despite all the papal strictures, the problem of curtailing the numbers of noncombatants was never resolved. It was virtually impossible to persuade those who desired to go that this was not a pilgrimage for the weak and unfit, and the astonishing fact is that huge numbers of noncombatants went on all the crusades.

The wealthy traveled with their extended families, including women, children, the elderly, and many servants; knights brought servants to push the carts carrying weapons, armor, and supplies; merchants and artisans came, as did clerics, camp followers, the poor, and pilgrims who were usually dependent on the rich for food and other necessities. The pope asked that the rich help the many poor who went East, but their sheer numbers constituted a considerable drain on finances. The noncombatants slowed progress and were the most likely to die en route. In every regard the crusade was an extremely expensive undertaking.

The Preparations Begin

August 15, 1096, the day when the Feast of the Assumption was celebrated, was the day set by the pope for the departure of the crusading armies; the intervening months gave the participants time to raise funds for the purchase of horses, the necessary armor and equipment and to settle their affairs before leaving. The crusaders, who would travel east in separate groups, were to gather at Constantinople before setting out for Jerusalem. This was not a unified or cohesive army, led by a single commander. The groups formed to go to the Holy Land on this first crusade were brought together by nobility from different parts of Europe, particularly France, though not exclusively so, and were each quite independent. They joined at Constantinople and from then on were under the nominal leadership of Adhemar of Le Puy, until his untimely death. But there was no power that could force them to stay together. In addition, there was a grassroots movement that inspired several bands of people to go east in advance of the formal crusading armies.

Before the council closed, the pope instructed the clergy and monks to go home and preach the crusade. He himself spent the whole of the next year traveling through France and Italy to arouse enthusiasm and enlist support for the crusade. The preaching was to be done—and indeed was done—by the bishops, priests, and monks who, by virtue of their offices, were legitimately empowered to transmit the pope's message. They were also able to hear confession and accept the vow of a person assuming the cross.

In the eleventh century, another kind of preacher had become a familiar figure on the religious landscape—the itinerant preacher who made his way through the towns and villages, extolling the spiritual values of the early Christians and preaching to people who found these men more sympathetic than the formal clergy. These wandering preachers spoke directly to the deep religiosity of the men and women who heard them. Occasionally these evangelists asked for and received the equivalent of a papal license to preach; most, however, did not.

Peter the Hermit's "Crusade"

At the time of the First Crusade, the most famous evangelist was Peter the Hermit. He was born in Amiens, France, and at some point became a hermit; beyond that his early life is a blank. His fame revolves around the role he played in the so-called Peasants' (or People's) Crusade, a misnomer, as it turns out, but one that has been difficult to dislodge. The people Peter gathered around him were knights and middle-class burghers, along with some poor to be sure, but his so-called crusade was by no means exclusively, or even predominantly, a peasants' crusade. The groups joined together under the general umbrella of the People's Crusade were not all led by Peter himself. There were actually five separate groups; the most famous was Peter's army, and it is his name that is most prominent. His preaching was, without doubt, the catalyst for the People's Crusade. The story that Peter had gone to Jerusalem as a pilgrim some time before Clermont and had brought back a letter from the Patriarch of Jerusalem to Urban asking for help has been discredited by most historians, although it resurfaces from time to time with some persistence. According to that story, it was Peter who persuaded the pope to undertake the crusade.

An eyewitness account described Peter as wearing "a woolen shirt, and over it a mantle reaching to his ankles; his arms and feet were bare. He lived on wine and fish; he hardly ever, or never, ate bread."[14] His cape, his bare feet,

---

[14] Guibert of Nogent, "The Deeds of God through the Franks," *Urban and the Crusaders*, trans. Dana C. Munro (Philadelphia: U of Pennsylvania P, 1895) 20.

2.1 Peter the Hermit riding his donkey. From an illuminated manuscript, ca. 1270.

and the mule he rode were all the outward signs of the apostolic poverty he had embraced and were recognized and revered by his listeners. He was, without doubt, a charismatic preacher, "For in whatever he did or said it seemed as if there was something divine."[15]

Peter began urging the crusade before the end of 1095. He traveled through northern France, visiting many cities and towns along the way, and then crossed into the Rhineland, stopping in Cologne to celebrate Easter. By the time he reached Cologne he had gathered in his train some fifteen thousand people—a mixed group of knights, foot soldiers, peasants, women, and the elderly. The people who followed Peter, for the most part, believed, as he did, that the Day of Judgment was near and that the necessity to rescue Jerusalem from the infidel was therefore urgent.

Peter's preaching in the Rhineland had several consequences, none of them anticipated or desired by Urban II. Peter had enlisted several of his followers to preach in places he himself could not visit, with the result that new bands were enlisted for the crusade that were not under Peter's control. Peter's preaching inspired lesser German knights and middle-class burghers (as well as Frenchmen), all eager for the chance to make the pilgrimage and to fight. A contingent of French recruits, led by Walter Sans Avoir (called, erroneously, the "Penniless") was so eager to go East that Walter did not wait for Peter but went on ahead to Constantinople. Peter and his troops soon followed. German bands spoiling for a fight remained behind. It was these Germans who committed the massacres of the Jewish communities in Speyer, Worms,

---

15 Guibert of Nogent, Munro 20.

Mainz, and Cologne—the infamous destruction of the Ashkenazic (northern European) Jews who, for a century, had lived and flourished in the Rhineland.

During the eleventh century, the Jews had migrated into the Rhineland, where they formed new settlements and participated in the general revitalization of life in northern Europe. They were mainly engaged in trade and economic life, becoming, among other things, money changers and ultimately moneylenders. Their communities became vibrant intellectual and social settlements, and the Jews had the privilege of practicing their own religion, with certain restrictions, such as the prohibition against any attempts to convert Christians. Until the spring of 1096 they remained essentially free of overt persecution. Nevertheless, the Jews were always fearful that the latent anti-Semitism in Europe, never far from the surface, would explode into active violence, as it did when the unruly German bands were left to their own devices.

A. The Massacres of Jews in the Rhineland

Peter may have participated in some early threats to the Jewish communities in France, although that is not well documented, and in any event he departed for Constantinople before the slaughters occurred in the Rhineland. However, the sermon Peter delivered on Easter Sunday in Cologne, in April 1096, was an incendiary reminder that the Christians believed that the Jews had been responsible for the crucifixion of Christ; it was, in its effect, a call to arms against the Jews, if, indeed, one was needed. The widespread violence in Europe, the fervor unleashed by the crusading ideal, the presence of a non-Christian minority living among Christians and far more accessible than the Muslims, combined with the desire of these crusading bands to get their hands on the Jews' wealth, all erupted in the atrocities committed in May 1096.

The first attack against the Jews took place in Speyer; it was, fortunately for the Jews, a small and badly planned attack, and although eleven Jews were killed, it was a tiny fraction compared to those who died in the major atrocities committed at Worms, Mainz, and Cologne. At Speyer the Jews were protected by the bishop, and the mob quickly moved on.

The next attack took place at Worms. The Jews there hoped and expected to depend on the townspeople and the local bishop, who had promised to help them. Some Jews remained in their homes; others fled for safety to the bishop's residence, but in the event none were spared. By May 20, the entire Jewish community had been eliminated, either by the crusading bands or by the hands of the Jews themselves. The Jews who had stayed in their homes were all killed, and then the mob went after those in the bishop's residence. When the Jews there realized that they would also be killed, they chose martyrdom rather than wait to be murdered by infidels. "They slaughtered brethren, relatives, wives, and children. Bridegrooms [slaughtered] their intended and merciful mothers their only children.... As they commended their souls to their Creator, they cried out: 'Hear O Israel! The Lord is our God; the Lord is One.' "[16]

The story was repeated at Mainz, the cultural and intellectual center of early Ashkenazic Jewry. It was here that the hated and hateful Count Emicho, a German count from Leiningen, made his appearance; a religious fanatic and a bloodthirsty warrior, he was determined to murder all the Jews. And the Germans succeeded, in this case with the collusion of the burghers who opened the gates for Emicho's army. The first Jews who were attacked, in an outer courtyard of the bishop's residence, chose not to attempt to escape; instead they remained where they knew they would die. "Rather with love they accepted upon themselves the judgment of heaven." The crusaders were wild and unmerciful, killing men, women, children, and infants still nursing in the vilest possible ways. When those who were hiding in an inner chamber saw that their brethren had stayed to be killed, they chose to martyr themselves. "All cried out: 'There is nothing better than to offer ourselves as a sacrifice.' There women girded themselves with strength and slaughtered their sons and daughters, along with themselves.... They offered up their children as did Abraham with his son Isaac.... They [all] stretched forth their necks for the slaughter and commended their pure souls to their Father in heaven." When Emicho and his men found their bodies, they stripped them and buried them naked. "That day," a Hebrew chronicler lamented, "the crown of Israel fell."[17]

The band went next to Cologne. Although the town's Jews had fled to other smaller towns to escape destruction, they were found and not spared. Once again those who survived took their own lives.

Before each act of destruction, the Jews were offered the opportunity to save themselves by converting to Christianity, and there were some who chose to convert, for life itself is sacred to the Jews. In other cases Jews were forced on pain of torture and death to convert. But the Jews who chose martyrdom raised the whole episode to an extraordinary level of religious and emotional intensity; their story has lived on and has an important place in the annals of Jewish martyrdom.

For many centuries historians believed that these massacres were the beginning of the end for European Jewry, that they presaged the large-scale and widespread destruction of the Jews that was to come in later centuries, that the history of the Jews and the history of anti-Semitism were from 1096

---

[16] Solomon ben Simson, "Hebrew First-Crusade Chronicle," *European Jewry and the First Crusade*, trans. Robert Chazan (Berkeley and Los Angeles: U of California P, 1996) 243–61.

[17] Solomon ben Simson 255–56.

onward one and the same. The newest evidence and interpretations of these sorry events, however, provided by Robert Chazan's responsible scholarship, points instead to the fact that these outbursts were isolated events, limited in time and space to the unfortunate Rhineland Jews.[18] These Jews were tragically caught in the uncontrolled brutality and fanaticism associated with the warlike bands who operated at the extreme edges of the crusading movement.

After annihilating the Jewish communities in the Rhineland, Emicho started out for Constantinople, choosing the northern, overland route that went through the Christian kingdom of Hungary. The King of Hungary, knowing Emicho's reputation, refused him safe passage through his kingdom. Emicho besieged a Hungarian stronghold for three weeks, but his army was defeated, his men dispersed, and Emicho was forced to turn back to Germany. His crusading career was finally and abruptly finished. "So the hand of the Lord is believed to have been against the pilgrims, who had sinned by excessive impurity and fornication, and who had slaughtered the exiled Jews through greed of money, rather than for the sake of God's justice."[19] This fitting epitaph to Emicho's lifework was written by a Christian chronicler.

Two other German bands attempted the route across Hungary but were forcibly turned back, and they also dispersed.

B. The People's Crusade Goes East

While Emicho was engaged in the Rhineland, first Walter Sans Avoir and then Peter the Hermit had begun the march toward Constantinople. The major problem Walter and Peter had to face was endemic to all the crusading armies and a constant during the whole crusading era: raising money for supplies and feeding people on the long march east. The soldiers had to be kept supplied with armor, weapons, horses for the knights, and fodder for the horses, and, above all, there had to be food for everyone, including the noncombatants who in some instances doubled the size of the military force. Three possibilities existed for obtaining food: carrying enough for such a long distance, which was extremely difficult; buying it en route; or plundering the countryside as the armies marched.

Both Walter and Peter followed the overland route most commonly used by pilgrims in the centuries before the crusades. The route went from Germany along the Rhine to the Danube River; along the Danube through

---

[18] Two books by Robert Chazan are strongly recommended for his full and lucid discussion of the history, sources, and implications of the subject: *European Jewry and the First Crusade* (Berkeley and Los Angeles: U of California P, 1987) and *In the Year 1096: The First Crusade and the Jews* (Philadelphia: The Jewish Publication Society, 1996).

[19] Albert of Aachen, "Chronicle of the First Crusade," in Allen and Amt 52. Albert's full account of the Peasants' Crusade begins on page 47.

the Kingdom of Hungary to the frontier at Semlin; across the Sava River, which formed the boundary between Hungary and Bulgaria; from Bulgaria to Belgrade, through the forests to Nish, passing Sofia and Adrianople; and finally arriving at Constantinople. The Kingdom of Bulgaria, which had been a fierce enemy of the Byzantines for several centuries, had been subdued and annexed to the empire early in the eleventh century, and a Byzantine governor ruled from Nish. The province was far from peaceful, however. The large Slavic population in Bulgaria was warlike and restless, and a Turkish tribe known as the Pechenegs, which had settled along the Lower Danube in southwestern Russia, raided regularly during the eleventh century, challenging Byzantine control in Bulgaria. So it was a troubled and unpredictable part of the world the crusaders had to traverse.

Walter Sans Avoir and his followers, consisting of a substantial number of foot soldiers and only eight knights, seem to have been well supplied to begin and had the money to purchase food and arms at the markets they passed. Walter's army made its way easily through Hungary, having been accorded safe passage by the Christian king. Their troubles began in Bulgaria. Walter and his army left Hungary at Semlin. Unbeknown to Walter, a small group of his men remained in Semlin, intending to purchase arms and supplies. Instead they were robbed by some Hungarians and had to make their way to Walter's camp at Belgrade bereft of all their possessions, including the clothes on their backs. There soon ensued a battle between Walter's men and the Hungarians, which ended badly for the crusaders. At Belgrade, Walter was not allowed to purchase food, so some of his men went off to forage. That event also ended badly; some sixty pilgrims in Walter's entourage were burned to death in a church in retaliation for the pillaging. The wrongs Walter had suffered were ultimately redressed by the Byzantine governor Nicetas at Nish, and Walter and his band were able to buy food and were given an escort for the rest of the route. They marched without further incident to Constantinople, where they arrived on July 20 and settled down to wait for Peter the Hermit to arrive.

Peter had been able to raise money and purchase supplies before he set out with an army that had swelled to perhaps as many as twenty thousand men. His preaching in Germany had brought large numbers of Germans into his ranks as well as Frenchmen. As always, any numbers given for the crusading expeditions have to be taken with a large dose of skepticism: both the lack of accurate numbers and the strong inclination of many chroniclers to exaggerate have to be taken into account. However, that Peter had a sizable force is not in doubt. — a force, one chronicler wrote, "innumerable as the sands of the sea."[20]

---

[20] Albert of Aachen in Allen and Amt 50.

Peter's knights, of course, rode on horseback, some of his men went down the Danube to Semlin on boats, the majority went on foot, and Peter rode his donkey all the way to Constantinople. He had in his train large numbers of pilgrims and noncombatants and many carts carrying supplies—among them a chest containing the treasure he had amassed. He was accorded a safe passage through Hungary, and all went well until he reached Semlin. There his men saw the clothing and arms that had been taken from Walter's men and left hanging on the city walls. Some of his men became so angry that they stormed Semlin and took the city, but Peter, always hoping for a peaceful journey, quickly led his men out of Hungary. When he reached Nish, Nicetas, who was prepared to defend the city, was persuaded to allow Peter to buy food if he left hostages to ensure the city's safety. All went smoothly, and the hostages were duly returned. Unfortunately, some Germans set fire to a few mills outside the city walls; Byzantine troops then attacked the baggage train and captured women and children, leading to further fighting. In the end Peter lost a sizable portion of his group, perhaps as many as a quarter of those who had started out with him.

Once he reached the Byzantine cities of Sofia, Philippopolis, and Adrianople, Peter found a warm welcome; so moved were the citizens of Philippopolis when he told the stories of his woes that they showered him with gifts. At Adrianople, Peter received a message from the emperor urging him to hurry to Constantinople, for Alexius had heard about Peter and was eager to meet him. Alexius undoubtedly was also eager to see what this strange army was that had entered his empire. Peter arrived on August 1; the journey had taken three months and eleven days.

At Constantinople, Peter joined Walter and his army, and they added to their company some Italians who had come to the East to trade or act as mercenaries in the Byzantine army. Alexius welcomed Peter, gave him gifts and good advice. He enjoined Peter to wait for the main crusading armies before proceeding toward Jerusalem, and Peter agreed. After a few days outside Constantinople, Peter's army was taken across the Bosphorus and overland to the Byzantine fortification at Helenopolis, the town the French called Civitot. Alexius warned Peter not to enter Turkish territory, which was close to their camp, and for two months Peter and his men heeded that advice. The location provided plentiful food so long as Peter could afford to pay for it. After two peaceful months, either because their money had run out or because they had become bored with inaction, many soldiers ignored Peter's admonitions and began to plunder the countryside, moving closer and closer to Turkish territory. In the end the army was ambushed by the Turks, the soldiers and the women and children with them all slaughtered. Only Peter himself and a few followers survived, because Peter had gone to Constantinople

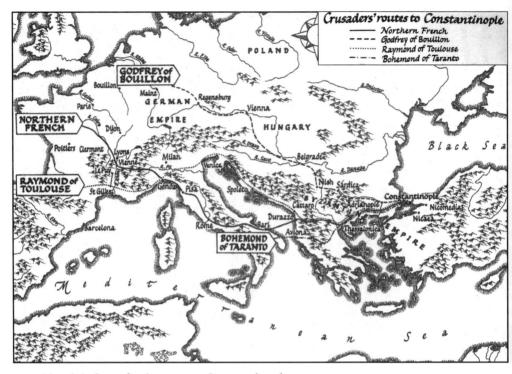

Map 2.1 Crusaders' routes to Constantinople.

to beg the emperor for help when he knew the Turks were approaching. In another version of the event Peter was rescued from Civitot by the emperor's navy, but, whichever is true, the People's Crusade ended in an unmitigated disaster, and Peter lived to witness it.

The Crusading Armies Leave for Constantinople

Within a few days the first regular crusading armies began to arrive at Constantinople. Anna Comnena, Emperor Alexius's daughter, wrote a remarkable history of her father's reign and included in it the history of the First Crusade from—needless to say—the Byzantine perspective. Although she recorded these events some thirty years after they occurred, Anna was an eyewitness to many of them and an intelligent, well-educated observer, researcher, and writer. About the crusaders' advance she wrote, "there is something strange about it, which intelligent people at least would notice. The multitude did not arrive at the same moment, nor even by the same route... but they made the voyage in separate groups, some first, some second, some after them.... Each

2.2 Crusader embraced by his wife. Twelfth-century sculpture from the cloister of the priory of Belval in Lorraine, France.

army ... was preceded by a plague of locusts, so that everyone ... came to recognize locusts as the forerunners of the Frankish battalions."[21] She may have exaggerated the plague of locusts, but she was correct about the way the armies came east. Response to the pope's call had come quickly; mobilizing the armies and raising the necessary funds took several months, as did the long march to Constantinople.

The cost of crusading, however measured, was remarkably high, for these were bloody wars, and the routes to the Holy Land were fraught with difficulties. In human terms the numbers of dead, wounded, and sick, which could easily reach as high as between one-quarter and one-half of the army that started out, are impossible to calculate with exactitude. We have an understanding of the cost in human misery during the crusades themselves from the chroniclers who recorded the events. But first there were the heartwrenching separations as the crusaders prepared to leave their families. "Oh how much grief there was! ... How much weeping among loved ones when the husband left his wife so dear to him as well as his children, father and mother, brothers and grandparents, and possessions however great!"[22]

The courage of the people who undertook the journey is astounding: to march for months across mountainous country and through thickly forested regions, to endure freezing cold and drought so severe that no water was available, to suffer from hunger, disease, the death of friends and loved ones — all these and more were constant companions on the journey east.

The cost in financial terms was extremely high. Urban's appeal had been first and foremost to the nobility — the counts, dukes, and barons, who could presumably afford the enormous expense involved. The nobles were expected to support their household knights; supply armor, weapons, and food; and provide horses and the grooms to care for them. Mercenaries formed an important part of every army, and they were expensive to hire.

Pride of place in the armies was given to the knights. By the close of the eleventh century, these mounted, armed, and highly trained warriors had emerged as a social class in Europe. Their origins were quite diverse: many came from noble families; others rose from the peasantry to take the training and the oath that initiated them into knighthood. Whatever their backgrounds, the bond that joined them was loyalty to their prince and to each other; the mark of their status was personal bravery. The knights wore body armor made of chain mail (called hauberks), which had a split skirt, so that their thighs would be protected, and a conical steel helmet, usually with a covering for the nose and face. They carried a shield for protection and a

---

21 Anna Comnena, *The Alexiad*, trans. E.R.A. Sewter (London: Penguin Books, 1969) 310.
22 Fulcher of Chartres, McGinty 23.

lance and spear—these last the weapons used in combat. All this they brought with them to the Holy Land, a heavy burden in both weight and expense.

The specially bred and trained horses that carried the knights into battle were the most expensive part of the knight's equipment—the biggest purchase he might be called on ever to make. In the best of times in Europe, feeding these horses was a difficulty. For the long journey east, supplying adequate grain was a major problem and was coupled with the hazards faced by horses who had to walk across unfamiliar, often treacherous terrain. It was customary for knights to bring more than one horse, usually a second horse for riding and also draught horses. The very wealthy princes—and few could afford this—might bring two or three chargers, to spare the main charger, and because many horses perished even before the crusade reached Jerusalem or were simply too fatigued to ride into battle. A large complement of grooms was required to look after the horses. To help with transport and the care of the armor and other equipment, the knights customarily brought servants.

Each army had a sizable contingent of foot soldiers, considerably greater in number than the knights. The trained infantrymen carried bows, crossbows, spears, a shield for protection, and they wore armor. Their role as archers was pivotal, and the funds they required were not inconsequential. This was a movable group; knights whose horses had died joined them, and many men untrained for battle were of necessity given arms and required to fight.

The entourage that accompanied and sustained the army—the servants, the artisans, the blacksmiths, the bakers, and all the people whose labor kept the army moving and in good working order—had to be supported. Wives and children of nobility and knights went on the crusades and so did their clothing, jewels, maidservants, even seamstresses. Carts to carry people and goods, draught animals to pull them, tents for sleeping—all had to be provided. Provisioning for the noncombatants was a major burden, and every army had in its train a large number of clerics, the poor, women, children, the elderly, and many, many pilgrims.

A few among the nobility, such as the Count of Toulouse, were sufficiently wealthy to underwrite their expenses, but most had to work hard to raise adequate funds. Mortgaging and selling assets, commonly land, and taking out loans were the usual ways to raise funds. We know that Godfrey of Lorraine, for example, sold several of his castles and lands, including Verdun, to the church in order to finance his crusade, and even the Duke of Normandy, Robert Curthose, had to pawn his duchy to join the First Crusade.

The sacrifices made by the nobility were mirrored at every social level. The knights who went independently, the foot soldiers who were not necessarily part of a noble's household, the merchants, the artisans hoping for work,

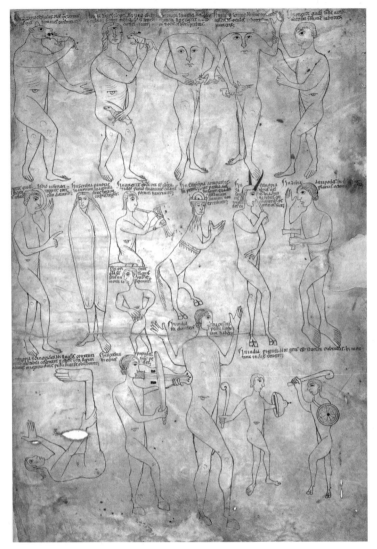

2.3 "Monstrous Races of the World." A graphic depiction in a twelfth-century crusader handbook illustrating what many crusaders envisioned awaited them.

the pilgrims and clerics ... all those who took the cross had to make sacrifices. For many it became a family and even a community affair, and many pooled their resources to subsidize the crusaders as they prepared for war. Once the crusader left, the burden of caring for the home, farming the land, even running a business, was shouldered by the women and sometimes by the church or a nearby monastery. Crusading was not, in any event, a private affair.

A. Hugh of Vermandois

The first crusading army to leave, in mid-August, was led by Hugh of Vermandois, the younger brother of King Philip of France. Philip had been excommunicated by the pope because he had left his wife and married the love of his life, neglecting, however, to divorce his legitimate wife. As an excommunicant Philip certainly could not take up the cross, although there are indications that he desired to go on the crusade. Hugh's resources came from his marriage to the heiress of the County of Vermandois and were not very great. The French chronicler Fulcher of Chartres wrote that Hugh started out with a "scant army," which seems unlikely, but it is certain that he arrived at Constantinople with an army that was by then definitely scanty. Hugh had elected to follow a route that would be taken by several crusading armies after him; he crossed the Alps into Italy and marched south to the port of Bari, and from there he sailed across the Adriatic to Durazzo. The Byzantine stronghold at Durazzo guarded the beginning of the old Roman road, the Via Egnatia, which was the most direct route to Constantinople and therefore the best one to follow.

A storm came up while Hugh's army was at sea and he lost a large number of men and ships; he and his depleted army were in a sorry state when they finally arrived at the headquarters of the Byzantine governor at Durazzo. The governor gave Hugh an escort for the march to Constantinople — a march that was longer than it might have been because, according to Anna Comnena, her father had instructed the governor to send Hugh through Bulgaria to Philippopolis rather than take him on the Via Egnatia directly to Constantinople. The reasons the emperor gave for his choice of route were flimsy; it seems likely that Hugh's arrogance offended him. Hugh had written to alert the emperor of his coming in "letters full of swollen insolence." " 'You are now permitted to greet me,' " Hugh wrote to the emperor, " 'and to receive me with magnificence, as befits my nobility.' "[23] Accurate or not — this is, after all, the Byzantine emperor's daughter writing — Hugh does seem to have given offense. But when Hugh actually reached the imperial court he was treated with kindness and respect. A somewhat different story of his arrival was told in the context of the next group to leave for the East.

B. Godfrey of Bouillon

The second army also departed soon after August 15. It was led by Godfrey of Bouillon, Duke of Lorraine, and included his brothers, Eustace and Baldwin of Boulogne. After some political difficulties in Germany, Godfrey had finally

---

[23] Anna Comnena, in Krey 78.

been able to take control of the duchy that had been left to him by an uncle. He had personal wealth but rather less than one might expect from the duchy itself, so he was forced to sell some of his own lands to finance his sizable army. Although a good deal is known about Godfrey's role during the First Crusade, his character remains an enigma. Godfrey achieved a reputation for piety based on his actions in Jerusalem that adheres to him to this day, but there is little, if any, evidence for piety in his early years.

Godfrey chose to follow the overland route through Hungary and Bulgaria; he encountered trouble in Hungary, which slowed his advance, and he did not reach Constantinople until two days before Christmas of 1096. While still en route, Godfrey purportedly heard a rumor that Hugh was being held prisoner by Alexius, but, if true at all, Hugh was released by the time Godfrey reached Constantinople. That rumor, coupled with the warning given him by some Franks that the Greeks could not be trusted, caused Godfrey to refuse the Byzantine emperor's invitation to enter Constantinople and come to his court. The emperor was furious and would not allow the crusaders to buy supplies. The crusaders retaliated by threatening to plunder. An uneasy peace was made and lasted for the few days that Christmas was celebrated. Soon after the holiday the issue was joined again, although Godfrey had acceded to the emperor's request to move his army some thirty miles (forty-eight kilometers) away from the capital. The distance did not stop the enmity from boiling over into several nasty battles between Godfrey's men and the Greeks.

Peace was again restored shortly before Easter, and Godfrey finally took the oath of allegiance to the emperor. The crux of the oath, which Alexius soon demanded of all the crusading leaders, was fealty to the emperor and the promise that whatever lands were captured from the Muslims that had been Byzantine territory—all towns, farmlands, castles, fortresses, and villages—be returned to the empire. When Godfrey accepted the oath, Alexius gave him money, gold, and jewels, enabling Godfrey to purchase the supplies he needed. All in all, however, it was not exactly a promising start to this new chapter in the relationship between the crusaders and the Greeks.

C. Bohemund of Taranto

Two weeks after Hugh sailed, he was followed by the third contingent, led by Bohemund of Taranto, the formidable eldest son of a formidable father, Robert Guiscard, who until his death was the Norman ruler of southern Italy and overlord of Sicily.

The Norman role in the crusades was pivotal, as was their role in the European political theater during the eleventh century. The conquest of England by the Norman Duke William is of course well known. The Norman expansion into southern Italy and Sicily during the eleventh century, although less dramatic, had equally significant repercussions on Italy, Byzantium, and the eastern Mediterranean.

According to a legend—which may hold a kernel of truth—some Norman pilgrims returning from Jerusalem arrived on the south Italian coast late in the tenth or early in the eleventh century. Southern Italy was regarded by Byzantium as an imperial possession, which indeed it once had been, although the Byzantines had lost control of it. By the time the Normans arrived, southern Italy was highly disorganized, divided among several warring factions. Sicily, once also a Byzantine possession, had been taken by the Muslims in the tenth century. Both areas were grist for the Norman mill, and gradually Norman mercenaries, sensing opportunity, joined the first arrivals, overcame the several feuding factions, and took possession, first of southern Italy and then of Sicily. By the mid-eleventh century Robert Guiscard had emerged as the preeminent Norman soldier–politician in Italy, and a colorful—and ruthless—pirate in the Mediterranean.

Guiscard's most cherished goal was the acquisition of Byzantium, and in 1081 he began a war against the empire that lasted until his death in 1085. His son Bohemund fought by his side, and Bohemund's courage and leadership abilities secured his reputation as a man of remarkable military talent. The war was a drawn-out affair, with first one side then the other seeming victorious until 1085, when Norman victory was certain. Alexius and his empire were saved by a typhoid epidemic that took Robert's life; soon after that Bohemund and the Normans returned to Italy. From the Norman point of view this was a temporary setback, and the Byzantines had good reason to be suspicious of Bohemund's motives for returning to the East.

Bohemund was besieging Amalfi (in southern Italy) when he learned of the crusade. In a flamboyant gesture he ordered his most valuable cloak to be cut up and made into crosses. True or apocryphal, the story is quite in keeping with Bohemund's larger-than-life personality. Caught up in Bohemund's enthusiasm, most of the knights present at the siege immediately took the cross.

Bohemund's followers included an impressive group of the most prominent Norman nobility in southern Italy and Sicily and several powerful members of Bohemund's own family, among them his nephew Tancred, an independent and hotheaded twenty-year-old whom Bohemund made his second-in-command. To these were added groups of Italians and Lombards—all with their own large armies. The author of a colorful history of the Normans and the First Crusade also accompanied Bohemund. Known simply as the Anonymous, this author was Bohemund's vassal, a layman who had been knighted and had firsthand experience of the battlefield. He was devoted to Bohemund, so his history is nakedly prejudiced in Bohemund's favor until events at Antioch caused him to leave Bohemund's army. But that is a later chapter in the Norman story.

Bohemund sailed from southern Italy across the Adriatic and marched overland by a circuitous route to Thessaloniki and on to Constantinople. All along the land route the Normans faced the recurrent problem of securing food — by purchase, if possible, or by plunder. Bohemund tried, with little success, to prevent his men from pillaging, but their need was great and he acquiesced at least once on the march when his men stole oxen and horses and probably pillaged the land as well, and another time when his men burned down a castle and killed all the inhabitants. When Bohemund went on ahead to Constantinople, Tancred remained with the army and continued to stir up trouble between the Normans and the Greeks.

Bohemund arrived in Constantinople on April 10, most of his army finally assembling in the capital a week later. Bohemund's first task was to convince the emperor that he came as a friend — a difficult proposition since the deep distrust and enmity between the two men was palpable. Bohemund is the villain in Anna's history, and she repeatedly refers to his "hidden and deceitful dealings." "Never, indeed," she wrote, "have I seen a man so dishonest. In everything, in his words as well as in his deeds, he never chose the right path." Alexius believed Bohemund to be "a man of wicked intention and perverse mind."[24] Among the first generation of crusade leaders Bohemund was the one most feared and despised by the Greeks.

For his part, Bohemund was so fearful that Alexius was trying to poison him that when Alexius prepared a feast for him he refused to eat the cooked meat and gave it instead to his men. They all survived. Ultimately Bohemund took the oath of featly to Alexius, but it was, at best and for a short time only, a wary alliance.

D. Raymond of Toulouse

On April 21, Raymond, Count of Toulouse, leader of the fourth group, arrived at Constantinople; his army followed several days later. Raymond likely knew of Urban's plans before the council at Clermont and was the first secular lord to take the cross. He was the wealthiest crusade leader: his own lands in southwestern France were plentiful and rich, and he commanded the largest army that went East. Raymond had more than sufficient funds to support his knights and was known for supporting the many clerics, poor, and noncombatants who accompanied him. The pope's legate, Adhemar of Le Puy, traveled with Raymond, and his entourage included his wife (actually his third), his young son, and his chaplain, Raymond of Aguilers, who wrote a history of Raymond's crusade.

---

[24] Anna Comnena, in Allen and Amt 59–60.

Raymond did not start until October, and his army had to travel during the winter months. He took the route through Italy, but rather than cross the Adriatic, he took a land route along the eastern Adriatic shore into Dalmatia, where he quickly encountered terrible weather and a landscape Raymond of Aguilers described as "so pathless and so mountainous that we saw in it neither wild animals, nor birds for three weeks." The local tribes were so hostile that "they even butchered like cattle ... the feeble aged and weak poor, who because of their weakness followed our army at a distance."[25] It was a perilous and gloomy march.

Despite Raymond's goodly supplies at the beginning, food began to run out and was impossible to buy or pilfer. When the hungry and exhausted army at last entered Byzantine territory they were given an imperial escort consisting of mercenaries who guarded the army's every move and watched to be sure the crusaders did not cause any trouble. The crusaders were attacked constantly by tribesmen roaming all along their way — Pechenegs, Bulgarians, even Turks, among others. The papal legate was abducted by Pechenegs, who threw him from his mule and beat him. He was rescued and soon recovered, but it was a sorry episode. The army was ambushed once, and there was fighting several times between the Byzantine mercenaries and Raymond's men. Nevertheless, Raymond accepted the emperor's invitation to enter Constantinople unarmed and, except for a few men, unprotected.

He no sooner had gone to Constantinople than his army began foraging in the countryside; they were attacked by mercenaries supplemented by Byzantine soldiers and suffered a serious defeat. The depleted army then made their way to Constantinople.

Raymond was over fifty-five when he made the journey east. He had already had an illustrious career in Europe and had a reputation for valor gained in his warfare against the Muslims in Spain. He was the logical choice to lead the crusading armies, and he very much wanted the command, but the pope, desiring his own ecclesiastical representative, had instead appointed Adhemar. For as long as he lived Adhemar was the moral center of the crusade, and he even took up arms when necessary, but one of the gravest problems for this first crusade was the absence of a supreme military authority. Inevitably Bohemund also wanted the command and was Raymond's only serious rival. The competition and enmity between the two men was exploited by Alexius, who certainly preferred Raymond to Bohemund.

The final group to leave Europe departed soon after Raymond, also in October 1096. There were actually three groups, each led by an important member of the nobility: Robert, Duke of Normandy (known as Robert Curthose), who was William the Conqueror's oldest son; Robert II, Count of

---

25 Raymond of Aguilers, "The History of the Franks Who Captured Jerusalem," in Krey 64.

Flanders, Curthose's cousin; and Stephen, Count of Blois, who was married to William the Conqueror's daughter Adela. This was not entirely a family affair, however, and soldiers from Brittany, Scotland, and England joined these armies. Fulcher of Chartres, a priest whose chronicle of the crusade is one of the most impartial records we have, was a member of Stephen's entourage.

The armies marched through Italy, stopping at Lucca, where they were met and blessed by Pope Urban; they then visited Rome and finally reached southern Italy. The plan was for them all to sail from Bari across the Adriatic, but only the Count of Flanders seems to have had great enthusiasm for the crusade; he left the others behind and went on ahead to Constantinople. His trip was uneventful; he sailed in December, managed to avoid many of the winter squalls that usually came up on the Mediterranean, and reached Constantinople in April.

Stephen and Robert spent the winter in southern Italy and in early April, judging the weather good for the crossing, at last embarked from Brindisi. A ship still near the shore suddenly and inexplicably broke apart. Some four hundred people were drowned at once and still others, who had managed to reach the water alive, perished soon after. Horses, mules, and money — all were lost. So disheartened and frightened were many who watched from the shore that they abandoned the pilgrimage and returned home. According to Fulcher's account, those bodies that were recovered were found to have crosses imprinted on them. "For it was fitting that this same symbol of victory, which they had worn on their clothes while still living, should remain by the will of God as a token of faith upon those thus occupied in his service."[26]

For those who continued on, the crossing went smoothly, and, except for one accident when a few pilgrims drowned in a stream, the march was essentially without incident. They reached Constantinople in the beginning of May.

During the month before they arrived, Alexius had invited the crusade leaders, one by one, to come to his palace and swear the oath of fealty to him. After much prevarication most of them acquiesced. It was rumored that Bohemund had offered to pledge himself to Alexius, to serve as his representative — an offer that Alexius, with great cunning, turned aside. Alexius had respect and affection for Raymond of Toulouse and recognized him as an ally against Bohemund, should the need arise. Raymond had initially refused to swear fealty to Alexius, but after much negotiation he and the emperor reached a compromise, a watered-down version of the oath that satisfied them both and also gave Raymond an ally against Bohemund. Tancred crossed the Hellespont while no one was watching and thus evaded the whole issue.

---

[26] Fulcher of Chartres, *A History of the Expedition to Jerusalem, 1095–1127*, trans. Frances Rita Ryan (New York: W. W. Norton & Co., 1973) 76.

At the Gates of Constantinople

Anna vividly recalled the crusading armies as they approached her city. "One might have compared them in number to the stars of heaven or the grains of sand poured out over the shore; as they hurried towards Constantinople they were indeed 'numerous as the leaves and flowers of spring' (to quote Homer.)"[27] How numerous these crusaders in reality were is difficult to assess. The armies suffered huge attrition as they trudged east, and this would be true during all the later crusades. Many died on the way, killed in battle or overcome by hunger, thirst, and disease. The terrors of the journey were inescapable, and many deserted. At the same time new recruits joined the armies as they passed through Europe and imperial territory. This was an army whose numbers were always in flux.

The estimates given by the chroniclers are illusory, either far too high or far too low to be credible. As the warfare went on the numbers given by the medieval writers become more reliable and are often confirmed by two or three sources. We shall discuss those in the context of the fighting. The great crusades scholar Sir Steven Runciman, after careful analysis, reckoned that, including Peter the Hermit and his men and including the noncombatants, "in all from sixty to a hundred thousand persons must have entered the Empire from the West between the summer of 1096 and the spring of 1097."[28] It is likely that something closer to the lower figure is nearer the mark.

Constantinople was awe-inspiring to the crusaders. The huge walls that girded the city; the paved streets adorned with statues and monuments; Byzantine churches with their glorious domes and mosaics; the magnificent harbor filled with merchant vessels loaded with silks, damasks, spices, carpets, and every imaginable luxury; the merchants, traders, and visitors from all over the Mediterranean and even from Asia; the sumptuousness of the imperial court — nothing in Europe could compare in size or splendor to the city Constantine had built on the foundation of an ancient Greek city named Byzantium.

Constantinople was perfectly sited on a triangular promontory and straddled Europe and Asia. The city was surrounded on the southern side by the Sea of Marmora, which could be entered only through either of two straits, the Bosphorus (which separated Europe from Asia Minor) or the Hellespont (known also as the Dardanelles); it was protected on the northeast by an inlet called the Golden Horn. The massive walls built on the land side were, through most of the thousand-year history of the empire, virtually impregnable.

---

[27] Anna Comnena, Sewter 324.

[28] Steven Runciman, *A History of the Crusades*, vol. 1 (New York: Harper & Row, 1964) 169. See also John France, *Victory in the East* (Cambridge: Cambridge UP, 1994) 122–24. France's estimate is about sixty thousand people.

2.4 Muslim soldier with his heavy sword.

Alexius allowed small groups of the rank and file—no more than six at one time—to enter through the walls, and to them the luxury, the sights, and smells of the city, the colorful clothing, the strange, incomprehensible language were incredible and dismaying and served to underscore the distrust the crusaders felt for the alien culture.

The Armies Advance toward Nicaea

The first military objective, agreed on by Alexius and the crusade leaders, was the city of Nicaea in Asia Minor. It had been for centuries a Byzantine city with an illustrious history; it was at Nicaea that Constantine presided over the first major Council of the Church in 323. It was a well-fortified city with one side protected by the waters of Lake Ascanius. In the 1080s Nicaea had been captured by the Turks, and it then became their capital under the Seljuk Sultan Kilij Arslan I. The Byzantines had tried several times without success to retake the city, and now, with the crusading army to fight with them, the

2.5 Knight kneeling in prayer.

Byzantines saw their opportunity to reclaim it. For the crusaders the capture of Nicaea was crucial, because Nicaea controlled western Asia Minor and the route across Anatolia that would take them to the Syrian-Palestinian coastal road to Jerusalem.

At the end of April, even before Robert of Normandy and his followers had arrived, the crusading armies, accompanied by imperial troops, began to advance on Nicaea. What a polyglot army it was when they gathered outside the walls of Nicaea. "Whoever heard of such a mixture of languages in one army? There were present Franks, Fleming, Frisians ... Bavarians, Normans, English, Scots ... Bretons, Greeks, and Armenians.... But though we were of different tongues we seemed, however, to be brothers in the love of God and to be nearly of one mind."[29] At last, with the siege of Nicaea imminent, the First Crusade began in earnest.

---

[29] Fulcher of Chartres, Ryan 88.

CHAPTER 3

The First Crusade: From the Siege of Nicaea to the Triumph at Jerusalem

In late April 1097 the first army, led by Godfrey of Lorraine, began the march to Nicaea. Godfrey followed the route taken earlier by Peter the Hermit; in the valley where so many of Peter's men had been slaughtered, the crusaders were greeted by the horrifying sight of the bones and severed heads that the Turks had left to rot. The defile the army had to pass through was overgrown and too narrow for the soldiers to use, so Godfrey sent three hundred men ahead to clear and widen it; when they finished they marked the way with wooden and iron crosses. Godfrey reached Nicaea on May 6.

Siege Warfare in the East

The time had now come for the crusaders' first confrontation with the Turks, their first experience of siege warfare in the East. The crusaders were experienced in siege warfare; the most recent research has shown that it was in fact the dominant mode of warfare in Europe and had been for centuries, extending back to the Roman era.[1] The principles of siege warfare are simple enough to understand; their application was fraught with difficulties.

A fortified site, whatever its size, was built to be a bulwark against invasion and usually erected at a strategic location from which a large area could be controlled. The first move of an enemy commander was to demand — or negotiate — the surrender of a castle or city. When successful, a negotiation

---

[1] See, for example, the excellent book by Randall Rogers, *Latin Siege Warfare in the Twelfth Century* (Oxford: Clarendon Press, 1992) and also Ray Bradbury, *The Medieval Siege* (Woodbridge, UK: The Boydell Press, 1992).

meant that the takeover would be fairly painless. This was rarely the case. The goal was then to capture a city by storm, to destroy a place in the walls large enough for soldiers to pass through and take the city by force. Even when they used the full strength of their siege engines, the picture of men hurling themselves against virtually impregnable walls is terrifying to contemplate. For both sides the hope was that reinforcements would arrive: an army to aid the besiegers or an enemy army to defeat them on the ground. Success in defeating an army in the field was many times critical for the outcome of the siege.

One alternative was to take a city by trickery or bribery, usually with help from a traitor within. When that tactic failed, the besieging army blockaded the city, intending to remain until the inhabitants were starved into surrender or the attackers could mount a successful siege. More often than not the advantage lay with the defenders. So long as food and water lasted, or supplies could be delivered, the likelihood of being able to hold out against a besieging army was quite high.

The problem of securing adequate supplies could quickly become acute, since it became commonplace for the defenders to destroy crops in the surrounding areas and to stop up wells and poison the streams. So the peasants who lived on the land also suffered; they were the innocent bystanders for whom the collateral damage, as we have taken to calling it, was disastrous. Sieges were hazardous affairs for everyone concerned and required huge reserves of courage, unanimity of purpose, and discipline. The necessity to break the siege before determination, food, and water all gave out was paramount.

The crusaders could not, of course, carry their machinery with them and had to build equipment before a siege could begin, which meant finding materials and labor. Noncombatants formed part of the workforce, and women and children helped as well, if only to bring water and food to the builders. With the help of Byzantine engineers and ultimately their own experience in the field, the crusaders improved their equipment considerably as time went on.

The main siege machinery included the simple battering ram, a large wooden beam, sometimes with an iron tip, used, as its name indicates, to batter the walls, and hurling machines of various sizes and weights used to pitch rocks and combustible mixtures over the walls. To undermine the walls the crusaders used a variety of digging machines. The purpose was to remove foundation stones and in their place insert wood to which they set fire, hoping in this way to cause a part of the wall to collapse.

The diggers, or sappers as they are called, worked within a temporary structure made of wood, with walls on all sides and a flat roof made of metal and sometimes of shields strung together. In theory the armored roof was an excellent idea; the first time it was used at Nicaea it was a disaster. The defenders threw heavy rocks from the ramparts onto the top of the armored

3.1 Siege scene with mangonel. The mangonel was a kind of catapult used to throw heavy stones (as shown) against or over a city's walls. The siege engine is sometimes identified as a *petraria*, basically a rock hurler, so it has the same function as the mangonel.

roof until it caved in and killed all twenty knights working within. An inventive Italian then figured out that a sloping roof would afford far better protection than a flat roof, and the armored roof was subsequently built that way.

The many-storied siege tower, made of wood and placed on wheels or rollers, became one of the most valuable pieces of the crusaders' equipment; the highest storey carried archers and soldiers who could hurl incendiary devices and rocks over the walls, and since the tower was movable, it could be brought right up against the city walls.

The Siege of Nicaea

Despite the crusaders' experience with siege warfare, the Near Eastern cities were daunting. Nicaea was enclosed by four miles (6.5 kilometers) of massive walls, fortified by more than two hundred towers and surrounded on three sides by a moat filled with water. On the fourth, western side, the walls reached down to Lake Ascanius, which provided added protection against invasion. Control of the lake also allowed the Turks to receive supplies sent from the eastern shore and enter or leave the city unimpeded.

By May 16, when this first siege undertaken by the crusaders would begin, Godfrey's men, supplemented by the Duke of Flanders's army and Peter the Hermit with the remnants of his group, faced Nicaea's northern wall; Bohemund, Tancred, and the Normans faced the eastern wall; and Raymond of Toulouse, accompanied by Adhemar of Le Puy, had deployed his forces against the southern wall. The Byzantine emperor sent a small group of soldiers and engineers, led by Manuel Butumites, to assist Raymond.

Alexius was canny, highly intelligent, and experienced in war and politics. Time and again during his tumultuous reign Alexius's ingenuity—to some it was his cunning—had benefited the Greeks. So it would again at Nicaea.

Until the Seljuk Turkish conquests had begun in earnest in the second half of the eleventh century, Anatolia had been a vital part of the Byzantine Empire, and Alexius wanted it back. To begin, he wanted Nicaea returned to him. The city had been fortified by the Greeks and it stood at the beginning of the major road across Asia Minor. It was an ancient and venerable city, famous as the place where the Emperor Constantine held the First Ecumenical Church Council in 325 and decided a theological question that had threatened to divide the church in the Byzantine Empire. The bargain Alexius made with the crusaders was that they would regain Nicaea for him in exchange for his help. However, Alexius had a deeply ingrained suspicion of the Franks and their motives and was so distrustful of them that he never personally joined them and kept his distance from Nicaea, close enough to receive reports and to send help when he deemed it necessary, but never too close. The Latin chroniclers who described the siege were reluctant to credit Alexius with the aid he gave to the crusaders, although it came at critical moments and was in fact invaluable.

The crusading armies had suffered enormous losses before they reached Nicaea. Thousands were killed or had died of starvation and thirst on the roads to Constantinople, and there were burial sites all along the way. Some crusaders, daunted by the hardships, had chosen to defect and return home. Although, as always, precise numbers are unreliable, the army that gathered at Nicaea was certainly sizable. "Who could have counted so great an army of Christ?" a chronicler asked. "No one, as I think, has ever before seen so many distinguished knights, or ever will again."[2]

At Nicaea the crusaders faced an acute food shortage; the grain that was available was sold at prices so inflated that the poorer crusaders could not afford to purchase it, and many more people died of starvation. The problem of supplies was partly solved by Alexius, who arranged for Greek merchants to bring food from Civetot, transported on Byzantine ships and sold at rea-

---

[2] "Gesta Francorum," in Krey 102.

3.2 The siege of Nicaea. Depicting the Turks and crusaders throwing heads over the city walls—and with some obvious glee (see the bottom left corner).

sonable prices. Even so, many people did not have enough money to do more than keep starvation at bay. As always there were large numbers of noncombatants—priests and pilgrims, women, the aged, ill, and very young—who had to be cared for and fed.

The sultan, Kilij Arslan I, who ruled Nicaea and much territory beyond it, was away fighting on his eastern frontier when the crusaders assembled outside his city. He was so unafraid of the Latins, having led the army that had easily and cruelly destroyed the People's Crusade, that he had left his wife, his children, and his considerable treasure at Nicaea in the care of the Turkish garrison. The city population was still largely Greek and Christian, governed by the Turks, who immediately sent to the sultan for reinforcements. Before he could turn his entire army around, the sultan sent a small advance party, which was handily defeated by Raymond of Toulouse and quickly retreated. Alexius seized the opportunity and sent Butumites to negotiate a truce with the Turks at Nicaea, but as soon as the Turks saw their sultan's army approaching, they stopped all negotiations and prepared to fight the crusading armies.

The battles that ensued were fierce, with huge losses on both sides. Both armies were merciless, since the aim was to kill, not take prisoners; the desecration of the bodies, carried out by Turks and Christians alike, was vicious, all the more so because it was done with unabashed glee. They taunted one another, hoping to frighten the enemy into submission. The Turks threw down from the ramparts the heads of Christians they had killed, and the crusaders catapulted Turkish heads over the city walls. When they killed Turks, the crusaders often "fixed [their heads] upon spikes and spears, offer[ing] a spectacle joyful to the people of God."[3]

The crusaders were victorious over the sultan's forces, and Kilij Arslan decided to remove his army and leave Nicaea to fend for itself. The crusaders then went back to undermining the city walls. They succeeded in causing a portion of a wall to fall, but the Turks repaired it during the night and fortified it so strongly that the Franks could not breach it.

The Turkish garrison was still able to receive reinforcements and supplies from across Lake Ascanius. Lacking naval support of their own, the crusaders turned to Alexius for help in blockading the lake. In a remarkable move, the emperor had his men bring ships overland the seven miles (eleven kilometers) from Civetot to Lake Ascanius. Some ships were dragged by oxen, others were taken apart, brought by cart, and then put back together. Along with the ships Alexius sent a contingent of fighting men; he also sent many more standards than there were men, to fool the Turks into thinking the force was considerably larger than it actually was. The Greeks floated the ships during the night, and when the Turks saw the flotilla the next morning, "they were frightened even to death, weeping and lamenting; and the Franks were glad and gave glory to God."[4]

Two versions of the events leading to the surrender were recorded by the chroniclers. According to the version favored by the Latins, the sight of the crusaders' preparations for their final assault, planned for June 19, was so terrifying to the Turks that they immediately capitulated. In the second and

---

3   Anselm of Ribemont, "To his reverend lord, Manasses," in Krey 107.
4   "Gesta Francorum," in Krey 103.

authentic version—since we know the outcome—the Byzantine emperor secretly sent an envoy to ask the Turks to turn the city over to him in return for a safe-conduct for the sultan's wife and family and the court officials. Nicaea surrendered to Alexius on June 19. To their surprise and resentment, just before the crusaders could begin their assault, they saw the Byzantine imperial standards on the city ramparts.

Alexius brought the sultan's family and the Turkish officials to Constantinople, where, to the total dismay of the Latins, he treated them with courtesy and respect. The officials were able to ransom themselves, and the sultan's family was returned to him without penalty. Alexius took the treasure he found in Nicaea for himself. Although he was exceedingly generous in the gifts he made to the crusaders—gold, jewels, and horses to the knights; copper coins and food to the soldiers; and immense amounts of his own treasures to the leaders—his gifts did not mitigate the distrust the Latins felt for the Greeks and their anger at how deceitfully Alexius had behaved. They did not forget or forgive the way he snatched the city from them. The extravagant gifts Alexius made to the princes came at a price: once again he exacted an oath of loyalty from the leaders, particularly from those who had not previously taken the oath.

The Road to Antioch

The real prize the emperor hoped the crusaders would win for him was Antioch. Prosperous, beautiful, and strategically located in a valley between a mountain and a river, Antioch had a long history as one of the most important cities in Asia. After its founding by one of Alexander the Great's successors, it had been conquered several times—first by Romans, then by Muslims, then by Byzantine Greeks, and in 1085 by Turkish Muslims. The population was composed of Greek, Armenian, and Syrian Christians. Antioch was revered throughout Christendom as the place where the name Christian was first used and where St. Peter had founded his church. Alexius believed it was rightfully part of his empire.

For the crusaders to reach Jerusalem it was imperative that they capture Antioch, since it guarded the road that led down the Syrian-Palestinian coast to the Holy City. They left Nicaea filled with optimism, on the whole relieved they had been spared a punishing siege and, as it turned out, overly confident about the future. In a famous letter from Stephen of Blois to his wife, Adela, he wrote in a prescient sentence near the end, "I tell you, my beloved, that in five weeks we will reach Jerusalem from Nicaea...unless Antioch resists us."[5]

---

[5]   Stephen of Blois, "Letter to his wife," in Krey 109.

After the crusaders had rested they separated into two groups and began the march across Anatolia. Bohemund, Tancred, and the Normans, with Stephen of Blois and his army, were in one group; all the other crusaders were in the second group. It is not certain what led them to separate, but for two days the armies marched apart and out of sight of one another. On the third day a huge Turkish army, appearing seemingly out of nowhere, "howling and shouting like demons,"[6] attacked Bohemund's armies.

Nothing in their experience had prepared the Latins for the extraordinary skill of the Turkish mounted archers. The Turkish nomads had for centuries lived on horseback, and their expertise was bred in the bone. Their horses were smaller, lighter, and swifter than the Western horses, and their mobility was remarkable. The Turks used a short bow made of wood, horn, and sinew that could deliver an arrow with enough speed and force to pierce a crusader's armor and mortally wound him. At close range they fought with swords and spears quite like those of the Franks. Their main tactics consisted of surprise attacks, ambushes, skirmishes, and feigned retreats to lure the enemy to follow so that they could then whirl around to attack once again. In a pitched battle the Turks customarily encircled the enemy and tried to separate the vanguard from the rear.

The shock of the ambush that took place on June 1 on the plain near Dorylaeum, the overwhelming numbers of Turks, together with Arabs, Persians, and other pagans — as the Franks called them — raining arrows on them, terrified the crusaders. In the initial attack many crusaders were wounded, the rest, driven back to their tents, "huddled together, indeed, like sheep in a fold, trembling and frightened."[7] When they believed themselves to be near death, they rallied and began to press forward against the Turks. Bohemund had already sent word of the attack to the second army, led by Raymond of Toulouse, who rushed to their rescue. The sight of this larger army and the surprise appearance of another body of troops led by Adhemar of Le Puy, persuaded the Turks to retreat. They left behind tents, camels, horses, and provisions that the crusaders seized.

Their victory in no way lessened the respect the crusaders had for the Turkish archers. Quite the opposite. "What man, however experienced and learned, would dare to write of the skill and prowess and courage of the Turks?... Yet, please God, their men will never be as good as ours."[8] The victory at Dorylaeum gave the crusaders renewed courage and purpose. It also

---

[6] *Gesta Francorum, The Deeds of Franks and Other Pilgrims to Jerusalem*, trans. and ed. Rosalind Hill (Oxford: Clarendon Press, 1962) 18.

[7] Fulcher of Chartres, Ryan 117.

[8] *Gesta Francorum*, Hill 21.

gave them access to the road they would take to cross Anatolia and reach Antioch. The route they followed was, for many, fatally dangerous; for everyone the hardships seemed, and indeed were, infinite. Alexius had sent Taticius as his representative with a group of guides to lead the way, and the crusaders blamed the Greeks for the perilous route they followed. Yet they had little choice if they were to avoid going through territory controlled by the Turks or their allies.

After the battle at Dorylaeum, the Turks, fleeing ahead of the Franks, laid waste the land, and neither food nor water could be had even before they reached the Anatolian desert — "a land which was deserted, waterless and uninhabitable, from which we barely emerged or escaped alive."[9] The crusaders marched all summer in heat that could easily reach 110° Fahrenheit (43° Celsius) or more. Their only food was prickly plants, presumably thistles. Somehow the men managed to survive, but many horses died of thirst and hunger. Knights were forced to walk as foot soldiers, and goats, sheep, and even dogs were forced to carry baggage.

By the middle of August the army finally reached fertile country in the area surrounding Iconium, a city formerly held by the Turks. For the moment the Turks had withdrawn, and the parched, half-starved, and exhausted crusaders remained there for two days recouping their energies and finding plentiful food and water.

The leaders' independence, their rivalries and quarrelsome natures, their thirst for personal glory and spoils, held in abeyance at Nicaea and Dorylaeum, surfaced soon after the crusaders reached Iconium. While the main army stayed to rest, Bohemund's nephew Tancred and Baldwin of Boulogne, with their respective armies, went off on their own. They went south toward the Cilician coast, passing through countryside and towns held by Armenian Christians. Several towns willingly surrendered to them, until they reached Tarsus, the birthplace of St. Paul. Although Tarsus was held by the Turks, the population was made up of Armenian and Greek Christians who very much wanted the crusaders to rescue them from the Turks and take the city for themselves.

Tarsus was wealthy, and Tancred and Baldwin immediately began quarreling over who would have control of the city. Baldwin offered to share the city and its spoils with Tancred, who flatly refused. The Turks, realizing they were outnumbered, fled from Tarsus during the night, and Tancred, recognizing the superior strength of Baldwin's army, withdrew, leaving Tarsus to Baldwin. Neither man even considered returning Tarsus to Alexius, despite the fact that Tarsus had belonged to the Byzantine Empire. Baldwin left a garrison at Tarsus and marched farther east toward the Euphrates River, capturing towns as he went.

---

[9]   *Gesta Francorum*, Hill 23.

A. Baldwin Captures Edessa

As he moved successfully eastward, Baldwin's reputation spread and he came to be regarded as a hero to the Armenian Christians, who saw him as their savior from the Turks. In the late winter of 1097 Baldwin was approached by an embassy from Thoros, the Armenian ruler of Edessa, a rich and famous city situated some twenty miles (thirty-two kilometers) east of the shore of the Euphrates River. Thoros was fearful that the Turks, who were already assembling a large army to save Antioch from the crusaders, were likely to attack Edessa first. He was fearful also of the people of Edessa, who thought him quite hateful. Through his ambassadors Thoros offered to adopt Baldwin and make him his heir if he would come to help him keep and protect Edessa.

Baldwin went to Edessa and in a public ceremony was legally adopted by Thoros, who had no children of his own. The ceremony was, for Europeans, decidedly odd. Both Thoros and Baldwin stripped naked to the waist and embraced; Thoros then sealed the adoption by kissing Baldwin. Soon afterward Baldwin left Edessa to besiege a neighboring city; when he returned he discovered that the local nobles had revolted against Thoros and intended to kill him. At this point in the story Baldwin's role in the events becomes murky. The chroniclers who liked Baldwin wrote that he had no knowledge of the revolt and tried to save Thoros from death. Those who were not so fond of Baldwin said that he engineered the incident in order to become ruler of Edessa without waiting for Thoros to die a natural death. In the end Thoros was murdered and Baldwin established himself as overlord of the first crusader state in the Middle East. His would not be the last crusader state.

Baldwin's difficulties were not quite over. He had word of a revolt planned against him by the citizens, and he ordered his followers to appear everywhere in the city, even in church, in full armor, letting it be known that he was aware of the plot. He accused the leaders of treason and forced them to confess. As punishment "some had their feet cut off, some their hands, others their ears and noses ... and all of them were castrated and sent into exile.... Baldwin then experienced the rewards and happiness"[10] of his acquisition. Beyond the city Baldwin controlled a large area, known as the County of Edessa, which extended on both sides of the Euphrates. He was the first leader to leave the crusade to take command of his own territory. His conquest was the first of the lands that would form the Latin Kingdom when the crusade ended. It also was a preview of things to come, when crusade leaders would put their own ambitions before the primary aim of the expedition.

Soon after Baldwin and Tancred had left Iconium, the main body of cru-

---

[10] Guibert of Nogent, *Gesta Dei per Francos: The Deeds of God through the Franks,* trans. Robert Levine (Woodbridge, UK: The Boydell Press, 1997) 71.

saders marched to Caesarea and from there to Coxon, their last stop for food and water before they began the hazardous journey across the Anti-Taurus Mountains, finally to Antioch.

All along the route to Coxon the Latins had encountered Turkish armies and in every case defeated them. As it turned out, the dangers from the Turks were as nothing compared with the dangers lurking at every step on the mountain. The path, such as it was, was narrow, strewn with rocks, and covered with slimy mud from the rains that had recently fallen. The crusaders slipped and stumbled nervously along in single file, and a great many horses and pack animals lost their footing and plunged over the precipice to a horrible death. Bereft and unprepared to cope, the knights whose horses had died "stood about in a great state of gloom, wringing their hands because they were so frightened and miserable, not knowing what to do with themselves and their armor."[11] They tried first to sell their armor and weapons, but when that failed they simply threw them over the side of the mountain. In that wretched state the crusaders finally descended the mountain and came to the Armenian Christian city of Marash, whose inhabitants gave them food and supplies. Only a valley now lay between the crusaders and Antioch.

The Crusaders Reach Antioch

In the third week of October the crusaders entered the plain that brought them in sight of Antioch. The city had been built between the Orontes River and Mount Silpius, which rose majestically behind it. The Orontes flowed twelve miles (thirty-two kilometers) through a fertile valley to the Mediterranean Sea, and to reach Antioch the crusaders had first to cross the so-called Iron Bridge, which spanned the river. The Turkish army they encountered at the bridge was quickly overcome; the Turks fled, leaving behind horses, camels, grain, and wine, which the crusaders carried off.

Although they surely knew something of the size and strength of Antioch, the crusaders were amazed when they actually saw it. The city was built on the slope of Mount Silpius, surrounded by formidable walls fortified by four hundred towers. Within the city there were two mountains; the imposing citadel, which could be seen from a great distance, was built on the top of the higher mountain, the way up to it so precipitous that it was almost impossible to reach. "This city," a chronicler wrote, "two miles in length, is so fortified... that it fears the attack of no machine and the assault of no man, even if every race of man should come together against it."[12]

---

11 *Gesta Francorum*, Hill 27.
12 Raymond of Aguilers, in Krey 127.

The Siege of Antioch

So the decision was made. An assault on Antioch was out of the question and the crusaders settled in for a siege of attrition, hoping to starve Antioch into submission. It would not be an easy matter. Antioch was blessed with such an abundance of crops that the Antiochenes had already harvested, good grazing land, and plentiful water that the city could withstand a siege for several months.

The siege began in late October. The crusaders were well supplied at first and were even profligate about how much they ate and drank, believing they could forage in the countryside. In time, however, their supplies began to dwindle, and they had to go farther and farther afield to find food, which brought them close to, and finally into, Turkish territory, where they were regularly attacked. To add to their difficulties, the crusaders had to swim across the river to reach new supplies and laden with burdens, return the same way. In time they built a wooden bridge, which helped considerably but did not end their troubles. At Antioch the Turks manning the walls made quick sorties through the city gates to harass and kill people in the camp.

By mid-November the cold winter had come, and by Christmas food was scarce. Hunger, thirst, disease, and the harsh weather became the most feared enemies. Soon after Christmas, Bohemund volunteered to lead a contingent of soldiers into Turkish lands to look for food. His army was ambushed, and, although many of his men were killed, Bohemund actually succeeded in routing the Turks. The victory was cause for celebration when he returned to camp. So eager were the crusaders for some success that a chronicler reported that a mere forty knights had routed a Turkish force of over sixty thousand men! Yet they had come back empty-handed, and more people died of starvation or became seriously ill.

People were reduced to eating stalks they found in the fields; thistles; and "horses, asses, and camels, and dogs and rats. The poorer ones ate even the skins of beasts and seeds of grain found in manure."[13] The famine bred disease. Horses died for lack of fodder, and it has been estimated that, even before the siege ended, no more than a thousand horses remained for the knights. The situation was far worse than anyone could have imagined and worsening with every passing day; the visions of fighting for a blessed cause were quickly losing their appeal.

Suffering from great hunger, exposed to freezing weather—their tents had rotted in the rain—with little hope of help or supplies, many crusaders deserted. Nor was it only the poor and needy who fled, hoping to reach the mountains or Edessa or Cyprus. Peter the Hermit attempted to escape, along with his com-

---

[13] Fulcher of Chartres, McGinty 44.

3.3 The siege of Antioch. The illustration shows the heavily fortified walls surrounding the city and the ferocity with which Antioch was defended.

panion William, known as the Carpenter. They were caught by Tancred and brought back to camp; William was forced to lie on the floor of Bohemund's tent all night while Bohemund berated him in front of the Franks. He might have killed William as an example had the Franks not intervened on his behalf. William gave his word that he would remain with the army until Jerusalem was captured, but before long he slipped away and was never seen again.

The expense of supporting the siege became so dear that Bohemund announced he would have to leave for lack of funds. It was later believed by some of his contemporaries that it was a ploy because he had set his sights on becoming lord of Antioch and intended to bargain for it. He remained, but the desertions were a clear sign of how desperate things had become.

Taticius, Alexius's representative and the crusaders' guide, offered to go to the emperor for aid and to return with reinforcements and supplies, so the crusaders agreed that he should leave. Taticius never returned, and his treachery deepened the animosity the Franks felt toward the Greeks. Count Stephen of Blois, feigning illness, deserted with his men exactly one day before the siege was ended; his reputation never recovered.

In retrospect what seems incredible is not that there were deserters, but that anyone should have persevered. For some the hope for military glory and acclaim still lingered, as did the thirst for spoils and the excitement of battle. For most if not all of those who stayed, the determination to reach Jerusalem at all costs—the conviction that they were doing God's work—sustained them, and they searched for reasons to explain their misfortunes. Many believed, as Fulcher of Chartres wrote, "that these misfortunes befell the Franks, and that they were not able for so long a time to take the city [Antioch] because of their sins. Not only dissipation, but also avarice or pride or their rapaciousness corrupted them."[14]

The dissipation Fulcher spoke of was the crusaders' sexual behavior and the temptations posed—for the men—by having women on the crusade. Among the women were wives and daughters, pilgrims, nurses, maids, care-givers, and camp-followers (that is, prostitutes). Given the close living quar-ters shared by men and women and the hothouse conditions, instances of adultery were hardly surprising and were regarded as particularly sinful. Captured women were often raped. As an example of sexual restraint, Fulcher of Chartres recorded one instance when the crusaders found Turkish women who had been abandoned after a battle and "the Franks did nothing evil to them except pierce their bellies with their lances."[15]

The asceticism of the reformed papacy in the eleventh and twelfth cen-turies focused much attention on the evils of fornication, so it is not surpris-ing that the crusaders believed that God's disfavor also focused on their sexual behavior. The treatment of women on the crusades and in the Latin Kingdom will be discussed in detail in a subsequent chapter. Suffice it to say for now that the extremes of licentiousness, followed by remorse and repentance, were characteristic of the crusaders. When they were convinced that their sexual misconduct merited God's punishment they took drastic measures to restore themselves to God's good grace.

Given the dire circumstances at Antioch, "after holding council, they drove out the women from the army, both married and unmarried, lest they, stained by the defilement of dissipation, displease the Lord."[16] If Fulcher is to be believed, the women then found shelter in neighboring towns. In a more detailed description of the same events, William of Tyre wrote that the leaders "put away from the camp all the light women of ill-repute"—which seems more likely. He went on to write that "adultery and fornication of every description was forbidden under penalty of death, and an interdict was placed on all reveling and intoxication."[17] Gambling, games of all sorts, swear-ing…all were forbidden. The sources did not bother to notice—or mention—the return of the women, although they must have come back to the camps.

---

[14] Fulcher of Chartres, McGinty 43.
[15] Fulcher of Chartres, McGinty 54.
[16] Fulcher of Chartres, McGinty 43–44.
[17] William of Tyre, vol. 1, 220.

Then, for the Franks who were already starving to death, Adhemar of Le Puy proclaimed a three-day fast as penance for their sins. For the Franks their penance carried a spiritual benefit. Nonetheless, it is sad to think of those poor hungry souls fasting and praying for three whole days in the hope that God would forgive them and deliver them from their misery.

The siege lasted from late October until June 3. During those seven and a half punishing months, in addition to the deaths from famine, illness, and exposure to the elements, in addition to the desertions, the crusaders had to face almost daily skirmishes with the Turks guarding Antioch and two major attacks by Muslim armies that had come in an attempt to relieve Antioch. Yet somehow they survived. Then, in the last weeks of May, the crusaders heard that the strongest Muslim leader, Kerbogha of Mosul, was advancing on Antioch with a huge army, and the crusaders, with good reason, feared certain defeat.

A. The Franks Take Antioch

In the little time before Kerbogha arrived, Bohemund struck a secret bargain with a traitor within the city who contrived to let the Franks into Antioch. The man was in command of three towers, which he was willing to hand over to Bohemund in return for riches and honor. The traitor was identified either as an Armenian Christian (in the Muslim sources) or a Turk (in the Latin sources). Before Bohemund told the crusaders of the ruse he had engineered, he exacted the promise that the first leader to enter Antioch would be given possession of the city. The main dissent came from Raymond of Toulouse, but he was ill and unable to rally support to resist Bohemund, so the promise was given.

On the night of June 3, the traitor helped twenty of Bohemund's men to climb over the walls of Antioch; they then opened a gate to let the armies into city. A bloodbath followed. "All the streets of the city on every side were full of corpses, so that no one could endure to be there because of the stench, nor could anyone walk along the narrow paths of the city except over the corpses of the dead."[18] The cruelty unleashed at Antioch presaged even more terrible cruelties to come.

The Turks' possessions were taken by the Franks—gold, jewels, horses, everything of value, including their wives and daughters. Some inhabitants were able to escape and others fled for refuge to the citadel, which still remained in Turkish hands. The Muslim ruler of Antioch fled in panic, although by the morning after he left he "repented of having rushed to safety instead of staying to fight to the death. He began to groan and weep for his

---

[18] *Gesta Francorum*, Hill 48.

desertion of his household and children. Overcome by the violence of his grief he fell fainting from his horse."[19] According to the Muslim version, the ruler's men were unable to seat him on his horse again, and they left him on the road. He was found, on the verge of dying, by an Armenian shepherd, who killed him and brought his head to the Franks.

Kerbogha had wasted three fruitless weeks in an attempt to besiege Edessa before he went on to Antioch, and his delay kept him from reaching Antioch until two days after the Latins had taken it. So the crusaders had a temporary reprieve. Although they built a stone wall to separate themselves from the citadel, they were hemmed in and attacked by the Turks in the citadel and quickly found themselves besieged by Kerbogha outside the walls. Food was scarce in the city and the crusaders were hungry, frightened, and despairing, and many more deserted. It was at that juncture that the Holy Lance—the lance believed to have pierced Christ's side—was discovered.

B. The Discovery of the Holy Lance and the Frankish Victory

A poor man named Peter Bartholomew—some thought he was a priest—who had accompanied Raymond of Toulouse's army, came before the count and the Bishop of Le Puy and told them he had had several visions in which St. Andrew had appeared, revealed where the lance was buried, and directed him to dig it up. Although the bishop was skeptical, Raymond believed him and a few days later went with Peter and twelve men to dig for the lance, which, according to the revelation, would be found below the altar in the Church of St. Peter. They dug all day without finding it until a young man—it may even have been Peter—jumped into the pit and emerged with the lance. The Latins were unrestrained in their joy at beholding the miracle. Adhemar of Le Puy remained unconvinced of the lance's authenticity, but he was in a minority. The great majority of crusaders and noncombatants were in no doubt that one of the holiest of all Christian relics had been found, and it strengthened their resolve and gave them the courage to continue.

Other, pragmatic considerations undoubtedly played into the decision to engage Kerbogha's army—against all the odds. The hope still remained that Alexius might come to aid the crusaders. He had actually started out to do just that, but was persuaded to turn back to Constantinople by some refugees from Antioch who mistakenly informed him that Antioch was already lost. Bohemund also seems to have been aware that there was dissension in Kerbogha's camp that made the enemy army more vulnerable than it might have

---

[19] Ibn al-Athir, in *Arab Historians of the Crusades*, trans. Francesco Gabrieli (Berkeley and Los Angeles: U of California P, 1969) 6–7.

been. Finally, what was abundantly clear to the crusaders was that they could not hold out much longer, and to wait until the Muslims came to slaughter them seemed far worse than making one last bold attempt to defeat them.

On June 28 the crusaders marched out of Antioch, protected by the Holy Lance, commanded by Bohemund, and following a strategy he devised. The priests, standing barefoot on the walls, watched them leave and prayed for victory.

Save for a small contingent guarding the city, the entire army left Antioch through a single gate. Kerbogha then made a serious miscalculation. He believed the crusaders were fleeing and therefore did not try to kill them or at least stop them, as he might have done, as they marched forward. When he finally realized that they intended to fight, he was forced to meet the crusaders in a pitched battle. It was what Bohemund had hoped. By this time he had learned how to counter Turkish tactics in the field and was able to outmaneuver them, despite the great size and energy of Kerbogha's army and the small numbers and fatigue of his own. The Turks fanned out, intending, as was their custom, to encircle the Franks. But time after time the crusaders held the line against the Turkish charges in a remarkable display of courage and discipline that was a tribute to Bohemund's charismatic leadership.

In an amazing turnaround, the crusaders defeated Kerbogha and routed his army. It was a stunning victory. On hearing the news, the Turks holding the citadel surrendered, and Antioch, at long last, was in Latin hands.

The crusaders had been so outnumbered, so starved and weak, that it is small wonder they were convinced their victory was a miracle, possible only because God had intervened. One chronicler reported that God had so multiplied the crusading army that it had actually become larger than Kerbogha's. "There came out of the mountains, also, countless armies with white horses, whose standards were all white. And so, when our leaders saw this army ... they recognized the aid of Christ.... This is to be believed, for many of our men saw it."[20] Much credit of course was given to the miraculous powers of the Holy Lance.

Of the many signs and visions that appeared throughout the crusades — and were accepted without question—the lance and the visions connected with it are the most unusual and perplexing because, from the first, opinion about it was sharply divided, and there were people who thought it a fraud. Yet the belief in relics and their powers and the belief that God communicated to men through Christ and His saints operated at a profound level of Christian experience; in the aftermath of the battle the doubts, for a time, were stilled.

---

[20] "Gesta Francorum," in Krey 184.

Although modern historians have tried to find more mundane reasons to explain the outcome at Antioch, we will probably never know why the Latins were able to win. The Arab historians, writing soon after the loss of Antioch, blamed Kerbogha for his decision not to kill the crusaders as they emerged from the city — a fateful blunder that cost the Muslims Antioch.

C. The Aftermath of Victory

Two important questions then had to be decided. The one uppermost in everyone's mind was the date for starting the march to Jerusalem. The princes agreed that the armies should stay in Antioch until the heat of the summer had passed and they could be assured of finding water on their route. They chose November 1 for the departure.

The second question involved the far more contentious issue of who would control Antioch. Bohemund, naturally enough, wanted the city, believing he had been promised it and that he had certainly earned it. Raymond of Toulouse objected strenuously to ceding Antioch to him. The rivalry between Bohemund and Raymond had been festering since they arrived at Constantinople, each man vying for Alexius's favor, hoping to be named commander of the First Crusade. At Antioch their antagonism erupted into open hostility.

In experience and temperament the two men had little in common. Bohemund had neither an illustrious lineage nor adequate financial resources for the crusade, but he was a true Norman and, like his Norman forebears, was restless, ambitious, and hungry for territory and adventure. He began his military career at an early age and had a well-earned reputation for bravery. His men admired him, and they trusted his judgment on the battlefield, even when he took extraordinary risks. He lied, he was duplicitous, he was tricky, yet with all that he was magnetic. Even the emperor's daughter, Anna Comnena, who despised him, had to admit that "a certain charm hung about this man."[21] Nothing we know of Bohemund indicates that he was motivated to participate in the crusade for the good of his soul, the Church, or the Holy Land.

Raymond IV was cut from different cloth. He came from an old and prominent noble family and in 1088, when his father died, had become Count of Toulouse and of St. Gilles, the latter title for the family's rich lands south of Nîmes. He has generally been credited with religious motives for undertaking the crusade. In the years before the First Crusade, Raymond was active in church reform and a staunch partisan of the reforming popes. He met with Urban and became privy to the pope's plans before the crusade was formally announced and was the first secular ruler to take the cross.

Raymond was an honorable, responsible man who shouldered many bur-

---

[21] Anna Comnena, Sewter 422.

dens and expenses in the course of the crusade. He was not entirely immune from personal ambition, but overall he was admirable. Unfortunately, Raymond was not loveable. He was thought to be a cold and distant man, and his personality did not inspire affection or friendship, either from his own men or from the princes.

Raymond and Bohemund had in common the vice of pigheadedness, and from Antioch on the crusade suffered from the intransigence of the two rivals.

When the crusaders took Antioch, Raymond was the first prince to reach the citadel, which he demanded the Turks surrender to him. But Bohemund, whose talent for intrigue was boundless, had previously reached a secret agreement with the leader of the Turkish garrison, who refused to surrender to anyone other than Bohemund. Raymond took control of a palace and the Bridge Gate and would not relinquish them.

In his appeal to the princes about the disposition of Antioch, Raymond took the high road, arguing that Antioch was part of the Byzantine Empire and should be returned to Alexius. Adhemar of Le Puy supported Raymond, and with his help the stalemate was temporarily broken. Hugh of Vermandois was dispatched to Constantinople to find out whether Alexius would actually come to claim Antioch.

The crusaders were trapped in a strange limbo with nothing really settled, and the situation within Antioch started to deteriorate. On August 1, Adhemar of Le Puy died of typhoid fever. His death was a terrible tragedy. On a personal level he was loved and respected by everyone for his sanctity and his leadership, and he was greatly mourned. Moreover, Adhemar was the one person with the moral authority to maintain order among the princes. In the aftermath of his death the crusade's major weakness was exposed: there was no one commander who could count on the loyalty of the rival princes and their armies, no one leader acknowledged by all the crusaders.

The typhoid epidemic that had taken Adhemar's life spread through Antioch, claiming many lives. The princes began to leave, partly to escape the fever, but mainly to exploit their victory and scout the countryside for towns and cities they could take for themselves. The people remaining in Antioch became restive and, without any authority to curb them, began to steal. There were outbursts of violence. Once again the food supply was dwindling.

By early September the worst of the epidemic had passed, and one by one the princes returned to Antioch, where they met to draft a letter to Pope Urban II, telling him about their successes and also of Adhemar's death. They implored the pope to come to Antioch to be the first Latin bishop of St. Peter's Church and to assume the leadership of the crusade. The business of the church and papacy was too consuming for Urban to leave Rome, so he declined.

The crusading army's effectiveness was severely hampered by its limited numbers. The will to fight was strong—for the most part—but death, desertion, and illness were the army's constant companions, and the lack of manpower would plague the Franks throughout the crusading era. For the moment, the problem that most rankled was that of the men who had taken the crusaders' vow and never left home. In their letter to the pope the princes begged him to send the malingerers to the East. "Those who put off that journey ought to receive neither counsel nor anything good from you until they have fulfilled the journey which they began."[22] That problem was not quickly addressed or easily solved.

When November 1 came and it was time to leave for Jerusalem, it was certain that Alexius was not coming. What followed is a shameful—and prolonged—episode in the history of this first crusade.

Neither Bohemund nor Raymond would yield on the question of Antioch, and the other princes were not strong enough to settle the disagreement or were simply unwilling to take sides. So the march to Jerusalem was postponed, and the princes left again to continue ransacking Syria, without choosing another date. Yet they had not counted on the anger of the rank-and-file crusaders, who, after enduring extraordinary hardships for so long, were not prepared to relinquish the goal of reaching Jerusalem. They actually threatened to tear down Antioch's walls, hoping to goad the princes into leaving. Still the delay continued.

The Road to Jerusalem

Finally shamed into taking action, Raymond and Bohemund reached an uneasy accord and agreed that they would set out together—leaving the fate of Antioch unsettled. Raymond left first, successfully attacking Syrian cities and taking them captive easily until he reached Ma'arra, some forty miles (sixty-four kilometers) southeast of Antioch, at the end of November. At Ma'arra Raymond's force met with strong resistance, and it was not until Bohemund arrived with help that the city was taken.

A. The Siege of Ma'arra

The crucial factor in the successful siege, however, was a movable tower that Raymond, at great expense, had constructed. The distinguishing feature of this tower was that it was taller than the city walls and enabled the soldiers to stand on top of it and, using pikes and rocks, attack right down into the city. It was so huge that it took one hundred knights to push it up against the walls.

---

[22] "Letter of the Crusading Princes to Pope Urban II," in Krey 195.

The wall-dominating tower proved to be a formidable weapon and became a mainstay of the crusaders' siege equipment from Ma'arra on.

The crusaders' behavior when they entered Ma'arra was ugly. They killed the inhabitants with such enthusiasm that "no corner of the city was free from corpses of the Saracens, and [they] could scarcely go anywhere in the city without stepping on the Saracen dead."[23] Everyone looted, from the poorest foot soldiers to the leaders, until there was nothing of consequence left anywhere. Bohemund promised to spare the lives of the Saracen leaders and their wives and children if they would assemble in one palace and bring their valuables with them. He then proceeded to murder them or send them to Antioch to be sold into slavery. The valuables he naturally appropriated for himself.

The arguments between Raymond and Bohemund escalated; they now quarreled over control of Ma'arra as well as Antioch. Once again the ordinary soldiers pressured the leaders to set out for Jerusalem. It was by then Christmastime, and Bohemund said he would go in March. The crusaders turned to Raymond and begged him to lead them and to leave soon or else give them the lance and they would go on alone. Raymond finally agreed to go—but first, before announcing a date, he met with the other princes in a city halfway between Antioch and Ma'arra to convince them to join him. They refused, and although Raymond resorted to bribery to persuade them, even that failed. He decided to post a garrison in Ma'arra to protect his interests after he left; when the crusaders heard this they were furious with Raymond for reducing the already small size of the army. Still they did not leave for Jerusalem.

As the weeks passed and the winter weather arrived the situation in Ma'arra became grave. A famine had set in, and by some accounts the crusaders were so starved that they were reduced to eating the rotting flesh of dead Saracens. They also burned the dead Saracens to retrieve the gold they had swallowed from their stomachs.

The ordinary crusaders were so angry and frustrated that they decided to destroy the city walls of Ma'arra so there would be no cause left for arguments about its ownership. Even "the weak and sick arose from their beds, and, armed with clubs they went to the walls."[24] Although Raymond was furious when he saw what had happened, he was finally convinced that he had no choice but to continue on to Jerusalem. On January 13, 1099, he left the city as a pilgrim, barefoot, to lead the weary and hungry crusaders to

---

[23] "Gesta Francorum," in Krey 206. The term *Saracen* was first used by the Greeks to refer to an Arab tribe before the coming of Islam. It was subsequently used throughout the medieval period—and after—to refer to all Muslims indiscriminately.

[24] Raymond of Aguilers, in Krey 213.

Jerusalem. A year and a half had elapsed since the crusaders had arrived at Nicaea in May 1098.

The Muslims in southern Syria were disorganized and so reluctant to fight the Franks that many towns and cities surrendered to Raymond without a struggle, and the crusaders were able to find food, water, and even gold, and replenish their supply of horses. By mid-February some of the princes had decided to join Raymond—but not all of them. As soon as Bohemund knew that Raymond was on the move and too preoccupied to challenge him, he threw Raymond's garrison out of Antioch and became sole ruler of the city. He finally had achieved his heart's desire. He started out to join Raymond's army but, after consulting his own interests, thought better of it and returned to Antioch, where he remained. For a time Godfrey of Bouillon and Robert of Flanders procrastinated at Antioch; Baldwin chose to remain at Edessa.

The delaying, the waiting for the seasons to change, the stops and starts, the lack of discipline, and even the desertions were all part of warfare as the crusaders had known it in Europe. But in the East, en route to Jerusalem, the delays, the suffering, the lack of sustained activity and purpose became unbearable for the rank-and-file crusaders.

B. 'Arqa and Peter Bartholomew's Final Trial

While Raymond of Toulouse waited for other armies to join him, he sent his men to besiege the city of 'Arqa, thinking to capture spoils and to keep his men occupied. However, 'Arqa had excellent fortifications and a strategic location that made it difficult to attack, and siege engines proved useless against it. The siege dragged on for almost three months. Godfrey and Robert of Flanders came to help, but even so the crusaders were never able to capture the city. At the beginning of May they simply gave up and left, having lost time and manpower in a useless struggle. It was the last major setback before the crusaders reached Jerusalem.

The plain outside 'Arqa was the scene of the final chapter in Peter Bartholomew's history. Raymond was Peter's protector and the most stalwart champion of the lance, which Peter had given to him for safekeeping. For his part, Peter had supported Raymond by reporting revelations that promised success for Raymond and his army. As time went on his revelations took on an increasingly political cast and in fact became so brazen that he began to lose his popular support. That Peter was so nakedly partisan undoubtedly helped provoke his ordeal, but the hostility against him crystallized around the question of the lance's authenticity and the truth of his revelations. Peter became so angry that he insisted on going through a trial by fire to prove that the lance was genuine.

When the day came, on Good Friday, in early April, the fire was built, and

Peter knelt before the bishop, in front of a multitude of people who had come to watch, and swore that the lance was the true one. Then, with the Holy Lance in his hand, "after invoking the sign of the cross upon himself, [he] went forth boldly and without fear into the fire. He stopped for a brief moment in the midst of the fire, and thus by the grace of God passed through."[25]

When he had come through, the people were so overwhelmed by emotion that they "dragged him along the ground and almost that whole multitude stepped upon him, each one wishing to touch him, or to take some piece of his garment.... And thus they made three or four wounds on his legs, cutting off the flesh; and trampling upon his backbone, they broke it."[26] Twelve days later, in fearful agony, Peter died. A different eyewitness, who had never believed the lance was a true relic, reported that Peter actually died of the burns he suffered as he passed through the fire. However Peter died, the fact is that the lance was from then on largely discredited, although there remained always some stalwarts who clung to their belief in the relic, and the lance's authenticity was debated for generations to come.

Before the debacle at 'Arqa, Raymond had been recognized as the leader of the crusade, but his difficult personality, his foolish decision to besiege 'Arqa, his unwavering loyalty to Alexius, and his commitment to Peter Bartholomew eventually cost him his command. Allegiances shifted at all levels, and the knights and ordinary soldiers moved at will from one leader to another. Bohemund's nephew Tancred, who had pledged himself to Raymond, switched to Godfrey of Bouillon, who became the popular choice to lead the march to Jerusalem.

On May 13, the crusaders left 'Arqa and headed south to Tripoli, where the independent Muslim ruler generously gave them supplies and gold to hasten them on their way. He even offered to become a Christian if the crusaders could defeat the Egyptians, break their hold on the coastal cities along the Mediterranean, and capture Jerusalem.

The crusaders now had two routes to choose from: one led inland to Damascus, which would have taken them across Mount Lebanon — not impossible, but difficult; the other was the coast road that went from Tripoli to Beirut and on past Sidon, Tyre, and Haifa to Caesarea. Their hesitation to take the coast road was caused by the fact that, once they left Tripoli, they would be entering territory controlled by the Fatimid Caliphate in Egypt.

For several decades during the eleventh century, the Egyptians had suffered rebellions within their own country and had lost considerable territory to the Turks, including many cities along the Mediterranean coast and, in

---

25 Raymond of Aguilers, in Krey 231.
26 Raymond of Aguilers, in Krey 232.

1071, Jerusalem. The Egyptian caliph then called on Badr, the Governor of Acre, for help. Badr was an exceptionally effective Armenian general, who was able to quell the internal uprisings in Egypt; institute a strong government; and then, one by one, restore Sidon, Tyre, and Acre to Egypt. In 1098 he took back Jerusalem.

As a footnote to the main events, while the crusaders were still in Tripoli, the Egyptians had sent an embassy to negotiate with them, but the terms the Egyptians proposed—to allow unarmed crusaders in small groups into Jerusalem—were simply out of the question.

The threat from the Fatimids seemed real enough; they had a navy patrolling the Mediterranean, they controlled the coastal cities south of Tripoli, and, most important of all, they held Jerusalem. Nonetheless, the crusaders took the coast road.

Two factors considerably mitigated the threat from Cairo; the first, which came as a surprise, was that the Egyptians had not made sufficient preparation to defend the coastal cities. The second was the willingness of Beirut, Sidon, Tyre, and Acre to make separate treaties with the crusaders, as Tripoli had done. The crusaders were in a hurry to reach Jerusalem before the Egyptians could coalesce their forces and in this final stage covered more territory more rapidly than they had before. They bypassed the major cities and fortifications, and on May 26 they reached Caesarea, where they celebrated Pentecost. Four days later they left and marched to Ramla, which was deserted. The inhabitants, having been alerted to their coming, had abandoned all their possessions and food and fled. The crusaders rested there until June 6.

Jerusalem at Last
From Ramla to Jerusalem is a distance of only fifteen miles (twenty-four kilometers). "As they approached still closer and could gaze upon the Holy City now so near at hand, the pilgrims, most of whom were walking barefooted, gave utterance to their spiritual joy with heartfelt tears and sighs. With ever-increasing fervor, they pressed on towards their goal and, in a short time, were standing before Jerusalem."[27] The date was Tuesday, June 7, 1099.

Jerusalem is in arid land. The drinking water for the inhabitants was mainly rain water, collected in cisterns during the rainy season and used during the hot months. Outside are only a few springs and, at a short distance from the city, the Pool of Siloam. Jerusalem was one of the best-fortified cities in the East. The walls were two and a half miles (four kilometers) in circumference, too long and the terrain too difficult to surround on all sides. In some places the strongly built walls were fifty feet (fifteen meters) high, and long

---

[27] William of Tyre, vol. 1, 338.

sections were surrounded by a second, outer wall that had to be breached before the inner city wall could be attacked. The deep ravines formed by the Kedron Valley on the east and the Valley of Hinnom on the south made the approach to the city from either side virtually impossible for an invading army.

The Fatimid garrison defending the city was strong and well prepared. It included Turks and warriors from the Sudan; in addition, the entire Muslim population had been mobilized to fight the Franks. The native Christian population had been sent away, since it was assumed that the Christians would defect to the Franks. Some left voluntarily, although some remained, among them the Eastern Orthodox clergy who were there when the Franks took the city. The Jews remained and fought alongside the Muslims, preferring the rule of the Fatimids to what they anticipated would be intolerance, or worse, from the crusaders. The garrison had been assured that a relief army from Egypt was on its way and would arrive in fifteen days—a piece of information the crusaders had as well, so they were under the pressure of time to capture Jerusalem.

When the armies reached Jerusalem, their numbers had been so depleted that they had only between 1,200 and 1,500 mounted knights and some 12,000 foot soldiers, the latter number likely including noncombatants, many of whom were ill. Raymond positioned his troops southwest of the city, on Mount Zion, where Christ is believed to have had the last meal with his disciples and where the Virgin Mary died. Godfrey of Bouillon, Robert of Normandy, Robert of Flanders, and Tancred positioned their troops along the northern wall. On June 13 they attacked the city, but they quickly learned that without scaling ladders it was hopeless to continue. On the fifth day of the assault they gave up and went to the countryside to find materials and workmen to build siege engines.

Once again their faith was severely tested. Food was scarce and lack of water was a desperate problem. It was hot summer, and the Franks, their horses, and their pack animals were parched and many were dying of thirst. The Saracens had destroyed the springs outside the walls, so the only good drinking water came from the Pool of Siloam, at the foot of Mount Zion. The water flowed at irregular intervals, and when it did people were in such a rush to get to it that they pushed each other out of the way and people and animals were shoved into the water. Pack animals and horses drowned in the pool, which thus became contaminated. The crusaders were forced to go six miles (ten kilometers) to find water and carry it back to camp in bottles that they fashioned from the hides of oxen, buffalos, and goats... if they were lucky enough to reach camp. The Saracens were usually lying in wait for the Franks and frequently killed them.

For ten days the crusaders were almost entirely out of food, until they received some supplies brought by ship from Genoa to Jaffa. Even so, conditions remained terrible. Tempers were short and the leaders reverted to quarreling. They argued heatedly over who should be King of Jerusalem. The priests objected to a secular ruler in so sacrosanct a city, and the disagreements became so acrimonious that the debate was postponed until after Jerusalem had been taken.

The princes were also angered by Tancred's behavior. Soon after the crusaders left Ramla they came to Emmaus, where they received a delegation of Christians from Bethlehem who implored the crusaders to rescue the Christian population from the Turks. Tancred rode off with a hundred knights and seized Bethlehem. When he succeeded in winning Bethlehem, Tancred treated the Church of the Nativity as his own personal property and placed his standard on the roof. The princes thought Tancred's behavior offensive, though it is more likely that they were jealous because Tancred was in sole possession of an important sacred city; however, he soon rejoined the crusade and participated in the assaults on Jerusalem.

All in all, it was a gloomy and dispirited time, and the crusaders seemed to have lost all heart for their mission. At that juncture a visionary revealed that Bishop Adhemar had appeared and counseled him to urge the crusaders to cleanse themselves of sin by praying, fasting, and marching barefoot around Jerusalem. If they did this and then made a heroic assault on Jerusalem on the ninth day, Adhemar promised that they would be successful. The priests insisted that the crusaders also forgive their enemies and be reconciled to them. After this was all accomplished, the crusaders went forward with renewed energy and hope.

Siege engines were built, although when the Muslims saw them they strengthened the city's fortifications. Raymond of Toulouse built his tower on Mount Zion, facing the southwestern wall. Godfrey and his men, in full view of the Turks, built a great tower facing the northern wall at a place that was strong and well defended. The night before the final siege, the night of July 13–14, Godfrey's men, under cover of darkness, took apart the tower and carried it, piece by piece, to the eastern section of the north wall, which they knew to be less well defended and where the ground was more level. By morning they had put it back together. When the Turks realized what had happened they were startled and dismayed at having been so outmaneuvered.

At daybreak on July 14 the assault began. Although the crusaders fought bravely, the Muslims put up a fearsome defense and by nightfall nothing had been decided. The night brought its own terrors. The Turks were afraid the crusaders would storm the city in the dark, and the Franks worried that the Turks would set fire to their siege towers. "So on both sides it was a night of watchfulness, labor and sleepless caution."[28]

---

[28] Raymond of Aguilers, in Krey 259.

The Franks Win Jerusalem

Early the next morning the Franks assaulted again. The Muslims hurled rocks and fire down onto their machines until they were badly shaken apart or burned. By midday the crusaders were weary and so disheartened that they were on the verge of withdrawing. But they had one last, incredible surge of courage; Godfrey's men shot firebrands over the walls, driving the Turks back so that one of Godfrey's knights was able to climb to the top of the wall. Then Godfrey released the drawbridge on his tower, and he and his army scrambled across it, onto the battlements and into the city.

While Godfrey's men were pursuing their enemies through the streets, Raymond and his men were still struggling to breach their side of the wall. As soon as it was known that Godfrey was in the city and that the enemy was on the run, the emir in charge of David's tower surrendered to Raymond and his men entered Jerusalem.

A. The Crusaders Ravage the Holy City

The intensity of the cruelty that then occurred strained the descriptive powers of the chroniclers who witnessed it. Although the precise words they used are somewhat different, they all reported the same degree of horror that ensued. "Some of our men (and this was more merciful) cut off the heads of their enemies; others shot them with arrows, so that they fell from the towers; others tortured them longer by casting them into the flames.... In the Temple and porch of Solomon, men rode in blood up to their knees and bridle reins."[29] Women and children were slain before the grisly slaughter at last began to abate. In a fitting peroration another twelfth-century historian wrote, "Still more dreadful was it to gaze upon the victors themselves, dripping with blood from head to foot, an ominous sight which brought terror to all who met them."[30]

Yet the crusaders were in no doubt of the suitability of what they had done, no doubt at all that God would rejoice with them. The Muslim holy places were piled high with the dead and mutilated bodies—a just end, they believed, for God's enemies, who had defiled Christian holy places with their pagan rituals. Then, having washed off the blood, suitably clothed and bare-foot, the crusaders went as pilgrims to the Holy Sepulchre to give thanks to God for their victory and to celebrate it. "This day," Raymond of Aguilers wrote, "will be famous in all future ages, for it turned our labors and sorrows into joy and exultation; this day ... marks the justification of all Christianity."[31] That day, Friday, July 15, was the culmination of all their hopes and the end— they believed—of all their hardships.

---

[29] Raymond of Aguilers, in Krey 261.
[30] William of Tyre, vol. 1, 372.
[31] Raymond of Aguilers, in Krey 261.

Jcome uos auce oṗ lı
peletın quı gnt met
ner auoıent ce ıṗof
ſeıoꝛneꝛent en la uılle
ꝗ lı baron ceuſoıent
les aſaures ce la cıte.
Cnguꝛınt toıe cemoꝛerent ṗlleue ·vıı·

**3.4 Pilgrims
praying at the
Holy Sepulchre.**

The massacre in Jerusalem went on with uncontrolled fury for three days. After the killing and after the praying, the crusaders ransacked the city and found treasures of all kinds and plentiful food and water. The city was stripped bare of all that was valuable. Any crusader who was first to enter a house was able to keep it; whether he was rich or poor before the crusade, he now had his own home — often a quite grand home.

The Muslim population was decimated. Some had managed to escape, but those who survived the massacres were captured and before they were sold into slavery were forced to clear the city of the decaying bodies and limbs and the blood, which were causing a dreadful stench. Raymond was the only one to spare the inhabitants; he permitted most of the people who had taken refuge in the Tower of David when it surrendered to him to go to Ascalon, still held by the Turks, under a safe-conduct.

The Muslim refugees who managed to escape fled to Baghdad, arriving on the eve of Ramadan. "On Friday they went to the Cathedral Mosque and begged for help, weeping so that their hearers wept with them as they described the sufferings of the Muslims in that Holy City.... Because of the terrible hardships they had suffered, they were allowed to break the fast."[32]

According to both Latin and Muslim chroniclers, the Jewish population was either burned to death or captured and forced to work with the Muslims to remove the bodies, cleanse the city, and then build funeral pyres outside the walls to burn the dead. Afterward they were also sold into slavery. For centuries historians were convinced that the Jews of Jerusalem had been completely eliminated. Although it is true that no Jews remained in Jerusalem after the Franks captured it, their story turns out to have been more complex.

A letter written in 1100 by a Jew originally from Ascalon found in the valuable collection of documents discovered in Egypt, known as the Cairo Geniza, reveals a good deal about the fate of a segment of Jerusalem Jewry.[33] The letter was sent to the Jewish community in Alexandria, the second-largest Jewish community in Egypt, after Cairo. The letter describes how the Jews in Ascalon raised money to ransom as many Jerusalem Jews as they could—likely those taken by Raymond in the Tower of David. Once ransomed, the refugees required medical care, food, and shelter, so it was an expensive undertaking. With the threat of a Frankish invasion looming, money was also needed to transport the refugees to the safety of Egypt. The costs had become burdensome, so the letter is an appeal for financial help for the Jews and for money to buy back the religious books the Franks had seized from the synagogues and were prepared to sell.

The letter fleshes out the story of the Jerusalem Jews. Although the majority were certainly murdered or sold into slavery, we now know that some, at least, were saved. Of those who went to Egypt—or attempted to reach Egypt—many died from exposure and starvation, but others actually managed to survive.

Thus was Jerusalem denuded of its inhabitants.

The Holy City Is Christian Again

Seven or eight days after the city was cleansed, the princes and bishops met to discuss the kingship. It was by then imperative that a ruler be chosen. The bishops still insisted that a patriarch be chosen first or they would not accept a secular ruler. The princes were angered by this and went ahead with their election. The two obvious candidates were Raymond of Toulouse and Godfrey of Bouillon. The kingship was offered first to Raymond. Although he wanted it, he turned it down on the grounds that he did not want to wear a crown in the city where Christ was crucified. He was also aware that he did not have

---

[32] Ibn al-Athir, in Gabrieli 11.

[33] The material about this particular document is based on S.D. Goitein, "Contemporary Letters on the Capture of Jerusalem by the Crusaders," *Journal of Jewish Studies* 3.4 (1952): 162–77. It is an illuminating article by the great scholar of the Cairo Geniza and includes his translations.

the wholehearted support of the princes; even his own men were opposed to his becoming king, mainly because they wanted to go home. So Godfrey became the first ruler, and the title he assumed was Defender of the Holy Sepulchre rather than king. "It was in a spirit of humility," William of Tyre wrote, "that he declined the crown which would perish, in the hope of attaining hereafter one that would never fade."[34] In effect, Godfrey had bested his rival.

A. Jerusalem under Godfrey of Bouillon

Raymond, having lost his chance for the title, refused to relinquish the Tower of David to Godfrey, and there was a real fracas until he agreed to give the tower to a bishop as a temporary measure until a judgment could be rendered by a council. Without waiting for a judgment, the bishop gave the tower to Godfrey. Raymond stormed off, leading his men to Jericho, where they took palms and went to the Jordan River. It had become customary to bring home palm fronds from Jericho as evidence that the pilgrimage had been completed. Instead of leaving, however, Raymond and his men, dressed only in shirts and breeches, crossed the Jordan in a raft made of twigs—something Peter Bartholomew had told them to do—and remained at Jericho.

In the meantime the bishops and princes appointed a Latin Patriarch of Jerusalem. The princes and bishops intended to supplant the Eastern Orthodox clergy, beginning with the patriarch, and replace them all with Latins obedient to the Roman see. The first Latin Patriarch was Arnulf of Chocques, a Norman who was Robert of Normandy's chaplain and the choice of the Norman French and of Godfrey. This highly political appointment was vehemently opposed by many clergy because Arnulf was only a subdeacon and because he had a well-known reputation as a womanizer. The new patriarch was an ambitious man, and a self-serving one, and the opposition to him continued until, months later, he was actually deposed. Before that happened Arnulf found what was purportedly the True Cross on which Christ had been crucified.

Arnulf had been outspoken in his conviction that the Holy Lance was a fraud, so it is ironic that he devoted himself to finding the True Cross, which he was certain had been hidden in Jerusalem. After he pressed the Eastern Orthodox citizens and clergy to tell him where it was, they finally relented, dug it up from its hiding-place in the Church of the Holy Sepulchre, and brought it to him. Although Arnulf claimed to have in hand the entire True Cross, all that could have been found was the shaft or simply fragments, since pieces had been removed several times in the course of the preceding centuries. Nevertheless, the relic was greeted with great enthusiasm and was later carried into battle to afford divine protection for the armies.

---

[34] William of Tyre, vol. 1, 393.

In early August, Godfrey, the bishops, and a group of princes gathered to write a letter to Rome, giving the pope a brief report describing the main highlights of the crusade. Sadly, Urban II never received the news he had so longed to hear; he died on July 29, just days before the letter was sent.

The immediate danger Godfrey faced was an Egyptian invasion. Early in the first week in August, an enormous, well-equipped Egyptian army, led by the vizier, al-Afdal, arrived in Palestine and camped near Ascalon, about to move forward to besiege Jerusalem. There was neither sufficient manpower nor sufficient food and water for the Holy City to withstand a siege, so Godfrey made the decision to go out to meet the Egyptians on the plain near Ascalon—a brave and seemingly foolhardy decision, since the Latins were greatly outnumbered and their leaders were at odds with one another. Raymond was still camped at Jericho, and the enmity between him and Godfrey was not healed. When Godfrey sent word to Raymond asking for his help against the Egyptians, Raymond at first refused to believe there was going to be a battle. After some of his men had gone to spy on the Egyptians and reported that it was indeed true, Raymond joined Godfrey.

At the sun came up on the morning of August 11, the crusaders approached the camp where the Egyptian forces were just waking up, unaware that the Latins were about to attack. Caught off-guard and unprepared to fight, the Egyptians did not put up much resistance. It was a total rout. The Franks killed thousands of Egyptians; al-Afdal fled to Ascalon and quickly returned to Egypt. The outcome was undoubtedly a surprise to both sides.

What happens immediately after any victory is crucial. Had the Franks followed up their victory by taking Ascalon, they would have had a port city they sorely needed, and the history of the next several decades would have been different. Instead, owing to the hostility between Godfrey and Raymond, the opportunity to win Ascalon was lost. The Muslims in Ascalon were willing to surrender, but only to Raymond. Ever since he had given his safe-conduct to the people in the Tower of David, the Muslims trusted in Raymond's clemency. Godfrey, however, was a cipher to them. Godfrey would not agree, and so Ascalon remained in Muslim hands until the mid-twelfth century, when the Christians, after a difficult siege of five months, finally captured the city.

To offset the regrettable loss of Ascalon, the crusaders found animals and other needed supplies outside Ascalon, which they brought to Jerusalem. Their victory considerably reduced the likelihood of any immediate Egyptian aggression, but the major coastal cities—Acre, Tyre, Sidon, and Ascalon—were still in Egyptian hands, and the Egyptian fleet still had command of the coastal waters.

B. The End of the First Crusade

Once Jerusalem had been conquered, the crusaders counted their pilgrimage a success. They had fulfilled their vows to recover the Church of the Holy Sepulchre and were now free to leave. The battle outside Ascalon delayed them, but as soon as it was over they began preparations to return home. Robert of Normandy, Robert of Flanders, and Raymond of Toulouse with their armies left Jerusalem to march toward the coast near Antioch, to sail from there to Constantinople and finally to France and home.

Bohemund had not yet seen fit to come to Jerusalem. Fulcher of Chartres excused his delay by explaining how essential it was for the Franks that the lands to the north, taken from the Turks, be safeguarded from future attack. Although there was truth in that, in fact Bohemund was involved in his own local war with Byzantium. The emperor had for months been sending letters to Bohemund demanding that he return Antioch to him, a demand that Bohemund naturally refused. According to the emperor's daughter Anna, Bohemund claimed that Alexius had forfeited his rights to the city when he failed to aid the Franks at the siege of Antioch. In any event, Bohemund was not giving up Antioch.

Although he was secure behind the walls of Antioch, the Byzantines had control of the coastal cities that were Antioch's outlets to the sea. Of the port cities, the one closest to Antioch and the strongest was Latakia. Bohemund knew that unless he could capture it, the Byzantines would be able to maintain their formidable fleet along the coast and prevent him and the Franks from reaching the sea. He therefore decided to besiege Latakia.

Bohemund then had a piece of luck, or so he thought. Unexpectedly a fleet from Pisa arrived at Latakia, presumably come to aid the crusaders in the Holy Land, but now willing to help Bohemund and engage the Byzantine navy on his behalf. Accompanying the fleet was the Archbishop of Pisa, a man named Daimbert, who was cheerfully willing to fight the Byzantines. Daimbert claimed to have been appointed papal legate to replace Adhemar by Urban II. Some contemporary historians have thought that Daimbert was dishonest about his putative appointment, since he was ambitious, but it seems certain that his appointment was legitimate.

For once Bohemund's luck did not hold. As he was preparing for the onslaught against Latakia, Raymond of Toulouse, Robert of Normandy, and Robert of Flanders arrived with their armies on their way home. They were all appalled at the idea of fighting the Byzantine Empire and vehemently opposed Bohemund's plan, particularly Raymond, who had remained faithful to Alexius throughout the crusade. Finally understanding that he would have no support from the princes, Bohemund reluctantly gave up the idea…for the moment. As the emperor's daughter wrote, "He [Alexius] had long experience of Bohemund's cunning and his stratagems…and the count's traitorous, rebellious nature was well understood."[35] Alexius knew that the postponement would be short-lived.

The confrontations and near confrontations between Bohemund and Alexius, the lightly veiled distrust between Greeks and Franks, as well as between Greeks and Normans, in time developed into something infinitely more serious and damaging. The effect of the growing animosity, when it surfaced full-blown, was pernicious for Greeks and Latins alike.

Once the issue of Latakia had been settled, Robert of Normandy and Robert of Flanders and their armies set sail for Constantinople and home. Raymond's men went home too, although Raymond stayed in Latakia and eventually went to visit with Alexius in Constantinople. He remained in the East and was a participant in the next chapter in the history of the crusades.

C. Bohemund Comes to Jerusalem

Bohemund finally decided that the time had come to go to Jerusalem. He encouraged Baldwin to come from Edessa to join him and Daimbert, who was also going. When the company assembled, Fulcher of Chartres estimated their number at twenty-five thousand people—including women, unarmed men, knights, and foot soldiers. They marched in November and much of December, so they suffered the hardships imposed by the cold, freezing rains, the difficulty of finding food, and occasional ambushes by the Turks. Along the way they happened on a plant that was unknown to them; they thought it was called wood honey because it seemed woodlike and yet, when they chewed on it, was sweet. They had accidentally discovered sugarcane.

They reached Jerusalem on December 21. After visiting the Church of the Holy Sepulchre and the other holy sites, they went to Bethlehem to celebrate the mass on Christmas Eve. Bohemund, despite his normally un-Christian behavior, spent the entire night in the Church of the Nativity and attended three masses.

D. The Sorry State of the Holy City

The situation in Jerusalem when Bohemund arrived was grim. The Franks were surrounded by their enemies, virtually captive in Jerusalem. Although Bethlehem, Ramla, and Lydda were in Christian hands, the city walls had been so weakened or destroyed during the conquest that the Muslims could easily break into the towns and steal, even kill the inhabitants. The Franks were also surrounded by Muslims, and the roads were extremely dangerous. The Muslim peasants refused to work the land, hoping to starve the Franks, so food was scarce. The only seaport the Franks controlled was Jaffa, and the Egyptian navy routinely thwarted any ships coming from the West carrying supplies and the few pilgrims who were hoping to visit Jerusalem.

---

[35] Anna Comnena, Sewter 359.

Godfrey's most pressing problem was the need for manpower. He hoped that Bohemund and Baldwin would provide help while they remained in Jerusalem and afterward leave men behind; he was willing to go to great lengths to secure their support. Wily and resourceful as ever, Bohemund made good use of the short time he spent in Jerusalem. With Bohemund's encouragement, Godfrey arranged for the deposition of Arnulf of Chocques and replaced him with Daimbert, who was now elevated to the Patriarchate of Jerusalem. Daimbert then gave Jerusalem to Godfrey as a fief, and Antioch to Bohemund as a fief. The investiture gave each ruler legitimacy and, in Bohemund's case, freedom from control by the Patriarch of Antioch and the Byzantine emperor, although what use the overlordship of the Latin Patriarch in Jerusalem—for them or for the patriarch—would be in actual practice remained to be seen.

Bohemund's nephew Tancred had also made good use of his time after the conquest of Jerusalem. He had moved into northern Palestine and captured Tiberias and Nazareth and the whole of the Galilee, which had not been well fortified or defended by the Muslims. He then received Tiberias and the Galilee as a fief from Godfrey and was given the title of Prince of the Galilee.

On New Year's Day 1100, Bohemund and Baldwin went to Jericho to collect palm fronds and the next day they started north, choosing to follow the Jordan River to Tiberias to see the Galilee and visit other places known to them from the Bible, before separating, Bohemund going to Antioch and Baldwin to Edessa.

In Jerusalem the gravest difficulty facing the new ruler was how to replenish the severely depleted population. No Muslims or Jews were ever permitted to live in Jerusalem while the Franks held the city. The native Christian population had been so severely reduced that their number was too negligible even to count. With the loss of the crusaders who had gone home, there were not enough people to defend the city or bring it back to life. Even with the addition of some men left behind by Bohemund and Baldwin, all the chroniclers agree that there were only three hundred knights and a thousand foot soldiers.

E. The Death of Godfrey

Godfrey had just begun to address the many problems confronting him when he was struck down by an incurable disease, most probably typhoid fever. After ruling for only one year, Godfrey died on July 18, 1100. During his short reign he attempted to extend his control over the Mediterranean ports, beginning with an unsuccessful siege of Arsuf, a town just north of Jaffa. When that siege failed, he took to ravaging the countryside, making it impossible for towns such as Arsuf, Acre, and Tyre to find sufficient food for their inhabitants—a maneuver that was more successful. The towns began to pay tribute to Godfrey, and he established reasonably friendly relations with his former enemies.

The repercussions from his ill-advised actions in Jerusalem were less fortunate, although less enduring. Godfrey had finally acceded, with some notable compromises, to the Latin Patriarch's demands that he turn over to him, as head of the Latin Church, the cities of Jaffa and Jerusalem. The compromise was to give the patriarch one-fourth of Jaffa and all of Jerusalem, the latter only after Godfrey's death, should he die without heirs.

Godfrey's untimely death was a sad epilogue to the First Crusade. He was buried, fittingly, in the Church of the Holy Sepulchre, "thereby obtaining the monument which he had liberated."[36] After an interval of three months, Godfrey's brother, Baldwin of Edessa, was elevated to the kingship. He took the royal title, and under his inspired leadership a new phase in the history of the Latin Kingdom began.

Suggestions for Further Reading

The following are particularly relevant for the topics covered in Part One, although many are useful for Part Two as well:

Armstrong, Karen. *Islam: A Short History*. New York: Modern Library, 2000.

Asbridge, Thomas. *The First Crusade: A New History*. New York: Oxford UP, 2004.

Brundage, James A. *Medieval Canon Law and the Crusader*. Madison: U of Wisconsin P, 1969.

Bull, Marcus. *Knightly Piety and the Lay Response to the First Crusade*. Oxford: Clarendon Press, 1993.

Chazan, Robert. *European Jewry and the First Crusade*. Berkeley and Los Angeles: U of California P, 1987.

———. *In the Year 1096: The First Crusade and the Jews*. Philadelphia: The Jewish Publication Society, 1996.

Cole, Penny J. *The Preaching of the Crusades to the Holy Land, 1095–1270*. Cambridge, MA: The Medieval Academy of America, 1991.

Constable, Giles. "The Second Crusade as Seen by Contemporaries." *Traditio* 9 (1953): 213-79.

Cowdrey, H. E. J. *The Cluniacs and the Gregorian Reform*. Oxford: Clarendon Press, 1970.

———. "The Genesis of the Crusades: The Springs of Western Ideas of Holy War." *The Holy War*. Ed. Thomas P. Murphy. Columbus: Ohio UP, 1974.

Daftary, Farhad. *A Short History of the Ismailis*. Princeton, NJ: Markus Weiner Publishers, 1998.

---

[36] Guibert of Nogent, Levine 149.

———. *Ismailis in Medieval Muslim Societies*. London and New York: I.B. Taurus Publishers, 2005.

Denny, Frederick Mathewson. *An Introduction to Islam*. 2nd ed. New York: Maxwell Macmillan International, 1994.

Douglas, David C. *The Norman Achievement, 1050–1100*. Berkeley and Los Angeles: U of California P, 1969.

———. *The Norman Fate, 1100–1154*. Berkeley and Los Angeles: U of California P, 1976.

Esposito, John L. *Islam: The Straight Path*. 3rd ed. New York: Oxford UP, 1998.

Goitein, S. D. "Contemporary Letters on the Capture of Jerusalem by the Crusaders." *Journal of Jewish Studies* 3.4 (1952): 162–77.

Mango, Cyril, ed. *The Oxford History of Byzantium*. Oxford: Oxford UP, 2002.

Morris, Colin. *The Papal Monarchy: The Western Church from 1050–1250*. Oxford: Clarendon Press, 1989.

Norwich, John J. *A Short History of Byzantium*. New York: Alfred A. Knopf, 1997. (This is based on his monumental three-volume work; it is extremely readable and informative.)

Peters, F. E. *The Children of Abraham: Judaism, Christianity, Islam*. Princeton, NJ: Princeton UP, 2004.

———. *The Distant Shrine: The Islamic Centuries in Jerusalem*. New York: AMS Press, 1993.

Phillips, Jonathan. *The Second Crusade: Extending the Frontiers of Christendom*. New Haven, CT, and London: Yale UP, 2007.

———. "Who Were the First Crusaders?" *History Today* 47.3 (1997): 16–22.

Riley-Smith, Jonathan. *What Were the Crusades?* 3rd ed. Basingstoke, Hampshire, UK: Palgrave Macmillan, 2002.

Sumption, Jonathan. *Pilgrimage: An Image of Medieval Religion*. London: Faber & Faber, 1975.

On military history, see especially:

Bachrach, Bernard S. "Medieval Siege Warfare: A Reconnaissance." *Journal of Military History* 58.1 (1944): 119–33.

Bradbury, Jim. *The Medieval Siege*. Woodbridge, Suffolk, UK: The Boydell Press, 1992.

France, John. *Western Warfare in the Age of the Crusades*. Ithaca, NY: Cornell UP, 1999.

Nicolle, David, *Crusader Warfare*, vol. 1. London: Continuum Books, 2007.

Rogers, Randall. *Latin Siege Warfare in the Twelfth Century*. Oxford: Clarendon Press, 1992.

Smail, R. C. *Crusading Warfare (1097–1193)*. 2nd ed. Cambridge: Cambridge UP, 1956. (This is an early classic in the field and still excellent.)

Part Two

CHAPTER FOUR

Baldwin I and the Early Years of the Latin Kingdom

The Reign of King Baldwin I

When Baldwin of Edessa was told of Godfrey's death and learned that he was to succeed him, "he grieved somewhat at the death of his brother but rejoiced more at his inheritance."[1] He turned Edessa over to his cousin, Baldwin of Le Bourg, and set out in October 1101 for Jerusalem with an army, according to Fulcher of Chartres, who accompanied him, of "nearly two hundred knights and seven hundred footmen."[2] It was a hard journey. The army was ambushed by Turks in a dangerous pass near Beirut—the Dog River pass—and it was only with supreme effort that Baldwin and his men defeated the Turks and were able to continue.

They arrived at Jerusalem in early November. "All the clergy and people came out from the city to meet them, Latins as well as other nations, and to the accompaniment of hymns and spiritual songs, with rejoicing they led the count into their city as their lord and king."[3] Daimbert, the Patriarch of Jerusalem, had stayed away.

Because there was bad blood between the two men, Daimbert refused to crown Baldwin in the Church of the Holy Sepulchre; he had at first refused to crown him at all. The issue between them was the bequest of Jerusalem Godfrey had made to Daimbert. Baldwin had no intention of honoring it. Daimbert wanted Jerusalem to be an ecclesiastical city under his exclusive authority, and the fight between him and Baldwin went on for several years.

---

[1] Fulcher of Chartres, Ryan 137.
[2] Fulcher of Chartres, Ryan 137.
[3] William of Tyre, vol. 1, 425.

4.1 The coronation of Baldwin I.

For the short run a truce was negotiated by intermediaries and Daimbert agreed to crown Baldwin, although not in Jerusalem. Instead the coronation took place in the Church of the Nativity in Bethlehem on Christmas Day 1101. Baldwin ruled until his death in 1118.

The future of the Latin Kingdom was not promising. The antagonism between the king and the patriarch, serious though it was, was only one of the difficulties Baldwin faced. The need for manpower; the need to repopulate the city and make it viable again; the need to expand the kingdom to secure seaports and make the entries to Jerusalem safe; the need to settle the issues revolving around the Latin church—all these and more crowded in upon Baldwin when he was elevated to the kingship. A lesser man might well have given up.

Fortunately, Baldwin was temperamentally well suited for his role, and he proved to be an excellent ruler. He was brave and tough-minded; he inspired the loyalty and affection of his men; he was intelligent and, when necessary, he could be quite cunning. Baldwin was also impetuous, a weakness that on occasion clouded his usual good judgment and led him to take risks he would have done well to avoid. Overall, however, he was a ruler of political acumen and foresight. He had a vision of what his kingdom should be, and he immediately set about, against appalling odds, to ensure its future.

At the time of Baldwin's accession, the Latin Kingdom, soon to be known as Outremer—"the land beyond the sea"—included the Kingdom of Jerusalem itself, the counties of Antioch and Edessa, and the principality of the Galilee.

Antioch was more than three hundred miles (160 kilometers) north of

Jerusalem, and the lands between the two cities were occupied primarily by Muslims and menaced by nomadic groups of Bedouin and marauding Turkish tribes. In addition to fending off regular Muslim attacks, the counts of Antioch had to contend with the Byzantine emperor's serious attempts to recover Antioch, the lands surrounding it, and Antioch's ports on the Mediterranean. Edessa was even farther from Jerusalem, 160 miles (256 kilometers) northeast of Antioch. The county had no natural boundaries and was more exposed and more vulnerable to attack than the heavily fortified city of Antioch. For centuries Edessa had been the bulwark which protected Byzantine territories from the Muslims, and now Edessa stood as a shield between the Muslims and crusader Antioch.

During Godfrey's rule, Bohemund's young, ambitious nephew Tancred had conquered Tiberias and the whole of the Galiliee in the interior of Palestine, which was added to the Latin Kingdom as the principality of the Galilee. Tancred had also conquered Haifa, although Baldwin refused to let him keep it and had given it as a fief to one of his own men.

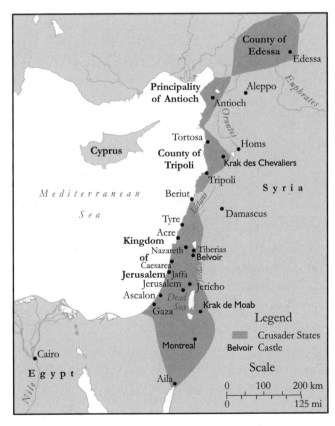

**Map 4.1
The Crusader
States, ca. 1140.**

Tancred had held a grudge against Baldwin since early during the First Crusade when Baldwin had bested him over control of Tarsus. He opposed Baldwin's becoming king, and his hostility continued to pose a problem for Baldwin. It was solved by an unexpected turn of events.

In August 1100, Bohemund and a small contingent of his knights were on an expedition to the upper Euphrates River when they were ambushed near the city of Melitene by the troops of the Danishmend Turkish dynasty. Bohemund was captured and held prisoner for almost three years until he was ransomed by the Franks. To keep Antioch secure during his absence it was imperative to have a strong ruler, so in March 1101, Tancred was offered the regency, which he accepted. Before going to Antioch, Tancred gave the principality of the Galilee to Baldwin for what he intended to be a limited time. Even after Tancred's return, Baldwin refused to give it back. Tancred never recovered the lands he had taken in the Galilee.

One of the strangest and longest-lasting agreements between the Muslims and Christians was actually effected by Tancred soon after he had originally taken control of the Galilee. He and his men had marched farther east, coming almost to Damascus itself, and they threatened Damascus by destroying the city's crops and herds and cutting off its supply lines. The ruler of Damascus agreed to an arrangement that divided the area of the Golan, east of the Galilee, into three parts: one-third of the income from the crops and herds went to the Franks, one-third to Damascus, and the final third to the peasants who lived on the land. So the Golan became a free zone. The agreement was honored by the Franks and Damascenes and, even allowing for several lapses, actually endured until 1187, when Jerusalem fell once again to the Muslims.

In 1109 the difficult task of capturing the port city of Tripoli was accomplished by Raymond of Toulouse's descendants. Count Raymond had begun the siege in 1103, but he died in 1105. The siege was continued by his successor, his cousin William Jordan. In the spring of 1109, Raymond's son and heir, Bertram of St. Gilles, came to claim his inheritance. In the struggle between Bertram and William that ensued, Bertram prevailed. In July 1109 he captured Tripoli. The principality of Tripoli was formed and added to the Latin Kingdom. Just as well, perhaps, that Raymond did not live to see that happen, since he had envisioned the principality as his own property.

As ruler of his kingdom, Baldwin, in effect, wore two hats. He ruled Jerusalem and the surrounding areas as king, and he ruled the counties and principalities as a feudal overlord. It was the form of governing the Franks were familiar with, and they transplanted it to the East. Enforcing the relationship between the king and his feudatories was, as we shall see, no easy task. Communications among the separate parts of the kingdom were extremely difficult, and since Antioch and Edessa had their own problems to contend with, they were unable—and sometimes unwilling—to offer regular help to Jerusalem.

In the Kingdom of Jerusalem itself, in addition to the Holy City, Baldwin possessed only the inland cities of Bethlehem and Ramla and the coastal cities of Jaffa and Haifa. The most immediate danger came from the Fatimid dynasty in Egypt, which still held the strongly fortified port of Ascalon, just forty miles (sixty-four kilometers) from Jerusalem. From Ascalon the Egyptians could send reinforcements and supplies into Palestine and maintain control of the eastern Mediterranean coast. (See Color Plate 1.)

Baldwin understood full well that the only way his kingdom would survive was if men and supplies could come from the West through the ports on the coast. This also meant making the roads safe. So Baldwin's first goal was to take control of the cities along the Mediterranean and to clear the roads.

4.2 Pilgrim being attacked. Graphically depicts the pilgrims' worst fears.

Jaffa was Jerusalem's single port of entry, and the road leading through the Judaean hills to Jerusalem was so dangerous as to be almost impassable. An English pilgrim who visited the holy sites in 1102–1103 described the dangers: "For the Saracens, always lay in snares for the Christians ... always on the lookout for those who make an attack on account of the fewness of the party, or those who have lagged behind their party through weariness.... Oh, what a number of human bodies ... lie all torn by wild beasts!" People were so fearful for their own lives that the dead were left unburied. If a person were so foolhardy as to stay alone to dig a grave, "he would be making ready a grave for himself rather than for his companion."[4]

Even so, some pilgrims and soldiers were able to get through Jaffa if they came into the port stealthily, in single ships or by twos and threes. Although they were warmly welcomed in Jerusalem, few stayed, and the need for manpower remained urgent. "We were in need of nothing," Fulcher of Chartres wrote, "if only men and horses did not fail us. The men who came by sea to Jerusalem could not bring horses with them, and no one came to us by land."[5]

The road between Jerusalem and Ramla was equally dangerous. "This country was infested by bandits and robbers. These scourges of the high-ways,"[6] William of Tyre called them, had to be cleared out before the road was safe. Even before his coronation Baldwin had gone after these bandits. He set fires all around their caves and hiding places to force them out into the open, where his men killed them on the spot. Those who could, fled, and the roads and the countryside around were simply abandoned ... at least temporarily.

The first coastal city Baldwin attacked was Arsuf. He succeeded in capturing it because he had the support of the Genoese navy, which besieged Arsuf by sea while Baldwin besieged it on land. Baldwin would certainly not have prevailed without the Genoese.

Baldwin secured the help of the Genoese by promising them one-third of all the spoils taken in any city they captured together. Moreover — and this was the important arrangement — the Genoese would have extraterritorial rights in every city they helped capture, allowing them to live and trade freely in the ports in the Latin Kingdom. It was the first of what would be a pattern of extraterritorial rights granted to the Italian naval cities. Pisa and Venice soon followed suit. The arrangement between the king and the Italians was essential for Baldwin, even though the extraterritorial privileges meant that the Italians who came to live in the Holy Land were free of the king's authority. The price the Italians eventually exacted for their help was often quite high.

After taking Arsuf, Baldwin laid siege to Caesarea, which was heavily fortified and put up a fierce fight, but, once again, with Genoese help, Baldwin was victorious. During the conquest of Caesarea, in June 1101, a large part of the population was massacred. "How much property of various kinds was found there it is impossible to say," Fulcher of Chartres wrote, "but many of our men who had been poor became rich." He then described how the

---

[4] Saewulf, *Pilgrimage to Jerusalem and the Holy Land*, trans. Bishop of Clifton, London: Palestine Pilgrims' Text Society, vol. 4, 1896 (New York: AMS Press, 1971) 8–9.

[5] Fulcher of Chartres, Ryan 150.

[6] William of Tyre, vol. 1, 426.

inhabitants' bodies were burned in order for the Franks to retrieve the gold coins that had been swallowed or hidden on their persons. Even women had hidden gold coins in places Fulcher felt it was too shameful to recount.[7]

Soon afterward news reached Baldwin that a huge Egyptian army was assembling outside Ramla, preparing to attack Jerusalem. So dire had the manpower shortage now become that Baldwin told his men to make each of their squires a knight. Then the waiting began. Finally, in early September, Baldwin decided to attack first. With the squires who were now knights, according to Fulcher of Chartres, Baldwin still had only "about two hundred and sixty [knights] and our footmen about nine hundred. At the same time eleven thousand knights and twenty-one thousand footmen opposed us."[8] Even if the latter figures were exaggerated, as undoubtedly they were, Baldwin was seriously outnumbered.

The king made a wonderfully stirring speech to his men before they went into battle, and he ended it with a piece of hard truth, reminding them that should they want to leave, France was very far away. Largely owing to Baldwin's inspired leadership, the Franks were able to defeat the Egyptians and force them to flee. It was a startling result for both sides. Then, as was customary, there was no fighting during the winter months, but the Franks knew that the danger from the Egyptians was far from over.

While Baldwin and his men had been valiantly trying to secure the coastal cities, their manpower shortage was acute. Time and again the Franks sent to the pope and the European nobility begging for help. Mindful of the manpower crisis, Pope Paschal II (1099–1118) was tireless in his efforts to win recruits to aid Jerusalem. He preached, he sent out legates to preach and to convene councils, even holding one (at Poitiers) on the anniversary of the Council of Clermont, in his efforts to organize what would be known as the Crusade of 1101.

The Crusade of 1101

Enthusiasm for the new crusade ran high. It can be attributed partly to the victory in Jerusalem, partly to the tales of courage and spiritual reward brought home by returning soldiers and pilgrims.

For everyone—nobles and knights as well as the poorer folk—the trip home had been arduous, long, and expensive. Those who could afford it attempted the voyage by ship, but even that was perilous; ships capsized and people often drowned. Those who retraced the land routes they had taken in

---

[7]   Fulcher of Chartres, Ryan 154.
[8]   Fulcher of Chartres, Ryan 156.

1096 returned worn out, ill, most of their booty used up by their expenses. Those who reached home were understandably all greeted as heroes.

Once the welcome had worn off, however, returning crusaders had serious problems to face. Those who had mortgaged property to finance the crusade now had to repay their debts, and many farms and businesses were in disarray. Life had been hard for the families left behind, and harder still was the problem of getting news of the fate of crusaders. Since no official list existed with names of the dead or wounded, families had to depend on word of mouth to learn what happened to their loved ones, and it could take months before they knew anything.

Although few men brought home any of the fabled riches of the East, some brought back holy relics, which were highly coveted and greatly prized: pieces of the True Cross, pieces of the Holy Lance, a ball of hair from the Virgin Mary's head, and relics of many other saints. Belief in the miraculous powers of the relics to cure the sick and restore sight to the blind, to right a wrong, to intervene on a person's behalf with God, to provide spiritual enlightenment all ensured their value to Christian Europe. The demand for relics grew during the crusading era, as did the supply, which raised questions about their authenticity and whether it was proper to move relics from one place to another. Whatever the Church's unease about certain relics, finding and selling them became a big and lucrative business.

Tales of the first crusaders' exploits spread throughout Europe; poems were written and songs sung about their heroism, and their example encouraged others to join the new crusade. Some chose to go back a second time. Many families who had sent one son on the First Crusade now sent off a second son, and crusading, particularly in France, began to be a family tradition.

In response to Paschal's pleas, armies were formed in Lombardy (in northern Italy) and in Germany. As Urban before him, Paschal II had great success in France. Contingents of knights and soldiers came from northern and eastern France and from Aquitaine and Burgundy, which had contributed only small armies for the First Crusade. Paschal wrote to all the prelates in France urging them to send soldiers and "especially [to] compel those who have assumed the sign of the cross in pledge of this journey, to hasten thither." He was fierce in his condemnation of the crusaders who had fled from Antioch: "let them remain in excommunication, unless they affirm with certain pledges that they will return."[9] Some famous defectors joined this new crusade — undoubtedly shamed into it — among them Stephen of Blois, whose wife insisted that he go, and Hugh of Vermandois.

---

9   Pope Paschal II, "Letter on the Capture of Jerusalem," in Allen and Amt 78.

As before, the armies were sizable. Despite papal strictures against noncombatants, a large group in every army was made up of women, children, and clerics. We will never have an accurate count, but all the chroniclers agree that the numbers altogether were substantial—as great, and perhaps even greater, than the numbers who left for the First Crusade. The several armies were led by high-ranking nobility: William IX, duke of Aquitaine; William II, count of Nevers; and Odo, duke of Burgundy, among many others. There was a large ecclesiastical contingent as well, and the armies were well financed.

This new wave of crusaders had learned very little from the examples of the First Crusade. They were better provisioned at the beginning and able to purchase food as they traveled. That apart, they had no single leader in charge; they followed the same perilous routes overland; they appear to have had no real plan about how to proceed once they reached Constantinople. All in all they replicated the worst errors of the earlier crusade and added a few of their own.

The Lombards were the first army to arrive at Constantinople, probably reaching the capital in late February 1101. Earlier, when they entered Bulgaria, which was Byzantine territory, the soldiers, or perhaps noncombatants with the army, had stolen food and generally pillaged the land; they compounded their actions by desecrating some Greek shrines, so they were on bad terms with the Emperor Alexius even before they arrived at Constantinople. They intended to wait at Constantinople for the other armies, but after two months the soldiers began pillaging again, and they rioted when Alexius cut off their supplies. He wanted the army to move to Nicomedia, as the first crusaders had done, and they finally went, but only after their relationship with Alexius was salvaged with the help of Raymond of Toulouse. Raymond had remained on good terms with Alexius and was in Constantinople when this group arrived. He ultimately joined the Crusade of 1101 as advisor, though his good advice was not taken.

By June the Lombards had been joined by several French armies, including the one led by Stephen of Blois. The Lombards knew of Bohemund's capture, knew he was being held in Pontus (in Asia Minor, near the Black Sea), and were determined to rescue him from the Turks. Although Alexius, Stephen, and Raymond strongly opposed this endeavor, they did not prevail. So rather than separate the armies, the French who were present joined the Lombards in this extremely foolhardy venture. To reach Bohemund, the armies had to cross enemy territory and rough terrain. After several inglorious encounters with the Turks, and severe food shortages, the crusaders were defeated by a Turkish army in early August, and they fled in panic.

The next wave of crusaders, convinced that they should catch up with the previous armies, hurried into Turkish territory. Ultimately they were ambushed by the Turks in the hinterlands of Asia Minor and suffered huge losses. Many who survived were taken captive and sold into slavery. And Bohemund continued to languish in a Turkish prison.

The men who escaped made their way to Antioch. With Tancred's help and the addition of some crusaders who had managed to flee from the first disaster, a new army was formed, which included Raymond of Toulouse, Stephen of Blois, and a complement of great nobles, among them the duke of Aquitaine and Raymond's brother, Hugh de Lusignan. They left Antioch in February 1102, finally en route to Jerusalem.

First, however, they laid siege to Tortosa, on the coast, roughly halfway between Latakia and Beirut. Tortosa had been taken during the First Crusade and subsequently retaken by the wealthy emir of Tripoli. Tortosa was strategically valuable, and this new group of crusaders was able to regain the city. Raymond of Toulouse decided to remain in Tortosa. He had been thwarted twice in his hope for land—once when he challenged Bohemund for control of Antioch and then when he lost the kingship of Jerusalem to Godfrey. So now he had the opportunity he longed for, and he began the conquest of all the lands controlled by Tripoli.

The rest of the crusaders continued on and were met by King Baldwin at the perilous pass near Beirut. He had waited over two weeks for the crusaders to arrive in order to ensure their safe passage. When they met, the king and nobles "rushed into each other's arms and exchanged gracious greetings with the kiss of peace. Pleasant converse with one another so refreshed them that their hardships and losses seemed to have slipped from their minds."[10] Nonetheless, refreshed though they were, many in this group quickly went home after celebrating Easter in Jerusalem. Poor Stephen of Blois, who was regularly quite luckless, tried to sail home, but the winds were against him, and he was forced to return to Jaffa. Thus it happened that some crusaders were still in the Holy Land, although few were in Jerusalem, when the Egyptian army began to approach Ramla from their base in Ascalon in May 1102.

Baldwin should have been cautious. But he was eager for action, and he badly underestimated—or perhaps had not wanted to know—the size of the Egyptian army. He rode out to meet the Egyptians and only when it was too late to turn back did he realize his error. His army was surrounded, and his soldiers broke ranks and ran; those who were not killed managed to flee to Jaffa or, as Baldwin did, to Ramla.

Baldwin escaped from Ramla with the help of an Arab who owed him a favor. After hiding in the hills, Baldwin finally reached the comparative safety of Arsuf. Soon after his escape, the Egyptians attacked Ramla. The city was

---

[10] William of Tyre, vol. 1, 442–43.

weak and poorly fortified, and the outcome was predictable; most of the crusaders and the population of the city were killed or taken to Egypt. Stephen of Blois was among the nobles who were killed. His death helped somewhat to restore his reputation, which had been tarnished when he deserted at Antioch.

Baldwin led one more attack against the Egyptians outside Arsuf; that battle was inconclusive and both sides withdrew.

With only a few exceptions, the crusaders of 1101 who survived went home. They had accomplished nothing for Baldwin, their only achievement having been the capture of Tortosa. The crusade was a dismal failure, and a sad story altogether. Fulcher of Chartres's description rings true; he termed it a "pitiable pilgrimage,"[11] when he saw the survivors of this crusade straggle into Jerusalem early in 1102. Unfortunately, the failure was a preview of things to come during the twelfth century, a presentiment of subsequent crusading failures. For the foreseeable future, Baldwin's hopes for reinforcements from the West were dashed.

Baldwin I's Further Campaigns

Still he soldiered on, determined to win control of the coastal cities. In the spring of 1103, Baldwin made his first unsuccessful attempt to take Acre. Acre had all the advantages that Jaffa lacked: built on a natural harbor, it had been fortified with two sets of breakwaters — an outer wall and an inner wall — so it was safe for ships in any weather and exceedingly difficult to attack, since it was a double port. It had the added safeguard of a tower built in the sea, known as the Tower of Flies. This port was so huge that it had room for as many as eighty ships at a time. When Baldwin made his second attempt to take Acre in 1104, he had the decisive aid of a large fleet of Genoese ships. Once in Frankish hands, Acre would become the most important commercial port in Outremer, the second-most important city in the kingdom, and the harbor for naval vessels that would eventually come from abroad to aid the Franks.

With the further help of the Genoese, Baldwin captured Beirut, and soon after he took Sidon. For that battle he had support of a fleet of Norwegian crusaders, led by the king of Norway's brother. The Norwegians had a grand adventure and a triumphal tour on their way home, including a visit to Constantinople. How serious they were about the spiritual aspects of crusading is difficult to assess, but their aid was invaluable.

Baldwin's determination to secure the coast never flagged. By 1112 he had taken all the coastal cities with the exception of Tyre and Ascalon. Tyre was as large and well fortified a harbor as Acre — some thought it even better fortified —

---

[11]   Fulcher of Chartres, Ryan 164.

and in 1112 Baldwin was forced to abandon his siege. Because of Ascalon's strategic location, the Egyptians were resolute in their defense of it. Not until just after the mid-century could the Franks capture this vital port. Nonetheless, and even without considering Baldwin's perilous situation when he became king, his military accomplishments were amazing.

Jerusalem Restored

His successes would not have been of much value to Jerusalem if the population crisis within the city had not been addressed. By every account the Holy City was "almost destitute of inhabitants. There were not enough people to carry on the necessary undertakings of the realm.... The people of our country [that is, the Franks] were so few in number and so needy that they scarcely filled one street, while the Syrians who had originally been citizens of the city had been so reduced...that there [sic] number was as nothing."[12] As already noted, no one who was not of the Christian faith was permitted to live in Jerusalem, so Baldwin had to wrestle with the question of where to find new inhabitants who would make the city come alive again.

Baldwin learned that there were Oriental Christians living beyond the Jordan River under very harsh conditions. What little income they could eke out from their lands and herds had been heavily taxed. Baldwin promised them much-improved conditions if they would settle in Jerusalem. In a short time, these families, their kinsmen, and their herds began arriving in the Holy City. Thus, within only a couple of generations following Baldwin's wise decision, the population grew and the city began to flourish.

Gradually other settlers came: pilgrims from the West who stayed to make their homes in Jerusalem, noncombatants who arrived with later crusading armies, sons of the nobility, traders, artisans, monks, nuns, and businessmen. The population increased until by mid-century, or soon after, it reached about thirty thousand inhabitants, a number at least as large as the population when the Muslims controlled the city. Thanks to Baldwin's initiative, Jerusalem under Latin rule became a thriving city.

There is a large kernel of truth in the often repeated truism that the Latin Christians lived surrounded by a sea of Muslims, but it is not the whole truth. The majority of the population in the East of course was Muslim, but scattered among the Muslims were many people professing different faiths, coming from different cultural backgrounds, and speaking different languages.

The most ancient were the Jewish communities, some of which could be traced back to the time of the Second Temple. The main concentrations of Jews in the Latin Kingdom lived in Tiberias or in small agricultural settlements

---

[12] William of Tyre, vol. 1, 507.

in the Galilee: in Ramla, and in Tyre, Acre, and the other smaller Mediterranean coastal cities. We have already seen the fate of the Jerusalem Jews. Except for Jerusalem, the Franks permitted the Jews to remain where they had settled, if they chose to do so, and throughout the decades of Frankish rule, Jewish pilgrims were permitted to visit the Holy City.

In the Latin Kingdom the Jews were always a tiny minority, although their settlements were gradually augmented by pilgrims and visitors from Europe. The largest, most important, and wealthiest Jewish communities were still in Muslim lands, in Syria and Egypt, and in Ascalon as long as it was held by Egypt.

Oriental Christians lived throughout the lands captured by the crusaders. In Antioch the population was almost entirely Greek-speaking and Orthodox, and it remained so after the Latins came. The largest groups of Armenian Christians lived in Asia Minor and in Edessa, where they remained after Baldwin became its first Latin ruler. Sectarian Christian churches were entrenched all over the East: the Syrian Christians (also called Jacobites); Copts and Maronites, who were Monophysites; and Nestorians, all dating their origins to the early Christian centuries.

The whole array of Eastern Christians came to worship in Jerusalem, to build their own churches and chapels, and to live in the Holy City. The immigrants encouraged by Baldwin to settle in Jerusalem were drawn mainly from the poorer among these Oriental Christians. To the Franks these non-Latin Christians — apart from the Greeks — were essentially fungible, and they lumped them together and called them all "Syrians."

For the most part the Franks were disdainful of the Oriental Christians, their disdain often turning to outright dislike and hostility. The popular sentiment is conveyed in the excerpts from brief descriptions given by an anonymous pilgrim in the twelfth century, who wrote that the Greeks "are cunning men, not much practiced in arms, and they err from the true faith." Of the Syrians, he wrote, "These are useless in war.... Others are Armenians. They have some slight skill in arms.... They have a language of their own and there is an irreconcilable hatred between them and the Greeks."[13] And on it went.

The Latin Christian population was also mixed, although it was predominantly French and French-speaking, to the dismay of those who were not francophiles. A German priest who made his pilgrimage in 1170, deploring the fact that no credit for taking Jerusalem was given to his German countrymen, wrote that "the taking of the city [Jerusalem] is attributed to the French alone.... [And] the entire city has fallen into the hands of other [i.e. non-German] nations — Frenchmen, Lorrainers, Normans, Provencals, Auvergnats,

---

[13] Anonymous Pilgrim V, trans. A. Stewart, London: Palestine Pilgrims' Text Society, vol. 6, 1894 (New York: AMS Press, 1971) 27–29.

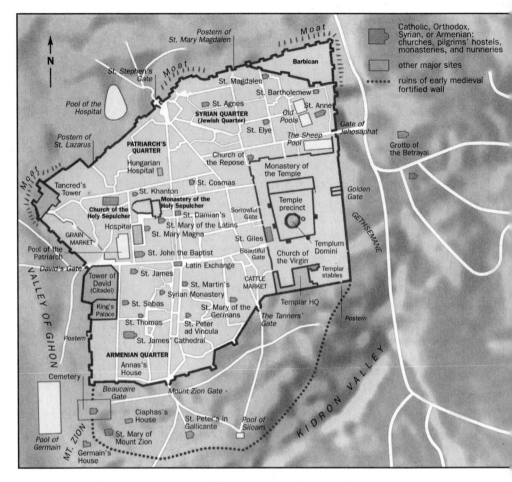

Map 4.2 Jerusalem in the twelfth century under crusader occupation.

Italians, Spaniards and Burgundians, who took part in the crusade ... And the glory of delivering the Holy City was ascribed to the Franks alone; and they at this day, together with the aforesaid nations, bear rule in the aforesaid city [Jerusalem] and the neighboring country."[14] He exaggerated, one suspects, to make his point, because there was, at least soon after this pilgrim's visit, a street in Jerusalem called the "German Street" and undoubtedly some Germans settled there. Nevertheless, his point is well taken and basically true.

---

[14] John of Wurzburg. "Description of the Holy Land." Trans. A. Stewart. London: Palestine Pilgrims' Text Society, vol. 5, 1896 (New York: AMS Press, 1971) 40–41.

Jerusalem was divided into four quarters: the Armenian Quarter, with its large Cathedral of St. James, populated by other Eastern Christians in addition to Armenians; the two quarters where the Jews and Muslims had lived and that were deserted until Baldwin encouraged the newcomers to move into them; and, the most important quarter for the Latins, the Patriarch's Quarter, later called, as it is to this day, the Christian Quarter. The centerpiece was the Church of the Holy Sepulchre.

The crusaders' first impulse, what they felt to be an immediate necessity once their victory was assured, was to transform Jerusalem into a Christian city, to beautify the Christian holy sites, and to eradicate the Muslim sites or convert them to Christian use. Their attention naturally turned first to the Church of the Holy Sepulchre.

The church, which had been rebuilt by the Byzantines following its destruction by the mad Caliph al-Hakim, was in good repair. It was a round church. "Its roof... built of beams and rising aloft and interwoven with most skilful workmanship into the form of a crown, is so constructed that it is always open to the sky.... Under this wide opening lies the sepulchre of the Saviour."[15] In addition there was the site of Calvary, the cave in which St. Helena had discovered the True Cross, and several smaller chapels associated with Christ's Passion. All these the Franks enclosed in a single church in the beautiful Romanesque style that they knew from Europe. In the large area where Constantine's basilica had once stood, the Latins built a cloister and a convent for the canons of the cathedral.

In this first generation the Franks strove to recreate Romanesque architecture. The essence of Romanesque lies in its simplicity—in the massive stone walls, the sense of spirituality conveyed by the half-light that infuses the church, and the separation of the sacred space from the intrusions of the outside world. The interiors are richly decorated with mosaics, wall paintings, and statues—altogether a feast for the senses.

As the Franks became familiar with the forms of Eastern architecture and the beautiful mosaics and paintings created by Byzantine and Muslim artists, their own style began to change. A new style gradually emerged, known as the crusader style or, more simply, crusader art, an art that was neither completely European nor completely Eastern, but a blend of the two.

Planning for the Church of the Holy Sepulchre began soon after the Franks arrived, although the actual work did not begin in earnest until the 1130s and took several decades to complete. The church was, appropriately enough, dedicated on July 15, 1145—the fiftieth anniversary of the capture of

---

[15] William of Tyre, vol. 1, 343.

Jerusalem—although the church was not yet finished. Until 1131 the coronation church had been in Bethlehem. Beginning in 1131, when the third king
of Jerusalem was crowned, the coronations took place in the Church of the
Holy Sepulchre. All the rulers of the kingdom, from Godfrey on, were buried
in the church in Jerusalem.

The first major conversions of Muslim holy sites to Christian use were the
Dome of the Rock and the al-Aqsa Mosque. The Dome of the Rock had
been placed over the ground where Solomon's Temple stood and was
adorned "with a wondrous casing of marble, [and] has the form of a beautiful
rotunda, or rather of a circular octagon ... with a wall decorated on the outside from the middle upwards with the finest mosaic work, for the remainder
is marble."[16] The site became a church named the *Templum Domini*—the
Temple of the Lord—and all who came to see it were awestruck by its beauty
and the sight of a Holy Cross placed on one wall.

The al-Aqsa Mosque, traditionally identified with Solomon's Palace, was
converted into a Christian royal palace, where the first three rulers lived and
governed. It "was an imposing edifice of surprising beauty and grandeur,
paved with marble slabs, supported on arches, and furnished with copious cisterns. The apartments were artistically decorated with mosaic and superb rows
of beautiful marble columns."[17]

The Christian Church was soon present everywhere. All over Jerusalem
chapels and churches sprang up, some built into Muslim sites, some newly
erected. The same was true throughout the conquered territories in Palestine
and Syria. "Old churches were repaired, and new ones were built; by the
bounty of Princes and the alms of the faithful, monasteries of regular monks
were built in fitting places; parish priests and all things appertaining to the
service and worship of God, were properly and suitably established everywhere."[18] Many of these churches were, naturally enough, Oriental Christian
churches and monasteries.

The Franks intended to have control over all Christian churches, whatever
the denomination. In both Jerusalem and Antioch, the Greek Orthodox
patriarchs were replaced by Latin Christian patriarchs. The Orthodox patriarch
in Jerusalem was actually expelled from the Church of the Holy Sepulchre.
The first Easter after his expulsion a strange and disturbing incident occurred—
or, more precisely, did not occur.

The miracle of the Descent of the Holy Fire happened, or was believed to

---

[16] John of Wurzburg, 15.

[17] *The Pilgrimage of the Russian Abbot Daniel*, trans. C. W. Wilson, London: Palestine Pilgrims' Text Society,
vol. 4, 1895 (New York: AMS Press, 1971) 21.

[18] Jacques de Vitry, "The History of Jerusalem," trans. A. Stewart, London: Palestine Pilgrims' Text
Society, vol. 11, 1896 (New York: AMS Press, 1971) 26–27.

have happened, every year on the eve of Easter. A pilgrim who witnessed the miracle early in Baldwin I's reign described how "the divine grace comes down unseen from heaven, and lights the lamps in the Sepulchre of the Lord.... At the end of the ninth hour [on the Holy Saturday] ... a small cloud, coming suddenly from the east, rested above the open dome of the church.... It was at this moment that the Holy Light suddenly illuminated the Holy Sepulchre, shining with an awe-inspiring and splendid brightness.... Man can experience no joy like that which every Christian feels at the moment when he sees the Holy Light of God."[19]

In the year the Franks summarily dismissed the Orthodox patriarch, the Holy Fire did not appear. Many people believed that the failure was punishment for the absence of the Orthodox patriarch, so he was invited to return and was able from then on to celebrate mass in the Church of the Holy Sepulchre every day, using the Greek liturgy. The following year the Holy Fire returned.

On the whole, the Eastern Orthodox communities throughout the Latin Kingdom continued as they had before the crusaders arrived. As time went on, the Franks grew more tolerant and accepting of the Eastern Christians. Living as a minority, the Franks understood the need to establish a rapport with all the diverse people living in the Holy Land—whether they liked them or not.

Meanwhile, Baldwin had not been neglecting his fight with Daimbert and his desire to rid Jerusalem—and himself—of the patriarch. He harassed the patriarch for months, until Daimbert left Jerusalem and went to his chief supporter, Tancred, in Antioch. In the company of Tancred and Baldwin of Edessa, Daimbert returned to Jerusalem for the last time. He was briefly restored to the patriarchal throne, but the king insisted that Daimbert be brought before a church synod of inquiry into his behavior. In December 1102, the synod removed Daimbert from office.

Daimbert was not so easily defeated. He returned to Antioch and in 1104, following Bohemund's release from prison, went with Bohemund to Italy in search of papal confirmation for his position in Jerusalem. We will never know whether he received it; he died on his way back to Jerusalem in 1107. Although the papacy did not give up the right to intervene in ecclesiastical elections in the Holy Land, by the time Arnulf of Chocques, who was Baldwin's friend and great supporter, was appointed patriarch by the king in 1112, the papacy understood that Jerusalem would never become an ecclesiastical state.

Arnulf had already achieved a reputation for political intrigue and sinfulness and, as William of Tyre wrote, "continued to conduct himself as he had done before and even committed many worse offenses." Nepotism was among the least of his sins; "even while he was patriarch Arnulf led an unchaste life,

---

[19] *Pilgrimage of ... Abbot Daniel,* 74–79.

and his shame was a matter of common knowledge."[20] As patriarch he was closely involved in Baldwin's marital affairs and was blamed for Baldwin's most egregious behavior toward the women in his life, although Baldwin probably needed little encouragement.

A. The King's Marital Life

Baldwin's first wife, who had accompanied him on the crusade, died and was buried at Marash in the fall of 1097. After Baldwin took Edessa, he married the daughter of a wealthy Armenian noble. The marriage helped Baldwin cement his position in Edessa, and he expected she would bring a rich dowry. Her father never paid it. We know very little about this second wife; she is mentioned infrequently in the sources and is known as Arda, although even her name is uncertain. She and Baldwin started out for Jerusalem together, but after passing Antioch they separated, and Arda sailed to Jaffa and arrived in Jerusalem some time later than Baldwin did. Although she was indeed the first Queen of Jerusalem, there is no mention of her having been present when Baldwin was crowned.

Within a few years Baldwin simply set her aside. The stories that circulated about why he did this were quite offensive to the queen. Rumors of her infidelities were bandied about, and in one popular version the writer claimed that Arda had been captured by pirates and raped. When she was released and returned to Jerusalem, "the king, suspicious, and not unreasonably, of the Barbars' sexual incontinence, banished her from his bed, changed her mode of dress, and sent her to live with other nuns in the monastery of St. Anne."[21] Somehow she escaped to Constantinople, where she joined her parents and, as far as we know, lived a luxurious life until her death.

Perhaps Baldwin was angry because she had brought him no money; perhaps he was disappointed that she had not borne any children; or perhaps she simply hampered his own indiscretions. He "is said to have struggled in vain against the lustful sins of the flesh,"[22] although the sins were kept from the public eye. In any event, Baldwin never bothered to divorce Arda, or even to annul the marriage, so the next so-called marriage he made was bigamous. It caused quite a stir.

In 1112 the most eligible queen in Europe was Adelaide, the former Queen of Sicily, widow of the Norman king, Roger I, and sister-in-law of Bohemund's father, Roger Guiscard. She had served as regent for her son until he came of age in 1112, was an extremely wealthy woman with an

---

[20] William of Tyre, vol. 1, 489.
[21] Guibert of Nogent, Levine 164.
[22] William of Tyre, vol. 1, 416.

unblemished reputation, and was well connected in Italy as well as Sicily. Her main attraction for Baldwin was undoubtedly her money, since he had so little left that he was unable even to pay his knights. The match was made on condition that if Adelaide and Baldwin were childless, the throne of Jerusalem would pass to Adelaide's son, Roger II.

Adelaide was handsomely outfitted for her voyage to Acre, and she brought with her a great deal of money. Soon after her arrival, the patriarch married Adelaide and Baldwin. "It is impossible to deny that she was misled, since, in the simplicity of her character, she supposed that the king was in a position to marry her legally." As William of Tyre observed, "Things that have a bad beginning rarely end well."[23]

The beginning, however, was good for the kingdom, since Baldwin availed himself of her money, paid his knights, and restored and strengthened Jerusalem's fortifications. Her attraction for Baldwin lessened as her money dwindled. Since the royal couple remained childless, the lords in the Latin Kingdom feared that Roger II would someday claim the throne of Jerusalem and join Outremer to the Norman Kingdom of Sicily. How much they feared for the king's immortal soul is difficult to assess, but it was a consideration that went into the mix, along with their intense dislike and distrust of the Latin Patriach, Arnulf of Chocques. When a papal legate arrived in Jerusalem, he called a synod, which deposed the patriarch. Arnulf then went to Rome and managed to persuade the pope to reinstate him. He had to promise that he would see to it that Baldwin and Adelaide separated.

Baldwin fell ill in 1116 and, fearful that he might die in sin, decided without any prompting to cast off Adelaide and reinstate Arda. Adelaide "was highly indignant that she had been called from her country to no purpose.... Sad and sorrowing over the insult offered to her as well as over the futile waste of her wealth,"[24] she departed for Sicily.

The repercussions were considerable. Her son never forgave the insult, nor did his descendants. When the kingdom needed the help, ships, and money that Sicily could have provided, Sicily's Norman rulers refused to give them. The marriage agreement between Adelaide and Baldwin gave Roger a claim to the throne of Jerusalem. Although Roger did not press it, his successors never forgot it. Arda quite sensibly refused to return to Jerusalem.

B. The Battle of Harran

No one had been in a hurry to pay ransom for Bohemund. On the other hand, whatever their personal grievances, the Frankish leaders, including

---

[23] William of Tyre, vol. 1, 497.
[24] William of Tyre, vol. 1, 514.

the king, could not let him remain in a Turkish prison forever. Although Bohemund had to add funds of his own, the ransom was finally paid, and he was released in May 1103. Only Tancred had not participated in ransoming his uncle. Bohemund returned to Antioch, removed Tancred, and took control of the city again.

Fighting in Syria continued unabated during the next year—Muslim against Muslim, Franks against Muslims—until, in May 1104, the Franks suffered a major defeat at the Battle of Harran. Harran's strategic value to both Muslims and Franks lay in its close proximity to Edessa. Since it was held by Muslims, Harran presented a real threat to Edessa. So Count Baldwin of Edessa and Bohemund, aided by Tancred and Baldwin's cousin Joscelin of Courtenay, who had recently arrived in the East, assembled their considerable forces and marched toward Harran, intending to blockade the city.

The blockade was successful and the city was ready to surrender. Instead of taking the city immediately, however, the Franks delayed, and by the next morning, on May 7, a large Turkish army had come to relieve the siege. In the ensuing battle the Christian armies were virtually annihilated, and the Count of Edessa and his cousin Joscelin were captured. "Never during the rule of the Latins in the East, whether before or after this event, do we read of a battle so disastrous as this one, which resulted in so terrible a massacre of brave men and so disgraceful a flight of the people of our race."[25]

William of Tyre blamed the disaster on an argument between Count Baldwin and Joscelin over who should have control of Harran. The dissension revealed how fragile the alliances were among the Franks and how easily their unity could be fractured. The inability of the Franks to press their advantage at Harran and their huge loss of manpower meant that Edessa was more than ever vulnerable to Muslim attack and that the Latins were prevented from extending their kingdom farther east. The defeat was a bad omen for the future.

For the Muslims their victory was also a turning point because, as a Muslim chronicler wrote, "the hearts of the Muslims were strengthened, and their zeal for the victory of the Faith and the war against the heretics was whetted and sharpened."[26]

Bohemund's Attack on Byzantium

Bohemund and Tancred escaped to Edessa, where Bohemund gave Tancred authority to govern until Count Baldwin should return. It is therefore not

---

[25] William of Tyre, vol. 1, 459.

[26] Ibn al-Qalanisi, *The Damascus Chronicle of the Crusades*, trans. H.A.R. Gibb (London: Luzac & Co., 1967) 61.

surprising that Tancred was content to leave the count and Joscelin in Muslim prisons; they remained in captivity for four years.

After settling his affairs in the East and appointing Tancred as his regent, Bohemund set sail for Italy. In Anna Comnena's version of his departure, Bohemund, fearing the Byzantines, spread the word that he had died and then sailed off hidden in a wooden coffin with air holes so that he could breathe. He even had a cock killed and placed in the coffin with him so that the stench from the putrefying cock would convince everyone that it was Bohemund's body that was rotting. "In the world of our generation this ruse of Bohemund was unprecedented and unique, and its purpose was to bring about the downfall of the Roman Empire."[27] The story may be apocryphal, but Anna was correct about Bohemund's purpose.

Of all the schemes devised during the first decades of Outremer, none had more serious long-term consequences than Bohemund's attempt to organize a crusade against the Byzantine Empire.

The crusaders of 1101 had felt it necessary to find a scapegoat for their failure, so they blamed Emperor Alexius and Raymond of Toulouse, though neither one was at fault. However, the rumors fueled the animosity the Latins had toward the Greeks and helped prepare the ground for Bohemund's actions. He appealed to Pope Paschal II and apparently convinced the pope to proclaim a new crusade, which the pope's legate did at Poitiers in 1106. Although it was formally a crusade to defend the Latin Kingdom, the pope had certainly not opposed Bohemund's plan to go to war against Byzantium. Bohemund made a successful tour through France, gathering support wherever he appeared, even securing a daughter of the French king as his bride and sending the French king's illegitimate daughter to be Tancred's bride.

In the fall of 1107 Bohemund crossed from Apulia to the eastern shore of the Byzantine Empire. He had a huge army and navy and was confident that he would accomplish what he and his father, Robert Guiscard, had failed to do before the First Crusade. Bohemund planned to seize Durazzo and then march his army along the old Roman road that led to Constantinople. His goal was the capture of Constantinople itself.

Alexius's troops and his navy were waiting for him, and the battle at Durazzo was Bohemund's Waterloo. It was long and drawn out. His army suffered huge losses in the actual fighting, as well as from disease, lack of food, water and military supplies. When Bohemund knew that his army was truly defeated, he sent envoys to the emperor to sue for peace. Alexius "invited" him to come to Constantinople.

---

[27] Anna Comnena, Sewter 367.

Alexius's first demand was for the return of Antioch, which Bohemund, naturally enough, at first refused. After some persuasion by Anna Comnena's husband, and aware that he had no choice, Bohemund swore a lengthy oath of loyalty to Alexius and his heir. Bohemund became Alexius's vassal and, to avoid any misunderstanding, his obligations were enumerated in great detail. In return, he could hold Antioch and some of his other territories, ruling under the authority of the emperor. He had to remove the Latin patriarch and reinstate a Greek one. The treaty also included Tancred, against whom Bohemund promised to wage war unless he handed over the emperor's territories which he had seized and agreed to abide by the terms of the treaty. It was an ignominious ending to the career of one of the greatest—and most arrogant—heroes of the First Crusade. Not long afterward Bohemund returned to Apulia, where he died in 1111.

Anna Comnena's description of Bohemund is a fitting epitaph. She hated him, but she recognized and even admired the characteristics that made him a worthy opponent for her father. "There was a certain charm about him, but it was somewhat dimmed by the alarm his person as a whole inspired; there was a hard, savage quality in his whole aspect, due, I suppose, to his great stature and his eyes; even his laugh sounded like a threat to others. Such was his constitution, mental and physical, that in him both courage and love were armed, ready for combat."[28]

Bohemund's chief legacy was that he had taken to a new and dangerous level the hostility between the Latins and the Greeks. He had opened a Pandora's box of distrust and antagonism that could not be closed. William of Tyre's comment about Baldwin's bigamous marriage is also unfortunately apt for the closing years of Bohemund's career: "Things that have a bad beginning rarely end well."

Baldwin's Last Triumphs

King Baldwin was zealous in his determination to expand and secure his kingdom, and he never rested. In 1115 he crossed the Jordan into the area known as Transjordan, and on elevated land south of the Dead Sea he built a fortress that overlooked the major road between Egypt and Syria. It was named Le Krak de Montreal—the Royal Mount—in the king's honor, although it is also known by its Arabic name, the castle of al-Shaubak. The garrison stationed at the Royal Mount was able to harass the caravans traveling between Damascus and Cairo and the pilgrims to Mecca who used the road to reach Arabia.

In the following year, Baldwin went even farther south, to the Red Sea,

---

[28] Anna Comnena, Sewter 422–23.

where he occupied a town called Aila, at the Gulf of Akaba. He then crossed to an island in the Red Sea and established fortifications on the island and in Aila before he returned to Jerusalem. It was on his return that he felt so sick that he decided, for the good of his soul, to dismiss Arda. He survived his illness, and the expedition was a triumph. Baldwin had attained the southernmost boundary of the Kingdom of Jerusalem.

The immediate danger for Jerusalem was still the threat from the Fatimids, who had constantly harassed the kingdom from their base at Ascalon. In a bold move the king decided to invade Egypt in 1118 and, with as large a force as he could muster, captured Pharmia, an ancient city near the mouth of the Nile. The next morning his men caught fish in the Nile River for the king's breakfast; soon after eating, Baldwin became severely ill. He was too weak to ride, so his men made a litter for him and set out for Jerusalem. When they had gone about fifty miles (eighty kilometers) and reached the village of Laris, known to us as al-Arish, the king died. His grieving soldiers carried his body to Jerusalem.

They reached the Holy City on Palm Sunday, April 17, 1118, and "met the religious procession when it was descending from the Mount of Olives into the Valley of Jehoshaphat. At the sight of this and as if Baldwin were a kinsman, all who were present gave themselves over to mourning rather than song, to grief rather than joy ... even the Saracens who saw it grieved also."[29] Baldwin was buried next to his brother Godfrey in the Church of the Holy Sepulchre.

The New Kingdom Is Formed

In less than twenty years Baldwin had brought the kingdom of Jerusalem to almost the full extent of its territory. He was midwife to the rebirth of the Holy City and the expansion of the Latin Christian churches in the Holy Land. With exceedingly good sense and little rancor in his dealings with the counts and princes in his realm, Baldwin had earned their respect for his kingship of Outremer. The first lines of his epitaph, recorded by Fulcher of Chartres, read: "When the king died the pious race of the Franks wept, For he was their shield, their strength and their support. He was the right arm of his people, the terror and adversary of his enemies."[30]

During the years of Baldwin I's rule the Latin Kingdom had begun to take on the form it would ultimately have. The early decisions that were made, the areas that were settled, the buildings that were constructed were signposts on the road the Franks would follow as they established themselves in the East.

---

[29] Fulcher of Chartres, Ryan 222.
[30] Fulcher of Chartres, Ryan 222–23.

The laws governing Outremer evolved over time and as circumstances demanded, but from the beginning the hierarchy was never in any doubt. At the top of course were the Franks and presiding over them all, the king.

The position of the king was based on the traditional European ideas surrounding kingship, the deep-seated respect and even reverence for the kingly office. In Jerusalem the kingship was further enhanced by the fact that the royal seat of governance was in the Holy City and that the king was anointed by the patriarch of the most revered church in the Latin Christian world. In the early decades the monarch's prestige was increased by the king's strong leadership in warfare and his own personal bravery. The first kings in Jerusalem also were wealthier and controlled more territory than the rulers of Antioch, Edessa, and Tripoli.

Immediately below the king were the great nobles who held their lands directly from the crown and were his chief vassals. These nobles formed the High Court of the kingdom, to which were added the highest-ranking ecclesiastics, who also controlled land. Once the Italian communities were settled in the coastal cities, they were able to send representatives to the meetings of the High Court. The court's main functions were to pass laws, to hear cases involving their own members, and to consult or intervene, depending on the circumstance, in royal elections.

Next in the hierarchy came the class of knights, who, with few exceptions, had no pedigrees. Most of them had come on the First Crusade in the retinue of a lord, and in the Latin Kingdom they were vassals in the service of a noble. The knights often were given a living in the cities or on rural estates; they manned the garrisons in cities and forts and owed military service to their overlord. Most were not rich men, but as they were necessary for defense they were highly respected.

Just below the knights were the burgesses, as the armed foot soldiers on the crusades became known. The largest groups of men who found a new life, new status, and social advancement in the East came from among the burgesses. They were mostly peasants who had worked the land in Europe and led a hardscrabble existence before the First Crusade. For them the possibilities of a free life either in the cities or rural settlements opened a world of opportunities. They, and their descendants, became the backbone of the new kingdom, working on the rural settlements or in the cities as glass-blowers, tanners, bakers, and in other useful trades, some eventually able to buy their own shops to sell goods in the bazaars.

Marriage between Christians and Muslims was expressly forbidden by law, but marriages between Latins, Oriental, and Eastern Orthodox Christians were permitted and became quite usual. These marriages occurred at every social level: King Baldwin I had married an Armenian princess, as did his successor, Baldwin II, whose wife was an Armenian who followed the Greek Orthodox religion. The Frankish nobility and the burgesses frequently married local Christian women. To swell the ranks of the burgesses, women were brought from Apulia in southern Italy to marry them.

The offspring of these marriages and their descendants were called *pullani* or *poulain*—a word that has been translated as "colt" or "pullet," in either case denoting a new, young people to differentiate them from the older, indigenous peoples. In 1124 or thereabouts, Fulcher of Chartres wrote a romantic description of the way the European settlers had succeeded in becoming a new society in so short a time: "For we who were Occidentals have now become Orientals. He who was a Roman or a Frank has in this land been made into a Galilean or a Palestinian.... Some already possess homes or households by inheritance. Some have taken wives not only of their own people but Syrians or Armenians or even Saracens who have obtained the grace of baptism.... He who was born a stranger is now as one born here; he who was born an alien has become as a native."[31] It is a vivid passage and, once read, his description is hard to dislodge. It is more likely a reflection of Fulcher's own optimism about the future of the kingdom than a completely realistic picture of how far the society had come, and may also have been intended to induce Europeans to come to settle in the Holy Land.

The founders of Outremer had neither experience nor precedents to guide them in establishing their relations with the indigenous population. Below the Franks in the hierarchy were the Oriental Christians, and at the bottom the Jews and Muslims. The Jews, Oriental Christians, and Muslims were all required to pay a poll tax to the Franks. For Jews and Christians this was not so different from the taxes they paid when Muslims ruled. For the Muslims the tax was an insult and a sure sign of their subjugation. The taxes varied from place to place; that they were burdensome is well attested. In return for the taxes, the Jews, Muslims, and the Oriental Christians were allowed to maintain their own houses of worship and their own religious practices and, for most disputes, have recourse to their own traditional law courts.

Those Muslims who could afford to do so fled from the Franks to the suburbs of Damascus, but the peasants remained, as did many middle-class traders and small businessmen. The rural settlements of Muslim peasants who worked the soil were largely undisturbed by the Franks. Following the European practice, the peasants were now considered serfs, tied to the land. They settled into acceptance, however grudging, of new overlords to whom they paid their taxes and to whom they sold their produce. There is no evidence of resistance to the conquerors once the initial, brief period of trying to starve

---

[31] Fulcher of Chartres, Ryan 271–72.

the Franks in Jerusalem was over. Any impulse to rebel was surely held in check when the Franks began erecting their forts and castles in the countryside.

Save for those who fled to Ascalon and Egypt when the crusaders sacked Jerusalem, the Jews also stayed. They lived in relationship to the Franks much as they had lived under the Muslims—a minority with rights as long as they paid their taxes. They lived primarily in the coastal cities, although some continued on the land. From as far back as the eighth century there are records attesting to the role of Jews as merchants and traders, and under the Christians they continued to trade, and they remained in the businesses with which they were most closely identified: dyeing, tanning, and butchering. They were a tiny minority always. A little past the mid-twelfth century the estimate for the number of Jews living in Tyre was somewhere between four hundred and five hundred people—and that was the most sizable Jewish community in Palestine. Jewish pilgrimage to the Holy City continued and soon after the mid-twelfth century reached substantial numbers.

During the Frankish conquests, the inhabitants of besieged cities were usually given the opportunity to surrender peacefully, in which case the Muslim and Jewish inhabitants were allowed to remain or go into exile. Thus in many cities Jews, Oriental Christians, Muslims, and Franks lived in close proximity to one another. For the first time in their lives Franks were awakened to the sound of the muezzin calling Muslims to prayer.

Encounters between Franks, Muslims, and Jews were frequent in the cities. As trade developed in the Mediterranean coastal cities, Muslim caravans arrived, carrying pepper and spices, carpets, jewels, gold, and beautiful fabrics, destined for the markets for luxury goods that were emerging in Europe. These caravans traveled peacefully through Frankish territory, and trade agreements were negotiated among the Muslims, the Franks, and the Jews who were involved in trade. Non-Christian visitors in Frankish cities shared the bathhouses, bought their food in the open markets, and found places to stay in Frankish inns.

Until recently historians were convinced that the Franks settled in the fortified cities they had conquered, safe behind their walls and towers, and that they kept themselves separate and apart from the rural population, only collecting an income from the lands they controlled.

It is true that the greater proportion of Franks lived in the cities and that the security of living in fortified cities was a strong attraction for them. The Franks adapted easily to the comforts of urban living: to the bathhouses, the bazaars, the water systems, and the public squares. They learned to enjoy living in the square stone houses, built around a courtyard with a fountain in the center, that they had taken from the Muslims. The walls and fountains were protection from the summer heat, and beautiful carpets insulated the houses from the winter cold. The cities afforded many opportunities for becoming wealthy in trade and manufacture. "Those who were poor in the Occident, God makes rich in this land. Those who had little money there have countless bezants here, and those who did have a villa possess here by the gift of God a city."[32]

Recent research, particularly the work of archaeologists, has revealed, however, that the Franks settled in rural areas as well as in cities.[33] It has been estimated that there were some two hundred or more Frankish rural communities, that the Franks learned the art of irrigating the unfamiliar soil, and that their agricultural settlements flourished. Villages and towns sprang up, each with its church, its mill, and its olive press. The Franks preferred, where possible, to live close to the Oriental Christian communities, and they often worked the land side by side, each speaking his own language—the Oriental Christians speaking Greek or, more usually, Arabic, and the Franks their various dialects of French.

The knowledge that the Franks did not hold themselves apart from the native population raises important questions about how deeply the Franks were influenced by their contacts with their neighbors and how profoundly the contacts may have penetrated Frankish attitudes. Did the Latin settlers, as it was once assumed, develop a culture that had few traces, other than superficial ones, of the way of life they found in the East, or did they fashion a new, mixed Frankish-Oriental society and culture? These are questions we will answer as we follow the development of the Latin Kingdom over the next several decades.

The Franks had conquered a multi-layered world. In every aspect of life, they inherited a many-layered landscape: the foundations and walls of Roman, Byzantine, and Arabic cities, built one on top of the other; city institutions and modes of governing that in some form had continued from the Roman, Byzantine, and Arabic periods; churches and monasteries of Roman and Byzantine origin; discarded marble columns; ancient wells and traces of biblical cities. All these and more were the visible, often rebuilt and reused vestiges of the long history that molded the landscape the Franks now ruled.

On this ancient landscape the Franks were compulsive builders. Along with their churches and chapels, they began to build castles and fortifications. What is astonishing, given the shortage of manpower and money and the vicissitudes of life, is how extensive the building undertaken by the Franks was and how quickly they built forts and fortresses, castles and churches. The magnitude of the building during the crusader era is extraordinary. ,

---

[32] Fulcher of Chartres, Ryan 272.

[33] For example, Ronnie Ellenblum, *Frankish Rural Settlement in the Latin Kingdom of Jerusalem* (Cambridge: Cambridge UP, 1998).

The Franks had to find solutions to many practical problems: where to find materials, where to find masons and craftsmen, artists, engineers, and architects. The solutions were determined by what they found in this unfamiliar landscape.

For their buildings the Franks used the varieties of limestone and sandstone that were prevalent throughout the East and had been used for centuries by one civilization after another. When they wanted to add marble for columns and decorative features, they did what their predecessors had done and reused the marble from columns, sarcophagi, and decorative arches that had been brought from Greece and Rome by the early Greek, Roman, and Byzantine invaders. The work itself was usually done by combinations of Franks, Armenians, Syrian Christians, and Greeks. The plans in the early years most often followed the design of European buildings, although they were soon influenced by the Byzantine and Islamic buildings that were all around them.

Funding came from many sources: the royal families, the wealthy families, the monasteries, the local nobility, and money raised abroad by the Church. As we will soon see, the new military orders became the most affluent builders of all.

The castles and fortifications are the footprints the crusaders left behind. Even in a ruined condition and desolate, the castles that can be seen to this day remain the most characteristic and impressive images of their presence.

Although daily life, trade, and agriculture all went on and even increased during the first century of Frankish rule, the essential fact was that the Franks lived with wars and raids by nomads and robbers as their constant companions. Over time they covered their kingdom with fortifications of various kinds and sizes.

The Franks built small forts, basically towers, in each of their towns and villages, so that if a raid occurred in the countryside, the people could take refuge in the tower. These small towers were not intended for offense, but simply to keep the local population safe for as long as the tower could hold out against an assault—sometimes not longer than a few hours. They were modeled on the towers the early crusaders knew from home, although adapted to the new conditions they found.

In Europe, in the eleventh century, the towers were mostly made of wood, since it was easily available, and preferably located on an elevated site if one was available. If not, then an artificial elevation, known as a *motte*, was made of earth and surrounded by a moat filled with water. The tower stood in the midst of a courtyard, or *bailey*, in turn surrounded by wood and a gatehouse of some kind. In the Holy Land, where stone was so ubiquitous and water was usually not available at all, the towers were made of stone, usually on flat, arid land.

Castles were of different sizes, built to serve a variety of purposes. When, for instance, Raymond of Toulouse was attacking Tripoli, he found it so well defended that the only way he—and later his heirs—could capture it was to build a castle on a hill facing Tripoli, and from its protective walls emerge to torment the inhabitants of Tripoli until they finally succumbed. Building such a counter-fort was a common tactic in the first half of the twelfth century. The Pilgrim Castle, as Raymond named his, was the largest of the early crusader castles, and when Raymond fell ill, in 1105, he went there to die.

Many castles were located in rural areas, where they encouraged settlements to grow up around them. They functioned as administrative centers as well as protective fortifications and as refuges for the neighboring people. The lords who owned and controlled them collected taxes, settled local disputes, and made sure the castle was well provisioned to withstand a siege or to strike out aggressively. No matter the size (and some were quite small), the castle stood as the embodiment of power in a region.

4.3 Krak des Chevaliers.

The greatest number of castles—and the most stunning—were built after the 1130s. These include the famous Krak des Chevaliers and Belvoir, which we will discuss in the context of the time they were erected. Even so, it has been estimated that some twenty-two castles were built in the years before Baldwin I's death; only eight of these were built anew, the rest rose on the remains, and integrated the forms, of earlier Roman, Byzantine, and Arab fortifications.[34] To the extent possible, the castles were erected in inaccessible places, on high land or on promontories, and were strongly fortified with towers and sometimes double walls.

---

[34] For an extensive discussion of castles and where they were built, see Ronnie Ellenblum, *Crusader Castles and Modern Histories* (Cambridge: Cambridge UP, 2007).

For decades Ascalon remained the major threat to the Kingdom of Jerusalem. The Franks decided to encircle Ascalon with fortresses to protect themselves and from which they could harass the Egyptian garrison stationed in Ascalon as well as the citizenry. Accordingly they built three fortresses. The first, which William of Tyre described, was near Ramla "on a hill slightly raised above the plain...they built a fortress of very strong masonry with deep foundations and four towers. From the old buildings of which many vestiges remain to the present day, an abundant supply of stones was obtained. The wells of olden times...also afforded an abundance of water."[35] This was the castle named Ibelin; it was given by the king to the family that took its name from the place.

Castles designed for one purpose were often turned to a second purpose. Such was the third fortress, which was built to encircle Ascalon. When the White Watchtower, as it was named, was completed, the king took it under his own protection, garrisoned it with experienced soldiers, and provisioned it with food and weapons. "The result was that those who dwelt in the surrounding country began to place great reliance on this castle, and...a great many suburban places grew up around it.... The whole district became much more secure, because the locality was occupied and a more abundant supply of food...was made possible."[36]

The nature of warfare during the crusading era was based on the intention of an invading army to capture the fortified cities and fortresses held by the enemy. If the invaders could successfully besiege a city or castle, control of the surrounding territory passed to the victor. The problem for both sides, as we have seen, was that the destruction of land, and therefore food supplies, weakened both invader and invaded. Since a battle meant moving the army out of the castle and leaving few men behind to defend it, the tactic was to avoid a pitched battle if at all possible. On those occasions when battles occurred, they were usually bloody massacres. So castles, fortified cities, and even small forts all had a role in the defense of the Latin Kingdom.

The question that has perplexed historians for centuries is whether the castles and forts were placed according to a carefully conceived plan, that is, whether the Franks had in mind the idea of a fortified frontier before they ever began building. Based on the sources contemporary with the events, it seems unlikely that they had formulated an overall program. The guarded answer, for the time being, is that we cannot be certain about what they intended. But the Franks were quick to respond to circumstances, and they certainly built when and where the need for fortifications arose.

---

[35] William of Tyre, vol. 2, 130.
[36] William of Tyre, vol. 2, 132.

The Passing of the First Generation

At the death of Baldwin I, there was no law governing the election of a successor to the kingship. The higher nobility in the kingdom and some important prelates gathered to decide what to do. A good argument was made for offering the kingship to Baldwin's remaining brother, Eustace, Count of Boulogne, who was then in France. Given how successfully his two other brothers had ruled, and given the general acceptance in Europe of the principle of hereditary succession, this was hardly a surprising choice.

Quite coincidentally, however, Baldwin Le Bourg, Count of Edessa, had come to Jerusalem to visit King Baldwin and to see the holy sites, and he was present when Baldwin I died. At the urging of Joscelin, Lord of Tiberias, and of the Patriarch Arnulf, the other members of the conclave were convinced to offer him the throne. In the spring of 1118, Baldwin of Edessa was consecrated as his cousin's successor, and in the following year he and his Armenian wife, Morphia, were both crowned in Bethlehem. He reigned until his death in 1131.

Eustace had reached southern Italy on his way to the East when he heard that Baldwin was chosen in his stead. Preferring not to cause dissension in Jerusalem, he graciously relinquished the crown and returned to his own lands.

In the same year that Baldwin I died, the Emperor Alexius also died, as did Pope Paschal II, the unfortunate Adelaide, and Arnulf. Most of the greatest men associated with the First Crusade had already died: Bohemund, Raymond of Toulouse, Tancred, Pope Urban II and his legate, the beloved Adhemar, and many, many others. Only Count Joscelin of Courtenay and Baldwin II survived. With the passing of nearly all the first generation, the first stage in the history of Outremer was ended. What the next generations would make of their inheritance was far from certain.

The succession in the counties and the principality of Antioch had not passed without serious difficulties and even civil wars, but by 1118 the following rulers were in place, at least for a time: Joscelin was count in Edessa; Raymond's son, Bertram of St. Gilles, was Count of Tripoli; and Roger of Salerno ruled Antioch until his death in 1119. These were new men in the East.

King Baldwin II was a fine ruler. He was a wise and temperate man who had experience governing his own often troubled county, as well as experience in warfare. He was also deeply religious — so much so that, according to William of Tyre, "he had callouses on his hands and knees from frequent religious exercise and constant kneeling."[37] Baldwin was not a young man — his birth date is not usually given, but the evidence is that he was fifty when he came to the throne, and all the sources remark on his advanced age. Nonetheless,

---

[37] William of Tyre, vol. 1, 522.

Baldwin II was energetic and worked hard to build on the foundation his predecessor had secured. There was much to be done.

At his accession, his kingdom, from the Gulf of Akaba to the county of Edessa, was roughly five hundred miles (eight hundred kilometers) long. At the southern border of Tripoli, it was only twenty-five miles (forty kilometers) wide; in the southernmost border of the kingdom, its greatest width was seventy miles (112 kilometers). Not a huge kingdom, but a troubled one. The north still suffered the worst of the Muslim attacks, and the fighting in Syria and the county of Tripoli continued almost nonstop, save during the winter months, when the bad weather provided some surcease.

In the south, the Egyptians, as always, were a potential—sometimes real—menace; roving tribes of Bedouins, Arabs, and bands of robbers harassed travelers and settlements, and the possibility of violence was omnipresent. Overall, however, the situation in the Kingdom of Jerusalem was more stable, and the Franks were somewhat more secure than they were in the north.

In just under two decades, this new kingdom had been established. It was a kingdom of a most peculiar kind. It had no firm political link to any kingdom in Europe, so there was no ruler with a special responsibility for the Latin Kingdom. Historians have sometimes discussed Outremer in the context of nineteenth-century colonialism, but it had none of the aspects of a colonial dependency; this was not India in the British Empire, nor Algeria in the French.

Paradoxically, the kingdom was at one and the same time independent of any European power and completely dependent on Europe for manpower, for ships, for supplies, and for funds. Throughout its troubled history the crusader kingdom had to rely on papal proclamations for new crusades, on the moral support of the papacy, and on the papal privileges given to those willing to die for Christ and his Holy Land.

It is a well-established truth that the triumphs of the First Crusade owed a substantial debt to the fighting among the Muslims themselves, that, in the words of a reputable Muslim historian, "It was the discord between the Muslim princes...that enabled the Franks to overrun the country."[38] The hostility between Sunnis and Shiites, the fighting between Turks and Arabs, and the rivalries among the several warlords continued to plague the Muslim world, and for a time the new kingdom was saved by the factionalism endemic in the East. This state of affairs was not to last.

---

[38] Ibn al-Athir, in Gabrieli 11.

CHAPTER FIVE

From the Reign of Baldwin II to the End of the Second Crusade

espite the many attempts to clear the roads from Jaffa to Jerusalem, they remained perilous. A Russian abbot named Daniel, who made the pilgrimage to the Holy Land in 1106–1107, wrote a graphic description of his experiences.[1] Dangers lurked everywhere. He was quite brave, but even so, he wrote frequently of his fears of being attacked and killed as he walked, barefoot, across the rocky, difficult roads. The Abbot Daniel was only one among the increasing number of pilgrims who were making their precarious way to the Holy City. The need to protect these unarmed pilgrims was acute and, as always, the lack of manpower was also acute. The solution came in an unusual guise.

The New Knighthood

A. The Templars

In 1118 or 1119 two French noblemen, Hugh de Payens and Godfrey de St. Omer, joined by seven other knights, went before the patriarch of Jerusalem and vowed that, for the remission of their sins, "as far as their strength permitted, they should keep the roads and highways safe from the menace of robbers and highwaymen, with especial regard for the protection of pilgrims."[2] At the same time they dedicated themselves to lives of poverty, chastity, and obedience.

King Baldwin II became their patron and gave them a portion of his own

---

[1] *Pilgrimage of … Abbot Daniel*, 1–82.
[2] William of Tyre, vol. 1, 524–25.

palace for their use, an area against the northern wall of the *Templum Domini*, from which they derived their name, calling themselves at first The Poor Knights of the Temple. This was the quiet, unheralded beginning of the movement that would develop into the military orders. It was an event of seminal importance.

Although both the first members, usually given as nine, and the poverty in which they originally lived are enshrined in the Templars' foundation story, the records indicate that they were neither so few nor so abjectly poor. When the order was confirmed at a church council in January 1129, the numbers had grown to at least thirty and likely more. The Templars received a benefice, or church living, from the king, and soon other grants and donations were given for their support. Nonetheless, the Templars maintained the tradition that they were so poor in their early years that two men had to ride on one donkey, and that they wore only cast-off clothing.

By the Council of Troyes, held in France in 1129, all that was changing. Before the council met, Hugh de Payens visited many counties and duchies in France, went to England and Scotland, and generally made a sweep of Europe to recruit members and solicit funds. His trip was highly successful. In addition to acquiring new members, the Templars received land and manors in Europe from which they could derive an income. They also gained some well-placed and well-connected supporters, not least of them Fulk, the Count of Anjou, who would one day be king in Jerusalem.

At the council in Troyes, the order received formal papal approval and was given a rule. The rule affirmed the Templars as Knights of Christ—men who combined monastic vows with fighting in defense of Christ and His Kingdom.

This new knighthood, in which fighting became a religious vocation, was unprecedented. Yet, in retrospect, in the context of the religiosity of the twelfth century, this synthesis of the warrior ethic of knights fighting for Christ and the spiritual life dedicated to Christ seems neither surprising nor strange. The language of spiritual warfare, which has a long history reaching back to the Bible, spoke of girding oneself in spiritual armor to do battle for God and one's soul. In the twelfth century, this spiritual armor and the armor worn by knights were joined. "He is truly a fearless knight and secure on every side, whose soul is protected by the armor of faith just as his body is protected by armor of steel. He is thus doubly armed and need fear neither demons nor men"[3] Those words were written by St. Bernard of Clairvaux,

---

[3] St. Bernard of Clairvaux, *In Praise of the New Knighthood,* trans. Conrad Greenia, Cistercian Fathers Series 19 (Kalamazoo, MI: 1977) 130. For an illuminating discussion of the subject, see Katherine Smith, "Saints in Shining Armor: Martial Asceticism and Masculine Models of Sanctity, c. 1050–1250," *Speculum*, 83.3 (2008): 572–602.

the man acknowledged throughout Europe as the greatest and most influential churchman in the first half of the twelfth century, as important, if not more so, than the pope.

St. Bernard's role as proponent of the Templars is one of many accomplishments for which he is famous. Early in his career he was instrumental in developing a new, rigorous monastic order, the Cistercian Order, named for its first settlement at Cîteaux, in France. The Cistercians were part of a reform movement within Christianity to return to the purity and simplicity of the early church. St. Bernard founded the second Cistercian monastery, at Clairvaux, in 1115, and remained its abbot until his death in 1153. The Cistercian Rule emphasized extreme asceticism, manual labor, and seclusion from the world. St. Bernard led an austere and contemplative life, and yet, because of his extraordinary talents, he was drawn from his seclusion to serve the Church on numerous occasions.

He was intimately involved in the formation of the Templars and instrumental in drafting the rule for the order, which in many aspects was influenced by the Cistercian Rule, particularly in its emphasis on strict obedience and austerity.

The Templars adopted a white robe as their habit, similar to the coarse, white habit of the Cistercian monks, to which the Templars affixed a double-barred red cross. They were required to sleep in their shirts and breeches, and to cut their hair and grow beards. The rule was particularly fierce on the subject of pointed shoes, since they were associated with Saracens "and recognized as an abomination." All their weaponry was to be without adornment of any kind. Each knight was allowed one horse at first, but soon was permitted three, as well as a squire. The monks were given two meals a day and were required to eat in pairs, to make certain that no one had too little, so as to become weak, or too much, so as to become greedy. The rule comprised seventy-one sections, each one defining the strict conditions of the Templars' daily lives.[4]

St. Bernard wrote eloquently on behalf of the Templars and the ideology of the military orders. At the close of his brilliant treatise in defense of this new knighthood, Bernard wrote: "Thus in an astounding and unique manner they appear gentler than lambs, yet fiercer than lions. I do not know if it would be more appropriate to refer to them as monks or as soldiers, or whether it would perhaps be better to recognize them as both, for they lack neither monastic meekness nor military might. What can we say about this, except that this is the Lord's doing, and it is marvelous in our eyes."[5]

---

[4]   For the complete rule, see *The Templars: Selected Sources.* trans. and annotated Malcolm Barber and Keith Bate (Manchester, UK, and New York: Manchester UP, 2002) 31–54.

[5]   Bernard of Clairvaux, in Allen and Amt 199–200.

In the top rank of Templars were the fighting monks, usually from wealthy families, and the only members of the order allowed to wear the white robe. Below them were the sergeants, whose job it was to serve the brothers, and who fought alongside the knights, although they were not necessarily from the knightly class. They wore either black or brown habits. In addition, secular knights were permitted to join as temporary members for a limited period of time, and they too were permitted to wear only black or brown.

The Templars vowed obedience to the head of their order, called the master, whose authority was absolute. They were placed under papal authority, which meant they were freed from control of local bishops and higher clergy, except in Jerusalem, where the master was responsible first to the patriarch and then to the pope. A few years after the order's formal recognition, priests were added to the hierarchy, freeing the Templars from dependence on local clergy.

The order was well respected in the beginning, and wealthy prelates, kings, and nobles made donations of land, goods, and money to enable the Templars to carry on the holy war. The papacy freed them from paying tithes to the church and taxes to secular governments, and they were permitted to keep the spoils they captured in war. As a result of these donations, exemptions, and privileges, the Templars amassed land and castles all over Europe—a formidable base, which assured them a supply of manpower, money, and provisions. In this way they became an international organization.

The Templars spent lavishly to enlarge the original portion of the palace given them in Jerusalem, and to which they added new buildings. Ultimately, they created an enormous compound, which included a church, room enough to house three hundred knights, and everything needed to make life secure and even pleasant. "Those who walk on the roof [of the palace]," a visitor wrote in 1172, "find an abundance of gardens, courtyards, antechambers, vestibules, and rainwater cisterns; while down below it contains a number of baths, storehouses, granaries." Of a new building alongside the palace, he wrote, "I could give the measurements of the height, length and breadth, ... but even if I did so, my hearers would hardly be able to believe me."[6] The knights' horses were kept in the very same stables believed to have been built for King Solomon's horses.

William of Tyre's assessment of the Templars, echoed by many chroniclers in the twelfth and thirteenth centuries, has usually been accepted by modern historians. After describing their wealth, "equal to the riches of kings," he wrote, "For a long time they kept intact their noble purpose and carried out their profession wisely enough. At length, however, they began to neglect

---

[6] Theodorich, *Description of the Holy Places*, trans. A. Stewart, London: Palestine Pilgrims' Text Society, vol. 5, 1896 (New York: AMS Press, 1971) 30–32.

'humility, the guardian of all virtues....' They withdrew from the Patriarch of Jerusalem...and refused him the obedience which their predecessors had shown him. To the churches of God also they became very troublesome, for they drew away from them their tithes and first fruits and unjustly disturbed their possessions."[7]

For the Latin Kingdom, the wealth that enabled the Templars to support and field a sizeable number of knights—sometimes reaching as many as six hundred—and build or expand castles and fortifications was a great blessing. The independence their wealth afforded the Templars became, as later events will show, a blessing well disguised. In light of the complex role they were to play in the Latin Kingdom and in Europe, William's summary seems quite apt.

B. The Hospitallers

The second religious order begun in Jerusalem was the Order of the Knights of St. John of Jerusalem, better known as the Hospitallers. Its origins were earlier than those of the Templars and of a much different nature.

During the eleventh century, Italian merchants from Amalfi who traded in the eastern Mediterranean and often visited the Holy City built or, more likely, restored the Church of St. Mary of the Latins in Jerusalem, and along with it a monastery. The monks associated with the convent were Benedictines. In the decades before the First Crusade, when pilgrimage traffic had increased and travel was punishing, hundreds of pilgrims arrived in Jerusalem "wretched and helpless, a prey to all the hardships of hunger, thirst, and nakedness."[8] From their own meager funds the monks built a hospital to care for them. They cared for so many pilgrims and sick people that the space proved inadequate, and they built another convent, dedicated to St. Mary Magdalen, for the care of female pilgrims. Soon after, they built a second hospice and a church dedicated to St. John. William of Tyre believed the patron saint was St. John the Almoner, known for his good works, but it is now accepted that the patron saint was St. John the Baptist.

The Amalfitans undertook support of the hospitals, but word of the monks' selfless generosity in caring for the "wretched and helpless" spread in Europe, and donations were made to the hospital even before the First Crusade.

The Hospitallers' reputation was enhanced during the First Crusade by the saintly reputation of the monastery's abbot and the hospital's administrator, a man named Gerald. As the Christian armies advanced toward Jerusalem, the Muslims extorted as much money as they could from the Christians before they fled. The Egyptian ruler believed that Gerald had a huge sum of

---

[7] William of Tyre, vol. 1, 526.
[8] William of Tyre, vol. 2, 244.

money hidden away, and he ordered Gerald captured and tortured to reveal the hiding place. He was so brutally tortured that, according to William of Tyre, "the joints of both his hands and feet were wrenched apart and his limbs became practically useless."[9] Gerald survived, however, to administer the hospitals during the early years of the kingdom — and to receive gifts of land bestowed on the hospitals by Godfrey and Baldwin I.

The Hospitallers were also relieved of paying tithes to the churches in Jerusalem and Caesarea. At some point they freed themselves from the governance of St. Mary of the Latins and became an independent entity. In 1113, they were confirmed as a monastic order by the papacy; they were henceforth subject only to the pope.

No specific date marks the moment when the Hospitallers became a military order. The change in their status came about gradually, in a number of papal decrees and bulls issued throughout the twelfth century. Nevertheless, many Hospitallers were bearing arms as early as 1120, when the second abbot, Raymond of Puy, led a group of Hospitallers to help defend the kingdom from an Egyptian incursion. He set the Hospitallers on the new direction the order would take, and by the 1130s they had a reputation as excellent warriors. When the King of Jerusalem built the three fortresses surrounding Ascalon in 1136, he turned the defense of the castle Bethgibelin over to the Hospitallers. From then on they were continuously engaged in warfare, along with their primary mission to care for the sick.

During the first half of the twelfth century, the order amassed an extensive network of property in the Holy Land and Europe, their wealth rivaling that of the Templars. The pilgrim who visited the Templar complex in 1172 also visited the Hospitaller complex and was again overwhelmed by what he saw. "No one can credibly tell another how beautiful its buildings are, how abundantly it is supplied with rooms and beds and other material for the use of poor and sick people, how rich it is in the means of refreshing the poor.... Indeed,... we were unable by any means to discover the number of sick people lying there; but we saw that the beds numbered more than one thousand."[10]

The dating of the Hospitaller Rule is uncertain. It was written sometime in the twelfth century by the second abbot, Raymond of Puy, and although its precepts are akin to an eleventh-century monastic rule known as the Austin Rule, it was undoubtedly influenced by the severity of the Cistercian discipline and the Templar Rule. The Hospitaller organization was similar to that of the Templars.

William of Tyre was as critical of the Hospitallers as he was of the Templars. In his book he went on for several pages enumerating all the com-

---

[9] William of Tyre, vol 1, 325.
[10] Theodorich 21–23.

plaints lodged against the order by the priests and bishops in the Holy Land, most of which can be subsumed under the heading of arrogance. They refused to pay tithes to any churches or cathedrals, and they disobeyed all the rules promulgated by the patriarch in an insulting and public manner. The worst offenses they reserved for the Church of the Holy Sepulchre. They erected a building at the very doors of the church, which overshadowed it, and as if that were not insult enough, "they carried their presumption to such extremes that, in a spirit of audacious fury, they armed and, breaking into the church beloved of God... hurled forth showers of arrows, as if against a den of robbers."[11]

Within less than a century of their founding, both orders were being vilified by many of their contemporaries. Even before their reputations turned sour, the role they played in the defense of the kingdom, though often vital for security, was many times not in the best interests of the kingdom. Unhappily, the good the military orders did—and it was considerable—was ultimately overshadowed by their problematic behavior, their independence, and their immense fortunes.

Warfare Continues

Although the warfare between Muslims and Christians was not carried on everywhere simultaneously, at any given moment there was fighting somewhere in the Latin Kingdom or on its borders. Not all their battles and skirmishes will be described in detail from now on. However, during Baldwin II's reign, three encounters warrant attention.

In 1118 the Muslim rulers of Egypt and Syria decided for the first time to overlook their religious differences and unite against the Franks. The Egyptians assembled a huge force, crossed the desert, and arrived at Ascalon, where they were met by the Syrians, who had crossed the Jordan River to join them. The formidable Egyptian war vessels were anchored at Ascalon and Tyre, prepared to attack from the sea. Baldwin II had summoned reinforcements from the north and was ready for the Egyptian attack, although he was greatly outnumbered. The end of the story is odd. Neither side wanted to attack, "because," Fulcher of Chartres wrote, "they preferred to live rather than to die."[12] The armies literally faced each other for three months, at the end of which time they all went home. Although the Syrian–Egyptian unity was not followed up immediately, it was an early warning of what was to come.

The second military event of Baldwin II's reign (in 1119) was a disaster for the Franks of such magnitude that it became known as the Field of Blood. The attack against the Franks was led by a dangerous enemy, Il-Ghazi, a Turkoman

---

[11] William of Tyre, vol. 2, 240.
[12] Fulcher of Chartres, Ryan 226.

leader with a long military career behind him, who had become ruler of Aleppo in 1118. Joined by the ruler of Damascus and several other armies in the north, he entered the country around Antioch, preparing for a full-scale offensive.

Roger of Antioch had sent for reinforcements from the king, who started to march north, but Roger was impatient, and he foolishly led his army out of Antioch toward Aleppo without waiting for help. His forces encountered the Turkish army in the field, and on June 28, his army was destroyed. Seven thousand of Roger's men were massacred, and Roger was also killed. Only twenty Turks died. The Muslims were justifiably proud. Inexplicably, they did not proceed to capture Antioch, which they might well have done. Nonetheless, the loss of so much manpower in a kingdom that had scarcely enough was a serious and lasting blow.

On his way to relieve Antioch, Baldwin encountered Il-Ghazi's army in a savage battle. "With scornful disregard of the laws of humanity, with burning zeal and insatiable hatred, both sides fought as if against wild beasts."[13] Although outnumbered, Baldwin's army was victorious, and he then went on to Antioch, where he was welcomed with gratitude by the Antiochenes.

By popular acclamation Baldwin was given the regency of Antioch until Bohemund's son, who was underage, should reach his maturity and come from southern Italy to claim his inheritance. The king provided for the orphans of men who had died in battle, and he provided husbands for the widows from among his own soldiers and any able-bodied men left in Antioch. He then returned to Jerusalem. Baldwin's own position was strengthened by his control of Antioch, but in the north his kingdom had been seriously weakened.

In the brief intervals between his wars, Baldwin made a decision for Jerusalem that provided more trade and prosperity for the city and won for him the affection of the citizens. He remitted unconditionally, and presumably forever, all taxes on imported and exported goods to and from Jerusalem. This economic freedom was extended to everyone, including Muslims, Oriental Christians, and Jews who traded in the Holy City. This decision also provided an incentive for people to move to Jerusalem.

Unfortunately, Baldwin was endlessly preoccupied with his northern problems. In 1122, Balak, the ruler of Aleppo, attacked Edessa, and although he did not capture the city, he defeated the Frankish forces and captured Joscelin, the count of Edessa. The next year Baldwin marched north to fight Balak; his army was also defeated, and this time the king was captured. Joscelin escaped, but Baldwin remained in prison until late in 1224, when he was ransomed and released.

---

[13] William of Tyre, vol. 1, 533.

The Taking of Tyre

Despite Baldwin's absence, the kingdom in the south had won a great prize. In February 1124, owing to the support of a huge flotilla of Venetian warships, the port city of Tyre was taken from the Muslims.

A. The Role of the Venetians

Venice is a city of the sea. Built on dozens of small islands, Venice was not even linked to the Italian mainland until the mid-nineteenth century, and then reluctantly. From early in their history the Venetians turned to the sea to make their fortunes. Venice's immense wealth derived first from piracy and then, by the late tenth century, from its growing trade in the eastern Mediterranean. Venice was, and remains, an eastern-facing city, greatly influenced by Byzantium. The crowning glory of Venice, the Basilica of San Marco, built in the eleventh century, with its rounded dome and interior mosaics, is to all intents and purposes a Byzantine church.

It was the Byzantine emperor Alexius who gave the Venetians their first real foothold in the eastern Mediterranean. When the Normans in Sicily threatened both Byzantium and Venetian supremacy on the Adriatic, Alexius and the Venetians formed an alliance. In return for naval support, Alexius granted the Venetians extensive trading privileges, the right to establish a colony in Constantinople, and freedom from all customs duties. Alexius was succeeded (in 1118) by his son John, who decided, in 1122, not to renew the privileges his father had granted. The Venetian warships immediately sailed from Constantinople and began successfully to attack the Greek islands in the Mediterranean; Corfu, Rhodes, Samos, and Lesbos all fell to Venice. By 1126 the emperor saw the error of his ways; he renewed the Venetians' privileges and they withdrew from the Greek islands.

Early in the twelfth century, the Venetians had invented an assembly line, the first assembly line we know of anywhere, for the production of their galleys. In 1104 they built the Arsenale, a huge factory where they could manufacture a galley completely outfitted and seaworthy in one hundred days. When the ship entered the water from the Arsenale, its entire crew was on board. Small wonder that the Venetian navy outstripped the other Italian maritime cities in the eastern Mediterranean.

The Doge of Venice himself commanded the Venetian fleet that went to aid the Latin Kingdom in 1123. The fleet was composed of forty galleys, twenty-eight *chatz*, which were huge beaked vessels, and four ships carrying supplies. The fleet encountered the Egyptian navy first at Jaffa and in a bloody battle defeated them. "For a circuit of two miles [three kilometers] around, the adjacent sea became blood red from the bodies thrown therein and from the blood of the slain which flowed from the ships.... The shores were so thickly covered with corpses...that the air was tainted and the surrounding region contracted a plague."[14]

The next question to be resolved was whether the Venetians should attack Ascalon or Tyre. The argument among the Franks and between the Franks and the Venetians was so acrimonious that, in the end, it was decided to draw lots. Two slips of parchment, one with *Ascalon*, the other with *Tyre* written on it were placed on a church altar, and a poor orphan boy was asked to pick one of them. He chose Tyre.

Since the king was in captivity, it fell to the nobles to make their agreement with the Venetians before they sailed to Tyre. The agreement, in brief, gave the Venetians the right to have their own streets, a church, a square, and other buildings in Jerusalem. In Acre, the Venetians were given an even larger area, and in Tyre and Ascalon, when they were taken, a third of each city. In all cities of the Latin Kingdom the Venetians were granted complete freedom from paying any taxes. These extraterritorial privileges were granted in perpetuity.

In February 1124, the Venetians sailed from Acre to Tyre, where the Venetian navy would besiege the city from the sea and the Franks would advance from the land side. Tyre was a seemingly impregnable fortress. On the water sides there were double walls fortified with towers; on the land side there were triple walls, also strongly fortified.

Tyre had two overlords, the Muslim rulers in Egypt and Damascus, but received little help from either of them. The siege began on February 16. Tyre was able to hold out for a considerable time, but the fighting was fierce on both sides, and finally the inhabitants of Tyre, worn out and starving, begged the ruler of Damascus to sue for peace. A peace treaty was signed, allowing the people of Tyre to surrender without further bloodshed and to have the choice of remaining or leaving freely. On July 7 the Franks and Venetians entered the city, and soon the flags of the Latin Kingdom and Venice flew over the ramparts. Now the only Mediterranean port remaining in Muslim hands was Ascalon.

The two Italian cities that had gained the most advantages in the early decades were Genoa and Venice. Amalfi did not have the navy necessary to participate in the warfare, and was in any event occupied elsewhere. Although Pisa had a substantial fleet, Pisa's fortunes were tied to those of Daimbert, who, as we have seen, did not fare well in the Holy Land. So the extensive commercial opportunities went to Venice and Genoa. Two questions have surrounded the role of these Italian cities: First, to what extent was their trade responsible for opening up the eastern Mediterranean to Western merchants? And second, how religiously motivated were the Italians? The first is easy to answer.

---

[14] William of Tyre, vol. 1, 549.

Research now shows conclusively that there was already trade in the Mediterranean before the First Crusade, and that it was growing slowly, but growing steadily. Although the Italians with privileges in the East following the First Crusade undoubtedly contributed to the momentum and the volume of that trade, the old view that the crusades opened up a new trade that had not previously existed is no longer valid.

The question of motivation is less easy to answer. There is evidence that many Genoese took the cross and went to the Holy Land as crusaders, and a case can be made for Venetian commitment to the idea of the holy war. On the other hand, the economic advantages were considerable, and the desire for material gain certainly weighed heavily in the Italians' decisions to go East. Given the Venetians' later behavior on the disastrous Fourth Crusade (in 1204), it is difficult to cast them in a favorable spiritual light. They were, after all, for several centuries mainly distinguished by their immense fortunes.

So it came about that before the mid-twelfth century the Latin Kingdom had in its midst two groups who were juridically independent of the King: the knights of the military orders and the Italians.

The Succession Problems in the Kingdom

Since Baldwin was far from young when he came to the throne, the question of the succession weighed heavily on his mind. Although he and Morphia had four children, all four were daughters. In the Latin Kingdom women in the upper classes had the same rights of inheritance as men. If there was no male heir, the eldest daughter could inherit a fief, and in the kingdom, absent a male heir, women could inherit the crown. The choice of a husband to rule with the queen and lead the royal armies was crucial. Baldwin's choice for his eldest daughter, Melisende, was the powerful, wealthy Count Fulk of Anjou, Maine, and Touraine.

Fulk was an experienced warrior who had several connections to the Holy Land. In 1120 he had made a pilgrimage to Jerusalem and, before he returned home, provided for the support of one hundred of his own knights, who remained in the kingdom for a year. Fulk's half-sister Cecilia had come to Antioch to wed Tancred, and when he died she married the count of Tripoli. Baldwin's choice was unanimously approved by the secular and ecclesiastical princes. In early June 1129, Fulk and Melisende were married in Jerusalem. As a wedding present the king gave them Tyre and Acre to govern. The next year Melisende gave birth to a son, the future King Baldwin III.

The years following Baldwin's release from prison were extremely trying for him. Not only did the king have to fight the Muslims, he had to deal with bitter feuding that had erupted between Joscelin, the Count of Edessa, and Bohemund II, the young Prince of Antioch. The quarreling between the two men became so fierce that Joscelin enlisted Turks to aid him in an attack on Antioch's lands. Baldwin went north, and in 1128 he was able to reconcile the two men. The ensuing peace was only temporary, and the situation in the north soon went from bad to worse.

Bohemund II of Antioch had married the king's second-eldest daughter, Alice, in 1127, and they had a daughter named Constance. In the early winter of 1130, Bohemund II was killed in a battle against the Turks, and his army was massacred. His legitimate heir, Constance, was only two years old. Baldwin had the right and responsibility as king to appoint a regent for her, but Alice immediately assumed the regency and soon made it clear that she wanted to rule Antioch herself. She sent an envoy to Zengi, the ruler of Aleppo, offering to make an alliance with him if he would help to keep her in power. Her envoy was intercepted by Baldwin, and her plot was revealed. In the ensuing struggle with her father, Alice actually prevented the king from entering Antioch for a few days. She was afraid for her life, but Baldwin was forgiving, and he and his daughter somehow made peace. He exiled Alice from Antioch and assumed the regency for his granddaughter. He put Joscelin in charge of guarding his arrangements in Antioch and returned to Jerusalem.

The Death of Baldwin II

Within a few months, the king became seriously ill. He was then, in 1130, in his sixty-second year, an old man by the standards of his time, and he had lived an exceptionally hard life. Aware that he was dying, Baldwin asked to be carried to the patriarch's palace so that he could die near to the Holy Sepulchre. He had his daughter Melisende, Fulk, and his grandson Baldwin, who was not yet two years old, brought to him, and he gave the three of them equal power to rule his kingdom after his death. The king died on August 21, 1131, having first taken monastic vows. He was buried alongside his two predecessors in the Church of the Holy Sepulchre. Baldwin was greatly mourned, even by his Muslim enemies, who held him in high esteem. Three weeks later, in mid-September, Fulk (1131–1143) and Melisende (1131–1152) became the first rulers to be consecrated and crowned in the Church of the Holy Sepulchre.

In the year following Baldwin's death, his friend and stalwart supporter, Joscelin, the count of Edessa, died under sad circumstances. He was seriously injured when a part of a tower his men were undermining fell on him. He never recovered from the severity of his injuries. His death was a great loss for Edessa, for the chances for unity among the quarrelsome Latin rulers in the north, and for any hope that they would willingly recognize the overlordship of the new king. Joscelin was the last of the original crusaders to die, the last of the rulers who had the security of the Latin Kingdom as their first care.

Joscelin was succeeded in Edessa by his son, also named Joscelin, a considerably lesser man than his father. Although known for bravery, he was also known for his licentious behavior and drunkenness. Unhappily, none of his contemporaries behaved commendably; none of them could put aside their greed and self-interest for the good of the Latin Kingdom.

King Fulk and Queen Melisende

King Fulk had many virtues and was personally well liked by the nobles in Jerusalem. He was physically brave, and more often than not his judgment was good. His major failing—and it was a serious one—was that he was weak when it came to asserting his sovereignty over Antioch and the counties in the north. On some important occasions he failed as well to assert himself with Melisende. "At his [Baldwin's] death," a Muslim chronicler wrote, "he was succeeded by a man who lacked his good sense and his gift for kingship.... Baldwin's death caused trouble and disturbance among the Franks."[15] He was perhaps overly harsh in his criticism of Fulk, partly out of respect for Baldwin II. "Trouble and disturbance," however, was an understatement.

Fulk was bombarded from several directions all at once: from the northern rulers, who wanted independence; from the Byzantine emperor, who wanted to take Antioch from the kingdom; and from the threatening Muslim counter-offensive.

No sooner had Fulk succeeded to the throne than Alice resumed her plan to abrogate the agreement she had made with her father, take control of Antioch herself, and free Antioch from the king's overlordship. She persuaded Joscelin II and Pons, Count of Tripoli, to join her rebellion. Fulk marched north with his army, invaded Antioch's territory, and, although he defeated the insurgents in battle, he was unable, or perhaps unwilling, to effect any permanent changes. Fulk forgave Pons and Joscelin II. He took over the regency of Antioch, but he had actually gained little, and he returned to Jerusalem with the northern problems unresolved.

Since Alice would not relinquish her intention to become independent, the need for a strong ruler in Antioch who would be loyal to the king became ever more pressing. Fulk arranged a marriage between the young princess Constance, who was not yet ten years old, and Raymond of Poitiers, a man thirty years her senior, the son of Count William IX of Aquitaine, who had been on the sorry crusade of 1101. To keep Alice in the dark about the plan, she was told by the patriarch in Antioch that Raymond was coming to marry her. After Raymond married Constance and her mother realized she had been tricked, Alice "pursued the prince with relentless hatred."[16]

---

[15] Ibn al-Qalanisi, in Gabrieli 40.
[16] William of Tyre, vol. 2, 79.

In her usual duplicitous manner Alice had made overtures to the Byzantine emperor, John II Comnenus, offering Constance in marriage to the emperor's son, Manuel, a marriage that would have effectively restored Antioch to the empire. When Constance was snatched away, John decided to take action. The marriage gave the emperor the excuse he needed to march against Antioch to assert his rights as overlord. In all his previous campaigns, mainly in Asia Minor, John had been successful, and he had a well-trained, hardened army under his command. He arrived at the gates of Antioch in August 1136, and immediately began to bombard the city.

King Fulk faced a difficult decision. At the same time that Raymond, now prince of Antioch, was appealing to him for help against the Greeks, the news had reached him that the fortified castle of Montferrand, in the County of Tripoli, was being besieged by Turkish forces and was desperate for the king's help. Fulk decided that Raymond should surrender Antioch unconditionally to the Byzantine emperor so that the king could turn his full attention to the Turkish attack. Thus Antioch became an imperial city once more. Raymond was permitted to rule as the emperor's vassal, and, in 1137, John II withdrew his army. Fulk set out to relieve Montferrand.

Resurgent Islam

For more than a decade after the crusaders settled in the Holy Land, the Muslims did not grasp the full import of the Frankish conquests, nor did they understand that the Franks intended to stay. But soon, here and there, sporadically at first, signs of a newly awakening consciousness in the Muslim world appeared. Two goals had to be accomplished for the overthrow of the Franks to be successful: the unification of the warring Muslim regimes and the reawakening of the *jihad*.

In Islam, the word *jihad* has two aspects. It means the inner striving to live a perfect Muslim life in accord with the Five Pillars of Islam, to live devoutly, and to wage an inner battle against worldly temptations. In its other meaning, it is the obligation to fight against non-Muslims, to wage holy war against the enemies of Islam. In this meaning, *jihad* is a responsibility that can be discharged only collectively, and it presupposes a legitimate caliph to call for a *jihad*.

There has always been disagreement within Islam about the role of *jihad* as a holy war, whether it was only to be a defensive war or an aggressive war, and whether, as some have contended, it should actually be considered the sixth pillar of Islam. The religious obligation to wage holy war had lain dormant for more than two centuries before the crusaders came to the East. The reawakening of the commitment to *jihad*, with the understanding that it was to be an offensive war, and then overcoming the rivalries among the several Muslim groups in order to unify them to fight against the Franks were not easy to achieve.

The first serious, successful counteroffensive against the Franks, the first that would have a continuous life, was led by the Sunni Turkish *atabeg* Zengi (1127–1145), who ruled in Mosul and subsequently in Aleppo. Mosul was the base from which Zengi initiated his expansion against the Franks and also Damascus, which he intended to conquer. His aspirations were boundless, and he was able to rekindle in many Muslims the religious fervor that was the spirit of *jihad* in its most militant form. To his supporters Zengi was the man "that God in His mercy to the Muslims was pleased to raise to power"[17] to defeat the Franks and save Syria from being overrun by Christians; he was, as he himself believed, the first effective leader of the *jihad*.

He began his military career by making several unsuccessful attempts to conquer Damascus, and he then turned to his war against the Franks. In 1137 he laid siege to the castle of Montferrand in the county of Tripoli.

The siege of Montferrand was horrific because the inhabitants had not had sufficient warning of Zengi's approach to provision themselves with enough food and water to withstand a lengthy siege. Zengi met the king's army in the field as Fulk marched toward Montferrand to relieve the castle. Zengi defeated the army, took the count of Tripoli prisoner, and forced the king and a small number of his men to withdraw into the castle. Soon the food gave out, and the people were forced to eat their horses. "After these were gone," William of Tyre wrote, "there was no food of any description. So even the strong and robust grew weak from hunger, and leanness, induced by famine, ravaged the strength of even the most vigorous."[18]

Fulk had sent messengers to Raymond of Antioch and Joscelin II of Edessa to hasten with their armies to join him. Before they could arrive, owing to Zengi's cunning, the castle surrendered. Zengi had learned that the Frankish relief forces were close, and, fearing that they might be joined by the Byzantine emperor and knowing the terrible conditions within the castle, he sent terms of surrender to Fulk. Zengi offered to let the people in the castle go free and even to return the prisoners he had taken, including the Count of Tripoli, if the king would relinquish the castle. Not knowing that aid was so near, Fulk capitulated.

The siege of Montferrand was a milestone in the counteroffensive led by Zengi, of whom a Muslim chronicler wrote that "He was the bravest man in the world... [who] never let a year pass without taking over a piece of enemy territory."[19]

---

17 Ibn al-Athir, in Gabrieli 41.
18 William of Tyre, vol. 2, 90.
19 Ibn al-Athir, in Gabrieli 55.

Zengi still had his sights set on Damascus and northern Syria, and so did the Byzantine emperor. Once John believed that Antioch was securely in his control, he gathered Raymond and Joscelin with their armies and laid siege to Shaizar, a fortified city south of Antioch, roughly halfway between Antioch and Tripoli. The emperor and his troops fought fiercely and bravely, but the outcome was negligible. The emperor was offered money to withdraw, and he did.

The real import of the siege is that neither Joscelin nor Raymond joined in the fighting. Raymond hated the emperor; Joscelin and Raymond distrusted each other; and, in any event, neither had the stomach, or the sense, to fight, even for their own interests. They stayed in their tent and played chess. (See Color Plate 2.) Had the Christians gained control of Shaizar, they would have been in a better position to block Zengi's advances. Zengi now had the upper hand. His reputation among the Muslims was growing, and he was rapidly winning allies. His next move was to be another attempt to capture Damascus.

However, both the Franks and the Damascenes wanted to prevent Zengi from taking Damascus, so, in a head-spinning turn of events, they made an alliance in 1139. The threat of the Frankish-Damascene alliance persuaded Zengi to leave Damascus, for the time being.

The Death of King Fulk

King Fulk was thrown headlong from his horse while he was out hunting in early November 1143. Three days after the accident he died. Melisende was "pierced to the heart by the sinister disaster. She tore her garments and hair and by her loud shrieks and lamentations gave proof of her intense grief.... The people of the household also manifested their grief by tears, words, and aspect."[20] Fulk was buried, with fitting ceremony, in the Church of the Holy Sepulchre. Melisende was crowned and consecrated queen. Since her son, Baldwin III, was only thirteen when his father died, Melisende then ruled as queen and as regent for her son.

The irony of Frankish history during Fulk's kingship was that the unity that Baldwin II had effected fell apart, and the Latins now exhibited the factionalism that had earlier characterized the Muslim world. With no one strong enough to hold it in check, the enmity between Joscelin and Raymond was out in the open, neither man willing or caring to help the other. It was an opportune moment for the Muslims, and Zengi made his move against Edessa. In late November 1144, he laid siege to the city.

---

[20] William of Tyre, vol. 2, 134.

The Loss of Edessa

Edessa was bereft of men to defend it, and with little food or water, the people in the city were soon starved. At the last minute Joscelin was finally impelled to act. He sent for help to Jerusalem and Antioch, but only the queen responded to his call. The prince of Antioch never came, and the royal army did not arrive in time to save Edessa. The siege lasted only four weeks. Edessa surrendered on December 24, 1144.

Thus, "through his lack of energy and in punishment for his sins, this Joscelin lost the entire land over which his father had ruled so ably."[21] Edessa was the first city to have been taken by crusaders, the first county administered by a Frank, and was strategically vital for the security of Antioch and the Latin Kingdom. Its loss was an unqualified disaster.

News quickly reached the West. Melisende sent a delegation to Pope Eugenius III, imploring him to send aid; bishops from the Armenian Christian Church, who were at the papal court, joined in the outcry for help; Raymond of Antioch sent messengers; and pilgrims and prelates of all denominations went to Europe to spread the story of the fatal siege and beg for help.

The Second Crusade Is Proclaimed

On December 1, 1145, Pope Eugenius III issued a papal bull calling for the Second Crusade. The pope accounted for the fall of Edessa in spiritual terms— "our sins and those of the people themselves requiring it, a thing which we can not relate without great grief and wailing."[22] His appeal for a crusade was heartfelt, but nowhere near as stirring as Pope Urban II's speech at Clermont, and it did not elicit an immediate response. The real work of preaching the crusade was done by St. Bernard of Clairvaux. Nevertheless, the papal bull marks the beginning of this new crusade.

At Christmastime in 1145, a few weeks after the pope had issued his bull, King Louis VII of France (1137–1180) brought the bishops and great lords to his annual Christmas court to reveal that he intended to go East to fight for Edessa. The first reaction to his announcement was dismay that he would leave his kingdom for a prolonged period. So it was decided that the decision would be referred to St. Bernard, who in turn referred it to the pope. It seems likely that the first papal bull had not been received at the French court when the king made his announcement. In any event, the king subsequently met with the pope, who enlisted Louis to be the leader of the crusade. The pope reissued his bull in March of 1146.

---

[21] William of Tyre, vol. 2, 53.

[22] This quote and the following ones are from Eugenius III, "Summons to a Crusade," trans. Ernest. F. Henderson, *Select Historical Documents of the Middle Ages* (London: George Bell & Sons, 1910) 333–36.

After exhorting people to join the crusade, the pope went on to enumerate the specific benefits that would accrue to them and their families. He granted remission and absolution of sins for those who went on the crusade: those "who shall devoutly begin so sacred a journey, and shall accomplish it, or shall die during it, shall obtain absolution from all his sins which with a humble and contrite heart he shall confess." He gave assurances that the wives and families left at home, and all their goods and possessions, would be protected by the Church; that those in debt would not have to pay interest for time past and the time away. All in all, the pope did everything possible to alleviate the financial burdens and risks of crusading. He then counseled those going not to be lavish in their spending and to take with them "none of the things which portend licentiousness," by which he meant no expensive clothing, no dogs, and no hawks, the last two presumably for hunting—nothing, in short, for pleasure.

Then, as had been arranged, a great meeting was held in the French town of Vézelay on the Sunday before Palm Sunday (in 1146). The assembled crowd was too large to fit into any building, including the church, so a wooden platform was erected out-of-doors and St. Bernard, with Louis VII by his side, addressed the people. "And when heaven's instrument poured forth the dew of the divine word, as he was wont, with loud outcry people on every side began to demand crosses."[23] When the cloth crosses St. Bernard brought ran out, he tore his own habit to make more. His preaching was an unqualified success. Among the many nobles who took the cross—and it was a roster of all the great noble families in France—was Eleanor, Queen of France, duchess of Aquitaine and Gascony, and countess of Poitou.

It would take a year of preparation before the crusade was ready to leave. In the meantime, Bernard began preaching all over France and Germany. Largely owing to Bernard's successful efforts, a remarkable enthusiasm for this new crusade erupted wherever he went, so spontaneous and so fierce that it could scarcely be contained.

A. Religious Fanaticism and the Jews

As happened at the beginning of the First Crusade, a religious fanatic came forward to preach against the Jews, once again perceived as the enemy closer to the hand. This time it was a Cistercian monk, an unauthorized preacher from northern France named Ralph (or Radulf), whose verbal onslaught against the Jews as enemies of Christ aroused people in northern France, in Flanders, and especially in Germany to attack the Jews.

---

[23] Odo of Deuil, *The Journey of Louis VII to the East*, trans. Virginia Berry (New York: Columbia UP, 1948) 9.

5.1 Guardians of the Holy Sepulchre. Sculpture from the tympanum of Strasbourg Cathedral. The knight on the left is lying on his shield, which carries the heads of two Jewish men, symbolically crushed under the Christian warrior's weight. This is one among several artistic examples of the prevalence of anti-Jewish sentiment.

However, St. Bernard came forward to silence Ralph in order to curtail the violence that threatened the Jews. St. Bernard planned to harness the fervor that Ralph had stirred up and turn it against the Muslims. He was on the whole successful, but, despite his early efforts, he could not squelch the monk. Bernard followed in Ralph's footsteps, going finally to the same cities in Germany where the Jews had suffered the most horrific massacres during the First Crusade. His letter to the Archbishop of Mainz set forth his explicit ideas about Ralph and, of more lasting importance, the Church's attitude toward the Jews. "I find three things most reprehensible in him [Ralph]," Bernard wrote, "unauthorized preaching, contempt for episcopal authority, and incitation to murder." What Ralph was preaching Bernard called "a foul heresy, a sacrilegious prostitution."

The nub of Bernard's argument to leave the Jews in peace was, for the Jews, a two-edged sword. "Is it not a far better triumph for the Church to convince and convert the Jews than to put them all to sword?... If she [the Church] did not hope that they would believe and be converted, it would seem useless and vain for her to pray for them."[24]

The Hebrew Chronicle of the Second Crusade, written by a man who was thirteen when the Jews in Germany were attacked, described some of the individuals who were killed, and the fear that seized the Jews when they heard Ralph's words and saw how he incited the mob against them. Remembering

---

[24] St. Bernard, "Letter to the Archbishop of Mainz," trans. Bruno James, in Robert Chazan, *Church, State, and Jew in the Middle Ages* (West Orange, NJ: Behrman House, 1980) 105.

the bloodbaths during the First Crusade, the Jews themselves knew that they had, for the most part, been spared. For this they were very grateful to St. Bernard.

According to the Hebrew Chronicle, Bernard spoke as follows to the mobs: "It is good that you go against the Ishmaelites. But whosoever touches a Jew to take his life, is like one who harms Jesus himself. My disciple Radulph [Ralph] who has spoken about annihilating the Jews, has spoken in error, for in the Book of Psalms it is written of them: 'Slay them not, lest my people forget.' "[25]

Although some Jews were killed as a consequence of Ralph's preaching, Bernard was at last able to send Ralph back to his cloister and divert attention away from the Jewish communities. So in Germany and France, and in England owing to the intercession of the king, the Jews were saved from worse persecution.

On the other hand, one should not be sanguine about the safety of the Jews in the mid-twelfth century. Episodic occurrences of anti-Semitism began to appear. In Norwich, England, for example, in 1144, the family of a young boy who had died accused the Jews of murdering him. The accusation was at first set aside by the sheriff, but surfaced again several years later, with details of how the boy was tortured before he died. The story spread, and a cult of the murdered boy was established. In Würzburg, in 1147, the Jews were accused of child murder in the case of a boy who was alleged to have drowned. Despite the coincidence of the timing, these and other like occurrences were not caused by the crusade. However, taken together with the forces unleashed against the Jews early in the crusade, they underscore how easily and quickly anti-Jewish sentiment could surface.

After quelling the anti-Jewish violence, St. Bernard went to Frankfurt to meet the German king, Conrad III (in 1147), and persuade him to take the cross. Conrad was at first reluctant because Germany was torn apart by civil wars, a situation virtually endemic in his kingdom. Bernard convinced Conrad to undertake the crusade by his gift for preaching and by the miracles he was believed to have performed at the king's court. So instead of a crusade led only by the French king, it became a joint enterprise led by two kings.

Not So Holy Warfare

In the months before the armies left for the Holy Land, three events occurred that, although unrelated to each other, expanded the theaters of war and began to influence changes in the ideology of crusading.

---

[25] *The Book of Remembrance of Rabbi Ephraim of Bonn,* trans. Shlomo Eidelberg (Madison, WI: U of Wisconsin P, 1977) 122.

A. In Spain

The first was the request made by King Alphonso VII of Castile to Pope Eugenius asking the pope to award crusading privileges for himself and the men who were going to fight against the Muslims in eastern Spain. This the pope did, and Alphonso's siege of Almeria, which he carried out with strong Genoese naval support in the fall of 1147, was successful. He then went on to conquer the last cities and outposts held by Muslims in Catalonia. Almeria was reconquered by the Muslims in 1154.

B. At the Siege of Lisbon

The second event was the conquest of Lisbon by a group of crusaders—primarily English, Flemish, Normans, and some Germans—en route by ship from England to the East. Opinion is still divided over whether the stop on the Portuguese coast at Oporto had been intentional. It seems likely from the sources that it was planned, but only in order to take a respite before going East. It is highly unlikely that there had been any prior discussion of the crusaders assisting the Portuguese king with the capture of Lisbon from the Muslims. In fact, the leaders who wanted to remain to assist King Alphonso had to overcome a good deal of resistance from the rank and file of crusaders.

The crusaders arrived outside Lisbon at the end of June 1147 and found Alphonso I of Portugal already there with his army. The king asked the crusaders to help with the siege of Lisbon and offered generous terms if they conquered the city. The king guaranteed that "If they [the crusaders] should, perchance, take the city, they shall have it and hold it until it has been searched and despoiled, both of prisoners for ransom and of everything else. Then, when it has been as thoroughly searched as they wish, they shall turn it over to me."[26]

The siege lasted for nearly seventeen weeks, until late October. After some negotiations, the Muslims capitulated and surrendered the city to the king and the crusaders. Once they had despoiled the city, the crusaders set sail for the East. Since its only link to crusading were the men who had taken the cross, it hardly qualifies as a crusade. However, this unplanned and unexpected victory was in fact the only successful conquest during the era of the Second Crusade.

C. Against the Wends

The third event was the north German warfare against the Slavic peoples known as the Wends, who lived on the eastern borders of Saxony. The German drive to expand their lands to the east and convert the pagans forcibly had begun

---

[26] "The Capture of Lisbon," in James A. Brundage, *The Crusades: A Documentary Survey* (Milwaukee: Marquette UP, 1962) 99.

in the late eighth and early ninth centuries. Although not continuously pursued, that drive for lands east of the Elbe River, and the conversion to Christianity of pagans living in those lands, was a recurrent theme in German history.

In 1147, while St. Bernard was at the emperor's court in Frankfurt preaching the Second Crusade, a group of Saxon nobles came to ask permission for a crusade against the Wends. They wanted the papal stamp of approval and the privileges accorded to crusaders fighting the Muslims. St. Bernard's response was decidedly in favor, and he wrote a strongly worded letter to the prelates and nobles in Germany, in which he said that "the might of Christendom was armed against them [the Wends], and that for the complete wiping out or, at any rate, the conversion of these peoples, they have put on the cross... and we, by virtue of our authority, promised them the same spiritual privileges as those enjoy who set out toward Jerusalem.... We utterly forbid that for any reason whatsoever a truce should be made with these people... until such a time as, by God's help, they shall be either converted or wiped out."[27]

The armies that set out comprised mainly Saxons and Danes, along with some Poles. The Saxons and Danes had different ideas about what the expedition should accomplish. On the whole, it seems that the real goal for the Danes was plunder and, for the Saxons, expansion and territory east of the Elbe River. Indeed, beginning in 1140, the Saxons were already pushing their frontiers eastward and sending colonists into areas where the Wends were settled. So the German expansion was already under way when they were given the crusading privileges in 1147.

The northern crusade, led by Duke Henry of Saxony, known as Henry the Lion, set out in mid-June, and by the end of September, it was ended. Some pagan places of worship were destroyed, and some conversions took place, although they usually lasted only until the crusaders left. Nothing of enduring consequence was accomplished, although the war against the Wends established an important precedent, as we will see. This first northern crusade fell pitifully short of any desire St. Bernard harbored for converting the pagans.

Conrad III, Louis VII, and Eleanor of Aquitaine on the Second Crusade

The Second Crusade itself was a catastrophe. Its beginnings, however, were auspicious. The armies were huge, larger than those on the First Crusade, their ranks swelled by Italians, Normans, English, Flemish, and Scandinavians. In fact, all of Europe was represented on this crusade, and its resources were substantial. There was every reason to look forward to a successful outcome, but these were disorganized armies, and the lack of discipline in both the French and German armies was manifest almost immediately. Again there were enor-

---

[27] Bernard of Clairvaux, "Letter of 1147," in Allen and Amt 269.

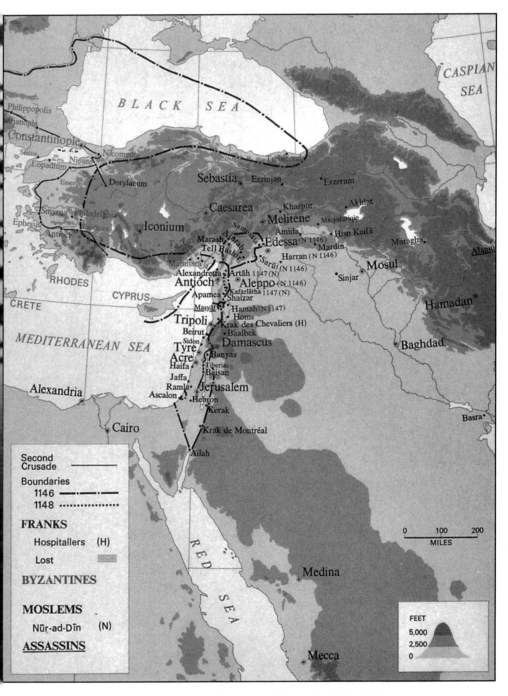

Map 5.1 The Near East during the Second Crusade, 1146–1148.

mous numbers of noncombatants to be fed and cared for, this time also including merchants and money changers, who expected to make their fortunes in the East, people seemingly less spiritually motivated than those who had gone on the First Crusade. These conditions, compounded by distrust, strategic errors, and staggering losses, brought about the unmitigated failure of the Second Crusade.

Two histories were written by men well placed to have inside information about the course of this crusade. For the French side there was Odo of Deuil, King Louis's chaplain, a man of so much prestige that, later in his life, he was appointed Abbot of St. Denis, the most coveted religious position in France. Odo accompanied the king at court and on the crusade and was privy to almost everything he described. The German story was told very briefly by Otto, Bishop of Freising, half-brother of Conrad III. Otto, who was intimate with the politics at the German court and accompanied Conrad to the East, was one of the most learned and admired European historians of the twelfth century. Otto included short references to the crusade in the early chapters of his book *The Deeds of Frederick Barbarossa*. He was so distressed at the outcome of the expedition, and so much preferred "to write not a tragedy but a joyous history, [that he left the Second Crusade] to be related by others elsewhere."[28]

Once it was settled that both kings would lead the crusade, they met to decide the route they would take. Conrad wanted to go overland, as the First Crusade had done, through Hungary into the Balkans to Constantinople. Louis's nobles were divided about whether to go by sea or land, and their debates were heated, but they finally decided to follow the Germans.

Conrad left in mid-May 1147, and Louis left a month later. They planned to meet at Constantinople. Before they started out, the kings and the pope had written to the Byzantine emperor to alert him to their coming and to negotiate the purchase of provisions along their route. The longtime Byzantine ruler John II had died in a hunting accident in 1143. He was succeeded by his younger son, Manuel (1143–1180), whom John had chosen over his older son because he believed Manuel to be more prudent.

Emperor Manuel had every reason to be wary of the crusading armies. The behavior of the prior crusading armies, the fact that he had not asked for help from the West, and the loss of Antioch fanned the flames of the emperor's distrust. Nonetheless, he had a bond with Conrad that made their relationship reasonably cordial. Manuel was married to Conrad's sister-in-law, a union which had been made to cement an alliance against the King of Sicily, who was threatening both the Greeks and the Germans.

---

[28] Otto of Freising, *The Deeds of Frederick Barbarossa*, trans. Charles C. Mierow (New York: Columbia UP, 1953) 79.

Nothing, however, relieved the bad feelings between the Greeks and the French. At every juncture they irritated each other. Manuel wanted assurances that the armies would swear fealty to him and that his possessions would be returned if the crusaders succeeded in taking them back from the Turks. In return he would promise that the armies would be able to buy food, and he would ensure a safe passage for them through his territory. The negotiations between Louis and Manuel's ambassadors were prolonged and unpleasant. In the end Louis agreed, but very grudgingly, that he and his nobles would swear fealty to Manuel.

Odo of Deuil claimed that the French were never given the markets they were promised, and he was angry and altogether disdainful of the Greeks. His anti-Byzantine attitude, reflecting the general French view, runs as the leitmotif through Odo's history. "Let no one think that I am taking vengeance on a race of men hateful to me and that because of my hatred I am inventing a Greek whom I have not seen. Whoever has known the Greeks will, if asked, say that when they are afraid they become despicable . . . and when they have the upper hand they are arrogant in their severe violence to those subjected to them."[29]

Odo had hardly anything favorable to say about Constantinople, although he admitted there were some beautiful parts of the city and that, presumably without the Greeks, it would be a nice place to live. Mostly he viewed it as squalid and dirty. "Constantinople," he wrote, "is arrogant in her wealth, treacherous in her practices, corrupt in her faith."[30]

Louis's difficulties were exacerbated by the behavior of his armies. He was simply unable to control them. The men under his command plundered; they burned homes; they incited the Greeks to fight; and, at least on one occasion, they committed murder. "The king frequently punished offenders by cutting off their ears, hands, and feet, yet he could not thus check the folly of the whole group. Indeed, one of two things was necessary, either to kill many thousands at one time or put up with their numerous evil deeds."[31]

Along the route to Constantinople the Germans also gave the French considerable trouble, taking everything from the markets, leaving nothing for the French to purchase, and getting into terrible fights with the French. "The Germans," Odo wrote, "were unbearable even to us." Thus, before encountering the Turks, King Louis had serious problems and had learned that he could not depend on his armies.

The most severe disaster the Germans suffered on their route was a flood,

---

[29] Odo of Deuil 57–58.
[30] Odo of Deuil 87.
[31] Odo of Deuil 67.

which came upon them suddenly after they had spent a peaceful night in a beautiful setting near the Hellespont, almost in sight of Constantinople. When the floodwaters rose, the men tried to cross the river on their horses, many tried to swim, and those who could not swim held on to those who could, causing them all to drown. It was the one tragedy Otto included in his book. You would have seen, he wrote, "some [men] ignominiously hauled along by ropes to escape the danger, some dashing in disorder into the river and sinking because they were hopelessly entangled with others."[32] Many, many men and horses lost their lives in the river. The remaining men, in some disarray, finally reached Constantinople.

The kinship between Manuel and Conrad notwithstanding, the Byzantine emperor sent the unruly Germans, who had arrived before the French, away from Constantinople as soon as he could. The Germans crossed the Bosphorus, intending to go to Antioch. At Dorylaeum they were met by a Turkish army, which annihilated them. Conrad was among the few who survived the massacre. Although he had been wounded, Conrad was able to make his way, with the remnants of his army, to the safety of Nicaea to wait for the French king. Small wonder that Otto wanted to draw a veil over the troubled German expedition.

The two kings decided to follow a longer route to Antioch along the coast rather than the more direct route across Asia Minor. At Ephesus, after a terrible journey, Conrad became ill. When Manuel encouraged him to come to Constantinople to recover, Conrad accepted the offer and abandoned the French king.

Louis and his armies soldiered on, but they were ambushed by Turks at every turn and had not nearly enough food. They marched to Adalia, on the southern coast of Asia Minor, where Louis planned to hire ships to transport him and his men to Antioch. The route to Adalia was far more perilous than the king had anticipated. Turks and Greeks together ambushed the armies as they attempted to cross a high ridge at the summit of a steep mountain. The men were frightened by the height and the slippery slopes, and they pushed and shoved one another and broke ranks in their rush to descend the mountain. Many died in the rampage or were slaughtered by Turks. Horses lost their footing and plummeted to their deaths. "The flowers of France withered before they could bear fruit in Damascus."[33]

At this terrible juncture Louis turned to the contingent of Templars who had joined his army in France and who had held fast and were disciplined. Therefore "it was decided that during this dangerous period all should establish fraternity with the Templars, rich and poor taking oath that they would

---

[32] Otto of Freising 81.
[33] Odo of Deuil 119.

not flee the field and that they would obey in every respect the officers assigned them by the Templars."[34] A wise decision, but one that revealed the king's inability to hold together his fractious armies. All the disasters the French suffered they blamed on the Greeks. They had kept to Byzantine territory on their march, hoping to find food and provisions, as the emperor had promised they would. Instead they were attacked all along the way and were not able to buy provisions or even find enough to plunder.

When finally the French reached Adalia, there were not enough ships available for the king and all his men. Louis and his entourage sailed to Antioch, leaving his armies to march overland. What remained of the French armies was almost totally wiped out by the Turks on the way to Antioch.

Louis arrived at Antioch in mid-March 1148, accompanied by Queen Eleanor. At the start of the crusade Eleanor and Louis had been married for ten years. It was not, by any account, a marriage made in heaven.

A. Eleanor of Aquitaine on the Crusade

When Eleanor was fifteen years old, in the spring of 1137, her father, Duke William X of Aquitaine, died. As his only surviving heir, Eleanor inherited the richest territories in what is now France: the duchies of Aquitaine and Gascony and the county of Poitou. Her inheritance, which stretched from the Loire River to the Pyrenees and from the Rhône to the Atlantic coast, was some four times larger than the lands ruled by the King of France. Eleanor brought her lands to France as her dowry. Keeping the queen and her land in France became a political necessity.

Eleanor's homeland was different in character and culture from the northern lands under the king's control. She came from a land bathed in sunlight, influenced by the advanced culture of Muslim Spain, and colorful. It was at Aquitaine that courtly love appeared and flourished, and romance, both literary and real, and the troubadours with their songs, and dancing, as well as a high level of education and good manners. The French spoken in the south, the langue d'oc, as it was called from the way it was pronounced, was different from the langue d'oeil spoken in the north. In the dialect of the south a vibrant and beautiful culture was produced. Eleanor's was a softer part of the world, and one in which women enjoyed more freedom than in the north. She never became accustomed to the stultifying atmosphere at the French court, the restrictions placed on her in her role as queen, and the expectation that she would produce a male heir to the French throne.

The crusade was a perfect outlet for Eleanor. She enlisted many noblewomen to join her, along with at least three hundred women of lesser rank.

---

[34] Odo of Deuil 125.

Her great advantage was that she had also enlisted a huge army of her vassals in the south, more numerous than the king's own vassals, and she was therefore virtually unstoppable.

Many tales circulated about Eleanor's entourage, how she dressed her ladies as Amazons and she herself rode out as Penthesilea, who, according to the myth, was the leader of the Amazons. Probably all this is legend, none of it supported by fact, but the story is telling for the way Eleanor was depicted by her critics, of whom she had many. Although barely mentioned in Odo's account—she was probably excised from Odo's work after she and Louis were divorced—Eleanor was at the center of a drama on the crusade that began at Antioch. It was at Antioch that the royal marriage fell apart.

Eleanor's uncle, Prince Raymond of Antioch, was a man known for his joie de vivre, his charm, his bravery and good looks, and the luxury of his court. In contrast, Louis was known for his piety and his seriousness; although admirable, he was quite lacking in charm. Raymond welcomed Louis and Eleanor with great ceremony and entertained them lavishly. Eleanor loved every minute of it; she spent much of her time in Raymond's company, and the rumors of an illicit affair between Eleanor and Raymond began to spread.

Raymond tried to persuade Louis to attack Aleppo and then recapture Edessa. Louis refused, insisting that he intended to go to Jerusalem. Raymond then asked Eleanor to take his part with the king. She did, but to no avail. Rumors of Eleanor's infidelity became increasingly serious, especially when she told Louis that if he did not join Raymond at Aleppo, she would remain in Antioch with all her vassals and, moreover, apply for an annulment of their marriage.

Louis was so upset that he physically forced Eleanor to leave Antioch with him. He and his followers left Antioch in secrecy. "Thus the splendid aspect of his affairs was completely changed, and the end was quite unlike the beginning. His coming had been attended with pomp and glory; but fortune is fickle, and his departure was ignominious."[35]

Raymond had reason on his side when he urged the French king to besiege Aleppo. In 1146 Zengi had been murdered and was succeeded by his son, Nur al-Din (1146–1174). Although young and untried, Nur al-Din soon proved singularly able to take his place as leader of the *jihad*. "Almighty God was pleased to crown his plans and decisions with glittering success, casting down the rebellious infidels [that is, the Franks] and hastening their death and utter destruction."[36] Nur al-Din was a religious man and the champion of Sunni Islam against the Shiites. He wanted to eliminate Shiism as surely as he

---

[35] William of Tyre, vol. 2, 181.
[36] Ibn al-Qalanisi, in Gabrieli 65.

wanted to eliminate the Latins. He fought against the Shiites, and he encouraged the spread and revival of Sunni Islam by founding mosques and schools and by strongly urging the unity of all Islam under the Sunni banner.

When Nur al-Din began to rule in Aleppo in 1146, his kingdom was divided. His brother and rival held Mosul, which together with Aleppo had been Zengi's base of power. To the dismay of the Franks, Nur al-Din had married the daughter of the ruler of Damascus, so it was only a matter of time before he took control of the city and the fragile alliance between the Franks and Damascenes would be ended. It was during the small window of time before Nur al-Din fully established his power that Raymond believed Aleppo could be taken from him.

It was not to be. Louis went to Jerusalem, and in mid-April 1148, Conrad joined him. The two kings and all the nobles on the crusade, all the nobility in the kingdom of Jerusalem, all the great prelates, and King Baldwin III, with his mother, the queen and regent, Melisende, met in Acre to decide what should be done next. It was finally agreed that the armies would attack Damascus. Any idea of recovering Edessa was now abandoned. The original reason for the crusade was simply ignored.

The Dismal End of the Second Crusade

The siege of Damascus should have been successful, but it failed, and failed shamefully. For reasons we will never know with certainty, the Latins withdrew their forces from a strong position facing the walls of Damascus where the city was not well defended, in an area where they had food and water. They moved to a well-defended portion of the walls, where there was no food or water to be had. The decision to move was blamed on traitors who had been paid by the Damascenes, on the Templars who had encouraged the move, on Raymond, and on just about anyone who had agreed to relocate. Unable to breach the walls and fearing the arrival of Nur al-Din's army, the crusaders abandoned the siege. It had lasted all of four days. They then retreated to Jerusalem.

Conrad soon left for Constantinople, where he remained for a time with Manuel, renewing his former alliance with the Byzantine ruler against the Normans in Sicily. Louis stayed longer in Jerusalem, still hoping to accomplish something, though what that would be is unclear. Although Abbot Suger implored the king to return to France, Louis spent almost a year in the Holy City before he set sail from Acre in the spring of 1149.

On the return voyage Louis and Eleanor sailed in separate ships owned by the Sicilians. Byzantium and Sicily were at war, and both ships were attacked by the Byzantine navy and then saved by the Sicilian navy. On the way to Sicily a storm blew Eleanor's ship off-course, and she disappeared for two months. No one seems to have known where she was, but she reappeared in time to join Louis to visit the pope in one of his palaces. The pope tried to convince the royal couple to stay married, even persuaded them to sleep together, but it was much too late.

In March 1152, the marriage was annulled on grounds of consanguinity — that they were cousins and too closely related to have married. Eleanor's inheritance was returned to her, and in May of the same year she and Henry, duke of Normandy and count of Anjou, were married, and her lands were joined to his already immense holdings. Overnight Henry became the richest lord in France. Two years later, in 1154, Henry was crowned king of England, and Eleanor's lands became part of the English royal domain.

Dismay at the failure of the crusade was widespread in Europe. Questions arose immediately about whose fault it was that such a promising expedition should have collapsed so miserably. The Greeks, naturally enough, were castigated. "To us who suffered the Greeks' evil deeds," Odo wrote, "there is hope of divine justice and vengeance. Thus we comfort our sad hearts and we shall follow the course of our misfortunes so that posterity may know about the Greeks' treacherous actions."[37]

The kings had not been united in their purpose, or strong in their leadership, so neither Conrad nor Louis emerged unscathed for his part in the outcome.

When King Louis visited Pope Eugenius III on his way back to France, he broached the subject of a new crusade, but Eugenius's despair at the outcome of the Second Crusade weighed too heavily on him. He perceived, rightly, that the Church had fallen into disrepute in many quarters, and that faith in crusading would have to be rejuvenated. Too much money had been spent, too many lives had been wasted on the battlefields, too many widows and children had been left to fend for themselves — and nothing had been accomplished.

Some outspoken critics believed that those who took the cross had been deceived by the preachers, that it was an error to have gone in the first place. It was further believed that the fault lay with the many people who went, not for religious reasons, but to make their fortunes, or to leave their debts behind and start anew, or to escape punishment for a crime.

The lion's share of blame fell on St. Bernard, for having so vigorously inspired and supported the crusade. The attacks on him were vindictive and personal. His response to the criticism was couched in religious terms, and he placed the responsibility for the tragedy on the people who had failed to understand what God required of them. It was thus the absence of faith, in his view, that led to the debacle.

---

[37] Odo of Deuil 99.

In his very moving apology to the pope St. Bernard wrote, "As you know we have fallen upon grave times, which seemed about to bring an end to not only my studies but my very life, for the Lord, provoked by our sins, gave the appearance of having judged the world prematurely, with justice, indeed, but forgetful of his mercy. He spared neither his people nor his name.... How, then, does human rashness dare reprove what it can scarcely understand?" He then gave biblical examples to demonstrate how man's sinfulness provoked God's wrath, and he closed by saying, "The perfect and final apology for any man is the testimony of his conscience.... I would rather that men murmur against us than against God...I shall not refuse to be made ignominious, so long as God's glory is not attacked."[38]

The wounds inflicted by the disastrous crusade did not readily heal. The animosity between the Latins and the Greeks increased, with baleful consequences in the next decades. Even allowing for some exaggeration by the critics, it is true that the Second Crusade displayed the weakness of spiritual commitment that would increasingly characterize further crusading in the thirteenth century.

One of the most troublesome and troubling outcomes was expressed by William of Tyre. He wrote this appraisal after the aborted siege at Damascus, but it applies even more to the sad result of the Second Crusade. "All too clearly they [the crusade leaders] perceived the treachery of those [meaning the leaders in the Latin Kingdom] to whose loyalty they had entrusted their lives and interests and abhorred the perfidy by which they had been deceived.... Henceforward, as long as they remained in the Orient, and indeed ever after, they looked askance at all the ways of our leaders.... Not only was this true in regard to themselves, but their influence caused others who had not been present there to slacken in love toward the kingdom."[39]

The crusaders could not understand the hostilities among the rulers in the Latin Kingdom, their unabashed desire to take each other's territory, and their reluctance to unite in the face of the Muslim advance. Nor did the crusaders understand, or approve of, the accommodations the settlers made with their non-Christian neighbors. A lamentable gulf had opened between the people who had settled in Outremer and the crusaders, who had rightly perceived that a new culture was emerging in the Latin Kingdom. This new culture, tinged with the Orient, also "caused [even] others who had not been present there to slacken in love toward the kingdom."

---

[38] Bernard of Clairvaux, "Apologia for the Second Crusade," in Allen and Amt 146–47.
[39] William of Tyre, vol. 2, 192–93.

CHAPTER SIX

Life in Outremer to the Fall of Jerusalem

he lives of those who remained in the Holy Land after the First Crusade had been chaotic. The kingdom was subjected to constant enemy attacks; plagues of locusts and mice that ruined crops and caused famines; earthquakes, and other natural disasters. In addition, serious social problems caused grave concern, paramount among them the relations between Christians and Muslims. "Since it was evident to all that the sins of the people had provoked God to wrath, it was decided by common consent that they must amend their wrongdoing and restrain their excesses."[1] To that end King Baldwin I and the patriarch of Jerusalem had called a council held in Nablus in 1120.

The Council of Nablus promulgated twenty-five canons designed to regulate Christian-Muslim relations and the sexual behavior of the crusaders, including adultery, homosexuality, and bigamy. The latter had become a problem because some crusaders married in the Latin Kingdom, having a family still at home in Europe. In all cases of misconduct the penalties were severe, although there was sometimes an opportunity for the guilty parties to repent and be given a second chance.

Marriage between Christians and Muslims was strictly forbidden unless the Muslim converted to Christianity. To prevent fraternization, Muslims were not allowed to dress as the Christians did. Punishments for Christian men who had relations with Muslim women included castration for the man and cutting off the woman's nose. The punishments were the same in the case of Christian women who had relations with Muslim men, unless they were raped, in which case only the man was punished. In cases of adultery, the

---

[1] William of Tyre, vol. 1, 535–36.

accused had to undergo ordeal by hot iron to prove innocence; if guilty, the man was castrated and the woman's nose was cut off. The kinder sentence was exile from the kingdom. Homosexuals were liable to be burned at the stake.

The Rulers and the Ruled: The "Great Miracle" in the Kingdom

As the years passed crusader society inevitably underwent changes, influenced by the cultures around it and the growing relationships between the Latins and their Oriental Christian and Muslim neighbors. Everywhere, and in all walks of life, the Franks rubbed shoulders with the native population. They fought against one another, of course, but in times of peace their relations were amicable, and they came to know one another. They did business together; the Franks hired Muslim servants, they bought their food from Muslim sellers in the markets and learned to go to Muslim doctors. Some Franks learned enough Arabic to do business with Muslims, to converse in the bazaars, and even to have friends among the Muslims.

Marriages between the Latins and the Oriental Christians were frequent and acceptable at all levels of society. Baldwin I and Baldwin II both married Armenian Christians, and Baldwin III, as we will see, married a Byzantine princess. Women brought their Oriental or Muslim servants with them, and their homes were filled with all the beautiful work done by the artisans in the East — the ceramics, carpets, glassware, and mosaic tiles all became part of daily life.

The Franks maintained the European style for clothing, to distinguish themselves from the indigenous population, but the local silks and linens, the handsome brocades and taffetas soon replaced the rough and heavy woolen garments they had brought from home. Although not normally seen on the streets in native dress, in private the Franks wore the loose, flowing robes typical of the East.

Their diet was more varied and more sophisticated than the one they had left behind, and their lives were more leisurely, owing to the warm climate and the necessity during the long summer to avoid going out-of-doors in the worst midday heat. The settlers learned to bathe frequently — something quite unheard of in Europe, where bathing was seldom done in the twelfth century. Bathing — and whatever was suspected of going on in the bathhouses — was considered by many Europeans who visited the Holy Land to be effeminate and even a vice.

The art and architecture surrounding the settlements was changing too and was the visible expression of the melding of Latin and Eastern traditions. By the 1130s a new generation of artists had emerged in the Holy Land, no longer wedded to designing exclusively in the Romanesque style the first generation had brought with them. The newer designs combined European styles with the traditions and techniques of Byzantine fresco painters and mosaicists, the forms of Byzantine and Islamic architecture, and the intricate

6.1 Crusader canteen. Thirteenth-century canteen, made in Syria, most likely by Eastern craftsmen. Its Latin Christian iconography is interspersed with Oriental Christian and Islamic designs.

decorative arts found in the East. These all moderated the European artistic sensibility in the Latin Kingdom. This blending of several styles and forms into one harmonious whole is what gave crusader art its unique character. At once familiar and different, the art underscored the transformation of crusader society.

"For we who were Occidentals have now become Orientals.... Some have taken wives not only of their own people but Syrians or Armenians or even Saracens who have obtained the grace of baptism.... People use the eloquence and idioms of diverse languages in conversing back and forth. Words of different languages have become common property known to each nationality.... You see therefore that this is a great miracle and one which the whole world ought to admire."[2]

---

[2] Fulcher of Chartres, Ryan 271–72.

Unfortunately, the whole world did not fully admire or appreciate this "great miracle."

The Latin Kingdom was little understood by the Europeans who came to visit after the Second Crusade, and newcomers were bewildered by what they found and sometimes actually repelled by life in the kingdom. A high-ranking and intolerant prelate, Jacques de Vitry, who in the course of an illustrious career became Bishop of Acre, was strident in his condemnation of the new society. The descendants of the first generation, he wrote, "succeeded to their fathers' property, but not to their good morals; they squandered the worldly wealth which their fathers had won by the shedding of their own blood.... Their children, who are called Pullani, were brought up in luxury, soft and effeminate,... addicted to unclean and riotous living, clad like women in soft robes.... They make treaties with the Saracens, and are glad to be at peace with Christ's enemies; they are quick to quarrel with one another.... Now, the pilgrims who come, with very great toil and at ruinous expense... are not only treated with ingratitude by these Pullani, but they... pour contempt upon these warriors."[3]

De Vitry was too angry and too righteous to be taken fully at face value, but there is an underlying truth in his writings. William of Tyre's assessment of the consequence of the Second Crusade was also harsh, but it held as well a real truth. "Henceforward, as long as they [the crusaders] remained in the Orient, and indeed ever after, they looked askance at all the ways of our leaders.... Not only was this true in regard to themselves, but their influence caused others who had not been present there to slacken in love toward the kingdom."[4] The crusaders' world had moved on in ways that were strange and disquieting to Europeans.

Nor was there any love lost for the newcomers on the part of the Easterners. "Everyone who is a fresh immigrant from the Frankish lands," a Muslim observer wrote, "is ruder in character than those who have become acclimatized and have held long association with the Moslems." [5] It was one of the gentler criticisms of the Europeans who came to visit the kingdom, since those who had chosen to make their lives in the East were considered by their neighbors—and themselves—to be vastly superior.

Nonetheless, Jerusalem remained the single most important pilgrimage site for Christians. Although uncertain of what they would find, knights, pilgrims, merchants, artisans, stone masons, monks, clerics, and the merely curi-

---

[3] Jacques de Vitry 65–66.
[4] William of Tyre, vol. 2, 192–93.
[5] Usamah Ibn-Munqidh, *Memoirs of an Arab-Syrian Gentleman*, trans. Philip K. Hitti (Beirut: Khayats, 1964) 169.

ous made the journey to the Holy Land during the twelfth century. Unfortunately, they never stayed in numbers large enough to keep the kingdom safe, or to ensure its future.

According to the best estimates, in the decades before 1187, there were one hundred and twenty thousand Franks living in the Latin Kingdom of Jerusalem. Of that number only between two thousand and three thousand were members of the Frankish upper class, and no more than a thousand of these were knights and barons; the rest were civilians, mainly wives, sisters, widows, and elderly relations.[6] This number was augmented by several thousand *poulains* (*pullaini*) and their descendants, the class formed primarily by the sergeants who had settled in the Holy Land. In addition there were Frankish peasants, who were the backbone of this society, along with craftsmen, workmen of all sorts, and a few hundred clergy. The several Italian colonies each had another few hundred people, and the knights of the military orders together numbered about six hundred. The population in all the northern states together was about the same as that of the southern kingdom.

In this man's world where heroism in battle was prized above all else, there were more women than men. Women lived longer: their average life span was forty-four years, while a man's life expectancy was between thirty and thirty-five years. Infant mortality was high, but for boys, oddly enough, it was higher than for girls.

Upper-class women had more responsibility and more freedom in the Holy Land than did their counterparts in Europe. Women whose husbands were killed in battle were widowed at an early age, and they assumed the guardianship of the family estates. On those estates that had to provide vassals for military service, it was necessary for widows to remarry. Unlike in Europe, where the dukes, counts, and kings had the right to choose a husband and force the woman to marry him, in the East, women and their families gained the right to choose from among three possible candidates. Under certain circumstances they could turn them all down.

Women were economically better off than in the West because, absent a male, the eldest daughter was able to inherit her father's property.[7] Widows also acted as guardians of their children and of their property, in effect becoming regents for their young children.

A Muslim observer was quite appalled at the freedom Frankish men allowed their wives and daughters. He could hardly credit that Frankish husbands stepped

---

[6] Runciman, vol. 2, 291–94. Exact numbers are difficult to know with any certainty, but Runciman's are generally accepted. See also Joshua Prawer, *The World of the Crusaders* (New York: Quadrangle Books, 1972) 73.

[7] This explains why Queen Melisende, for example, was able to inherit the crown and then confer the kingship on Fulk.

aside and permitted their wives to speak freely with another man and, if the conversation went on for a time, left her alone with the man and went on their way. "Frankish men," he concluded, "are void of all zeal and jealousy."[8] Women's greater freedom had to do in part with the nature of an evolving society that was making new law, in part with the numbers of women who were economically independent, and in part because there were simply more women.

In this new kingdom the Franks kept their own language, using their regional dialects, and the upper nobility could read and write Latin and usually French. There were schools in the Holy Land, some for the training of clerics, such as one run by the canons of the Holy Sepulchre, and schools attached to monasteries, where young men could receive an education, although the education was not at a high level. No schools existed that were as advanced as the great cathedral schools that had developed in Europe in cities such as Paris. Nor were there ever any universities. For higher education in law and theology students went to European universities, as did William of Tyre, who studied abroad for four years. The nobility and the royal family had tutors at home for their young children and their daughters, who were also educated.

Although some of the Franks learned to speak Arabic, with very few, if any, exceptions they never undertook the study of the corpus of Arabic philosophy and science. The vast, beautiful world of Arabic learning and literature was literally a closed book to them. The Greek language they disdained, Italian some of them knew slightly, and the Oriental languages that surrounded them — Syriac, Coptic, and the like — they simply ignored.

The Italians brought Italy with them. In the cities where they lived and traded they built Italianate palaces, or they moved into the grand buildings that had once been home to wealthy Muslim or Byzantine merchants and officials. They had piazzas that replicated the ones they left behind, around which were installed the shops and warehouses for their merchandise. They spoke the dialect of the various cities they came from, and their intense economic rivalries led to frequent wars between the Italian communes. Intermarriage between Italians and Franks took place, and on the familial level brought the two groups together. Broadly speaking, however, no real cultural exchange resulted from these connections. As much as they could, the Italians stayed to themselves; they knew only the most rudimentary French, which they pronounced badly when they spoke it at all.

Internal Problems in the Kingdom
Beginning in the 1130s, dissensions arose in the royal family and among the barons in the High Court, which, serious enough in themselves, were a fore-

---

[8] Usamah 164.

taste of the even more serious divisiveness that would plague the government until its collapse.

A. Queen Melisende's Role

The most formidable of all Jerusalem's queens, Melisende, was at the heart of the first two crises; whether her behavior actually provoked the first one (in 1132) is not certain. The immediate challenge to King Fulk's authority came from the queen's cousin, Count Hugh of Le Puiset, Lord of Jaffa. He was young and handsome and had lived at the royal court for several years. Rumors of an affair between the queen and Hugh circulated early. The rumors were brought to the king's attention by Hugh's stepsons (he had by then married a widow with children), who went so far as to accuse Hugh of plotting to murder the king. Hugh denied the accusation and agreed to a duel to settle the issue. The court was divided. Melisende, who took Hugh's part, was supported by many nobles as well as the patriarch of Jerusalem.

Hugh did not appear on the day appointed for the duel. He was pronounced guilty *in absentia* and sentenced by the king to three years in exile, a mild reproof, which Melisende probably engineered and which the king hoped would calm the situation.

Just before Hugh was scheduled to leave, he was stabbed by a knight who expected to find favor with Fulk by ridding him of his enemy. But Hugh survived, and when he had recovered sufficiently, he went to Apulia and remained in exile until he died. Fulk was blamed for the attack and saved his reputation only by apprehending the knight and turning him over to the High Court for punishment. The knight was tortured, and before he was killed took full responsibility for attempting to murder Hugh and declared that Fulk was in no way implicated.

Melisende was so angered by these events that, as William of Tyre reported, those who had "informed against the count and thereby incited the king to wrath... were forced to take diligent measures for their safety.... Even the king found that no place was entirely safe among the kindred and partisans of the queen."[9] Eventually Fulk and Melisende were reconciled, and from their reunion their second son, Amalric, was born.

Melisende was undoubtedly responsible for the next crisis. She was an unusually gifted woman, capable, intelligent, well educated in Latin and Greek, and she knew Armenian (from her Armenian mother, Queen Morphia) as well as French. She was also exceedingly ambitious and headstrong.

Melisende's older son Baldwin was thirteen when his father, King Fulk, died; her younger son, Amalric, was seven. William of Tyre admired Baldwin

---

[9]   William of Tyre, vol. 2, 76.

6.2 The coronation of Baldwin III. The coronation immediately followed Fulk's death. Baldwin was thirteen and his mother, as shown, was already queen.

hugely, and he went on at length to convey Baldwin's many gifts: his outstanding character, his physical beauty (in which he resembled his mother), his intelligence, and his natural abilities for leadership.[10] He was gracious to everyone, regardless of station or age, and eventually became the most popular ruler that the kingdom ever had.

Although Baldwin II had intended that Melisende and the future Baldwin III rule jointly until Baldwin came of age, Melisende pushed her son aside and took the reins of government into her own hands. She chose as constable and commander-in-chief of the army her cousin, Manasses, who through his connections to the royal family and an advantageous marriage was a wealthy and important nobleman. In time he became haughty and overbearing and was deeply resented by many barons for his power and his influence over the queen.

In 1145, Baldwin reached fifteen, the age at which, according to the law of the kingdom, he could legitimately assume the throne as sole ruler. Yet he remained, unhappily, under the queen's control. The tension between Baldwin and his mother festered for seven years until it erupted in 1152, when Baldwin was twenty-two.

---

[10] William of Tyre, vol. 2, 137–39.

B. Baldwin III Wins the Struggle for Power

The King's formal coronation was finally to take place on Easter day in 1152. Baldwin had been strongly advised by the patriarch, the prelates, and the barons, who wanted to avert a war, to share his coronation with Melisende. Baldwin refused. Instead he postponed the coronation and then demanded that he be crowned alone and in secret. When that was done, he informed his mother that he would divide the kingdom with her. With the help of intermediaries the division was made. The queen took Jerusalem and Nablus and all their dependent lands, and Baldwin took Tyre and Acre and their dependencies.

Baldwin, however, was not content with his portion, and he mustered his army and pursued his mother to Jerusalem, where she had retreated to the citadel for safety. In the end, after besieging the city for days, the king was admitted by the citizens, and the queen was forced to surrender and make a new agreement. She relinquished her claim to Jerusalem and retired to Nablus. The king promised on oath that he would leave her in peace in Nablus. "Thus they were restored to the good graces of one another; and as the morning star which shines forth in the midst of darkness tranquility again returned to the kingdom and the church."[11] The reconciliation brought the kingdom back from the edge of a full-blown civil war.

When the kingdom was first organized, the lands belonging to the crown were larger than any of the feudal domains—and wealthier by far. This fact, coupled with the strong personalities of the early rulers and their reputations for bravery, sustained the king's authority over his barons and royal vassals.

In time the barons began to seek more power for themselves. The nobility had elected Godfrey to be the first ruler of the Latin Kingdom, and from then on they maintained the right to elect the crown, or at the least approve the succession. This claim was further strengthened when the barons were able to exact an oath from the rulers that they would uphold the privileges of nobility.

The rulers, for their part, became more generous with their gifts of lands and towns to the nobility, hoping to gain their loyalty. The result was a gradual shift in the relationship between the crown and nobility, to the detriment of royal power. The weakness of royal authority then became the opportunity for the nobles to vie with one another for power.

Before the worst effects of the infighting became obvious, and soon after the settlement between Baldwin and Melisende, the southern kingdom had its greatest victory, its greatest cause for optimism. In 1153 the Franks were finally able to conquer Ascalon, the one Mediterranean coastal city still in Egyptian control.

---

[11] William of Tyre, vol. 2, 207.

The Victory at Ascalon

To the crusader kingdom, Ascalon was by far the most feared and threatening of Egypt's possessions: it was Egypt's most strongly fortified city; it held a large garrison, and was well supplied and protected by the Fatimid navy. However, by the mid-twelfth century the fortunes of the Fatimid caliphs, for internal reasons, had taken a turn for the worse, and their power was waning. The crusader kings, beginning with the first Baldwin, had all wished to conquer Egypt, and now so did the Sunnis, led by Nur al-Din. The fear of being crushed between Egypt and Syria was a real possibility for the crusader kingdom, and it became a matter of who would overcome Egypt first.

In 1149 or early 1150, Baldwin III ordered the ancient city of Gaza, ten miles (sixteen kilometers) south of Ascalon, to be rebuilt, intending to use it as a base from which to attack Ascalon. When a goodly portion was completed, the king turned it over to the Templars. In late January 1153, every prince and prelate in the kingdom assembled before Ascalon to begin the blockade of the city that was considered virtually impregnable. The siege lasted for seven months. The fighting was incessant and cruel, and on both sides there were tremendous losses.

Although at one point the crusaders received help from pilgrims who had unexpectedly arrived on the coast, they were so weakened and so dispirited during the course of the siege that they wanted to withdraw. When the king called a council to decide what should be done, the majority wished to give up, and even the king favored retreat. However, the patriarch, all the prelates, and the Grand Master of the Hospitallers favored continuing, and it was agreed that they would carry on. The Franks prepared for a final attack on Ascalon.

"Seized with a mad fury for extermination, they rushed upon the enemy and attacked them so fiercely that the foe marveled and stood dumbfounded before the evidence of our insuperable strength and indomitable perseverance. Although they made desperate efforts to retaliate, it was all in vain."[12]

The Ascalonites asked for a temporary truce so that both sides could bury their dead. Then, after consulting among themselves and recognizing that they could do nothing else, the Ascalonites sent an embassy to Baldwin telling him they would surrender the city if he would let the inhabitants leave in peace. The king gave the inhabitants three days to leave, although the people were so frightened that they vacated the city in two days. Baldwin gave them guides and a safe-conduct south to Al-Arish; from there they expected to cross into Egypt. Their disasters were not over. Once the king's guides had left, a band of Turks attacked the Ascalonites, stripped them of all their worldly possessions, and left them destitute in the desert.

---

[12] William of Tyre, vol. 2, 229.

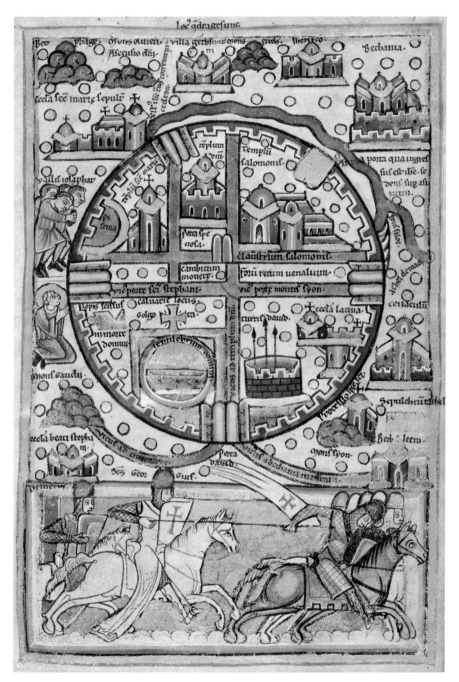

Plate 1 Map of Jerusalem. Twelfth-century map of Crusader Jerusalem and surrounding holy sites. Koninklijke Bibliotheek, The National Library of the Netherlands, The Hague. MS. 76 F5, fol. 1r.

Plate 2 Playing chess at Shaizar. Scene illustrating the story in William of Tyre's *History* of Joscelin II of Edessa and Baldwin of Antioch playing chess—which was wildly popular—while the siege of Shaizar was going on. Bibliothèque municipale, Lyon, France. MS 828 fol. 160v.

Plate 3 Page from the Melisende Psalter (ca. 1131–1143) depicting Christ's entry into Jerusalem. © British Library Board. All rights reserved. Egerton 1139, f. 5v.

Plate 4 Thirteenth-century decorated terra-cotta tile with roundels of Richard and Saladin. From Chertsey Abbey, Surrey. © British Library Board. All rights reserved/ The Bridgeman Art Library.

Plate 5 Women fleeing from mounted Muslim soldiers. © British Library Board. All rights reserved. ADD.27376 f45.

Plate 6 Saint Louis setting out on Crusade. Depicts the King of France leading his army on the Second Crusade and, in the lower half, the king departing from Aigues-Mortes. Bibliotheca Medicea Laurenziana, Florence. MS Plu.LXI.10, f.336v.

وعارض وهو في يده اليسرى وعمر على وسط خط الميدان حتى يصلوا الى وسط الموكب
ثم يتناول العنان مع الدرقة بشماله ويضرب بقائم السيف قبة الدرقة وثنى عليها
بالدبابه وىزد فرسك يمنا ويدرق بالدرقة بشان عن كفل الفرس ويرجع على خط الداىر

الكبير وىجى الخلفه يفعل كفعل الاول ورد فرسه شمالا على خط الداىر الكبير
وىجى الثالث يفعل كفعل صاحبه ورد فرسه يمنا وىجى الاول فيفعل كفعل الاول ولا ورد

Plate 7 Mamluk warriors in training. Four horsemen brandishing their swords; their circular shield is in the center. © British Library Board. All rights reserved. Add 18866, fol. 140.

Plate 8 The Nine Worthies. From a late-fourteenth-century manuscript showing Godfrey de Bouillon as one of the three Christian "worthies." Bibliothèque nationale de France, Paris. MS. Fr. 12559, f. 125v.

Plate 9 Charles and the Spectacle. The scene depicts a reception during the visit of the Emperor Charles V to the court of the King of France in the late fourteenth century. The emperor, his son, and the king are watching a play that is telling the story of the siege and conquest of Jerusalem (on the right). The illustration also shows a ship (on the lower left), which symbolizes the crusaders' fleets. Bibliothèque nationale de France, Paris. MS. Fr. 2813 f. 473v.

The siege had lasted from the end of January to August 22, 1153, and the costs in lives as well as money were incalculable. Yet it was a splendid victory for the Franks. The Latin Church quickly replaced the Muslim houses of worship. The True Cross, which had been carried at the forefront of the army, was brought into the largest mosque in the city, and not long after, a church was dedicated to St. Paul on the same site. Baldwin gave the city as a gift to his younger brother, Amalric, count of Jaffa, who would administer it.

Troubles in the North

In marked contrast to the south, where the mood following Ascalon had become optimistic, in the northern kingdom the years following the ignominious Second Crusade were exceptionally miserable. Led by Count Joscelin II of Edessa, the Latins made one final attempt to retake Edessa in the fall of 1146, but they were not well prepared and were handily defeated by Nur al-Din's army. Edessa was permanently lost, and the loss paved the way for Nur al-Din to stay on the attack. Their victories had emboldened the Muslims, who "mocked at the shattered strength and broken glory of those who represented the substantial foundations of the Christians."[13] Nur al-Din and his army soon began harassing the countryside around Antioch and finally threatened the city itself. In the battle that Raymond of Antioch foolishly undertook without waiting for aid, Raymond was killed and his army was massacred.

Baldwin III led his army north to relieve Antioch in 1149, which he did successfully. Although he then became regent in Antioch, Baldwin returned to Jerusalem to safeguard his interests in the southern kingdom.

Problems in the north continued unabated. Joscelin II was captured by Nur al-Din in May 1150 and taken to prison, where he soon died. So Baldwin went north again to help Joscelin's defenseless widow and provide security for Antioch. In the following year, Nur al-Din took Damascus without a struggle, and the northern kingdom was now in grave peril. With only some unimportant exceptions, Nur al-Din had all of Muslim Syria under his command, and from Edessa south the Muslims controlled the eastern frontier of the Latin Kingdom. Baldwin, meanwhile, had to contend with yet another troublesome situation that had arisen in Antioch.

After Prince Raymond of Antioch died in 1149, Antioch, as always, was in need of a strong male ruler who could protect it, and the king and his nobles were intent on his young widow, Constance, taking a suitable new husband. She refused all the candidates for marriage that were presented to her. Even the Byzantine emperor sent a candidate, a widower who had been married to the emperor's sister. Unfortunately Constance had fallen in love with one of

---

[13] William of Tyre, vol. 2, 196.

the most singularly dreadful men to come to the East, Reynaud de Châtillon.

Reynaud had come with Louis VII's army during the Second Crusade and decided to stay on and make his fortune. He was an opportunist, an adventurer, a man with no scruples who caused endless serious problems for the Latin Kingdom. He was known to be brave, was undoubtedly attractive, and had great success with women. Constance sent him to Ascalon to ask for the king's permission to marry her, which Baldwin granted. Perhaps it was the timing of the request, in the midst of the siege, that led the king to make what turned out to be a very ill-considered decision. The two were married in 1153.

6.3 Patriarch of Antioch exposed on the citadel by Reynaud de Châtillon.

The new prince was heartily disliked by the nobility and virtually everyone else in Antioch, especially the patriarch, who made no secret of his disapproval of the match. In retaliation Reynaud threw the patriarch into prison and, according to William of Tyre, "forced the aging priest...an almost helpless invalid, to sit in the blazing sun throughout a summer's day, his bare head smeared with honey. No one, for pity's sake, offered him any relief...or tried to drive away the flies."[14] When Baldwin learned of this, he sent messengers with a strongly worded letter telling Reynaud to release the prelate, which he did. A sensible man, the patriarch straightaway went to Jerusalem. The story is more significant for what it reveals about Reynaud than for any irreparable harm done the patriarch.

---

[14] William of Tyre, vol. 2, 235.

The next episode was even more telling about Reynaud's character and the trouble he caused. The Byzantine emperor Manuel had offered to pay Reynaud if he would subdue an Armenian noble who was plundering the emperor's lands. When Reynaud succeeded, the emperor, from Reynaud's point of view, was too slow to pay him what he was owed. As retribution for the perceived slight, Reynaud mounted an expedition in late 1155 or the beginning of 1156 against the Byzantine island of Cyprus. It was unprovoked and cruel. The Cypriots were peaceful, friendly to the Franks, and, moreover, most were Christians. The violence Reynaud unleashed was horrific. His men so ravaged the country, stole its treasures, raped the women, and despoiled the monasteries and churches that the island had great difficulty recovering.

Although Nur al-Din and Baldwin renewed an earlier truce in 1155 and extended it again in 1156, the Syrians were suffering repeated earthquakes, and it seemed (in 1156) a propitious time for the Latins to break the truce. The Frankish raids centered in the area around the frontier town of Banyas, at the base of Mount Lebanon. Nur al-Din responded with a successful attack on Banyas. Baldwin was able to force Nur al-Din to leave, but he and a part of his army were ambushed as they, too, left. "In less time than it takes to tell," a Muslim historian wrote, "the enemy was completely overwhelmed and the fighting was over. Almighty and all-conquering God had sent His virtuous supporters victory and condemned the infidel rebels to hell.... [O]ne authority says that not more than ten [Franks] survived, delivered from death for the time being, but overwhelmed with terror."[15]

The king barely escaped, and the warfare between the Franks and the Syrians continued. The Franks won a victory a year later, but Baldwin had good reason to fear further attacks by Nur al-Din, and he was sorely in need of an ally.

Baldwin found his ally in the Byzantine emperor, who also did not want to be overtaken by Muslim Syria. On the theory that the enemy of my enemy is my friend, the two rulers agreed to consider an alliance. Baldwin sent an embassy to the emperor to ask for a bride; after long negotiations, the emperor chose his thirteen-year-old niece, Theodora. She arrived in the Latin Kingdom in September 1157, and shortly after, she and Baldwin were married, and Theodora was consecrated and crowned queen. By all accounts she was an exceptionally beautiful young woman whom Baldwin came to love and to whom he remained faithful.

Baldwin agreed that Manuel should be free to take control of the citadel in Antioch and deal as he wished with Reynaud. It was a wise move on Baldwin's part and reveals how valuable the Byzantine alliance was to the king.

The Byzantine emperor led his army into Syria to subdue an Armenian

---

[15] Ibn al-Qalanisi, in Gabrieli 67.

rebel and then proceeded toward Antioch. His imminent arrival threw Reynaud into a panic, because he feared the emperor's reprisals for his destruction of Cyprus. Rather than wait for him, Reynaud chose to go to the emperor and beg his forgiveness. "He appeared before the emperor barefooted and clothed in a woolen tunic short to the elbows, with a rope around his neck and a naked sword in his hand. Holding this by the point, he presented the hilt to the emperor. As soon as he had thus surrendered his sword, he threw himself on the ground, where he lay prostrate till all were disgusted and the glory of the Latins was turned into shame."[16]

At Eastertime in 1159 the Byzantine emperor made a triumphal entry into Antioch, where he was welcomed by Baldwin and his royal entourage, including his younger brother, Count Amalric, and the now-forgiven Reynaud. Manuel's army took over the citadel, and, as Baldwin and Manuel had agreed, Reynaud was permitted to govern as the emperor's vassal. Manuel also wanted a Greek to be installed as patriarch in Antioch, although he did not press the matter. The important result of the negotiations between Manuel and Baldwin was the alliance against the Syrian Muslims and the emperor's promise to fight with the Franks against Nur al-Din.

Soon after Manuel left Antioch, Reynaud learned of an opportunity for rich plunder in the lands near Edessa, where there were flocks and herds mainly owned by Christians and no Turkish garrison close by. So he rode off and vandalized the countryside. He was informed that the Turkish ruler of Aleppo was on his way to force him to give up the stolen goods. Rather than leave the rich booty behind, Reynaud foolishly stayed to meet the Turkish army. His own army became so frightened at the sight of the Turks that most deserted. Reynaud was captured and brought to Aleppo, where he remained in prison for the next sixteen years. His captivity did nothing to temper his miserable qualities. When he finally was ransomed, he was still arrogant, impulsive, contemptuous of royal — or any — authority, and scornful of treaties and truces.

In his absence Antioch once again needed a male ruler to protect the principality, and once again Baldwin assumed the regency. When he arrived, Baldwin found that negotiations were already under way between Manuel and Constance for the marriage of Constance's daughter, Mary, to the emperor. Although the king, with good reason, was wary of the emperor's intentions, he acceded to the wedding.

The Death of Queen Melisende

In early September 1161, while Baldwin was at Antioch, his mother died, after a long illness. She was greatly mourned throughout the kingdom, and,

---

[16] William of Tyre, vol. 2, 277.

despite their earlier rupture, Baldwin was grief-stricken. The queen was buried outside Jerusalem, in the Valley of Jehoshaphat, in a stone crypt close to the sepulcher of the Virgin Mary.

Melisende's greatest legacy was her patronage of the arts and of the Church. Even during the most turbulent years of her reign Melisende spent lavishly to beautify existing churches and endow new buildings, and she participated in the design of many projects.

The ambitious plans for the reconstruction of the Church of the Holy Sepulchre were occasioned by the coronation of Melisende and Fulk in Jerusalem, and Melisende was involved in the plans as they developed. In Jerusalem, Melisende also gave generously to restore the Church of St. Anne, hallowed as the site of the Virgin Mary's birth. A little gem, simple, graceful, and truly lovely, St. Anne's is a perfect example of an early phase in crusader church building.

Among her many important gifts, Melisende founded a convent at Bethany, which she had built for her sister, Yvette, who had taken monastic vows. Bethany was a famous pilgrimage site, since it was the town of Mary, Martha, and Lazarus, and of Simon the Leper. The Tomb of Lazarus was there, and Bethany was also the place where the procession to Jerusalem on Palm Sunday started.

Melisende was known for her love of books. At Bethany and in the Church of the Holy Sepulchre, she supported and encouraged the work of the scriptoria—the places where manuscripts were copied and illuminated. Along with the scriptorium at Acre, the Bethany and Jerusalem sites produced the finest manuscripts in the Holy Land. It is therefore fitting that the manuscript associated with her name, the Melisende Psalter, is of surpassing beauty and is famous still. It is a small psalter, or prayer book, for personal use, covered in engraved ivory, with an embroidered silk binding on the spine. It contains twenty-four illuminations of New Testament scenes and a calendar with the signs of the zodiac. All the pages have gold initials, and throughout there is an abundance of gold, as well as incredible colors. An interesting feature of the psalter is the fact that the illuminations were done by four illuminators, each working in a different style, each influenced by Western or Byzantine styles and colors, or working with a combination of styles. (See Color Plate 3.)

The psalter is of such exceptional workmanship that the only person worthy of such a book must have been the queen herself. The most respected scholar of crusader art, Jaroslav Folda, believes that Fulk commissioned the manuscript for his wife and presented it as a gift when the two were reconciled in or soon after 1134.[17]

---

[17] Jaroslav Folda, *The Art of the Crusaders in the Holy Land, 1098–1187*, vol. 1 (Cambridge: Cambridge UP, 1995) 155.

The Death of Baldwin III

Not long after Melisende's death, Baldwin was taken ill. He had a severe form of dysentery, was in terrible agony, and wanted to be brought to Jerusalem. When the stricken king came to the county of Tripoli, the count sent his own doctor, a Syrian, to treat him. Baldwin remained for several months, but when it became certain that he would not recover, he and his entourage went on to Beirut, where the king died on February 10, 1163.[18] The rumors that he was poisoned by the Syrian doctor were generally believed throughout his kingdom.

Baldwin was only thirty-three when he died. He was so admired and loved that, as William of Tyre wrote, "There is no record in any history, nor does any man now living recall, that such deep and poignant sorrow was ever felt over the death of any other prince of our own or other nations."[19] The funeral cortege took eight days to travel from Beirut to Jerusalem, and all along the route people came forward to mourn the king. He was buried, with fitting honors, in the Church of the Holy Sepulchre.

Nur al-Din continued his attacks in the north, intending to capture Antioch. In the summer of 1164 he besieged a fortress only twelve miles (nineteen kilometers) from Antioch. The army that set out to relieve the fortress, led by Bohemund III of Antioch (Constance's son, who had replaced her the year before) and Raymond II of Tripoli, was almost entirely annihilated. Bohemund, Raymond, a Greek governor who had joined the Franks, Joscelin III of Edessa, and many other nobles all surrendered and were carried off to prison in Aleppo.

It is not only in retrospect that we can observe how desperate the northern Frankish situation had now become. In 1164 the Patriarch of Antioch, in a moving letter to King Louis VII of France, described the devastation and loss of manpower Nur al-Din had caused and in graphic terms wrote of how terrified the Christians were. He begged the king to come to aid the kingdom. "God is a witness," he wrote, "that the remnant which is left us is in no way sufficient to guard the walls night and day, and owing to the scarcity of men, we are obliged to entrust their safety and defense to some whom we suspect. Neglecting the church services, the clergy and presbyters guard the gates.... For we do not hope to hold out any longer, inasmuch as the valor of the men of the present day has been exhausted and is of no avail.... Above all, the only anchor which is left in this extremity for our hope is in you."[20]

---

[18] There is actually some confusion about the year of Baldwin's death, since William of Tyre gave it as 1162. The date of 1163 is now thought more likely to be correct.

[19] William of Tyre, vol. 2, 294.

[20] Aymeric, Patriarch of Antioch, "Letter to Louis VII of France," *Translations and Reprints from the Original Sources of European History*, ed. D. C. Munro, 1897, vol. 1, no. 4 (New York: AMS Press, 1971) 17.

But the Europeans were not yet in any frame of mind to embark on another crusade, and the kingdom was left to fend for itself.

The Reign of King Amalric

During the same years that the Latins in the north remained huddled in terror behind their walls, the southern kingdom soldiered on, still optimistic and, under their new ruler, King Amalric, expansionist.

Since Baldwin III and Theodora had no children, the late king's younger brother, Amalric, count of Jaffa and ruler of Ascalon, succeeded to the throne. Not, however, without a fight among the nobles, some of whom were unwilling to acquiesce to the principle of hereditary kingship and wanted an election. In the end the hereditary principle prevailed.

Many nobles disliked and distrusted Amalric's wife and were strongly opposed to her becoming queen. Amalric had been married for several years to Agnes of Courtenay, the daughter of Joscelin II of Edessa. They had two young children, Sybilla and Baldwin, who would later succeed his father as Baldwin IV. Agnes and Amalric were so closely related that there was a question about whether they should have married in the first place. Before Amalric could be consecrated, the marriage was annulled on grounds of consanguinity, and the two children were legitimized by the Church. Amalric was crowned on February 18, 1163, and ruled until 1174.

A few years into his reign Amalric invited William of Tyre to write the history of his kingship, an offer William reluctantly accepted. Once he started, he put all his intellectual gifts and training, his linguistic abilities, and his intimate knowledge of the Latin Kingdom into creating a masterpiece of historical writing. William eventually lived at the royal court, having been induced to tutor the king's young son, the future Baldwin IV, so he knew the cast of characters very well.

William admired Amalric; he thought him highly intelligent and second to none in his knowledge of law and how to administer the kingdom. He possessed the kingly virtues of bravery, endurance in the face of adversity, and piety. Amalric was an attractive man, good-looking and physically strong, although exceptionally fat. That did not stop him from being a womanizer, and quite a successful one at that. It was well known that he "abandoned himself without restraint to the sins of the flesh."[21]

Amalric undertook to relieve the churches of their wealth, something which certainly upset William of Tyre, who believed that the king's greed for money was altogether excessive. Although when necessary Amalric used the

---

[21] William of Tyre, vol. 2, 297.

money for the kingdom's safety, his demands left his subjects poorer than they were before he became king. His major personal drawback was that he lacked the ease his brother had shown when conversing with his subjects, the ability Baldwin possessed to charm people and to become so well loved. Whatever his personal failings, Amalric was to be Jerusalem's last great king.

A. Amalric's Egyptian Policy

Amalric was determined to expand the kingdom southward by conquering Egypt, and he began immediately to implement an Egyptian policy. Egypt was the prize sought by both Amalric and Nur al-Din. With its natural resources, its industries, and trade routes across the Mediterranean and the Red Seas, Egypt would be a rich trophy for the Franks and would offset the losses incurred in the north. For the Syrians, winning Egypt had the promise of enabling them to crush the crusaders between the northern and southern millstones of Muslim supremacy.

In 1163, Amalric led the first of five military expeditions into Egypt. He crossed the Isthmus of Suez and defeated an Egyptian army, which then retreated to Bilbeis. The Egyptians, fearing Amalric's further advance into Egypt, opened the dikes that normally kept the Nile from overflowing. Threatened by the floodwaters, the Franks were forced to withdraw.

Power Struggles in Egypt

Meanwhile the situation in Cairo was deteriorating. Egypt was in the throes of a civil war between two viziers, one of whom, Shawar, turned to Nur al-Din for aid. Shawar promised Nur al-Din that, if he were restored to power, he would pay an enormous yearly tribute and compensate the Muslim ruler for the expenses of the relief expedition. In the early spring of 1164, Nur al-Din sent his general, Shirkuh, to Egypt. Accompanying Shirkuh was his young nephew, Salah-ad-Din, more familiar in the anglicized form of his name, Saladin. Although Saladin's appearance in Egypt was not his first entrance into the public arena, after the Egyptian campaigns, the trajectory of his career was astonishing.

Once Shawar was restored to power, he reneged on the deal he had made with Nur al-Din and wanted to rid Egypt—and himself—of Shirkuh. Alliances shifted so quickly it is difficult to keep up with them. Shawar turned to Amalric, who agreed to come to Egypt (in 1164) to fight Shirkuh.

For the next few years the war between Nur al-Din and Amalric was fought on Egyptian soil, with first one vizier then the other calling on either the Syrians or the Franks to intervene in their civil war. After an initial set-back, the Egyptian war went well for the Franks, so well indeed that it seemed to Amalric the time was ripe for a fifth attempt to conquer the country. For that he needed help. So in 1168 he sent William of Tyre to Constantinople to ask the emperor to join him. Manuel agreed and in the fall of 1169 sent an imposing Byzantine fleet to Acre to support the Frankish land forces. Together they besieged Damietta, but the Muslims, commanded by Saladin, defeated the Greeks and Latins and forced them once again to withdraw from Egypt.

Amalric was still not ready to concede that the conquest of Egypt was hopeless. He undertook yet another embassy to Constantinople, where the emperor entertained him with great ceremony, their alliance was renewed, and the emperor promised to join the king in an attack on Egypt. In the end nothing came of Manuel's promise.

A. The Death of Amalric and the Rise of Saladin

Amalric then turned to the Normans in Sicily for help, and they agreed to provide their navy to support the Franks. Before the Sicilians arrived, Amalric was taken severely ill with dysentery, followed by a raging fever. On July 11, 1174, the king died in Jerusalem and was buried alongside his brother, Baldwin III, in the Church of the Holy Sepulchre.

After Saladin's victory at Damietta, circumstances in Egypt changed dramatically. Shawar, who had called on the Franks for help, was executed by Saladin's uncle Shirkuh, acting on the caliph's order. Shirkuh then became the vizier. After a little over two months in office, he suddenly died. In late March 1169, Nur al-Din invested Saladin with the office of vizier. By 1171 Saladin had dissolved the caliphate by having the caliph murdered, and the Fatimid Shiite caliphate was brought to an end. Egypt now was subject to a Sunni Muslim caliph—the Abbasid caliph in Baghdad. Saladin nominally held Egypt as a governor for Nur al-Din, who in turn nominally ruled Syria and Egypt as a commander for the caliph in Baghdad. In reality they all behaved as though they were autonomous.

Saladin was, for a time, occupied in Egypt putting down the resistance to his rule by the Fatimid army and their supporters. Relations between Saladin and Nur al-Din were becoming strained, possibly over their different views on the relative importance of protecting Egypt or northern Syria. In any event, the problems that might have intensified were avoided when Nur al-Din died in May 1174. The death of Nur al-Din and Amalric within less than three months of each other gave Saladin his great opportunity. He married Nur al-Din's widow, a prudent move indeed, and before the year was over, he ruled Damascus as well as Egypt.

We are fortunate to have several contemporary accounts of Saladin's life. Most were written by men intensely loyal to Saladin and close to him. Even a prominent Muslim historian who was less enthusiastic about Saladin was fair-minded about his career, so overall he has had exceptionally good press. Everything written about him reveals the nature of this extraordinary man, whose career dominated the East for decades, and who brought so much romance to the later stories of the crusading era.

Saladin possessed in abundance all the qualities required of a Muslim ruler. He was just, merciful, courageous, and generous to a fault, so much so that he had little property or wealth of his own left when he died. His character was impeccable: he was loyal to his friends, kind—sometimes even to his enemies—affectionate, and fearless.

The Jihad Resumes

Saladin was an orthodox Muslim devoted to his religion in its purest, that is Sunni, form and unwilling to tolerate any heresy. He was scrupulous in per-forming the prayers, almsgiving, and other rituals required of his faith, and he was learned in the Quran and *hadith*. Saladin had inherited Nur al-Din's mantle as leader of the *jihad*, and he dedicated his life to the pursuit of the Holy War.

He "was more assiduous and zealous in this than in anything else.... The Holy War and the suffering involved in it weighed heavily on his heart and his whole being in every limb; he spoke of nothing else.... For love of the Holy War and on God's path he left his family and his sons, his homeland, his house and all his estates, and chose out of all the world to live in the shade of his tent."[22]

Saladin faced challenges similar to those Nur al-Din had dealt with: to consolidate, if need be by conquest, all the Muslims under his command and to join them under the banner of Sunni Islam to fight the Franks. To these Saladin added the necessity to reclaim Jerusalem and his desire to rid all Palestine and Syria of the Franks. He even intended to pursue the Franks all the way to Europe, "so as to free the earth of anyone who does not believe in God, or die in the attempt."[23]

Since Jerusalem was third in their hierarchy of holy cities, the Muslims had to be persuaded that it was imperative to fight for it. At the beginning of the eleventh century, perhaps even earlier, a literature developed and spread, as much by recitation as in its written form, called "On the Merits of Jerusalem." These Merits were collections of sayings attributed to Muhammad in which he described the value of Jerusalem and the sanctity of the al-Aqsa Mosque. Here are two examples among many others: "On the authority of Abu Umamah al-Bahili it is reported: the Apostle of God said whoever makes pil-grimage to Jerusalem and performs the ceremonies and prays, and engages in the Jihad, and perseveres, he has become perfect in fulfilling my laws." And

---

22 Baha ad-Din, in Gabrieli 99–100.
23 Baha ad-Din, in Gabrieli 101.

according to another authority, "it is related: the most beloved thing about Syria in the sight of God is Jerusalem; and the most beloved thing about Jerusalem in the sight of God are the Rock and the Mount of Olives."[24] The Merits were a powerful religious factor in the enthusiasm Saladin aroused, or tapped into, among his followers to undertake the conquest of Jerusalem.

After consolidating his position in Egypt, Saladin had to reconquer the Muslim towns and fortresses in Syria, which had defected after Nur al-Din died. In the early years in the north two assassination attempts were made on Saladin's life, the first in late 1174 or early 1175, the second in May 1176. Both attempts were made by the Assassins while Saladin was besieging Aleppo, the major holdout against him.

A. The Assassins

High in the mountains of northern Persia, overlooking the Caspian Sea, there was a castle named Alamut, the virtually inaccessible home for more than one hundred and sixty years of the Ismaili Nizari Shiite sect in Islam known popularly as the Assassins.

The movement began in Persia as an Ismaili Shiite revolt against the Sunni Seljuk Turks who, by the end of the eleventh century, had conquered much of Persia, Iraq, Syria, and Palestine (as well as Byzantine Asia Minor). The first leader, Hasan Sabbah, was a remarkable man, who charted the course the Ismailis would follow in the East.[25] As his base of operations against the Turks, Hasan seized (in 1090) the stronghold of Alamut, which was so heavily fortified and so difficult to reach that it was unable to be captured until the Mongols finally succeeded in 1256. From Alamut, Hasan sent missionaries into Persia and Syria, established many more strongholds, devised the tactics, and commanded the resistance against the Turks. At the time of yet another crisis over the succession to the caliphate in Egypt, Hasan made the decision that brought the nascent Nizari sect to power in the East.

Although the caliph (named al Mustansir), who died in Cairo in 1094, had designated his elder son, Nizar, as his successor, for complicated political reasons his younger son was chosen in his stead. Nizar then went to Alexandria, where he waged an unsuccessful war to wrest the caliphate from his brother. In the course of the fighting Nizar was taken prisoner and killed. Nevertheless, his followers carried on the struggle. Hasan then made the crucially important decision to support the Nizaris and sever all ties with the caliphate in Egypt,

---

24 Al-Fazari, "The Book of Arousing Souls," in Peters, *Jerusalem* 337–38.

25 For the religious beliefs of the Nazari sect, see Farhad Daftary, *A Short History of the Ismailis*, especially chap. 4, and on the legends, by the same author, see *The Assassin Legends: Myths of the Ismailis* (London and New York: I.B. Taurus, 1994).

which was, in any event, in the period of its final decline. Thus a dynamic new sect was begun within Ismaili Shiite Islam. The Nizaris' rise to prominence, with their center now at Alamut, ushered in the second period of Ismaili greatness.

Once the crusaders settled in the East, they inevitably crossed paths with the Nizaris, as we will see, and biased accounts of the Assassins' behavior and beliefs reached Europe in stories reported by the chroniclers of the crusades. Much of what we know — or once thought we knew — about the Assassins is colored by the highly fantastical description left by Marco Polo, in his story of the fabulously beautiful gardens surrounding the stronghold in the mountains, and of how the Master of the Assassins, called the Old Man of the Mountain, fed his followers hashish — hence the name — and later sent them to murder an enemy, with the promise of everlasting paradise when they had succeeded.

The Assassins were, in fact, extremely well organized and in the course of the twelfth century had spread through Syria, Persia, and Iraq. They developed a religious doctrine based on their belief in a hidden imam, descended from Nizar, who would one day appear. It was a religion that demanded obedience and loyalty from its followers. The Nizari adopted assassination as a means calculated to strike terror in their enemies, a tactic in part used to make up for their lack of armies, and for which, it was popularly believed, they "earned immediate and eternal bliss."[26] The young men sent as assassins were well trained. Usually they worked alone or in pairs, and their murders were carried out, preferably, in public places so that they could inspire as much fear as possible. The Assassins made alliances with many rulers, including, when expedient, with the crusaders. Among their important allies were the Turkish rulers in Aleppo, who enlisted their services when Saladin besieged the city.

After the second attack on his life, Saladin took extraordinary precautions to preserve himself from the Assassins, eventually befriending them so he would be free to carry on his war against against the Franks, but first he wanted to seize Aleppo, which he did in 1183. Then, secure in his military strength and armed with the religious zeal to retake Jerusalem, Saladin was ready to move toward the Holy City.

Baldwin IV, the "Leper King"

Amalric had been succeeded by his young son, Baldwin IV (1174–1185), whose life was blighted and shortened by leprosy. His is a remarkable and surprising story. That he was acceptable as king in a period when lepers in Europe were being placed in leper houses, and the fear of contagion led to their increasing segregation from society, is astonishing.

---

[26] Bernard Lewis, *The Assassins* (New York: Basic Books, 1968) 48.

It is likely that there was a leper hospital in Jerusalem before the First Crusade; by the 1140s an Order of the Knights of St. Lazarus had been founded, attached to the Hospitallers. The leper hospital and the new order were patronized by Queen Melisende and King Fulk, and their properties were enlarged, although their numbers remained small. In the Latin Kingdom, those who had contracted the disease were treated more sympathetically than their counterparts in Europe, and leprosy was not even mentioned when the nobles met to affirm Baldwin's succession to the throne.[27] They were unanimously in favor of the young boy, who was not quite thirteen when he was consecrated and crowned.

William of Tyre had identified the boy's disease when Baldwin was nine years old. William watched him roughhousing with his friends and noticed that he did not feel any pain from the pinches and punches that hurt the other boys. When William inquired of Baldwin, he learned that the boy's right arm and hand were numb, an indication of the dreaded disease. "It is impossible to refrain from tears while speaking of this great misfortune. For, as he began to reach years of maturity...day by day his condition became worse. The extremities and the face were especially attacked, so that his followers were moved to compassion when they looked at him. Nevertheless...he was comely of appearance for his age, and far beyond the custom of his forefathers he was an excellent horseman.... In every respect he resembled his father, not alone in face but in his entire mien.... Like his father...he was well-disposed to follow good advice."[28] That good advice, more often than not, came from William himself, who was appointed both the king's chancellor and Archbishop of Tyre.

The history of the Baldwin IV's reign and the two years following his death—from 1174 to 1187—are overshadowed by our knowledge of the disaster at the end, the defeat of the Franks at the Battle of Hattin and the loss of Jerusalem to Saladin. While it is true that the kingdom ultimately faced a formidable and canny foe, the internal disputes that divided the kingdom must also be held accountable for the failure to take united and prudent action against Saladin.

Baldwin's youth when he came to the throne meant that a regent was necessary. After a brief regency held by a rival, Count Raymond III of Tripoli became regent in the fall of 1174. He was a good man and, as his later actions demonstrate, held the safety of the kingdom as his highest duty. He was descended from Raymond of Toulouse, one of the great leaders on the First Crusade, and was a cousin on his mother's side of King Baldwin III and his successors, so his connections were impeccable. Raymond was admired by the

---

[27] There is some doubt about whether the disease was actually recognized for what it was at the time Baldwin was crowned. The symptoms were certainly manifest.

[28] William of Tyre, vol. 2, 398.

barons descended from the original nobility in the kingdom, and William of Tyre thought highly of his abilities and character.

Raymond's regency ended when Baldwin came of age in 1176. From then on, despite the king's courage and talents, his youth and his illness made jockeying for power at his court irresistible. Before long there was a serious division among the barons.

On one side were the descendants of the original families who had settled in the kingdom, led by Raymond of Tripoli. On the other, the newcomer barons, adventurers, eager for their own fortunes. This was the generation William of Tyre called "a wicked generation ... sinful sons, falsifiers of the Christian faith, who run the course of all unlawful things without discrimination.... From such, because of their sins, the Lord justly withdraws his favor."[29] These barons were led by Agnes of Courtenay, the king's mother; the dispossessed Count of Edessa, Joscelin III, who was Agnes's brother; and, last but not least, the incorrigible Reynaud de Châtillon, who had been released from captivity in 1176.

The Fight for the Throne

The most serious problem was the question of the succession. Baldwin would perforce be childless, and how long he would live or be fit to rule was unpredictable. The hope for the succession therefore rested with the king's older sister, Sybilla, and the choice of her husband. Baldwin made a wise choice for Sybilla's first husband, the son of William of Montferrat, who came from France to marry Sybilla in 1177. Sadly, he died soon after the marriage, leaving behind a pregnant Sybilla. Their son was the future Baldwin V.

Sybilla's second marriage, to Guy de Lusignan, took place in 1180. Although Guy came from a fine French noble family, he had little to commend him except his good looks. He was inexperienced, foolish, and unpopular; as it turned out, he was a genuinely infelicitous choice. Raymond of Tripoli was so opposed to the marriage that he and Bohemund III of Antioch marched their armies to Jerusalem to try to prevent it. So, the marriage was performed in haste, during Lent, which was normally not permitted. The battle lines circling round the king were now drawn: Guy, Sybilla, and Agnes, the mastermind behind the intrigues, with their supporters on one side and the stalwarts among the barons, led by Raymond of Tripoli, opposing them.

In that same year, 1180, Baldwin and Saladin, at Baldwin's behest, concluded a truce that lasted for two years. For both men it was a point of honor to maintain the peace, and so they did, leaving the Latin Kingdom to enjoy a brief period of freedom from external threats. However, within Jerusalem the political infighting became more and more contentious.

---

[29] William of Tyre, vol. 2, 406.

The king had appointed Guy de Lusignan regent, which put him in charge of the army when Saladin crossed the Jordan in 1183 and attacked the Frankish city of Baisan. Although Guy commanded a substantial army, he never engaged Saladin, preferring to sit it out until Saladin finally withdrew his forces. Although Guy suffered the king's wrath for his decision, it was in keeping with the conventional wisdom that it was better not to fight a pitched battle if it could be avoided.

The king was so angry at Guy's failure to engage the enemy when, in the opinion of many, the Franks might have won the battle that the king removed Guy from the regency and took the kingdom into his own hands. Baldwin also tried to make certain that Guy could never inherit the throne by crowning Sybilla's young son in front of all the barons, who swore fealty to the next king. Baldwin V was only five years old. Baldwin IV also tried to have the marriage between Sybilla and Guy dissolved, but in this he was unsuccessful, and Guy's fury against the king only increased when he learned of the plan.

A. The Deaths of Baldwin IV and Baldwin V

By 1184 Baldwin was almost totally incapacitated by his illness, and, knowing that he could no longer rule, he chose Raymond of Tripoli to act as regent. After years of heroically fighting his debilitating illness, the "leper king" died in March 1185. A little over a year later, the young Baldwin V also died.

Baldwin IV had done all he could to prevent Guy de Lusignan from becoming king, including arranging a committee, which would include the pope, among other rulers, to decide about future elections to the throne. Nonetheless, fighting between Raymond of Tripoli and his allies and Guy and his supporters resumed immediately after Baldwin V's death. At the end of a dreary story of court intrigue and, on Sybilla's part, duplicity, she was crowned queen by the Patriarch of Jerusalem in the late summer of 1186, and then she herself crowned Guy.

Meanwhile, Saladin's armies were coming closer to Jerusalem and, despite repeated pleas to Europe for substantial aid, the little help that came was inconsequential. The Franks had also lost any possibility of help from the Byzantine Empire, once their only ally in the East.

Conflicts in Constantinople

The Latin traders in Constantinople, particularly the Venetians, had amassed great wealth and, for the most part, enjoyed many privileges throughout much of the twelfth century, a fact that aroused real animosity on the part of Byzantine merchants and traders competing for the same imperial favors. Imperial-Venetian relations had been badly strained in 1171, after the emperor had conquered the Dalmatian coast across from Venice, but it was not until after Manuel died, in 1180, that the popular hostility against the Latins broke free.

Manuel had been attracted to things Western; had married a Latin wife, Mary of Antioch; and had been on friendly terms with Baldwin III—all of which many of his subjects intensely disliked. On the other hand, however cordial on the surface, relations between the Greeks and Latins had been tense and suspect for centuries. Since Manuel's son and heir was underage when the emperor died, his mother became regent, and it was assumed that, being Latin, she would follow her husband's pro-Western policies. Within two years, Andronicus Comnenus, the emperor's cousin, led a revolt against her and her son. Much of the rebels' support came from the anti-Latin groups in the capital. These were the people, William of Tyre wrote, who had "for a long time cherished this hatred in their hearts and were ever seeking an opportunity, at least after the death of the emperor, to destroy utterly the hated race of the Latins in the city [Constantinople] and throughout the empire."[30]

There were eighty thousand Latins living in the capital. Warned of the plans against them, many were able to flee the city. In April 1182, almost the entire Latin population that remained was massacred or sold into slavery. The worst punishments were reserved for the monks and priests of the Latin Church, who were mutilated and tortured before they were killed. The Latins who fled on their galleys had managed to make off with huge amounts of gold and other valuables, much of it belonging to Greeks. It was small recompense and even smaller consolation for the horrendous destruction of the Latin communities.

Three years later, independent of the Venetian problems, the Sicilian Normans tried to conquer the Byzantine Empire. In 1185 an enormous Sicilian fleet, estimated at somewhere between two hundred and three hundred ships, with a huge land force, crossed the Aegean to Durazzo, where the garrison surrendered without a fight. From there the Sicilian army marched to Thessaloniki, on the Aegean coast. The combined land and sea assault began on August 15; by August 25 the Sicilians were in the city and a terrible bloodbath followed.

The violence was staggering. Few people were spared when the Sicilians took Thessaloniki, and nothing was safe from them. They stomped on the chalices and icons in the Greek churches, desecrated the altars, and, even worse, a Byzantine historian reported, some "exposed their shameful parts and sprinkled the holy places with their urine.... [For] the Latins, when they have vanquished and subjugated their adversaries, become an unbearable and indescribable evil." Small wonder, the Greek historian wrote, that "Between them and us a bottomless gulf of enmity has established itself."[31]

---

30 William of Tyre, vol. 2, 462.

31 Nicolas Choniates, "Historia," trans. Peter Charanis, in Kenneth Setton and Henry Winkler, eds., *Great Problems in European Civilization* (Englewood, NJ: Prentice-Hall, 1966) 115.

Leaving a garrison in Thessaloniki, the Sicilians then marched toward Constantinople. The Byzantine emperor, disliked by his subjects on many personal counts, and blamed for the loss of Thessaloniki, was overthrown by another royal cousin, Isaac Angelus. This change heartened the Byzantine army, and the Greeks were able to defeat the Sicilians before they reached Constantinople. The defeat encouraged the Thessalonians to rise up against the small Sicilian garrison, and the soldiers fled the city. Nonetheless, the empire had come within a hair's breadth of defeat.

The dreadful result of the "bottomless gulf of enmity" between the Latins and Greeks meant that the Kingdom of Jerusalem could never again count on the Greeks for aid — or even neutrality.

The Prelude to Hattin

In 1185 a truce had been concluded between Saladin and the Latin Kingdom. Raymond of Tripoli had been the architect of the truce when he was regent, and it was essential for the Latins that the truce be maintained, since they were in such internal disarray. Unfortunately, neither King Guy nor the barons had foreseen how the reckless and greedy Reynaud de Châtillon would destroy the fragile peace and force the encounter with Saladin.

After Reynaud's release from prison he had made another advantageous marriage, this time to the heiress of the Oultrejourdain, whose dowry included Kerak and Montreal, the two major fortifications south of Jerusalem, astride the road between Damascus and Cairo. From his castle at Kerak, Reynaud watched the caravans, which, according to the truce, were free to travel the road from Damascus to Cairo without harm. The caravans carried expensive wares and great riches for the markets, and after a time the tolls he exacted were not enough to satisfy Reynaud. In the early winter of 1187 he captured a caravan, took all the treasure, and imprisoned the Muslims. Guy failed to persuade Reynaud to return the booty and prisoners to Saladin, who was so enraged that he vowed to kill Reynaud. There was now no way to avert the war.

At the end of June 1187, Saladin crossed the River Jordan and set up his base camp at a village called Kafr Sabt, which had an excellent water supply and was halfway between Tiberias and the Frankish base camp and accessible to both. When all the armies from Saladin's vast empire had been summoned and gathered, he commanded a force of some 30,000 men, 12,000 of whom formed an elite cavalry.

Guy set up his camp at Sephoria (or Saffuriyah), in the Lower Galilee, an advantageous site that also had a good water supply and pasturage for the horses. Although the Franks had mustered all the available manpower they could, their cavalry was comprised of only 1,200 men, including 600 members of the two military orders; their foot soldiers numbered somewhere between 15,000 to 18,000 men. They were hugely outnumbered.

On July 2 Saladin sent a contingent of his men to besiege Tiberias. In short order they took the city and burned the lower town. The townspeople took refuge in the citadel, along with Raymond of Tripoli's wife, who sent a messenger to the Frankish camp asking for help. Guy was all for rushing off to Tiberias to meet the Muslim army in battle and take back Tiberias. It was Raymond who counseled against it. He believed it would be foolhardy for the crusading army to leave their good location and march in punishing heat to do battle with Saladin. He also believed the Muslims would become restive if there was no battle, and that in time Saladin would evacuate Tiberias, and his army would go home. Raymond carried the day. But during the night Guy was approached by the Grand Master of the Templars, who persuaded him to change his mind and march against Saladin. It was a fatal decision.

On the morning of July 3 the crusaders broke camp. Raymond of Tripoli led the van, the king led the center, and Reynaud and the military orders led the rear. It was fiercely hot, and the Frankish knights were weighed down by their weapons and heavy armor. Sweltering under all their metal, they were desperate to reach water, but Saladin had foreseen that and had drained the cisterns along their route. His forces harried the Franks all day under the blistering hot sun.

By nightfall the Franks had reached the plateau above the Horns of Hattin and could go no farther. They spent a long night, parched with thirst and worn out. As if the Franks had not suffered enough, the Muslims set fires on the hill, and smoke poured into their camp. By daybreak, on July 4, the Franks were completely surrounded. On that Saturday the two armies met in a long and anguished battle. On both sides it was a furious struggle.

In the course of the long day the Franks fought bravely against overwhelming odds, on more than one occasion pushing the Muslim forces back. In the end, there was no escape for the crusading armies, not from the numerical strength against them, not from the heat, nor from the thirst and the exhaustion.

Realizing that the situation was hopeless, Raymond of Tripoli left while he could and returned to Tripoli, where soon afterward he died in his sleep. Those who survived the battle, including the king, fled to a hill near the Horns of Hattin from which they could see, but were never to reach, the waters of Lake Tiberias. They hoped to regroup and defend themselves, but the Muslims fell on them and captured the king and all the men with him, including Reynaud and the Grand Master of the Templars.

That night Saladin had the king and Reynaud brought to his tent. Both men were quaking with fear and nearly dying of thirst. Saladin had ice water brought in a goblet, which he gave to the king. After the king had drunk his fill he handed the goblet to Reynaud, who also drank the ice water. "This

6.4 The Battle of Hattin. Saladin seizes the True Cross.

godless man," Saladin is reported to have said, "did not have my permission to drink, and will not save his life that way.... Then he rose and with his own hand cut off the man's head."[32] A few days later Saladin ordered all the captured Templars (except their grand master) and the Hospitallers to be beheaded.

Among all the tragedies of that famous battle, the most heartrending for the Franks was the capture by the Muslims of the relic of the True Cross. The cross had given them courage in battle and the promise of God's protection, and it was the most revered relic in Christendom. Its loss was incalculable.

The relic was brought to Damascus for all the Muslims to see, and the king and the barons whose lives were spared, and the grand master of the Templars, were brought to Damascus to be imprisoned. The countess of Tripoli, in the citadel in Tiberias, was allowed to go free and return to Tripoli with her companions.

The question of who made the decision to leave their good location and chase Saladin into the Galilee has engaged historians for centuries. It seems likely that Guy, Reynaud, and Gerard, the Grand Master of the Templars, were most responsible: Guy who wanted to be thought brave and Reynaud who was dangerously irresponsible. Guy had personal reasons for hating Raymond, so he rejected his sound advice in favor of Gerard's unsound advice to pursue Saladin. It may be that Saladin had attacked Tiberias expressly to draw the Franks out into the arid country. We may never know for certain.

What is certain is that the Franks made a grievous error when they pursued Saladin. They were hemmed onto a plain between the Horns of Hattin, and nearly all the fighting men either perished or were captured. Many foot soldiers were sold into slavery. Only the captured knights were treated more humanely by Saladin. Very few men were lucky enough to escape — among them Raymond of Tripoli and Balian of Ibelin, who would become the hero of the siege of Jerusalem.

"The number of dead and captured was so large," a Muslim historian wrote, "that those who saw the slain could not believe that anyone could have been taken alive, and those who saw the prisoners could not believe that any had been killed."[33]

During the two months after Hattin, Saladin conquered city after city and castle after castle on his march toward Jerusalem. By the end of the summer, all the important coastal cities, including Acre, Ascalon, Beirut, Sidon, and Jaffa, had fallen to his forces. Only Tyre held out against him; it became the haven for refugees fleeing from his army. In late September 1187, Saladin appeared before the walls of Jerusalem.

---

[32] Ibn al-Athir, in Gabrieli 124.
[33] Ibn al-Athir, in Gabrieli 123.

6.5 Saladin ravaging the Holy Land. Illumination shows burning and destroyed towns in the background.

Jerusalem Surrenders to Saladin

Saladin had allowed Balian to return to Jerusalem to rescue his wife and children before the siege began, on condition that Balian stay for only one night and never fight against him. Balian remained, however, and he led the resistance, such as it was, that Jerusalem offered to Saladin's army. The city had few men left to fight.

When it seemed certain the city would fall, Balian asked for a safe-conduct for the citizens in return for handing over Jerusalem. At first Saladin refused, since he was bent on destroying the Christians as they had destroyed the Muslims eighty-eight years before. Balian then threatened to kill all the Muslims in the city and to destroy the Muslim holy sites, including the al-Aqsa Mosque.

So an arrangement was negotiated whereby Saladin accepted payment for the Franks, who would then be allowed to leave without their weapons and horses. Many escaped the net, however, and were able to flee or bribe an official to let them go. Some seven thousand of the poorest people were paid for by Balian, who found funds in the city to do so, but others for whom there was no money were sold into slavery.

Saladin was careful to warn his troops to behave when they entered the Holy City, so the massacre that had followed the Latin occupation was not repeated. He ordered the Muslim shrines and holy sites, which had either been covered or converted to Christian use, to be restored to Islam. After much disagreement about its fate, the Church of the Holy Sepulchre was left to stand unchanged. It was given to the care of the Greek Orthodox Christians. Most churches and monasteries were turned into mosques and Islamic schools, and the Hospital of St. John became a Muslim hospital, though for a short time some Hospitallers were allowed to remain to care for the sick.

Thus Jerusalem became a Muslim city once more. "By a striking coincidence, the date of the conquest of Jerusalem was the anniversary of the Prophet's Ascension into Heaven. Great joy reigned for the brilliant victory won, and words of prayer and invocation were on every tongue. The sultan [Saladin] gave an audience to receive congratulations.... His manner was at once humble and majestic.... His face shone with joy, his door was wide open, his benevolence spread far and wide."[34]

Saladin's policies toward the Jews and the native Greek and Eastern Christians were sensible and amicable, much as the Muslim policies had been before the crusaders came. He seems to have wanted to disrupt life as little as possible. If they paid taxes to the Muslims, the Jews and the native Christians could live their lives peacefully under the new conquerors. Saladin encouraged Jews to settle in Jerusalem, and, since in the past the Jews had been on good relations with the Muslims, they were satisfied with the turn of events. The Greeks had always disliked the Latins and were content to live under Muslim rule. The Byzantine emperor congratulated Saladin on his victories and even made overtures for an alliance.

Sometime in 1184 William of Tyre had decided not to continue writing his *History*. He was in such despair over the disasters that had already befallen his country that he felt he simply could not go on. However, William was persuaded to resume his work and he began what would have been the twenty-third book of the *History*, but he died in the spring of 1185, with only a few pages written.

---

[34] Imad ad-Din, in Gabrieli 160.

Although he did not live to witness the capture of Jerusalem, he was pre-scient when he wrote, "In the acts of our princes there is nothing which seems to a wise man worthy of being committed to the treasure house of the mem-ory.... We who used to triumph over our foes..., now, deprived of divine favor, retire from the field in ignominious defeat after nearly every conflict.... It is therefore time to hold our peace; for it seems more fitting to draw the shades of night over our failures than to turn the light of the sun upon our disgrace."[35] A fitting epitaph indeed.

A New Crusade Is Proclaimed

News of Jerusalem's fall reached Europe quickly. Pope Urban III was so heart-broken at the news of the disaster that he died a few days later. His successor, Pope Gregory VIII, immediately issued a papal bull proclaiming a new cru-sade. It is a passionate letter, and the pope's sadness and his anger are palpable.

He described in detail the tragedy that had overcome Jerusalem, "the terri-ble severity of the judgments which the divine hand has exercised over Jerusalem and the Holy Land,"[36] and he then turned to his understanding of how it could have happened. "We ought to be persuaded that these reverses are only to be attributed to the anger of God, against the multitude of our sins.... We ought not then to attribute our disasters to the injustice of the judge who chastises, but rather to the iniquity of the people who have sinned.... Would to God that they then [before their defeat] had recourse to penitence."

The sinfulness that led to the fall of Jerusalem was to be overcome by penance—not only by those who, after confessing, undertook the new cru-sade, but also by those remaining at home. In this new understanding of why Jerusalem and the Holy Land had suffered, it was not only the inhabitants of the Holy Land who were at fault, but all Christendom. So now "it is every-where urgent to act, to efface our sins by voluntary penance, and, by the help of true piety to return to the Lord our God."

The penitential aspect of crusading had been integral to the movement from the beginning. Pope Urban II had tapped into the overwhelming sense of sinfulness that was so deeply embedded in the Christian worldview when he called for the First Crusade and had promised remission of their sins to the men who took the cross. Now, nearly a century later, all Christendom must do penance.

Among his other regulations, Gregory VIII proclaimed that the fast of Lent should be observed every Friday for five years, and that everyone should abstain from eating meat on every Friday and Saturday. To the men who took

---

[35] William of Tyre, vol. 2, 505-06.
[36] This and all subsequent quotes are from Gregory VIII, "Papal Bull," in Allen and Amt 164–65.

the cross he promised remission of their sins and a plenary indulgence for their faults, provided they were "determined to do so by motives of a sincere faith."

Pope Gregory's bull initiated the Third Crusade and extended the penitential nature of crusading to encompass all Christendom.

Suggestions for Further Reading

Barber, Malcolm. *The New Knighthood: A History of the Order of the Temple.* Cambridge: Cambridge UP, 1994.

Benvenisti, Meron. *The Crusaders in the Holy Land.* Jerusalem: Israel Universities P, 1970.

Boase, T.R. *Castles and Churches of the Crusading Kingdom.* London: Oxford UP, 1967.

Daftary, Farhad. *The Assassin Legends: Myths of the Ismailis.* London and New York: I.B. Taurus, 1994.

Edginton, Susan B., and Sarah Lambert, eds. *Gendering the Crusades.* New York: Columbia UP, 2002.

Ellenblum, Ronnie. *Crusader Castles and Modern Histories.* Cambridge: Cambridge UP, 2007.

———. *Frankish Rural Settlement in the Latin Kingdom of Jerusalem.* Cambridge: Cambridge UP, 1999.

Folda, Jaroslav. *The Art of the Crusaders in the Holy Land, 1098–1187.* Cambridge: Cambridge UP, 1995.

Forey, Alan. "The Military Orders, 1120–1312." *The Oxford History of the Crusades.* Ed. Jonathan Riley-Smith. Oxford: Oxford UP, 1999.

Kedar, Benjamin Z., ed. *The Horns of Hattin.* Jerusalem: The Israel Exploration Society, 1987.

Kennedy, Hugh. *Crusader Castles.* Cambridge: Cambridge UP, 1994.

Lane-Poole, Stanley. *Saladin and the Fall of Jerusalem.* 1898. London: Greenhill Books, 2002.

Lewis, Bernard. *The Assassins.* New York: Basic Books, 1968.

Lyons, Malcolm, and D.E.P. Jackson. *Saladin: The Politics of Holy War.* Cambridge: Cambridge UP, 1982.

Marcombe, David. "Lepers and Knights." *Leper Knights: The Order of St. Lazarus of Jerusalem in England, ca. 1150–1544.* Woodbridge, Suffolk, UK, & Rochester, New York: The Boydell Press, 2003.

Munro, Dana C. *The Kingdom of the Crusaders.* New York: D. Appleton-Century, 1935. (This is an early study that is still valuable and important.)

Nicholson, Helen. *Templars, Hospitallers, and Teutonic Knights: Images of the Military Orders, 1128–1291.* Leicester, UK: Leicester UP, 1993.

Prawer, Joshua. *The History of the Jews in the Holy Land.* Oxford: Clarendon Press, 1988.

———. *The Latin Kingdom of Jerusalem.* London: Weidenfeld and Nicolson, 1972.

———. *The World of the Crusaders.* New York: Quadrangle Books, 1972.

Riley-Smith, Jonathan. *The Knights of St. John in Jerusalem and Cyprus 1050–1310.* London: Macmillan & Co., 1967.

Roncaglia, Martiniano. *St. Francis of Assisi and the Middle East.* 2nd ed. Cairo: Franciscan Center of Oriental Studies, 1954.

Rozenberg, Silvia, ed. *Knights of the Holy Land: The Crusader Kingdom of Jerusalem.* Jerusalem: The Israel Museum, 1999.

Seward, Desmond. *The Monks of War.* London: Penguin Books, 1972 (revised ed. 1995).

Smith, Katherine. "Saints in Shining Armor: Martial Asceticism and Masculine Models of Sanctity, ca. 1050–1250." *Speculum* 83.3 (2008): 572–602.

Part Three

CHAPTER SEVEN

The Changing Ideology of Crusading in the Thirteenth Century

While Europe prepared for the Third Crusade, fighting continued unabated in the Holy Land.

Tyre was the only coastal city that the Franks had managed to keep from Saladin, but after Jerusalem fell, the people in Tyre were so certain they could not withstand Saladin a second time that they were on the verge of surrendering even before he arrived. The city was saved due largely to the talents of a newcomer to the East and partly to a mistake Saladin made.

Baldwin V's uncle, Conrad, Marquis of Montferrat, had started for the East in 1185 but did not arrive until 1187. The delay made him too late to save Acre from Saladin. As it turned out, he came in time to save Tyre. Many men who had fled before Saladin, or whom the sultan had permitted to leave when Frankish cities surrendered, had assembled in Tyre, but they lacked a leader and the will to confront Saladin. Conrad asked them to swear to give him—and only him—the city and its surrounding territories if he was able to defeat Saladin. In exchange for money Conrad had brought with him, they agreed to his terms.

To the Muslims Conrad seemed "a devil incarnate in his ability to govern and defend a town, and a man of extraordinary courage."[1] He was in fact an extraordinary leader. By the time Saladin reached Tyre, in November 1187, Conrad had so well fortified the city and had so coordinated his naval resources with the garrisons within the city that the Latins were able to capture half of Saladin's navy, destroy much of the rest, and inflict heavy losses on his army. Facing disaster, Saladin retreated.

---

[1] Ibn al-Athir, in Gabrieli 177.

He was severely criticized by many Muslims for that decision, although he may have understood that his troops were too weary and discouraged to carry on without a respite. In any event, the decision was a blessing for the Franks. Tyre gave them a seaport that men and supplies coming from the West could safely enter and from which they could send ships to besiege Acre.

Saladin had taken King Guy prisoner at the Battle of Hattin, and Guy was still imprisoned when Saladin besieged Ascalon in the late summer of 1187. In return for the surrender of Ascalon, Saladin had allowed King Guy, the Master of the Templars, and ten nobles to go free, provided they pledged never to fight against the Muslims. It was a merciful, although self-destructive, act. The promise was immediately broken. By the summer of 1189 Guy and Sibylla had reconstituted a small army and marched to Tyre. They were refused entry by Conrad. Once again a breach occurred in the leadership of the Latin Kingdom at a time when unanimity was so necessary. Guy then marched to Acre and began a long, tortuous siege in August 1189. Eventually, Conrad joined Guy in the fight for Acre, but their rivalry was only temporarily suspended.

The Third Crusade

Meanwhile in Europe, plans for the new crusade were under way. Three great men dominated the continent when the news of Jerusalem's fall reached them: Frederick I Hohenstaufen, called Barbarossa (or Red Beard), king of Germany and Holy Roman Emperor; Henry II of England; and Philip II Augustus of France. All three were willing to undertake the new crusade, although Philip was less enthusiastic than the other two.

A. Frederick I's Crusade

The Emperor Frederick I was the first to leave for the East. He had a large, well-trained, disciplined army and sufficient funds for provisions and supplies. Frederick was the senior statesman in Europe, his power and political and military successes acknowledged even by his enemies. He was senior as well in age, since he was close to seventy when he embarked on the crusade.

Although Frederick had been on the Second Crusade and knew the perils of the overland route, he decided to march East rather than try to outfit a navy sufficiently large for his army. Frederick's chroniclers reported the unlikely number of one hundred thousand men for the size of his army. Whatever the exact count, it was the largest ever to set out on a crusade.

Before he left Germany, Frederick sent an embassy to the king of Hungary, the Seljuk Sultan, and to the Byzantine emperor, Isaac Angelus, requesting safe passage through their territories. This was granted by all three, although the Byzantine emperor required assurances that Frederick was not planning to invade his empire. Frederick even wrote to Saladin, demanding that he return Palestine to the Christians. It was a demand, as one could well imagine, that was rejected, although as consolation Saladin offered to release some prisoners.

Having set affairs in his kingdom in order by the spring of 1189, Frederick and his troops started out from Ratisbon (modern Regensburg) in May 1189. They encountered no difficulties until they entered Byzantine territory. In a letter to Leopold of Austria, Frederick described the Greeks' heinous behavior toward his army, and the fact that the emperor had imprisoned the ambassadors Frederick had sent to him to arrange everything for their march. Eventually relations were restored, the ambassadors were set free, and promises of aid were made again. "Truly," Frederick wrote, "because the burnt child dreads the fire, we can in the future have no confidence in the words and oaths of the Greeks."[2] To make matters much worse, the Byzantine emperor had concluded an alliance with Saladin.

The alliance had been a long time in the making, and the Byzantine emperor and Saladin each sent the other lavish gifts as signs of friendship and ambassadors to work out the details of their arrangement. The obvious reason for the alliance was their joint fear and dislike of the crusaders coming East. The alliance only further enraged the Latins, who saw it as one more instance of Byzantine treachery.

Everything seemed to conspire against the German armies—harassment by the Greeks, by the Turks, and, most of all, the terrible terrain and the bad weather they encountered as they crossed Asia Minor. Starving and having lost men and horses, the Germans were nevertheless able to win a victory over the Turks at Iconium (in Asia Minor). From there they crossed the hazardous Taurus Mountain range, their route leading them to the sea. By the time of their crossing the weather had become intolerably hot. When they reached Seleucia, the emperor, against all advice, jumped into the River Saleph for a swim. He was caught in a whirlpool and drowned. His death on June 10, 1190, effectively ended the German crusade.

The emperor was greatly mourned, so much so that some of his followers were said to have been ready to follow him into the river to their deaths. His son, the Duke of Swabia, was chosen to lead the army, and he and his men carried Frederick's body to Tarsus, where his intestines were removed and buried. His body was buried in the Church of St. Paul in Antioch. The largest contingents of Germans returned home; many died en route, and only a small number remained to join in the siege of Acre.

---

[2] Frederick I, "Letter to Leopold of Austria," in Munro, vol. 1, no. 4, 21.

B. Richard and Philip Set Out for the East

It was not until July, a month after Frederick's death, that the French and English kings started East. Major impediments had to be removed before the two kings were willing to join forces. They were, on and off, but more on than off, at war with each other over the territory held in France by King Henry II, who was Duke of Normandy, Anjou, and the coastal areas of the channel separating France and England. Neither king was willing to leave Europe unless the other left also. They were at war in the summer of 1189 when Henry II died, on July 6. In September, his elder son was crowned King Richard I of England; in March 1190, Philip and Richard agreed to a truce and prepared to leave together.

Substantial sums of money were raised throughout Europe to finance the Third Crusade. In 1188, Henry II had imposed the so-called Saladin tithe, a tax of 10 per cent on all the property and movable goods owned by everyone in his kingdom, with few exceptions, so Richard inherited a rich treasury. Philip also levied the tax, although it was never as strictly enforced as it was in England. The papacy exempted the knights and clergy who went on the crusade from paying the tax; anyone else who defaulted was liable to be excommunicated.

Richard and Philip took the lessons of the earlier crusades to heart. They understood the expense and dangers of having huge numbers of weak and helpless noncombatants with them and discouraged them from going. They also knew that the safest and most practical way to travel was by ship, rather than marching hundreds of miles overland, prey to starvation, disease, and loss of men and horses.

Richard spent lavishly to acquire a naval force and pay for men and supplies. He sailed at first with a fleet of some 100 ships, which was later increased. Although Philip was poorer, he paid the Genoese to provide a fleet to transport 650 knights, 1,300 squires, and four times that number of foot soldiers and to supply them for eight months. Both kings marched first through France, where they met at Vézelay, and in July 1190, they set out for different ports, Richard to Marseilles and Philip to Genoa, to sail for Palestine.

Neither king seemed in any hurry to leave Europe. Richard made a leisurely tour through Italy, stopping in Rome, Naples, Salerno, and Sicily, where he was joined by Philip. They stayed in Sicily for some time, since Richard became embroiled in family politics on the island, and it was not until March 1191 that Philip sailed from Messina and not until early April that Richard left. By then the English fleet had been enlarged to 180 ships.

Philip sailed directly to Acre without incident. Richard's fleet was caught in a storm, and many ships were blown off course. Richard made a quick stop at Crete and then went to Rhodes, where he remained for several days. While there he learned that some of his ships had been wrecked off the coast of

Cyprus, the sailors who survived had been taken prisoner by the Cypriots, and the treasure the ships carried was stolen. So Richard went to Cyprus and conquered the island with little difficulty.

The capture of Cyprus, merited or not, proved to be a major boon. A perfect location for assembling crusading troops before they sailed to Acre or Egypt, it became a base from which to send supplies to the Palestinian coast. The seaport of Famagusta became a thriving trading center, and Cyprus remained a strong Latin Christian center for four hundred years, long after the Holy Land was lost.[3]

C. The Siege of Acre

7.1 The siege of Acre, 1190. Although it is highly unlikely that women actually participated in warfare, this illumination shows them playing at least a small part in the siege of Acre. Note that that they are not wearing any protection over their clothing.

Philip arrived at Acre and joined his cousin, Conrad of Montferrat, in the camp outside Acre seven weeks before Richard came. The Muslim chronicler reporting the events at Acre praised Philip and acknowledged him as "a great and honored ruler," although he was young—only twenty-five years old—and never really well. He was not a charismatic leader, although he took up his duties responsibly.

---

3   The island was actually sold twice. Richard sold it to the Templars, who were unable to support it, and they sold it to Guy de Lusignan, who became King of Cyprus.

It was Richard who made the more powerful impression. "His kingdom and standing were inferior to those of the French King, but his wealth, reputation and valor were greater.... His arrival put fear into the hearts of the Muslims, but the Sultan met the panic with firmness and faith in God."[4]

Richard and Philip each fell ill soon after they arrived; Philip recovered first and launched the attack against Acre. Again and again the besiegers were repulsed. On July 6, Richard was sufficiently recovered to join the attack. The Latin armies' camp was hemmed in between the seemingly impregnable walls of Acre in front and the Turkish army behind. Richard's siege engines hammered away at one great tower while his miners and sappers dislodged stones from the wall near the tower, placed timber in the opening left by the stone, and set fire to it. It was a slow and laborious job, so Richard offered a financial incentive to any soldier who would remove a stone from the wall—first two and then four pieces of gold for each stone.

The siege had gone on for nearly three years. Richard was on the point of breaching the walls, and without aid and supplies the garrison within the city could not hold out, so they sent word to Saladin asking him to allow them to surrender. Although Saladin did not want to relinquish Acre, it was too late to save the city. On July 12, 1191, the garrison requested terms for their surrender.

After some negotiation, Saladin and the two kings agreed upon the following conditions: the garrison in Acre was to be spared and ransomed—for a huge sum—by Saladin; the True Cross was to be returned to the Christians; a large number of Christians taken captive by Saladin were to be released; and hostages were to be turned over to the kings until the terms of surrender had been fulfilled.

Philip and Richard entered Acre together. As they had previously arranged, they divided the city, and each appointed a commander for his sector. As soon as this was accomplished, Philip decided to leave for home. He was castigated for the decision, but he was adamant, claiming that he was ill, and that he had fulfilled his vow. Since Richard did not trust Philip to leave his lands in France undisturbed, Richard asked Philip to swear an oath that he would not harm Richard's lands while the English king remained in the Holy Land. Philip took the oath, returned home, and almost immediately attacked Richard's lands in Normandy.

After weeks passed and Saladin still had not fulfilled the conditions of the surrender, Richard became increasingly impatient and angry. Finally, he decided to hang the hostages. "King Richard, aspiring to destroy the Turks root and branch, and to punish their wanton arrogance ... ordered 2,700 of the Turkish hostages to be led forth from the city and hanged; his soldiers marched forward with delight to fulfill his commands."[5]

---

[4] Baha ad-Din, in Gabrieli 212–13.
[5] "Itinerary of the Pilgrims and Deeds of Richard," in Allen and Amt 173.

7.2 Philip and Richard receive the keys to Acre, 1191. Illustration in *Grandes Chroniques de France* (fourteenth century), showing the humiliation of the Muslims when they surrendered.

Richard then led his army along the coast toward Jerusalem, pursued and harassed all along the way by Saladin's army. On September 7, just north of Arsuf, Richard and Saladin met in a pitched battle, the first time they fought face-to-face. The Muslims were not able to withstand Richard's mounted knights, and he won a decisive victory. It was a serious setback for Saladin that left his army depleted and disheartened.

Anticipating Richard's march to Jaffa, Saladin had destroyed the city walls, which Richard had to rebuild when he arrived there. He had expected to use Jaffa as his base from which to attack Jerusalem, but during the winter of 1191–1192, which Richard spent at Jaffa, he decided not to besiege Jerusalem. Richard did not believe his supply line between Jaffa and Jerusalem would hold; he was concerned by the news from home, where Philip had begun to advance against Normandy; and he was seriously ill. Richard actually marched toward Jerusalem during the winter, but he thought better of it and turned back when he was only six miles (ten kilometers) away. Saladin, believing that Richard was retreating, captured Jaffa. Richard immediately returned to save the city and, even though his forces were outnumbered, was able to inflict a stunning defeat on Saladin's army. Both sides were exhausted, and it seemed the opportune moment for Richard to ask for a truce.

Saladin was opposed to a truce, but his emirs and advisors all counseled it. "Look, too, at the state of the country, ruined and trampled underfoot, at your subjects beaten down and confused, at your armies, exhausted and sick."[6] They went on in that vein, also reminding Saladin that the Franks never kept their treaties for long. Negotiators went back and forth between Richard and Saladin until an agreement could finally be drawn that was acceptable to both. On September 2, 1192, Richard received Saladin's final offer for a treaty; he signed it and three days later Saladin signed. (See Color Plate 4.)

D. The Truce between Richard and Saladin

The most important terms of the truce were that for a period of three years and eight months Christian pilgrims would have access to Jerusalem to visit the holy sites unmolested, and Christian and Muslims could freely pass through each other's territories. The Franks would keep the coastal cities from Tyre to Jaffa. The sticking point was the disposition of Ascalon, which Saladin was adamant should be returned to him. It was finally decided that Ascalon's fortifications were to be destroyed before the shell of the city was turned over to him. The new crusader capital, until the end of the kingdom, was in Acre, now a crowded and uncomfortable place to live but a virtually impregnable fortress.

Before Philip and Richard left for home they adjudicated the claims made by King Guy and Conrad of Montferrat for the throne of the kingdom. The situation had changed in 1190, when Queen Sybilla died, as did her two daughters. Because Guy's claim to the throne was based on his marriage to Sybilla, his claim became tenuous after her death, and Conrad was a forceful opponent. He had strengthened his claim in a brutal way. The only surviving member of the royal family was Amalric's daughter Isabella, who was happily married. Conrad had her marriage annulled, and in November 1190, he forced Isabella to marry him.

The two kings decided that Guy should remain on the throne for his lifetime, and that when he died the throne would pass to Conrad. It was not a decision that made Conrad happy and would probably not have succeeded. However, fate took a hand. Conrad was accosted on a street in Tyre and murdered by two men on the evening of April 28, 1192. All the sources agree that the murderers were Assassins, although the reasons for the murder remain unclear.

---

[6] Imad ad-Din, in Gabrieli 236.

In May 1192 Isabella married the most powerful French lord in the Holy Land, Count Henry of Champagne. Henry was a fine leader who had played an important role in the siege of Acre, a charming man, and the nephew of both the French and English kings. Richard acquiesced to the marriage and Henry became the new king, although he never used the title, perhaps because Guy was still, at least in name, King of Jerusalem. Henry proved to be a capable ruler, quite the sanest and most pragmatic ruler the kingdom would have.

Guy de Lusignan died in 1194, and his brother Aimery took his place as King of Cyprus. Henry believed that Cyprus was a part of the Kingdom of Jerusalem and therefore subject to him. Aimery believed Cyprus should be separate and independent. The two quarreled until they decided that, in the best interests of the Latin East, they should make a lasting peace. Cyprus remained independent, with its own king, but the two kingdoms were on friendly terms.

Isabella turned out to hold the fortunes of the Latin Kingdom's rulers in her hands. After Henry of Champagne died, in 1197 there were two candidates for the throne of Jerusalem. Guy's brother Aimery had the strongest support, and he was chosen to be the new king. The much-married Isabella married Aimery and she and Aimery were crowned King and Queen of the Latin Kingdom. The marriage joined Cyprus and Jerusalem for as long as they ruled. Guy's wish had finally came true, and the royal title was restored to the Lusignan family, although only temporarily. In the next generation the kingdom was separated yet again.

E. The Deaths of Richard and Saladin

Richard sailed from Acre in October 1192. His voyage home was beset by disasters, culminating in his capture by Leopold of Austria, who turned him over to the Emperor Henry VI. Henry kept the English king prisoner until March 1194, when he was ransomed for an enormous sum, of which his mother, Eleanor of Aquitaine, paid a considerable part. Richard spent his last years fighting against Philip II to defend his possessions in France. During the course of a campaign, a boy standing on a castle wall shot an arrow that entered the king's shoulder. After Richard forcibly removed the arrow, the wound turned gangrenous. He died on April 6, 1199.

It is hard to know what to make of Richard. He was an impetuous and courageous warrior, in his glory in the field, and he earned the title the Lionheart while still young, even before he was crowned king. Despite his personal derring-do, he was a brilliant and prudent commander, astute about his options and careful for his men.

Richard has come down through the centuries as the model of a perfect knight, the embodiment of medieval chivalry. His reputation and his actions were not always well matched; his decision to hang twenty-seven hundred hostages is a case in point. Nonetheless, he was surely the most legendary European leader on the crusades. Although he spent only six months of his reign in England, the British revered him, and in the nineteenth century Parliament erected an equestrian statue to him in front of Westminster Palace. His place in history, legend, and literature is assured.

A few months after Richard left Acre, Saladin became gravely ill. His condition worsened rapidly until, on March 4, 1193, less than two weeks after his illness began, he died in Damascus. His chronicler, who had been in faithful attendance throughout Saladin's last days, recorded the immediate aftermath: "The day of his death was a day of grief for Islam and the Muslims, the equal of which they had not known since the days of the right-guided Caliphs. The citadel, the city and the entire world were overcome with a grief beyond words...[and] on that day I knew that if it had been possible to ransom him with our lives I and several others would have been ready.... After the midday prayer he was carried out in a coffin draped simply with a length of material.... He was laid in his tomb at about the hour of the evening prayer; God sanctify his spirit and illumine his sepulcher!"[7]

The praise heaped on Saladin by the Muslims was not without some reservations among his countrymen. To some he seemed a man bent on using the *jihad* for his own desire to expand his power and that of his family. And his generalship was called in question, particularly his inability—some thought reluctance—to take Tyre and the defeats he suffered in his battles with Richard. The criticisms seem churlish. He was the greatest opponent the Franks faced in the Holy Land. He was generous and chivalrous, even to his enemies. A chronicler's encomium seems more just: "He endured separation [from his infant sons]..., putting up with the discomforts of a life of squalor...in order to gain merit in God's eyes and dedicate himself to the Holy War against God's enemies."[8]

The result of the Crusade of Kings was mixed. Thanks largely to Richard, the coastal cities were under Latin control, Ascalon in its sorry state excepted. Possession of the coast, coupled with the strength of the Italian navies and the destruction of Saladin's naval force, gave the kingdom a powerful hold on the eastern Mediterranean, both for supplies and the rapid development of commerce. Yet Jerusalem was still not a Christian city.

A short coda followed the Third Crusade, not important enough to be given a number, but important enough to include briefly. Frederick I Barbarossa had been succeeded by his son, Henry VI, who decided to carry on what his father had died attempting to do. Henry took the cross in the spring of 1195

---

[7] Baha ad-Din, in Gabrieli 251–52.
[8] Baha ad-Din, in Gabrieli 105.

and called on his subjects to join him in a new crusade. By the spring of 1197, he had assembled a large army, ready to sail from either Sicily or southern Italy. Because Henry was taken ill before the crusade was to leave, he remained at his home in Sicily and the crusade was led by the Archbishop of Mainz.

The Germans reached Acre in September 1197 and went up the coast to Sidon and then to Beirut. The army had great success against the Muslims as they marched north, and by the time they reached Beirut, the Muslims had deserted the city, which was quickly taken by the German army. At Beirut the news reached the Germans that Henry VI had died, and the crusaders returned home.

Almost immediately on the heels of this brief and aborted effort, a new pope proclaimed a new crusade to recover the Holy City.

The Turning Point: The Papacy of Pope Innocent III

In the history of the medieval papacy, few men were as formidable, as far-reaching in their influence, and as overweening in their use of papal power as the man elected in 1197. Lothario di Segni, who took the name Innocent III, was only thirty-seven and the youngest member of the College of Cardinals when he ascended the papal throne. Innocent's character has come under scrutiny for centuries by historians: was he a politician with a thirst for his own power, or was he a deeply spiritual man with a strong conviction about the role of the Church within a Christian society, and with the tools to enforce his beliefs? What is certain is that he left his stamp on Christendom, and that during his fairly short pontificate—from 1197 to 1216—the course and nature of crusading were irrevocably changed.

The whole of the twelfth century was a period of such innovation that it has been called a Renaissance, in the literal sense a century of renewal. The rapid growth of population, the development of towns and cities, the expansion of Europeans into new lands—including Palestine and Syria—the emergence of strong central governments and effective administrative systems, the rebirth of classical learning, and the beginning of universities all made themselves felt throughout Europe. It was a century of great progress.

One aspect of the twelfth century above all affected the papacy and Innocent's view of his role in society. This was the deeply held belief that the ideal of a Christian society was unity under one ruler. This ideal of one world, ruled from Rome, came into being with the founding of the classical Roman Empire in the first century. The conviction that the greatness and glory of Rome were achieved because of its empire and in its imperial form did not die with the empire in the mid-fifth century. Although attempts were made to revive the empire in a reduced form in the course of many centuries, none was lasting. In reality the empire was basically moribund in the West until the goal of unity was revived in the twelfth and thirteenth centuries.

The all-important issue then became the question of whether the leadership of a unified society should be in the hands of the secular authority, that is the Holy Roman Emperor, or the sacred authority, that is, of course, the pope. In Innocent's perception of the papacy, there was no doubt that the greater power was his.

In the unequivocal expression of his authority in temporal as well as spiritual affairs Innocent had no equal. "To me is ... said in the person of the apostle, 'I will give to thee the keys of the kingdom of heaven. And whatsoever thou shall bind upon earth it shall be bound in heaven, etc.' (Matthew 16:19) ... thus the others were called to a part of the care but Peter alone assumed the plenitude of power. You see then who is this servant set over the household."[9] Innocent reiterated the grounds for his right to interfere in secular matters many times. In a famous bull he wrote, "Paul, too, writing to the Corinthians to explain the plenitude of power, said, 'Know you not that we shall judge angels? How much more the things of this world?' "[10]

The desire for unity went hand-in-hand with the desire for uniformity, which meant to the pope the purity of Christian belief. In Innocent's view, only a society free from sin could hope to restore the Holy Land and the Church of the Holy Sepulchre to its rightful place in Christendom. Innocent could tolerate neither heretics nor neutrals.

Such was the man who issued his call for a crusade in August 1198, eight months after he took office. Even before Innocent's call for the Fourth Crusade, a sizable group of French noblemen, led by Count Theobold of Champagne, had committed themselves to taking the cross.

A. The Fourth Crusade

In two important respects this new crusade was different from the previous two. It was led by nobles, primarily Frenchmen, rather than by kings, and the strategic decision was made to attack Egypt first and then go on to the Palestinian coast, rather than go directly to Acre and then Jerusalem. Richard had counseled this plan when he returned home, knowing that Egypt was in effect, the "soft underbelly" of the Muslim Empire and that conquering Egypt would make the capture of Jerusalem a real possibility. This meant that the crusade would go by ship and not attempt the overland route at all — a wise decision, since the Byzantine emperor could no longer be trusted to make the overland route secure or to provide food. However, it threw the crusaders into the arms of the Venetians, to whom the French turned for ships and supplies.

---

[9]   Pope Innocent III, "Letter to the Archbishop of Ravenna (1198)," in Brian Tierney, ed. and trans., *The Crisis of Church and State, 1050–1300* (Englewood Cliffs, NJ: Prentice-Hall, 1964) 132.

[10]   "The Decretal 'Per Venerabilem' (1202)," in Tierney 136.

Innocent wrote letters to encourage the crusade; he sent legates to preach the crusade; and he took the important step of raising manpower and money by insisting that all cities and all nobles raise a fixed number of men at arms and support them for two years. The higher clergy could send either men or, if they had no troops at their disposal, money.

The pope's most unusual financial act was to levy a tax of one-fortieth of the annual revenue collected by the clergy in their respective parishes and contribute it to the crusade. Innocent was at pains to explain to the clergy that this tax would not be permanent. Nevertheless, his decree proved difficult to enforce, and it is not certain how much money was raised this way.

The Fourth Crusade was a sorry, misbegotten venture altogether. According to Geoffrey de Villehardouin, an active participant in the negotiations during the crusade, the crusaders had contracted the Venetians to build enough ships to transport 4,500 knights, 4500 horses, 9,000 squires, and 20,000 foot soldiers. Geoffrey was an eyewitness to all the events until his death in 1207 and was the author of *The Conquest of Constantinople*,[11] the first history of the crusades written in the French language.

The ships and supplies were to be ready for departure by the end of June 1202. The amount the Venetians charged was based on the numbers given them by the crusade leaders, and it was far too optimistic. When the crusaders assembled in Venice, their numbers were reduced by a good third of their original estimate. So there was not enough money to pay the Venetians. The Doge then offered to defer final payment if the crusaders would sail across the Adriatic and take back for Venice the Christian city of Zara, once a Venetian vassal city, now held by Hungarians. It was the first step on the slippery downward slope that led two years later to the so-called diversion of the Fourth Crusade to Constantinople.

When Innocent learned of the plan to attack Zara, he immediately forbade it on pain of excommunication. Although there was some dissension among the crusaders about the wisdom of going ahead, they, with a host of Venetians, crossed to Zara and in November 1202, captured the city. Innocent excommunicated them all. The men then sent a delegation to the pope explaining the reasons for their action and begging his forgiveness. In order not to delay the crusade any longer, Innocent absolved them.

Meanwhile, before the crusaders had left for Zara, Alexius Angelus, a Byzantine prince whose father was a deposed and now imprisoned emperor, came to Venice to ask for help in restoring his father and retrieving what Alexius claimed was his rightful inheritance of the imperial throne. In return

---

[11] Geoffrey de Villehardouin, "The Conquest of Constantinople," in *Chronicles of the Crusades*, trans. M. R. B. Shaw (London: Penguin Books, 1963) 33.

he would pay the crusaders and the Venetians huge sums of silver from the Byzantine treasury and provide an army to help with the attack on Egypt.

An inordinate amount of ink has been spilled by historians trying to decide who was responsible for the diversion of the crusade to Constantinople. Assessing blame is less important, however, than the fact of the siege of Constantinople and its horrific aftermath. The crusaders and the Venetians, seduced by the young Byzantine prince, now had an excuse to go to Constantinople, and they all hoped to gain by the diversion.

There was serious disagreement among the French leaders about whether to pursue this course. Many elected to defect from the main body of crusaders and so, as de Villehardouin pointed out, the numbers going to Constantinople dwindled considerably.

B. The Siege and the Sack of Constantinople

In June 1203 the fleet arrived at Constantinople. The young Alexius Angelus had expected to be welcomed when he arrived at Constantinople; instead the gates were closed, and the crusaders had to breach the walls so that Alexius could enter. In a short time the reigning emperor deserted. Alexius's aged and blind father was released from his Greek prison, and he and Alexius were crowned co-emperors. Alexius IV, having secured his throne, no longer needed the crusaders or the Venetians, and he also discovered that he had no money in the treasury. So he reneged on his promises. While the Latins waited outside the walls to be paid, there was a revolt against Alexius IV, who was forcibly removed from his bedchamber and presumably killed. His father soon died. From then on, no one in Constantinople would negotiate with the Venetians or the crusaders, and no money was forthcoming. It was certain by the spring of 1204 that no money would ever be forthcoming. On April 9, 1204, the Latins began the siege of Constantinople, and by April 12, they were in the city.

The sack of Constantinople was inhuman. The crusaders pillaged, wrecked, raped, mutilated, and killed everyone and everything they could lay their hands on. The great Church of Santa Sophia was desecrated, and a "harlot ... sat in the patriarch's seat, singing an obscene song and dancing frequently.... [W]ith one consent all the most heinous sins and crimes were committed by all with equal zeal. Could those, who showed so great madness against God himself, have spared the honorable matrons and maidens or the virgins consecrated to God?"[12]

The wealth the crusaders found was beyond anything they could ever have imagined and could scarcely find words to describe. One of the most vibrant accounts of the Fourth Crusade is the chronicle dictated to a scribe by Robert

---

[12] Niketas Choniates, "Historia," in Allen and Amt 235–36.

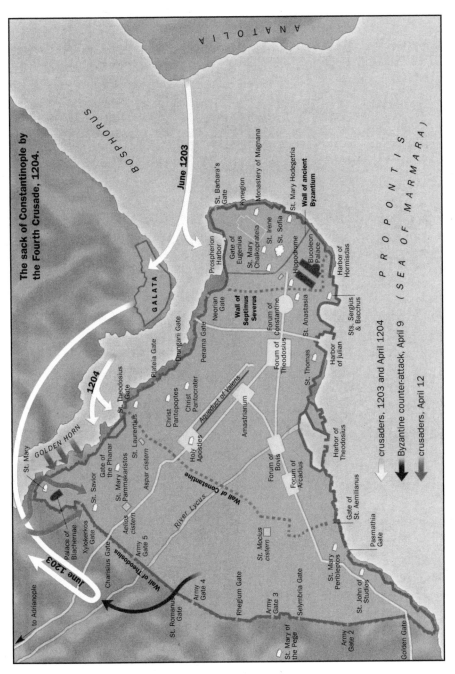

Map 7.1 The sack of Constantinople by the Fourth Crusade, 1204.

7.3 The siege of Constantinople, 1204. An illustration from Geoffrey de Villehardouin's *Chronicle of the Fourth Crusade.*

of Clari, a knight from Picardy, who was an eyewitness to most of the events. His chronicle is one of the first examples of Old French narrative prose, which developed during the thirteenth century. Robert was a humble soldier, not privy to the intrigues of the barons and Venetians, but aware of the results; he was acutely observant, an excellent reporter, and remarkably impartial. His descriptions of Constantinople itself and the riches and relics found in the city are invaluable.

After the nobles had taken the best houses in the city for themselves, leaving nothing for the humbler soldiers, they ordered all the spoils brought to a church, "[a]nd it was so rich, and there were so many rich vessels of gold and silver and cloth of gold and so many jewels, that it was a fair marvel.... Not since the world was made, was there ever seen or won so great a treasure."[13] Despite the presence of guards to preserve the treasure intact, it was set on by the nobles and stolen.

The crusaders took innumerable relics housed in Constantinople. Robert could not list them all, there were so many, but he included the most revered: "two pieces of the True Cross as large as the leg of a man... [and] the iron of the lance with which our Lord had His side pierced and two of the nails which were driven through His hands and feet... [and] in a crystal phial quite a little of His blood."[14] Altogether it was a booty of incalculable value. The consequence of such a stolen richness was that, over time, the cult of the

---

[13] Robert of Clari, *The Conquest of Constantinople*, trans. Edgar Holmes McNeal (New York: W.W. Norton & Co., 1964) 101.
[14] Robert of Clari 107.

saints and their relics began to change. As so many relics were brought to Europe, they soon became a commodity to buy and sell. Holy objects still, but transformed into objects of substantial commercial value. The sale of relics became big business.

C. The Latin Empire of Constantinople

In May 1204, the first Latin ever to sit on the throne of Constantinople was elected. Baldwin, count of Flanders, was chosen to be the first Latin emperor of what had now been renamed and reconstituted as the Latin Empire of Constantinople. The Venetians claimed the larger portion in Constantinople, including Santa Sophia, for themselves. The first Latin patriarch to ascend the throne of that venerable church was a Venetian. The Venetians and the Franks divided between themselves most of the Byzantine territories in Greece, the Balkans, and the islands. What little territory remained in Greek hands, particularly in Asia Minor, became the rallying point for the Byzantines who had gone into exile.

The Latin Empire lasted until the disaffected Greeks found the strength to return and expel the Latins from Constantinople in 1261. By that time, the Latin Empire had been so badly mismanaged, so denuded of its treasures, that Constantinople had become a poverty-stricken city, shorn of inhabitants, its last Latin ruler offering to mortgage or sell all he had—even a son—to keep the city afloat. Even in Latin hands, the empire at Constantinople was no help at all to the Latin Kingdom.

The long-run effects of the Latin devastation of Byzantium have provoked substantially different opinions from twentieth-century historians. To Steven Runciman, a famous Byzantine scholar, "There was never a greater crime against humanity than the Fourth Crusade. Not only did it cause the destruction or dispersal of all the treasures of the past ... and the mortal wounding of a civilization that was still active and great; but it was also an act of gigantic political folly."[15]

For the opposing, pro-European view, here is Richard Southern, a great medieval scholar: "In the whole sweep of European history, the fall of Constantinople in 1204 is only a minor landmark.... That their [the crusaders'] instincts finally led to the capture of Constantinople is deplorable, but not surprising... [since] it had been a standing temptation."[16] The fury unleashed in Constantinople was the final act in the drama that had been unfolding for more than a century.

The crusade that was not a crusade ended ignominiously. Needless to say the Greeks were lost to the Latin Kingdom as possible allies, and only their animosity could be counted on.

---

[15] Runciman, vol. 3, 130.
[16] Richard Southern, *The Making of the Middle Ages* (New Haven, CT: Yale UP, 1953) 61–62.

When Innocent learned the full extent of the damage caused in Constantinople, he was furious. In a letter he wrote to the papal legate, he vented his rage at the course of events and the role played by his legate. "For you, who ought to have looked for help for the Holy Land, you who should have stirred up others, both by word and example, to assist the Holy Land—on your own initiative you sailed to Greece.... Because of you, its [the Holy Land's] last state was worse than the first, for all its friends deserted with you.... We have just heard and discovered from your letters that you have absolved from their pilgrimage vows...all the crusaders who have remained to defend Constantinople.... Whoever suggested such a thing to you and how did they lead your mind astray?"[17] The pope was also furious because his hopes for the unification of the Greek and Latin churches were dashed. How could a reunion happen when "she [the Greek Church] now, and with reason, detests the Latins more than dogs?"

Innocent was nothing if not resilient, and he soon came to believe that what had happened was God's will and that the foothold secured in Constantinople would bring the Latins closer to Jerusalem and would soon lead to the recovery of the Holy City. He also came to believe that the reconciliation of the Greek and Latin Churches would, in time, be possible.

The diversion to Constantinople was certainly not planned. It simply happened step-by-step as the leaders reacted to each new problem. Nor could the diversion be blamed on the pope, although this first significant, and damaging, change in the crusading movement happened on his watch. Innocent soon moved on to deal with a different problem. The next crusade he called was his responsibility.

D. The Crusade against the Albigensians

In 1208 Innocent called a crusade against a well-entrenched heretical group in southern France known as the Cathars, or the Albigensians (from the name Albi, the area of their greatest strength).

We have seen how the popular desire for a meaningful spiritual experience and for the expiation of sin manifested itself in the enthusiasm for crusading, how the longing to embrace holiness led to the veneration of saints and their relics and the desire to undertake a pilgrimage. The heretical movements that became a grave concern for the papacy during the twelfth century sprang from the same well of spiritual feeling that permeated everyone's life in the medieval period. The serious difference was that the heretics followed a path that drew them away from the Church in Rome.

The largest and most successful heresy that Innocent confronted was the

---

[17] Pope Innocent III, "Letter to Peter, Cardinal Priest and Legate of the Apostolic See," in Brundage 208, 209.

Cathar heresy. The Cathar heresy was founded on the dualist belief that there was a God of good and a God of evil, who was Satan. Cathars believed in the strict dichotomy between spirit and matter, that Satan had created all matter and that matter was therefore evil. In this view all flesh was evil, so the Cathars refused to procreate because it would be adding another body to the world of matter. Jesus was therefore never made human, and the Church itself, being material, was also evil. The logical consequence of the Cathar belief was that the Church itself and all its sacraments were the work of Satan and should be abjured. At the highest rank of Cathars were the *perfecti*, those whose lives were so ascetic that they were perfect. The rank and file of Cathars could lead normal lives until they accepted the *consolatio*, or the consolation, which forgave them their sins and placed them among the *perfecti* and insured that they would live a life free from all sin until death. The heresy spread through all classes in society and attracted many noblemen and even more noblewomen, since women were able to be full participants in the Cathar communities.

Some of the Cathars' support came as a consequence of their rejection of the clergy and particularly their animosity toward those clerics who controlled great wealth, whose lives were devoted more to the care of their property than to the care of souls. The need for pastoral care was met within the Catharist communities. The simplicity and strict asceticism of the Cathars' lives was of a piece with the growing desire among many religious to return to the apostolic life of the early Christian communities.

From the Church's point of view, those who strayed from the orthodoxy, or right belief, of Christian doctrine were anathema and outside the pale of Christian society. Heresy was a disease that ate at the very fabric of Christianity and had to be rooted out. In the first line of offense against heretics were the local bishops, charged with finding and restoring heretics to the Church. Because the bishops in southern France had been desultory in discharging this responsibility, the heresy flourished. By the time Innocent came to the papal throne, Catharism had spread to northern Italy and to parts of the Rhineland and was most firmly entrenched in southern France, where the heretics had won support from some of the nobility.

In the years before Innocent called the crusade, he had sent papal legates to the south charged with stamping out the heresy. All efforts failed. As it became clearer that force was necessary, Innocent appealed to King Philip II Augustus of France to wage war in southern France. Philip, occupied with England and other personal affairs, was at first reluctant.

The final straw was the assassination of the pope's legate in the south, Peter of Castelnau. Innocent had been considering using force even before the assassination, but it then became imperative. In 1208 Innocent proclaimed a

7.4 The torture of the heretics. The scene depicts the pain and torture inflicted on the Cathars to persuade them to recant.

crusade against the Cathars. He granted to those who took the cross the same privileges granted to crusaders who went to the Holy Land, including remission of their sins and the assurance that their property would be protected while they were away. He also permitted the crusaders to confiscate the lands and cities that they took from heretics.

The summons was answered mainly by nobles and their knights from northern and central France. The crusade lasted for more than ten years after Innocent died. Although the heresy was not completely suppressed everywhere in Europe, most of the heretics in southern France had been eliminated when the Peace of Paris, a formal settlement ending the crusade, was signed in 1229.

The sad consequence of a violent and bloody story is that the beautiful culture and language of the Languedoc was destroyed. Ultimately the victor in this crusade was the King of France; the south of France was joined to the northern lands of the royal domain. The close relationship thus established between the papacy and French monarchy continued until the end of the century and greatly benefited the French as well as the papacy.

The use of the crusade against Christians and heretics was a perversion of the original crusading ideology, and Innocent had opened the way for later popes to use the crusade against their political enemies by denouncing them first as heretics. Innocent's reputation among his contemporaries did not emerge unscathed from the Albigensian crusade, nor from the attack on Constantinople. The use of force against heretics was questioned and criticized, as was the appropriateness of using force against a Christian country. None of this diminished Innocent's ardor for yet another crusade. Before he called the Fifth Crusade, one of the sadder and stranger instances of popular religiosity took place, in 1212–1213. This was the Children's Crusade.

E. The Children's Crusade

The Children's Crusade was not in any sense an official crusade. Rather it was a spontaneous movement, a chapter in the history of the religious enthusiasm and hysteria that gave rise, for example, to Peter the Hermit's huge success. Before, during, and after the crusading era Europe had its full share of popular preachers, evangelists who attracted followers ready to take the cross and free Jerusalem. Usually these outbursts were mercifully short-lived, but the religious fire was always smoldering just beneath the surface, ready to be rekindled.

The Children's Crusade was two movements, joined in the popular imagination into one crusade. The first movement was an outburst in France, in June 1212, led by a shepherd boy name Stephen, who had seen a vision of Christ, dressed as a pilgrim, telling him to bring a letter to the King of France. He gathered around him many boys and girls, but nothing is known about who they were or how many followed Stephen to Saint Denis. From what is known, it seems that the king sent them home.

In the story for which there is more evidence, the leader was a German boy, Nicolas, from Cologne, who inspired hundreds of children, many as young as six years old, to follow him to Jerusalem to free the city. The children marched across Germany and though the Alpine passes to Italy, heading for the sea and ships to carry them to the East. So many children joined this movement that a number as high as thirty thousand was given in the sources, though that is undoubtedly an exaggeration.

Most who survived the trip across the Alps went to Genoa. Since they could not find passage, they returned home, or were lost in Genoa or on the return. One contingent went to Marseilles, and their story, if true, is very sad. According to one often-repeated version, the children were betrayed by the sea captains who promised to take them to the Holy Land. Many were sold into slavery; others drowned at sea.

The Children's Crusade quickly became the stuff of legend, and much was written about it for centuries. The author of *The Chronicle of the City of Cologne* wrote: "In this year [1212] occurred an outstanding thing and one much to be marveled at, for it is unheard of throughout the ages." He described how thousands of children left their work in the fields and went off "despite the wishes of their parents, relatives, and friends who sought to make them draw back." But they continued on, certain that they were obeying God's will and that they would somehow reach Jerusalem. "What their end was is uncertain. One thing is sure: that of the many thousands who rose up, only very few returned."[18]

To many writers the movement was deeply disturbing and foolish in the extreme. "Those who had once passed through the land in crowds and never without a song of encouragement...now returned, singly and silently, barefoot and famished, held in scorn by everyone."[19] Nonetheless it had begun with great popular support, and even Innocent was among those who were moved by the efforts of these unfortunate children.

F. The Fourth Lateran Council

In April 1213, Innocent began sending out letters to prelates all over Europe, calling for another crusade and summoning them to attend a council that was to convene in November 1215. The Fourth Lateran Council was the high point of Innocent's papacy, indeed the highpoint of the medieval church. In his letter calling for the council, Innocent wrote:"Of all the desires of our heart, we long chiefly for two in this life, namely, that we may work successfully to recover the Holy Land and to reform the Universal Church, both of which call for attention so immediate as to preclude further apathy or delay."[20]

Four hundred and twenty bishops and eight hundred abbots and priors, plus innumerable other religious figures and representatives of kings, nobles, princes, and of free cities were in attendance when the council met in Rome. The council lasted for a month and issued seventy decrees, most dealing with the strengthening of faith, and matters of discipline, heresy, the conduct of the clergy, corruption in the church, and pastoral care. Four canons dealt with the Jews. Innocent's concern with uniformity and his fear that the Jews were in some way harmful, or potentially so, to a Christian society, led him to his inflexible attitude toward the Jews. Among other restrictions was the one that required Jews (and Saracens) to wear different dress in order to distinguish themselves from Christians.

For the laity the most important canon was the requirement to confess their sins and receive the sacrament of the Eucharist at least once a year. There then followed a series of decrees to do with the planning and organization of the Fifth Crusade.

Innocent's *Crusading Privileges* reveal how committed he was to this crusade

---

18 "The Chronicle of the City of Cologne," in Brundage 213.
19 "Annals of Marbach," in Allen and Amt 250.
20 Pope Innocent III, "Letter of Convocation, trans. C. R. Cheney and W.H. Semple, in Marshall Baldwin, ed., *Christianity through the Thirteenth Century* (New York: Harper & Row, 1970) 293.

and how much care he took to ensure its success. This new crusade would be fully manned, fully armed, well provisioned, and well financed. A large part of the financing, for the first time, would be borne by the Church. Innocent allocated a substantial sum from the papal treasury toward the crusade and decreed that "absolutely the entire clergy ... shall give a twentieth part of their ecclesiastical revenues for three years in aid of the Holy Land."[21]

Innocent made another major change when he enjoined the Christian community as a whole to participate, either by going to the Holy Land or, under certain permissible circumstances, redeeming their vows by making a suitable payment. "Let them [the prelates] beseech the kings, dukes, princes, marquises, counts, barons, and other magnates, as well as the common people of the towns, villages, and castles.... Let even the lesser people be pressed, for greater security." By participating in this war against God's enemies, in whatever way they could, everyone would be granted remission of their sins. He opened the way for women, children, aged men, and even the halt to undertake the crusade. Those who refused to take the cross, or who took the cross and then did not go on the crusade, were subject to excommunication.

Innocent also took the unprecedented step of permitting men to take the cross without their wives' permission. When Pope Urban II called the First Crusade he had made it very clear that no married man should take the cross unless his wife concurred. The central issue was the sacramental nature of the marriage vow and the obligations it imposed on a husband as well as a wife. Until Innocent's papacy, Urban's position on the wife's role prevailed. Innocent's decision to free the husband from his obligation to his wife, to subsume it under the now all-important crusader vow, was a marked and lasting change.

To ensure the full support of the entire Christian community at home, Innocent instituted monthly processionals, with prayers to be offered for the restoration of the Holy Sepulchre. The pope also decreed a general peace for at least four years, so that the crusading armies could leave unimpeded by warfare in Europe. Any infraction of the peace was punishable by excommunication.

The date for departure was set for June 1, 1217. The crusaders were to meet at either Brindisi or Messina to set sail for the East. Innocent planned to be present to bless them before they left, but he died an untimely death in Perugia on July 16, 1216.

It was a blessing for Innocent that he did not live to see what actually became of the Fifth Crusade, how few participants came from the upper nobility, how none of the major European kings joined, and how much trouble was eventually caused by his former ward, Frederick II.

---

[21] This and the following quotation from "The Crusading Privilege of Innocent III" are from *Select Historical Documents of the Middle Ages*, trans. E.F. Henderson (London: George Bell & Sons, 1896) 337–44.

The Fifth Crusade

Pope Honorius III was left to implement the plans that had been set in motion by Innocent. The Fifth Crusade has usually been divided into two parts, the first led by King Andrew of Hungary and Duke Leopold VI of Austria, the second the Crusade against Egypt. Leopold and Andrew sailed for Acre at the end of the summer of 1217, both with large armies. At Acre, they were met by Bohemund IV of Antioch and the King of Cyprus, as well as the titular King of Jerusalem, John of Brienne.

They had to decide whether to abandon the policy followed by crusaders throughout the twelfth century—attacking Jerusalem directly—or to follow King Richard's plan and attack Egypt, on the assumption that defeating the Muslims in Egypt was the only sure way to regain Jerusalem.

Saladin had designated his brother and his two sons as his heirs, with the provision that his empire be divided among them. Saladin's brother, al-Adil, shoved aside Saladin's sons and took all of the empire for himself. He then divided it into administrative units ruled by his own sons. The arrangements al-Adil made were fragile at best, and there was intense rivalry among the various princes, although it was generally accepted that al-Adil, as sultan of Egypt, was the highest official in the empire. Egypt still had manpower and wealth, but the fractiousness in the empire as a whole made it seem a propitious time for a campaign against Egypt.

Nonetheless, the Christian leaders could not agree about what to do, so they stayed on the coast near Acre and fought a few skirmishes, with little result. The King of Hungary decided he had fulfilled his vow, and he and his army left for home, followed soon by Bohemund IV and Hugh of Cyprus. The remaining armies and their leaders decided to wait for the arrival of the Emperor Frederick II, whom they expected imminently.

A. The Amazing Career of Frederick II

Frederick II was the grandson of Frederick Barbarossa, who had arranged a marriage between his son, the future Henry VI, to Constance, the heiress of the Kingdom of the Two Sicilies, which included Italy from Naples south as well as Sicily itself. Frederick was the only child of Henry VI and Constance and was four years old when he was orphaned and inherited the throne of Sicily. The marriage between Henry VI and Constance had been a diplomatic coup for the German monarchy. By virtue of the imperial position, the German emperors had a legitimate claim to the northern Italian cities and now, through marriage, controlled the south of Italy and Sicily as well.

The great fear that haunted Innocent and his successors was that the German emperors would squeeze the papacy between the imperial power in the north and south and thus so weaken papal authority that the emperor would become the supreme power in Christendom.

To avoid that happening, Innocent had enforced his right to designate the king in Germany, who would then be emperor-elect. During most of his pontificate he had supported Otto of Brunswick, one of two contenders for the throne, but he never actually gave him the crown, and for decades there was civil war in Germany. Innocent finally decided in favor of the young Frederick Hohenstaufen, and in 1215 the pope offered Frederick the imperial position on condition that Frederick separate the crown of Sicily from his northern Italian and German territories once he was emperor. Naturally enough, Frederick promised. Very soon afterward Innocent died, surely a happy man, with not an inkling of what lay ahead.

Frederick was so intellectually gifted, so much a polymath, that he was called *stupor mundi*—"the wonder of the world"—by his contemporaries. He was born in Sicily, and although he became the ward of Innocent III, he was raised and educated there. All his life he remained far more devoted to Sicily than to Germany. He knew Arabic, Greek, Latin, French, Italian, and German, and he absorbed the remarkable mixture of sophisticated cultures and learning in Sicily. Sicily had a large Muslim and Byzantine Greek population and attracted scholars from the Muslim world, who brought with them their advances in medicine, the sciences, mathematics, and philosophy. So Frederick learned from them, and he learned from his close acquaintance with both the Greek and Muslim communities a great deal about Islam and the Eastern Orthodox religion. He had a harem and a taste for the life of an Oriental potentate that greatly disturbed his Latin critics. Frederick was far more tolerant of other religions than his contemporaries, an attitude that was easily and often misunderstood.

The breadth of Frederick's intellectual interests was nothing short of amazing. To further education in his kingdom he founded the University of Naples, which became one of the earliest and greatest of Italian universities. He had an intimate knowledge of Rome and Roman law, and he wrote a law code and constitution for Sicily that was far more advanced than the laws of any other European country.

He was canny, brave, boundlessly ambitious, and arrogant. He was a fierce enemy, and time and again he showed himself to be quite untrustworthy. For all that Frederick was colorful, flamboyant, brilliant, and, finally, admirable—indeed the "wonder of the world."

B. The Fifth Crusade at Damietta

Although Frederick had taken the crusading vow in 1215, he was still in Sicily in the spring of 1218, when German and Frisian reinforcements, along with Genoese and Pisan ships, reached Acre. With his enlarged army, John of Brienne, the titular king of Jerusalem, joined by the duke of Austria and the master of the Templars, decided not to wait for Frederick and to invade Egypt. His goal was Damietta, a port city on the Nile, from which he planned to attack Cairo. The crusaders sailed from Acre to Egypt, where the armies, with their ships behind them, camped on the shore across the Nile from Damietta.

The singular impediment to the capture of Damietta was a formidable tower on an island in the middle of the Nile, known as the Chain Tower because enormous, heavy steel chains came down from it, effectively preventing men and ships from crossing the river. The crusaders tried for days on end to capture the tower, using all the weapons in their armory to no avail. They suffered heavy losses in the process, until finally, just as they were ready to give up, Oliver of Paderborn came forward with a design for a tower that could be mounted on two boats joined together. The tower that was erected was actually a fortress covered with skins to protect the crusaders from attack and from the enemy's use of Greek fire.[22] Many of the crusaders' siege machines were dragged to the top of the fortress. It was all a hazardous undertaking at best.

Oliver of Paderborn was one of several legates chosen by Innocent III to preach the Fifth Crusade. He subsequently joined the crusade and wrote a history of the siege of Damietta, in which he played a crucial role. His siege machinery was so artfully constructed that it was able to reach the tower. Against formidable odds the crusaders captured the Chain Tower on August 24, 1218.[23] Sultan al-Adil was so overcome when he received the news that he soon died of grief; he was succeeded by his son, al-Kamil. The Egyptian resistance proved so strong, however, that the crusaders were forced to begin a difficult blockade of Damietta, which lasted for eighteen months until, in early November 1219, they finally captured the city.

One of the more engaging stories to come out of this crusade — engaging, that is, to Christians — occurred while the Franks were besieging Damietta. It is the story of St. Francis of Assisi's visit to the sultan of Egypt, and his attempt to convert him to Christianity.

St. Francis's life is too well known to rehearse here in all its details: how he had a spiritual conversion from his secular, fun-loving life as the son of a wealthy cloth merchant in Assisi; how he chose a life of poverty; how he went

---

22 Greek fire was an incendiary liquid mixture invented in the seventh century by a Syrian in the Byzantine Empire. The liquid was placed in tubes or cups and hurled at the enemy. It was so highly inflammable that it could not be extinguished by water. The ingredients were kept so secret that to this day no one knows what went into the mix.

23 The whole undertaking is vividly described by Oliver of Paderborn in his book, *The Capture of Damietta*, trans. John J. Gavigan (Philadelphia: U of Pennsylvania P, 1948) 24–28. Although Oliver did not identify himself as the designer of the tower, it was certainly well known and was reported in other accounts.

out in the world among the people to preach the word of God to all God's children. In his desire to follow in Christ's footsteps, poverty, humility, simplicity, and prayer became the cornerstones of his existence. Although at first his preaching met with little response, even with disdain, he soon won followers, and in 1211 the new order, the Friars Minor, was confirmed by Pope Innocent III. From that time forward Francis committed his order to proselytizing and bringing Christianity to the Muslims.

Francis thought of going east as early as 1212, but for various practical reasons did not succeed until the summer of 1219. After a difficult, uncomfortable sailing he reached Acre, where he remained only briefly, and in July 1219, he arrived at Damietta. Although it seemed a foolhardy undertaking, Pelagius, the papal legate at Damietta, gave Francis permission to leave the crusader camp and cross into Muslim territory. How Francis actually accomplished this we will never know. Perhaps it was Francis's gentle personality, and how harmless he seemed, that convinced the sultan's guards to give him leave to see the sultan.

Francis was granted an interview with the new sultan, al-Kamil, and tried to persuade him to convert. Several versions written by Francis's followers described the interview, but again, we will never know with certainty what took place between the two men. It was a mission doomed to fail. The sultan provided Francis with a safe-conduct to return to the Franks' camp. Soon after, he left for the Holy Land, where he stayed for a time, and then he returned to Italy. Although Francis's own mission failed, its importance is twofold: it marks the beginning of Franciscan missionary work among non-Christians, an enterprise that took them all the way to China during the course of the thirteenth and fourteenth centuries, and it is an indication of what would later become the Franciscan involvement in the Holy Land, particularly in Jerusalem.

The crusaders had endured terrible losses during the long siege of Damietta, but their sufferings paled by comparison to what had befallen those they found inside the city. The people had been so starved during the blockade, and disease had carried off so many, that the first thing that greeted the Latins was "an intolerable odor, a wretched sight. The dead killed the living... by their odor.... Not only were the streets full of the dead, but in the houses, in the bedrooms, and on the beds lay the corpses.... Almost eighty thousand, as we learned from the report of captives, perished in the city from the beginning of the siege to its end; all except those whom we found, healthy or ill, about three thousand in number."[24]

---

[24] Oliver of Paderborn 53–4.

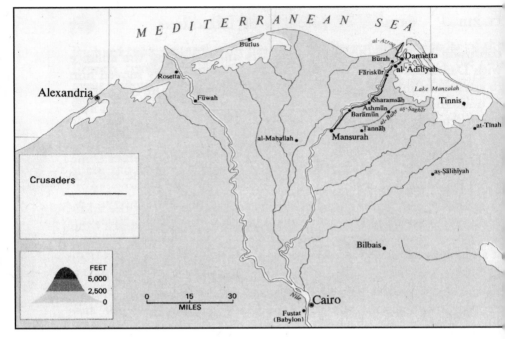

Map 7.2 The Fifth Crusade, 1218–1221.

The response in the Muslim world to the loss of Damietta was total panic. "All the rest of Egypt and Syria was on the point of collapse," a Muslim chronicler wrote, "and everyone was terrified of the invaders and went in anticipation of disaster night and day. The population of Egypt was even ready to evacuate the country for fear of the enemy."[25] Nevertheless, the Franks did not follow up their victory and instead remained in Damietta for the whole of 1220 and into the spring of 1221, dividing the wealth they found, which was considerable, arguing about what to do next and who should lead them.

In the course of the blockade and during their time in Damietta, the Franks received two offers of peace from al-Kamil, both with generous terms. The Muslims were willing to give up all of Saladin's conquests, including Jerusalem, keeping only the fortresses of Kerak and Shaubak (Montreal) in the Transjordan, since they protected the overland route connecting Damascus and Cairo. The Muslims even offered to return the True Cross, though they actually could not find it. The Franks were divided about what to do, and in the end, encouraged by the papal legate and convinced they would be able to defeat the Egyptians, they refused both offers.

---

[25] Ibn al-Athir, in Gabrieli 256.

C. The Disastrous End of the Fifth Crusade

By the summer of 1221 al-Malik had persuaded his brother in Damascus to come to his aid, and with the large Syrian army and his own, he fortified a camp at Mansurah, which protected Cairo. The Franks were certain they could defeat the Muslims again, and in late July they marched against Mansurah. The rest of the story is quickly told. The crusaders made the fatal mistake of camping between the Nile and one of its tributaries. When the Nile began to rise, al-Kamil opened the floodgates, and the crusading army was soon in danger of drowning. At the end of August 1221, the Franks gave up Damietta in return for peace and fled Egypt, and the Fifth Crusade came to its sorry and unnecessary conclusion.

As in the aftermath of the Second Crusade, there was a strong feeling in Europe that someone had to take the blame for the disaster in Egypt. The papal legate, Pelagius, who had encouraged the Franks to turn down the early peace offers, was blamed, as was Frederick, for his failure to show up. All during the Fifth Crusade, the Franks had clung to their conviction that Frederick II and his army would appear. In fact, Frederick sent German troops to Egypt in the late spring of 1221, but he himself did not come. In some fairness to Frederick, he had his own problems in Germany and Sicily to settle before he could safely leave. Nevertheless, he was severely criticized for his failure to aid the Franks. Pope Honorius came in for his share of blame, and he became increasingly angry with Frederick for his delay.

Frederick had been crowned Holy Roman Emperor in 1220 in a grand ceremony, during which he renewed his vow, made first in 1215, to go on a crusade. Although Frederick had promised that he would relinquish the throne of Sicily when he became emperor, Honorius allowed Frederick to keep it for his lifetime, on Frederick's assurance that in the next generation Sicily and Germany would be separated. The Pope was convinced that Frederick would fulfill his vow to leave for the Holy Land; in the spring of 1223, Frederick renewed his vow and promised to leave in June 1225.

D. Frederick II Claims the Throne of Jerusalem and Goes East ... at Last

Frederick did not leave in 1225. Instead, he did something far more in keeping with his own ambitions in the East; he married the young heiress to the Kingdom of Jerusalem, Isabella of Brienne, known also as Yolanda.

When King Aimery and his much-married wife, Isabella, had both died in 1205, the crown passed to Isabella's daughter Mary, who was a minor. The regent appointed for her was a French nobleman, John of Brienne, a sensible man and a good ruler. When Mary came of age, in 1210, she and John of Brienne married, though he was considerably older than she was, and they had a daughter, Isabella. The women in Mary's family all died untimely deaths, and Mary was no exception. She died in 1212, leaving her infant daughter heir to the throne. John of Brienne served as his daughter's regent.

John of Brienne's expectation, when he arranged Isabella's marriage, was that he would rule until his death, and that after he died, the crown would pass to his daughter and Frederick. The pope favored the marriage because he believed that it would encourage Frederick to fight for Jerusalem. The pope insisted that Frederick promise never to assume the kingship of Jerusalem himself, a promise that of course Frederick had no intention of keeping.

In late August 1225, the first marriage ceremony took place, although Isabella was in Acre, where it was performed, and her groom was in southern Italy. In November of the same year, when Isabella arrived in Italy, they were married again. Soon after the wedding Frederick sent his young bride to live in his harem, which he kept in Palermo. Poor Isabella gave birth to a son, Conrad, in 1228, and died a week later.

Meanwhile Honorius had extracted the promise that Frederick would leave in 1227. The emperor assembled his fleet and his army and prepared, at last, to sail from Brindisi in August of that year. However, southern Italy was struck by an outbreak of malaria, many of his men became ill, many died, and others left to avoid falling ill. No sooner had his own ship set sail than Frederick also became ill, and he returned home to recover.

During the summer of 1227 Honorius died and was succeeded by Gregory IX, a man far more intractable and implacable than his predecessor. He was so angered by Frederick's delays, and so unconvinced by Frederick's excuse, that he excommunicated the emperor at the end of September 1227. When Frederick sailed at the end of June 1228, he was excommunicated a second time for leading a crusade before the first ban of excommunication had been lifted.

By the time Frederick reached Acre, in September, after spending five weeks on Cyprus, he had already entered negotiations with the Egyptian Sultan al-Kamil for a treaty. Frederick did not have a large enough army to wage a full-scale war, nor did he have wholehearted support from the Franks, whom the pope had instructed not to have anything to do with plans pursued by an excommunicant. The sultan had his own internal problems; he was primarily concerned with reuniting under his command Saladin's empire, which was now divided. Both rulers were of a mind to make a peaceful arrangement, though neither was willing to lose face with his followers, so the negotiations were prolonged and delicate.

E. Frederick's Treaty with the Sultan

Frederick began by insisting that the favorable terms al-Kamil had offered the Franks when they were at Damietta be the basis for any new treaty; that is, that all Palestine save the fortresses in the Transjordan be returned. That proposal was too much for al-Kamil, but after much back and forth he and Frederick worked out a compromise. On February 18, 1229, the treaty, which would last for ten years, was signed at Jaffa. According to its terms, Jerusalem, Bethlehem, and Nazareth were returned to the Kingdom of Jerusalem, along with a strip of land from near Acre to Jaffa, giving the kingdom access to the sea. Much of the western Galilee was also returned.

Within Jerusalem, the Muslims retained the Temple Mount, including the al-Aqsa Mosque and the Dome of the Rock, and Muslims from all over were to have free access to their holy places. The Muslims who resided in the Holy City were permitted to remain, although many chose to leave, and few Christians came to resettle the city. Thus Jerusalem became neither a Christian city nor a Muslim one, but a peculiar mix of the two, sparsely settled, and unsatisfactory to everyone.

In addition, a sizable Jewish community was living in Jerusalem. After Saladin's conquest he had invited the Jews to return to the Holy City, and they came, apparently in large numbers: Jews from Ascalon, forced to flee along with everyone else when the city was destroyed; Jews from North Africa; and Jews from Europe.

Jewish pilgrimage had continued throughout the twelfth century, even when Jews were prohibited from living in Jerusalem. Coincidental with Saladin's victory, though not caused by it, a new immigration of European Jews to the Holy Land began, and it continued through the thirteenth century. To some extent Jews were motivated by the understanding that no one, Christian or Muslim, could seemingly hold the Holy City for long, and that it was time for them to return to the land that God had promised to Abraham and his descendants. Outbursts of Jewish persecution in Europe, which came later in the thirteenth century, also encouraged the growing Jewish migration.[26]

The Holy City was in a sorry state and defenseless. After Saladin's conquest, he had spent considerable time, money, and labor to rebuild the walls and fortifications that had been destroyed during the fighting. He was sufficiently concerned that the walls be well constructed that he came every day to oversee the work.

In 1219, when the Latin conquest in Egypt was going well, before the Franks foolishly lost Damietta, the sultan in Damascus had ordered Jerusalem's walls to be destroyed. He reasoned that if Jerusalem were to fall to the Latins again, it would be easy for the Muslims to recapture a defenseless city. The unfortunate souls living in Jerusalem had to watch their fortifications being torn down, presumably for the future good of the Muslims (and incidentally the Jews) living there. When al-Malik returned Jerusalem to the Franks, the

---

[26] See Joshua Prawer, *The Latin Kingdom of Jerusalem* (London: Weidenfeld and Nicolson, 1972) 243–46.

condition he imposed was that Frederick agree not to rebuild the walls. No one was happy with this arrangement.

The angry letter written by the Patriarch of Jerusalem immediately after the treaty was signed encapsulates the Church's response, and that of most Europeans, to both the treaty and Frederick. "It should be fully known how astonishing, nay rather, deplorable, the conduct of the emperor [Frederick] has been in the eastern lands from beginning to end, to the great detriment of the cause of Jesus Christ.... After long and mysterious conferences...he suddenly announced one day that he had made peace with the sultan.... Moreover, you [Pope Gregory IX] will be able to see clearly how great the malice was and how fraudulent certain articles of the truce which we have decided to send to you."[27]

The Muslims were equally upset. "The news swept swiftly throughout the Muslim world, which lamented the loss of Jerusalem and disapproved strongly of al-Malik al-Kamil's action as a most dishonorable deed."[28]

Frederick's ambition had been to win the Kingdom of Jerusalem for himself and add it to his empire in the West. He went so far as to organize his coronation as King of Jerusalem, but in effect he gave a coronation and hardly anyone came. The patriarch refused to crown him, so Frederick placed the crown on his own head. His action angered virtually everyone, and Jerusalem was placed under an interdict by the pope for acquiescing, to the extent that anyone did, to the coronation. Finally recognizing that he was personally disliked, distrusted, and almost totally rebuffed by the native population, Frederick prepared in secret for his departure. He was pelted with garbage by an angry mob when he set sail from Acre on May 1, 1229.

Among the Christians and their chroniclers, some understood how remarkable it was that Frederick could have restored Jerusalem without shedding a drop of Christian blood. They were few and far between, however, and the pope was surely not among them, nor were the military orders, the patriarch of Jerusalem, or even the majority of crusaders. Without the warfare that was for the Church the *sine qua non* of a crusade, Gregory IX had great difficulty swallowing the treaty, and he castigated Frederick for dealing with the Muslims as if they were friends. Frederick was exceptional in his understanding that Jerusalem was a holy city for Muslims as well as for Christians, and for that he was forever tainted in the eyes of the papacy.

The Papal Wars against the Hohenstaufens Begin

At the same time, before Frederick returned from the Holy Land, Gregory IX had gone to war against him by invading Sicily. Gregory IX and his successors

---

27 "Letter of Patriarch Gerold," in Allen and Amt 291–92.
28 Ibn Wasil, in Gabrieli 269.

were blinded by their hatred of Frederick and their fear of being trapped in the Hohenstaufen Empire, particularly in Italy. That possibility was to the papacy simply untenable.

The imperial title, from Charlemagne onward, had, at least in theory, included the Lombard towns and cities in the north. These were fiercely independent towns, and each new emperor had to fight to establish his power over them. If Frederick succeeded in controlling the Lombard towns, as he was determined to do, and kept Sicily and southern Italy, the largest part of Italy would be his. So while Frederick was in the East, Gregory IX attacked. The pope's appeal to the European rulers for help met with little response, and his own armies, drawn mainly from the papal states, were no match for Frederick's seasoned troops when the emperor returned. The pope had little choice; he reluctantly ratified Frederick's treaty and released the emperor from the ban of excommunication. The two made peace in 1230.

The attempt to take Sicily was the formal beginning of the war between the papacy and the Hohenstaufens that lasted until the last Hohenstaufen was killed in 1268.

Not surprisingly, it was Pope Innocent III who had planted the seed for these political crusades when he called a crusade in 1199 against Markward of Anweiler, the lord high steward under Frederick II's father, Henry VI, King of Germany and of Sicily. Markward had tried to keep land in central Italy after Henry VI died. When he was forced off the mainland by Innocent, Markward went to Sicily, where he attacked the men Innocent had appointed to serve as Frederick's regents. The crusade Innocent called was not enthusiastically supported by anyone in Europe, and it accomplished little. The situation was saved for the papacy when Markward died in 1202.

The example was not lost on the popes who succeeded Innocent. In the thirteenth century, five popes called crusades against the Hohenstaufens.

Despite all his promises, Frederick had no intention of separating Sicily from northern Italy and Germany, nor did his successors. In 1237 Frederick advanced on northern Italy and won a complete victory over the Lombard towns. He then went south to Rome itself, where he tried to persuade the Romans to fight alongside him against the pope. At that juncture, in 1239, Gregory IX excommunicated Frederick again, and a new stage in the pope's political activity began.

In 1239, or perhaps early in 1240, Gregory sent legates into northern Italy and Germany to preach a crusade against Frederick and the Hohenstaufen family. This political crusade, as it is known, and the others that followed, carried all the privileges given to crusaders fighting in the Holy Land. In the course of the struggle, two popes went so far as to encourage crusaders who had vowed to go to the Holy Land to fight the Hohenstaufen instead, retaining all the usual crusading privileges. Thus it came about that the objective and the nature of crusading changed in the late twelfth and the thirteenth centuries.

Gregory IX died in the late summer of 1241 and after a long interval was succeeded by Pope Innocent IV (1243–1254), who was even more intransigent than his predecessor. Innocent IV called a council at Lyons in 1245, at which he removed Frederick from his kingships in Germany and Sicily and renewed the crusade against him. Frederick retaliated on the battlefield, naturally enough, and also in letters to the pope, resisting his deposition.

His cleverest letter was sent to the rulers throughout Europe. "You and all kings of particular regions have everything to fear from the effrontery of such a prince of priests when he sets out to depose us who have been divinely honored by the imperial diadem…. In truth we are not the first nor shall we be the last that this abuse of priestly power harasses…. The copious revenues with which they are enriched by the impoverishment of many kingdoms, as you yourself know, make them rage like madmen."[29] Frederick touched on a nerve when he wrote about the revenues because, although the kings were not directly taxed to pay for the crusade, the church all over Europe was being heavily taxed and funds were being drained out of the kingdoms.

Frederick died in 1250 and was succeeded by his son, Conrad IV of Germany. Frederick's death did not change papal policy, which by the mid-century was whole-heartedly dedicated to eradicating the entire Hohenstaufen family. To accomplish this, the popes needed allies to fight alongside the Italian armies the pope could muster. They offered the Sicilian crown first to the English royal family, then to the French, then to the English again, until finally Pope Clement IV, who was French, negotiated a firm commitment from King Louis IX of France, which brought the king's brother Charles of Anjou, and the French, into Sicily. According to their agreement, Charles was given Sicily and all the lands from Naples south, to be held as a papal fief.

In January 1266, Charles reached Rome, and by August of the same year, he had defeated the last Hohenstaufen forces in Sicily. The kingdom was his. Charles's final opponent was Frederick II's grandson, Conradin, who had unexpectedly appeared to rally the Hohenstaufen forces. In the course of his conquest Charles captured Conradin, whom he had executed in Naples in the fall of 1268. Conradin was sixteen years old.

Although the Angevins, as the Anjou rulers were called, eventually lost Sicily to the Spanish in 1282, they ruled the Kingdom of Naples until 1442, when the Spanish ruler of Sicily, Alfonso V of Aragon, took it from the French. Under the Angevins, the Kingdom of Naples was a beautiful, wealthy, highly

---

[29] Frederick II, "Letter to the Kings of Christendom (1246)," in Tierney 145.

regarded city, frequented by poets and pirates and loved by the rich. The close relationship between the papacy and the French was a boon for both powers.

Germany, on the other hand, suffered greatly during and after the wars. The country had been on its way to being united under a strong monarchy during the reign of Frederick Barbarossa, but the opportunities for the leading nobility to rise up against the embattled monarchy in the thirteenth century were irresistible. Germany became fragmented, weakened at its center, and it did not regain its former prominence until many centuries later.

The popes found ways to justify their crusades against the Hohenstaufens. Nevertheless, they came under increasing criticism from within the church, and from rulers in Europe, for diverting funds and manpower away from the Holy Land and for fighting Christians on Christian soil.[30] The use of the crusade to fight Christians whose only sin was that they threatened papal power caused a far-reaching change in the crusading ideal.

---

[30] To the extent that there was, or may have been, widespread popular reaction against these and other crusades that were not associated with the Holy Land will be discussed in the following chapter.

CHAPTER EIGHT

Storm Clouds Gather over the East

During the decade following the truce that Frederick made in 1229, the Latin Kingdom and its Muslim neighbors enjoyed a period of reasonably peaceful co-existence.

Within the Muslim world the driving force of the *jihad*, so integral to Saladin's life and career, began to subside in the generation following his death. The prime objective of Saladin's nephew, the Egyptian Sultan al-Kamil, was to wrest Damascus and Syria from his brother, al-Mu'azzam, and reunite Saladin's empire under his control. For the time being that goal took precedence over fighting the Latins. Although the Muslims had been able to regain Damietta in September 1221, the long siege had cost them dearly, and they were fearful that renewed warfare would bring new crusading armies.

Al-Kamil also hoped to restore the flow of commerce that wound its way in Muslim caravans from India, China, and Syria, or that came on Egyptian ships to the Latin seaports on the Mediterranean and then was carried on Italian ships for export to Europe. This lucrative trade was valuable to both the Muslims and the Franks. A list of the duties imposed by the Franks on the many items that went through their ports gives an excellent idea of how diverse this trade was. Spices certainly, and silk, cotton, wool, sugar, salt and salt fish, ivory, oil, olives, saddles, camphor, incense, wine. The list is long and minutely detailed. Even the duty on the twigs and leaves of lavender was carefully calculated.[1] It was therefore in the best interests of both sides to keep the peace.

---

[1] "Taxes of the Kingdom of Jerusalem (Assises de Jerusalem)," trans. R. P. Falkner, in *Translations and Reprints from the Original Sources of European History*, 1907, vol. 3, no. 2 (New York: AMS Press, 1971) 14ff.

The Never-Ending Struggles in the Latin Kingdom

When Emperor Frederick II abruptly sailed from Acre in May 1229, he left behind his representatives and an imperial army to enforce his rule over the Kingdom of Jerusalem. He had intended that the Latin Kingdom would become part of his empire, governed under the same laws that he enforced in his European possessions. Open warfare immediately began.

The emperor's strength came from his armies in the Holy Land, the Order of Teutonic Knights (of whom more below), and the Pisans. He also had the support of Tyre, the only city that had remained loyal to Frederick. Although Jerusalem was ruled, to the extent that it was ruled at all, by regents appointed by Frederick, or by minors, it was in an exceedingly poor condition, and the small Christian population was opposed to Frederick. Frederick never came east again. Nor did his son or grandson come to claim the title of King in Jerusalem. The battles challenging Frederick's rule were fought by his army and its leaders.

Ranged against the imperial forces were the Templars, the Hospitallers at first, all the religious leaders in the kingdom, and the large majority of barons who were prepared to fight to the bitter end to defend their independence and maintain their traditional rights and power. Their leader was John of Ibelin, known as "the Old Man of Beirut" because of his lordship over that important city. He came from a family that was firmly established in the Holy Land and well respected. John of Beirut had a splendid military career, spent in recent years opposing Frederick's claims to Cyprus. An excellent and popular choice, he was the only leader who was capable of inspiring unified action against Frederick's armies.

Until Tyre finally fell to the barons in 1243, and imperial rule was ended in Jerusalem in the same year, constant civil war wrecked the kingdom, which was once again at the mercy of its ruinous internal struggles. The struggles continued despite the arrival of a new crusade.

The Barons' Crusade

The treaty Frederick had signed was due to expire in 1239, and as early as the fall of 1234, Pope Gregory IX began to call for a new crusade to the Holy Land. The largest response came from the nobility in northern France, led by Count Thibaut of Champagne and Duke Hugh of Burgundy. In England, the leader was Richard, earl of Cornwall. The short crusade, which lasted from 1239 to 1241, is known as the Barons' Crusade. Since the main difficulty was raising funds, Gregory taxed every person in Christendom a small sum, to be given to the local diocese on a weekly basis. That money, in turn, would be given to support the barons. There was apparently great confusion about the way the money was given out, but confusion was the hallmark of the Barons' Crusade.

The French host going to the Holy Land sailed from Marseilles in August 1239. Their first care, when they arrived in the Holy Land, was to refortify Jerusalem.

The more basic problem, however, was that there was no agreement between the local nobility and the European barons or among the factions within the crusader camp, about whether to proceed against Cairo or against Damascus. Their one piece of good fortune was that the sultans were fighting each other. Al-Kamil had captured Damascus in 1238 and died soon after. His son and his nephew, having apparently learned nothing from the civil wars in the previous generation, were at war again. A good case could be made for a Latin attack against one of them.

Instead of being able to decide, the crusaders reached an odd compromise and went to Ascalon to refortify that city's walls, planning ultimately to attack Damascus. The Egyptians were not sitting idle, however, and they met a part of the French army in two battles, the first a victory for the French, the second a total Egyptian success. The Egyptians followed their victory by attacking the small garrison defending the Tower of David in Jerusalem, and they took the Holy City again.

Thibaut was mainly busy trying to arrange a truce with either Damascus or Cairo. He succeeded first in a preliminary truce with Damascus, and when that met with disapproval from the local barons, he negotiated a truce with Egypt. He then went home. Richard of Cornwall's ships passed Thibaut's navy as Richard made his way to Acre. The two leaders never met. Richard had the good luck to conclude the truce with Egypt, thereby gaining credit for the work Thibaut had actually accomplished.

The strangest part of this whole crusade is that, even though there was a minimum of fighting, when it was over, the crusaders came home with a truce that restored Jerusalem, Bethlehem, Ascalon, Sidon, the whole of the Galilee, and a road from Ramla to the sea to the Franks. This enlarged territory came to them as the direct consequence of the hostility between Egypt and Damascus and had little to do with any military effort on the crusaders' part. Nonetheless, it was a felicitous, unexpected outcome. The Latin Kingdom of Jerusalem reached the fullest extent of its territory in 1241. It would not last for long.

The ongoing civil war in the kingdom was exacerbated by hostilities that had broken out in Acre. The city was overcrowded, filled with refugees, housing was expensive and at a premium, local residents were forced to give rooms to strangers, tempers were short, and the situation was incendiary. The Italian colonists were battling one another in the streets. Their commercial rivalry added to their bitter quarrel over whether to support the imperial claims. "Those men from the noble cities of Genoa, Pisa, and Venice," the Bishop of Acre complained, "would be very terrible to the Saracens if they would cease from their jealousy and avarice, and would not continually fight and quarrel with one another."[2]

Additional serious problems were caused by the military orders. Soon after their formal recognition as fighting orders, the Templars and Hospitallers had begun to change. Gradually, as their discipline, their expertise in warfare, and their dependability in the field were recognized and their wealth increased, their influence in the Latin Kingdom grew. With each threat to the kingdom, new fortifications and castles were built, in many cases turned over to the military orders to garrison and defend. The Hospitallers controlled the fortifications that ringed Ascalon; the Templars controlled Gaza.

In the late twelfth century more castles and fortifications were added along the borders and in key areas to protect the kingdom from Nur al-Din and Saladin. Safed, Krak des Chevaliers, Kerak, and many others were built, in some cases rebuilt, by the military orders, or were given to them by a king to garrison. Their fortifications dominated the Latin East along the pilgrim routes and in the north, where Templar castles protected Antioch and Tripoli.

By the end of the twelfth century, both orders had acquired huge properties all over Europe. Their well-organized and well-managed holdings were the principal source of the manpower, funds, and supplies needed in the East. Their wealth, and the kingdom's reliance on their armies and defenses, made the orders indispensable and independent. Their position was exceptional — not under the king's jurisdiction and yet a vital part of his kingdom.

The Order of Teutonic Knights

A new military order, the Teutonic Knights of the Hospital of St. Mary, was formed in 1198 and approved by Pope Innocent III. The order was the outgrowth of a small hospital, St. Mary of the Germans, founded in 1127 by a German family in Jerusalem to care for Germans who spoke and understood only their own language. When Jerusalem was captured by Saladin and the Germans were forced to leave, they moved to Acre, where they set up their hospital in a tent outside the city walls and cared for the wounded during the siege of Acre. After Acre surrendered to the Latins, they moved their headquarters into the city.

At Acre, they were joined by some German soldiers in the Holy Land, and together they created the Teutonic Order. Their rule was modeled on the Templar Rule, although their obligations to care for the sick were similar to those of the Hospitallers. They wore the white robe of the Templars, with a black cross on the front.

---

[2] Jacques de Vitry 66–67.

The Teutonic Knights won the special favor of Frederick II when he was in the Holy Land, and he endowed them with lands in southern Italy, Sicily, and Germany to support their work. They were also given funds by wealthy German nobles to establish their houses in the Holy Land. Their major fortification was the castle called Montfort, located northeast of Acre.

In the Holy Land, the Order of the Teutonic Knights was always considerably smaller than the Templars and Hospitallers and never had resources comparable to the other two orders. Although they sided with Frederick II in his wars against the barons, their impact in the East was considerably less than their impact on the Northern Crusades and German expansion eastward, as we will see.

The rivalry between the Templars and Hospitallers in the thirteenth century was in part owing to jealousy, in part to their different and strongly held views on the kingship and foreign policy. The Templars were against Frederick II, hated the treaty he had made, and favored going to war against Damascus. The Hospitallers, although initially opposed to Frederick, later supported him and favored fighting Egypt, not Damascus. Both orders were prepared to make separate treaties with one or the other Muslim sultan.

Fighting broke out in 1241, when the Templars stormed the Hospitaller house in Acre because they suspected that the Hospitallers had entered into a secret agreement to turn Acre over to Frederick's supporters. Although the barons and Templars defeated the Hospitallers, the fighting did not cease until, in 1243, the barons finally succeeded in capturing Tyre from the imperial armies and the last vestiges of imperial rule were removed from Jerusalem.

The Mongols Rise to Power

By then a new power was looming over the East, and the civil wars in the Muslim world and in the Latin Kingdom soon paled in the huge shadow cast by the Mongols, also called Tartars by the Europeans. A new period of armed conflicts, with new adversaries, began, and the upheavals that followed transformed the map of the East and of eastern Europe.

The astounding Mongol advance had begun in 1206, with the accession to power of Genghis Khan, the invincible Great Khan of the Mongols. He united under his command a huge conglomeration of Mongol and Turkic nomadic tribes from the steppes near the Altai Mountains and began the expansion of the Mongol Empire by attacking and subjugating northern China.

The Mongols were fierce, disciplined fighters; they moved swiftly on their fast horses and were utterly fearless. Every male was a trained warrior, and any warrior who tried to run away in battle was summarily executed. The way they traveled was something of a marvel to their enemies. The Mongols could ride for a week or more without stopping to eat or to rest. They were also clever. Their attacks were carefully planned, and they developed a reputation for deceitfulness, which in practice meant that they were more clever than their enemies. They would pretend to retreat and then return to slaughter their enemies, and they often appeared with women and children on horseback lined up beside the warriors, to make it seem as if they had a larger army than they actually did. It was a kind of cleverness that was not appreciated by the vanquished.

From China, the Mongols turned west, crossed Central Asia, and conquered south Russia. In the years following Genghis Khan's death in 1227, his sons and grandsons continued the expansion into eastern Europe and Syria-Palestine. In most places where the Mongols appeared, they devastated the land and the cities and in many places killed the inhabitants without mercy. Although contemporary historians are finding some evidence that the Mongols' destructiveness did not fall equally on all the areas of their vast conquests, it is undeniably true that "seen from the point of view of those who bore the brunt of them, [they] were undeniably catastrophic."[3]

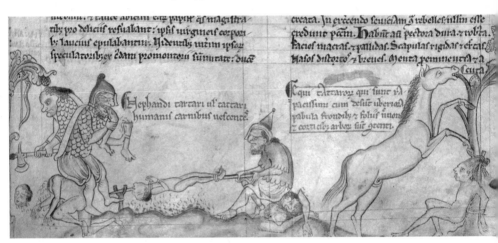

8.1 Depiction of the Mongols as cannibalistic savages. Illustration by Matthew Paris, from his *Chronica Majora* (ca. 1255).

Their rapid onslaught on Syria was so terrifying that, a Muslim chronicler wrote, "[for] some years, I continued averse from mentioning this event, deeming it so horrible that I shrank from recording it.... This thing involves the description of the greatest catastrophe and the most dire calamity... which befell all men generally, and the Muslims in particular.... For indeed

---

3   David Morgan, *The Mongols*, 2nd ed. (Malden, MA: Blackwell Publishing, 1986) 64.

history does not contain aught which approaches or comes nigh unto it." He then described in graphic detail the killing or enslavement of men and women, the total destruction of land and towns, stories "which the hearer can scarcely credit, as to the terror of [the Mongols] which God almighty cast into men's hearts."[4]

The only buffer between the Muslims and the Mongols was the Khwarismian Empire, which, in the early thirteenth century, literally stood in the way of the Mongol advance into Syria and Palestine. The Khwarismians were another of the nomadic tribes from central Asia, pushed out of the area by the disasters and fighting that with regularity afflicted the region. They had able commanders, a huge army, and a reputation for ferocity. By the end of the twelfth century, they had established a large empire, which extended to the borders of India and Anatolia and included Persia.

On the face of it the Khwarismians appeared to be a formidable obstacle to Mongol expansion. However, their empire was not built on a strong foundation, and the Shahs, as their rulers were titled, and their soldiers were hated by the people they subjugated. Piece by piece the Mongols conquered the Khwarismian Empire until, in 1230–1233, they captured its last strongholds in Persia. The defeated soldiers who were left alive became mercenaries. Sometime in the early 1240s, they sold their services to the Egyptian sultan, as-Salih, who was preparing to go to war to reclaim Damascus.

Since the Latins' survival in the region depended on having a strong ally, they were now faced with deciding which side to join. The Templars, the most forceful power in the kingdom, counseled an alliance with the sultan in Damascus. In return for the Frankish alliance in the coming civil war, the sultan ordered the Muslims to evacuate the Temple Mount, and the Templars were restored to their Jerusalem headquarters. The price the Templars paid was much too high. The alliance proved to be a fatal mistake.

The Latins Suffer the Loss of the Holy City

The final crisis for Jerusalem came in the early summer of 1244. The war between Cairo and Damascus resumed, and in June 1244, the Khwarismians began their rampage through Syria, into Palestine, to Tiberias and Nablus, and on July 11, they stormed into Jerusalem. Only the garrison in the Tower of David held out against them. In return for relinquishing the citadel, the garrison was offered a safe-conduct to leave the city. The garrison handed over the citadel on August 23, and the Jerusalemites decided that all the inhabitants should leave quietly and go to safety in Jaffa. After going a short distance, they

---

[4] Ibn al-Athir, in Allen and Amt 352–54.

turned to look at the Holy City and saw the Frankish standards raised on the city walls. Thinking that help had arrived and that it was safe to return, many started back, only to be trapped in an ambush.

The Master of the Hospitallers, who was present, described the ambush and the desecration of the holy places in Jerusalem that followed. He wrote that the enemy "slew and cut to pieces, according to a correct computation, about seven thousand men and women, and caused such a massacre that the blood of those of the faith, with sorrow I say it, ran down the sides of the mountain like water." When the enemy re-entered the Holy City, they slaughtered the nuns and everyone else who had taken refuge in the Church of the Holy Sepulchre, "perpetrating in His holy sanctuary such a crime as the eyes of men had never seen since the commencement of the world."[5]

For 673 years, from 1244 until 1917, Jerusalem remained a Muslim city. On December 11, 1917, the British General Sir Edmund Allenby, having accepted the Turkish surrender, entered the city to occupy it for the British. Out of respect for the Holy City the general dismounted outside the gates and walked, unarmed, at the head of his troops into Jerusalem.

As if the sack of Jerusalem had not been punishment enough, the most severe losses the Franks suffered, second only to those suffered in the Battle of Hattin, soon followed. At the Battle of La Forbie (or Herbiya) near Gaza, on October 17, the combined armies of the Franks and Damascenes were almost totally annihilated by the Khwarismians and Egyptians. Every able-bodied man, religious as well as secular, fought valiantly—even the Templars and Hospitallers rode together—but they were so outnumbered and outmaneuvered that the battle lasted only a few hours. The Master of the Templars was slain, as were most of the knights and foot soldiers. Some eight hundred prisoners, including the Master of the Hospitallers, were captured. Very few soldiers managed to escape; of the military orders only thirty-three Templars, twenty-six Hospitallers, and three Teutonic Knights survived. The conservative estimate for the total losses incurred is five thousand.

The manpower shortage was so acute after La Forbie that the only thing that saved the Latins for a time was the resumption of warfare between the Egyptians and Damascenes. The Egyptians had attempted to besiege Ascalon but, to everyone's surprise, the fortifications held, and the Egyptians had to wait for naval reinforcements. So the Latins had a brief respite.

The Mongols Advance into Europe

During those same years, Europe was suffering the full force of the Mongol invasions. After sweeping through Russia, the Mongols advanced into eastern

---

5   The Master of the Hospitalers [sic], "Letter to Lord de Melaye, 1244," in Munro, vol. 1, no. 4, 33.

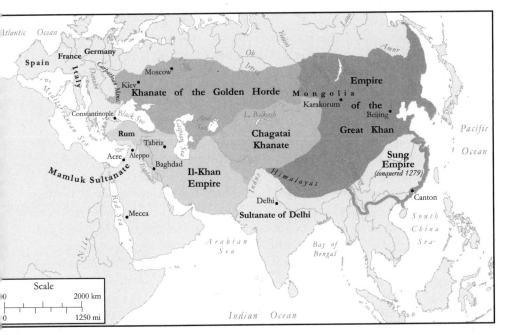

Map 8.1 The Mongol Empire, ca. 1260–1350.

Europe, and in 1240 and 1241 they overwhelmed Poland and Hungary. Hungary took the main brunt of the invasion; Hungarian lands were devastated repeatedly, and the country even endured a Mongol occupation for a time. The threat of a Mongol invasion into Germany and even farther west became a grave concern for Europeans, despite the fact that they did little to prevent it. In 1242 the Mongols returned to Mongolia for reasons that had to do with their own internal history, but it was not unrealistic to fear that the Mongols would return and that they were planning a massive attack on Europe as part of a plan to conquer the world.

King Bela IV of Hungary had appealed to the European kings for help, and although some promises were made that encouraged him to think he might actually receive aid, none was forthcoming. Finally, believing that a second wave of Mongols was imminent, Bela sent an impassioned plea to Pope Innocent IV in 1250 begging for help, since "Most of the kingdom of Hungary has been reduced to a desert by the scourge of the Tartars."

But the ruin of Bela's country was not the principal reason for the letter, or so he wrote. "It is rather against the whole of Christendom that their forces are unified, and, insofar as it is deemed certain by several trustworthy people, they have decided to send their countless troops against the whole of Europe soon." He described all that he had done to safeguard his kingdom and secure his borders, although he believed these efforts were hopeless unless he received substantial help. He also expressed amazement that the pope had sanctioned a new crusade (to be led by King Louis IX of France) and even more amazement that the pope offered help to the Latin Empire of Constantinople, "which if they [the lands in the East] were lost—God forbid!— would not harm the inhabitants of Europe as much as if our kingdom alone passed into the possession of the Tartars."[6]

The pope's response was to send an embassy to the Mongol court explaining why the Mongols should convert to Roman Christianity and cease their wars. The papal attitude toward the Mongols was ambivalent, and for decades it wavered between trying to find some accommodation with them, perhaps even an alliance against the Muslims, and planning a crusade to eliminate them.

Innocent IV seemed to have expected to come to some understanding with the Mongols. He was aware that the Mongols, though predominantly pagan, were tolerant of other religions and had many Eastern Christians living among them. Many were Nestorians, members of a Christian sect that had been declared heretical in the fifth century and, refusing to recant, went east from their patriarchate in Baghdad, spreading their religion through Persia and finally into China. Thus Christianity in some form was not unknown to the Mongols, which may have given the pope some cause for hope.

According to the Mongol law of inheritance, the conquered lands were divided among the descendants of the ruling family, so there were separate administrative centers of Mongol power. The most important was the Mongol capital at Karakorum, in the heart of Mongolia, which traditionally went to the youngest son. Innocent IV sent three separate embassies to the Mongols; the most important and best-known mission was entrusted to a Franciscan friar named John of Plano Carpini, who had been St. Francis's disciple and friend. John and several companions went first to the Mongol court on the Volga. From there, with only one other Franciscan for company, he made the incredible trek across Asia to Karakorum.

Friar John left Europe in March of 1245 and arrived in Karakorum over a year later, in August 1246. His whole journey there and back took two years. No European before him had ever made the punishing trip. Because the friars had to cross the high Altai mountains and the Gobi desert, they suffered extreme cold and fierce heat, in addition to the hazards of finding their way in alien territory. Fortunately, they received some help along the way and survived to see a new khan enthroned in Karakorum in 1246.

---

[6] King Bela IV, "Letter to Pope Innocent IV," trans. Piroska Nagy, in *Reading the Middle Ages*, ed. Barbara Rosenwein (Peterborough, ON: Broadview Press, 2006) 419–21.

Friar John carried two papal letters for the khan. In the first, Innocent IV explained why the Mongols should convert to Roman Christianity and expressed his hope that the khan would treat his ambassadors kindly and give them a safe-conduct for their return. In the second letter, the pope described in detail the horrors the Mongols had perpetrated and begged them to desist from further warfare: "Make fully known to us through these same friars what moved you to destroy other nations and what your intentions are for the future."[7] In both letters the pope made a plea for peace.

The khan's reply, which the friars carried back, was quite insolent. In essence he said throughout what he summarized at the end: "Thou thyself, at the head of all the princes, come at once to serve and wait upon us! At that time I shall recognize your submission. If you do not observe God's command [the Mongol God], and if you ignore my command, I shall know you as my enemy."[8]

The Mongols were not moved by the pope's entreaties. They were not of a mind to cease their attacks or to accept the Roman Church. It was more likely that they would convert to Nestorianism, if indeed they converted at all. Nonetheless, although the embassy was a failure, it was not the last attempt the Europeans made to come to an agreement with the Mongols.

King Louis IX's First Crusade

While John of Plano Carpini was traveling to and from Mongolia, a new crusade was being organized in Europe. King Louis IX of France took the cross in 1244, probably before he knew of Jerusalem's fate and the disaster at La Forbie. Whether he had heard the news, the immediate cause of his taking the vow was his recovery from a near-fatal illness and the promise he made to God that, if he lived, he would undertake a crusade to free Jerusalem. King Louis IX was the last great crusader to go East, and the crusades he organized and funded were the last great crusades.

A modern historian has argued that Louis's first crusade was in some measure his rebellion against his mother, Blanche of Castile, who had been regent since 1226, when her husband, King Louis VIII, died.[9] At the time of his father's death, Louis was twelve years old. Blanche was a strong-willed woman, extremely capable, and successful in suppressing many of the rebellious barons in France. She wielded great influence over her son, who was thirty in 1244 and, if Jordan's assumption is correct, eager to be free of his mother's control. She even interfered with Louis's marriage, doing everything

---

7   Innocent IV, "Second Letter to Guyuk Khan, 1245," in Allen and Amt 392.
8   Guyak Khan, "Letter to Innocent IV, 1246," in Allen and Amt 393.
9   William C. Jordan, *Louis IX and the Challenge of the Crusade* (Princeton, NJ: Princeton UP, 1979).

8.2. Blanche of Castile instructing Louis IX.

she could to keep the king and his wife apart. Although Blanche, along with the leading prelates and several barons, opposed the crusade and wanted the king to remain home to tend to his country, she helped Louis in his preparations and did as he wished while he was gone.

Louis IX was perfectly suited to his role as leader, organizer, and financier of the largest crusade ever to leave Europe. His kingly qualities complemented the piety for which he was sainted, and together they assured his steadfast devotion to his crusades once he had committed himself to restoring Jerusalem.

No crusade was better planned or provisioned. Four years elapsed from the time Louis took the vow until his armies left France in 1248. During those years he raised huge sums to build ships, to recruit and support knights and foot soldiers, and to purchase supplies and food. Much of the money was raised from a tax imposed by the pope on the clergy throughout Europe. They were now, for the first time, all to contribute a tenth of their incomes for the crusade. In France, the clergy raised the amount to a twentieth of their incomes. The king's lands, the towns throughout France, and the nobility all bore their share of the expenses. Louis had prudently arranged for enough provisions to be taken to Cyprus, or purchased and stored there, to feed his army for quite some time. His plan was to attack Egypt and from Egypt to go to Palestine.

Many of Louis's contemporaries, or near contemporaries, wrote about the king's crusades, among them, the most intimate description is the *Life of Saint Louis*, written in Old French by his companion on the crusade of 1247, Jean, Lord of Joinville. In the first part of his book Joinville described the character of the king, his love of God and justice, his bravery, the care he took of his people, and his humility. The second part of the book is devoted to the crusade.

In preparation for leaving, Louis had made a tour of his kingdom, and in late April 1248, he participated in the dedication of his beloved Sainte-Chapelle (see below). In May he went to the Cathedral of Notre-Dame, where he was given the traditional pilgrim's staff and scrip. He then walked barefoot, as befitted a pilgrim, to the Church of Saint-Denis, the church associated for centuries with the French monarchy, and was given the *oriflamme*, believed to be the banner Charlemagne carried into battle.

On August 25, 1248, the king sailed from Aigues-Mortes, a small fishing village on the Mediterranean coast, which Louis had had enlarged and fortified so that his ships would have ample room in the harbor and the townsmen could help outfit his ships. (See Color Plate 6.) Other crusaders sailed from Marseilles, some from other ports, and they all met on Cyprus.

The nobility who joined the crusade were the most important and wealthiest nobles in France; Louis's three brothers were among them, including Charles of Anjou, who would one day be King of Sicily. The young Queen of France, Margaret, was part of the king's entourage. Everything possible had been done to ensure the success of the crusade, and an overpowering sense of optimism attended its departure from Europe.

The king wintered on Cyprus until his armies had assembled. When they had all gathered, they set sail for Egypt in May 1249. "It was indeed a lovely sight to look at, for it seemed as if all the sea, as far as the eye could reach, was covered with the canvas of the ships' sails. The total number of vessels, both great and small, amounted to about eighteen hundred."[10]

A. Louis Captures Damietta

The crusaders made their landing on the banks of the Nile across from Damietta and immediately attacked the Muslims stationed there. The approach of Louis

---

[10] Jean de Joinville, "Life of Saint Louis," trans. M. R. B. Shaw, in *Chronicles of the Crusades* (London: Penguin Books, 1963) 201.

and his armies was so terrifying to the inhabitants of Damietta that they sent pigeons carrying urgent messages to the Egyptian sultan to come to their aid. The sultan did not reply because he was seriously ill, but the inhabitants thought they had been deserted, and they fled. "They abandoned the city," a Muslim historian wrote, "without a living soul in it, man, woman, or child. They all left under cover of night, accompanied by the troops.... The behavior of the people, of Fakhr ad-Din [the emir in charge] and of the troops was shameful."[11] The Franks occupied Damietta without striking a blow. Even the Greek fire that the Muslims had hurled at the Franks as they fled was blown back to Damietta by the wind. For the Muslims "it was a disaster without precedent."[12]

Instead of immediately following up their victory, the French remained in Damietta for the summer. The king and his barons spent precious time dividing up the booty they found, and the barons, probably out of boredom, "took to giving great banquets at which an excessive amount of food was consumed. As for the main mass of the troops, they took to consorting with prostitutes."[13] The Muslims harassed the men camped outside Damietta to guard the city. The king wanted to wait for his brother Alphonse, Count of Poitiers, to arrive with his army before deciding on his next move. It was an unfortunate delay.

The king had the choice of attacking either Alexandria or Cairo. The barons all favored Alexandria, largely because of its good harbor and the ease of getting supplies, but another of the king's brothers, Robert of Artois, made a strong case for going to Cairo. "If you wished to kill the serpent," he said, "you must first of all crush its head."[14] So the crusaders took the route that had been followed by the unfortunate Fifth Crusade to Mansurah on the Nile, which blocked their way to Cairo. Although the crusaders won some battles, in the end they lost the war. They fought heroically for months, but by the end of March, they had been brought to their knees by the superior numbers in the sultan's army and the difficulties of crossing the Nile River.

B. The Retreat from Damietta: The Failure of Louis's Crusade

The soldiers were suffering from a disease that afflicted many parts of the body, even their gums, and they were in terrible pain. The king also suffered from what Joinville termed the "army disease."[15] He endured prolonged bouts of dysentery and was in such agony that he often fainted because of it. The weakened, hungry, and depleted crusader army finally tried to retreat to

---

[11] Ibn Wasil, in Gabrieli 285.

[12] Ibn Wasil, in Gabrieli 286.

[13] Joinville 207.

[14] Joinville 210.

[15] Joinville 164. The disease was most likely scurvy. Many captives taken by the Egyptians died of it; according to Oliver of Paderborn the disease had also afflicted crusaders at the first siege of Damietta (32–33).

Damietta, but it was too late. The remnants of the crusading armies were captured and along with them King Louis, who surrendered to the sultan.

Queen Margaret, in the last months of a pregnancy, had been left behind in Damietta. She was scared to death. She was so sure that she saw Saracens enter her tent at night that she asked an aged knight to sleep on the floor beside her and made him promise to cut off her head if the Saracens should try to capture her. She gave birth to a son, Jean (called Tristram because of the sadness he was born into) in May 1250, while Louis was in captivity, and had to bribe the Genoese and Pisans with large sums of money and food not to leave her and the baby stranded in Damietta. They finally took her and the baby to Acre, where she waited for the king to be released.

The Saracens held only the nobility, the knights, and of course the king—the valuable prisoners who would presumably be ransomed. They killed all the sick and weak among the prisoners and routinely threatened the prisoners, even the king, with cruel tortures and death.

C. The Shepherds' Crusade

When the news of the king's captivity reached France, it provoked a spontaneous, emotional religious movement of shepherds and peasants, led by a preacher known as the Master of Hungary. This preacher, or "imposter," as the chronicler Matthew Paris called him, traveled through France claiming that "he had received orders from St. Mary . . . to assemble the shepherds and keepers of other animals, to whom, as he stated, was granted by heaven the power . . . to rescue the Holy land." He was wildly popular, and the shepherds abandoned their work and their homes to follow him. Matthew of Paris estimated that their number reached one hundred thousand, swelled by "thieves, exiles, [and] excommunicated persons" who joined the shepherds. They quickly became a frenzied band and nearly uncontrollable. At Orleans, violence broke out and many people were killed or injured; the same happened in Bourges and wherever they went, even Paris.

They were finally stopped outside Bordeaux by Simon de Montfort, Earl of Leicester, who threatened to send his army after them. Some of them "accepted the penance enjoined on them and reassuming the sign of the cross . . . duly proceeded on their pilgrimage." Most simply disappeared. The whole episode, known as the Shepherds' Crusade, had been horrifying and frightening. "Never since the times of Mahomet [sic], had such a fearful pestilence crept into the Church of Christ."[16]

---

[16] Matthew Paris, *English History*, trans. Rev. J. A. Giles, vol. 2 (London: Henry G. Bohn, 1853) 451–58.

SACRED VIOLENCE

D. Louis IX Surrenders Damietta and Withdraws to Acre

After long negotiations, the sultan's representatives and the king agreed that Damietta would be surrendered and the captives freed for the payment of an enormous sum of money, half before and half after the captives were released. The king and nobles were to be released on the same day that Damietta was restored to the Egyptians and the ransom was paid. When the ransom money was counted, it turned out that the French had fallen short, and the king requested the difference from the Master of the Templars, since it was well known that the Templars had the funds. The master refused, saying that the Templar rules would not permit him to release the money. In the end he allowed the king's men to take it from him, thus neatly absolving himself from any responsibility.

The sultan promised to care for the sick left behind in Damietta and to keep the salt pork, the armor and crossbows, and the machinery that had been stored in the city until the Franks could retrieve it. Instead the sultan killed all the sick in Damietta and he destroyed the salt pork and hacked to pieces everything else belonging to the Franks. When that was done, he set the whole on fire—a fire so terrible that it burned for three days.[17]

The king was ill and had neither clothes nor a bed on board his galley for the voyage to Acre. For six days he slept on mattresses and wore an outfit given him by the sultan. Joinville had less to wear, arriving in Acre in a short tunic made from a bed covering. Finally, on or about May 13, 1250, the king and his companions reached Acre, where Louis was welcomed by a great crowd who had come to the harbor to meet him.

The Queen Mother, Blanche, had written to the king imploring him to return to France, since the war between France and England was continuing and there was urgent need of his presence. His barons also begged him to return home, but Louis decided to remain in Acre.

During the nearly four years that Louis stayed in the Holy Land, he restored the defenses of Acre, Jaffa, Caesarea, and Sidon and was able to control the hostilities among the barons. He was instrumental in restoring calm and security to Antioch by removing a heartily disliked regent, Lucienne, the widow of Bohemund V. Lucienne's son was a little shy of the legal age to rule, but Louis, with the pope's blessing, elevated him to the principality and persuaded the young Bohemund VI to marry the Armenian king's daughter. The marriage cemented the relationship between Antioch and Armenia, and the Armenian king promised to aid Antioch when help was needed.

---

[17] Joinville 256.

Joinville included in his book a colorful report of an embassy sent to Louis by the leader of the Assassins, who was demanding tribute from the king. Joinville described the two well-dressed men who sat behind the emir, one who held three knives that would be presented to the king as an act of defiance if the emir's request was denied; the other with a roll of linen "which he was to present to the king as a winding-sheet for his burial"[18] if the king refused the demands. Since the Assassins were afraid of the military orders — the Templars and Hospitallers had both been receiving tribute from the Assassins to keep them from going to war — Louis used this as his leverage in bargaining with the Assassins. The Assassins' leader and Louis eventually exchanged elaborate gifts as tokens of their friendship, and the incident was closed.

While Louis was at Acre, a rumor that a Mongol prince had converted to Christianity encouraged the king to send a Dominican friar, William of Rubruck, as his envoy to Karakorum. Louis probably had some hope that an alliance against the Muslims might be arranged. In 1254 William of Rubruck reached the Mongol court. His account of Mongol life, which quite astonished him, is filled with wonderful anecdotes. He was surprised that they did not ever wash their clothes because they believed God would be angry with them; nor did they wash their bowls. Their marriage customs particularly appalled him. The Mongols believed that a widow should not remarry, since she would serve her husband when they met in the afterlife. The son, however, could and often did marry all his father's wives, except his own mother. "When therefore we found ourselves among these barbarians, it seemed to me ... that I had been transported into another world."[19]

In his report to King Louis, William wrote that the Mongols might well be receptive to a European proposal, but only if a proper ambassador was sent, meaning a person of high rank, not a humble friar. They would listen, William believed, to an appropriate ambassador, but "he must have a good interpreter — nay, several interpreters — abundant traveling funds, and so on."[20] He had discovered that the Mongols' interpreters mangled his words and had decided it was better not to preach to them at all than to have his meaning changed.

For Christians the real benefit derived from William's journey, and of the previous one undertaken by John of Plano Carpino and the subsequent ones to the Great Khan in the following decades, was to open the way for missionaries to cross central Asia and reach the Far East to spread Christianity. Trade followed religion, and the impulse for profit led adventurous merchants to stake their

---

18 Joinville 277.
19 William of Rubruck, "The Journey to the Eastern Parts of the World," in Allen and Amt 395.
20 William of Rubruck, in Allen and Amt 396–97.

capital and their lives to follow in the missionaries' footsteps. Direct trade routes to China were opened—without intermediaries—and slowly but surely the geographical horizons of Europeans began to expand. But here we are getting ahead of the story.

E. The Legend of Prester John

Hovering in the background of the European–Mongol relationships, such as they were, was the strange legend of Prester John. The legend began with a story that the historian Otto of Freising reported, which he had heard in Rome, of a Nestorian Christian ruler somewhere in the heart of Asia who descended from the same race as the biblical Magi. After many victories in the East, this priest-king, known as Prester John, had planned to ride to the aid of Jerusalem, but he was held back because his army was unable to cross the Tigris River.[21]

The next step in the dissemination of the legend was a letter purportedly written by Prester John to the Byzantine Emperor in 1165.[22] Prester John described his country as a place beautiful beyond imaging, wealthy and peaceful, where all people lived in harmony, unlike Byzantium or Europe. He also wrote of his intention to aid the Latin Christians and visit the Church of the Holy Sepulchre.

The relevance for the crusades is that Europeans unreservedly believed that Prester John and his armies would come to help the recovery of Jerusalem and the Holy Land. They also believed that, as the letter indicates, he would defeat the Mongols. So he was seen as a great deliverer, a genuinely hoped-for deliverer. Marco Polo, in his famous book recording his travels late in the thirteenth century, wrote of a great battle between Genghis Khan, whom Marco Polo greatly admired, and the Prester; in his version the Prester was killed and his army defeated.

The legend took hold, and for centuries the story of this mythical figure impelled a handful of hardy Europeans to find the mythical kingdom in the East over which it was assumed Prester John and his descendants ruled. Its location was placed variously in Ethiopia, India, or China. The legend was so deeply rooted in the European consciousness that it was not until well into the sixteenth century that it was finally dislodged. Even now some historians are still struggling to separate the fiction from whatever fact may be hidden behind it, to find a reality behind the myth.

---

[21] Bishop Otto of Freising, "Chronicon," in Brundage 83.

[22] There is general agreement that the letter was written by a European who was attempting to describe a utopian society in contrast to the Latin world, where there was much internal conflict. For more detail, see Charles E. Nowell, "The Historical Prester John," *Speculum*, 28.3 (July 1953) 435–45.

Louis would have liked to prolong his time in the Holy Land, but in 1252 Queen Blanche died, problems with England and the barons in France had resurfaced, and the regency of Louis's brothers was not proving satisfactory. Louis had succeeded in making a truce with the sultan in Damascus, although his hope to restore Jerusalem by arranging a truce with Egypt came to nothing. Finally, when a truce had been declared between Damascus and Cairo, he knew that it was time to leave. He sailed from Acre shortly after Easter in 1254. The king's ships embarked on his birthday, and Joinville told him "that he might in future say that on that day he had been re-born, for certainly he had entered on a new life when he escaped from that perilous land."[23]

The failure of the Sixth Crusade was a bitter disappointment in Europe, all the more so because it had started with such high expectations. For the king it was a personal failure as well as a public humiliation. Although he had left one hundred knights and their foot soldiers and squires, at his own expense, to defend the Holy Land, that was scarcely enough to ward off his deep feelings of remorse. After he returned to France, he became a penitent and, as much as possible, given his royal responsibilities, led an ascetic life with "a disregard for personal vanities."[24] The Holy Land was never far from his thoughts.

While Louis was still in the East, a palace revolution occurred in Egypt that would have long-term consequences for the Muslim world and the crusader kingdom.

When Louis IX invaded Egypt in 1249, the Egyptian Sultan al-Malik was already ill, and by the time the French captured Damietta he was too weak to command his army or even to move without help. He died in late November 1249. In the final battle between Louis IX and the Egyptians, it was the Bahrite Mamluks, as they were known, who defeated the French and took Louis captive.

The Mamluk Revolt in Egypt

For centuries it had been the custom for Muslim rulers to use Mamluks, or slaves (the word Mamluk in Arabic means "owned"), as the major component of their armies. These slaves were predominantly Turks and a lesser number of Kurds, who came from north of the Black Sea. They were bought when young, converted to Islam, and trained to be a powerful fighting force of archers and cavalrymen. In Egypt, the Mamluks were quartered on an island in the Nile, hence their name Bahrite, which derives from the Arabic word meaning river. They learned the military arts and became devout Muslims. (See Color Plate 7.)

---

[23] Joinville 318.
[24] Joinville 331.

The Mamluks' overthrow of the Ayyubid sultanate in the decade following al-Malik's death was led by the talented, legendary Baybars. During his training Baybars had shown such unusual military gifts that he was appointed to the Sultan al-Malik's bodyguard. His reputation was made early in his career when he commanded the Egyptian army that defeated the Franks at La Forbie (in 1244).

Soon after the defeat of Louis IX's crusade, Baybars murdered al-Malik's son and heir. Ironically, it was al-Malik who had brought the greatest number of Mamluks into Egypt, and now the Mamluks had forcibly removed his family from the sultanate. Egypt went through a ten-year period of unrest and uncertainty over the sultanate. During that decade, the first, most pressing business that faced the Egyptians was to confront the Mongols and halt their relentless advance into Syria and Palestine.

Under Genghis Khan's grandson, Hulegu, the Mongols had wiped out the Assassin strongholds in northern Persia and killed the last of the Assassins in 1256; in early 1258, they captured Baghdad, murdered the last Abbasid caliph and his family, and ransacked the city. The sack of Baghdad was a tragedy, for the Muslims who were all slaughtered, and for the beautiful city that had for centuries been the heart of the Sunni Muslim world. The next year, Aleppo fell to Hulegu's troops, then Damascus surrendered, and the Mongols descended on the Palestinian coast and on the fortresses held by the Muslims.

A. The Battle of Ain Jalut

In September 1260, the Mamluk officer Qutuz, who had taken over the sultanate for a short time, led the Egyptian army to a stunning and startling victory against the Mongols at the battle of Ain Jalut, near Nablus. The fact that the largest part of the Mongol army had returned to Mongolia to deal with the succession to the throne and that only a rump army remained to fight at Ain Jalut did not lessen the importance of the Mamluk victory. Ain Jalut was an epic event. The Mamluks had demonstrated to the world that the Mongols might actually be stopped, and they came away covered in glory.

The battle was a great victory for Islam. In time the Mongols converted to Islam, despite their attempts later in the century to secure a relationship with the Latins in Europe, and despite Christian missionaries to the Mongols. Perhaps they believed after Ain Jalut that the God of the Muslims was the stronger God.

Ain Jalut was a catastrophic portent for the Latin Kingdom. It now became only a matter of time before the Mamluks attacked the remaining Frankish strongholds. It is hard to put aside the thought that if the Latins in Europe and the East had taken advantage of the opportunity — or had made the opportunity—to ally themselves with the Mongols, the story might have had a different ending.

Ain Jalut assured Egypt's future as the strongest power in the Muslim world. Immediately after the victory Baybars murdered Qutuz, became the new sultan, and ushered in a new era in Egyptian history. He ruled from 1260 until his death in 1277. Under the Mamluks, Egypt experienced a rebirth of Sunni Islam and became a strictly controlled, well-run, and wealthy state. The Mamluks did not believe in hereditary succession, so the sultans were chosen by a small circle of Mamluk leaders. It was a military state—and a remarkable one, ruled by the sultan and an efficient Mamluk elite. Beginning with Baybars, the Mamluks built schools, grand mosques and hospitals and encouraged and supported trade and industry. They created an impressive and beautiful architecture and art; the Mamluk period was, and remains, renowned as the greatest period of Islamic art. Although later, during the fourteenth and fifteenth centuries, Egypt suffered from the destructive policies of the rulers, the Mamluks endured until 1517, when the Ottoman Turks conquered Egypt and hanged the last Mamluk sultan.

Baybars was regarded by Muslims, and by himself, as Saladin's true successor, in his devotion to Sunni Islam, his intelligence, his thirst for power, his determination to reunite Saladin's empire, and his desire to rid the East of the last vestiges of the crusader state.

Troubles in the East Worsen

From the fall of Jerusalem in 1244 onward nothing went well for the Latins in the East. Everywhere the Latins looked they were in extraordinary difficulties. Yet the divisiveness and deep-seated animosities continued unabated within the kingdom.

A full-scale war had broken out in Acre between the Venetians and the Genoese in 1256, ostensibly over the ownership of some property belonging to the monastery of St. Sabas, hence called the War of St. Sabas. The conflict brought in fleets from the mother cities on the Italian mainland. The Italian quarters in Acre were fortified, the entire city was dragged into the war, and the residents were forced to take sides. Ultimately, the whole kingdom was involved: the Templars and Teutonic Knights on the Venetian side, the Hospitallers and the barons inevitably on the Genoese side. The war ended in 1258, when the Venetian navy destroyed or captured roughly half the Genoese fleet. The Genoese then abandoned their quarter in Acre (to the Venetians) and went to Tyre. The Genoese fury at their loss led them to play an important role in the last years of the Latin Empire in Constantinople.

The Final Days of the Latin Empire of Constantinople

Even before 1244, the Latin Empire of Constantinople was showing all the signs of its impending demise. Conditions in the city, as everyone knew, were wretched. The city had never recovered from the wanton destruction caused by the Latins when they conquered Constantinople in 1204. The looting, followed by the incredibly bad management of the Frankish rulers, had left Constantinople impoverished and suffering acute food and manpower shortages. Constantinople was beset by outside invaders, especially the exiled Greeks determined to oust the Franks. The Latin Empire was, quite simply, in total disarray during the last twenty-five years of its existence.

The last Latin emperor of Constantinople, Baldwin II, who came to the throne in 1228, spent most of his reign touring Europe, his crown in hand, trying to raise funds. Although the empire was spared for a time by the Mongol threat from Russia, which distracted their Greek enemies, it was kept propped up principally by the Venetian fleet and the funds given by King Louis IX of France and his regent-mother, Blanche of Castile. Louis in fact was the only European monarch who really tried to save the shaky empire.

Among the possessions Baldwin sold or mortgaged was the single most priceless relic in Constantinople, the Crown of Thorns, which he mortgaged to the Venetians. Since Baldwin could not redeem the crown when his payment came due, Louis IX, who was an avid collector of holy relics, purchased it and had it brought to Paris. Louis built the beautiful Sainte-Chapelle on the Île de la Cité, in the center of Paris, to house it, along with the relics of the True Cross, which he redeemed on Baldwin's behalf from the Templars. Louis IX left many valuable legacies, but had he left only one, Sainte-Chapelle would suffice as the perfect metaphor for the reign of this sainted king. The chapel is a jewel box, suffused with the reflected colors of the incredibly lovely and rich stained glass.

The relics were not the only investment King Louis made in his attempt to salvage the tottering Latin Empire for Baldwin; he and Blanche gave regular infusions of money, all to no avail. Baldwin tried to mortgage his own holdings in France, on the whole unsuccessfully, and he even took the extreme step of mortgaging his young son, Philip, to the Venetians. The papacy tried to divert crusaders who planned to go the Holy Land to aid Constantinople instead, but there was never sufficient help given to ward off the final, inevitable collapse of the empire.

Soon after the Latins had taken Constantinople, the Greeks living in Asia Minor and on the islands in the Aegean Sea had begun planning their return. In the years shortly before 1261, the exiled emperor, Michael VIII, made careful preparations to invade Constantinople. In order to succeed he enlisted the support of the Venetians' long-standing rival, the Genoese, who supplied the ships and men to help him. In return he promised the Genoese exclusive trading privileges in the Greek coastal cities and to give back everything that had once been theirs in Constantinople. He promised to give them the Venetian possessions as well and to close the Black Sea to all of Genoa's enemies, which meant, of course, the Venetians.

As it happened, the Venetian ships and the Frankish garrison were away from the city on a military expedition when, unbeknown even to Michael, who was not present, the leader of a small Greek contingent found a tiny, unlocked entrance into Constantinople. Once inside, he opened a gate, and on the morning of July 25, 1261, the Byzantine army was in the city. The Latins fled.

Baldwin II and many Venetians were rescued by Venetian ships that were still in the harbor, although many refugees died of starvation on board ship because there was not sufficient food for them.

In mid-August 1261, Michael VIII Palaeologus arrived in Constantinople, and he and his wife were crowned in Santa Sophia. The misbegotten Latin Empire had come to its sad end. Michael made an attempt a few years later to reconcile with the Roman Church for political reasons, but his own countrymen refused to accept it. Until the present day, although there have been sporadic attempts at reconciliation, the churches remain separate. The extent to which the Latin conquest so weakened Constantinople that it could not withstand the Ottoman Turks in the mid-fifteenth century is still debated today.

Baldwin spent the rest of his life trying to find support so that he could return to Constantinople — a hopeless, absurd gesture.

The Invincible Baybars

The decade of the 1260s was altogether terrible for the Latin East. Baybars wasted little time after defeating the Mongols, and he moved swiftly to exterminate the Latin settlements. He advanced into the Galilee in 1263; in 1265 he captured both Caesarea and Arsuf, and in 1266 he took the great Templar castle of Safed. Although Baybars promised the Templars a safe-conduct to leave if they surrendered, when they emerged the sultan beheaded them all. In 1268 he captured Jaffa, and in the same year he invaded Tripoli, causing much damage, although he did not stay to capture the city. Instead he turned his army toward Antioch.

Antioch was the city the Latins believed could never be taken from them. This was the city a chronicler described when the Latins saw it during the First Crusade as "so fortified ... that it fears the attack of no machine and the assault of no man, even if every race of man should come together against it."[25] Baybars took the city in four days.

---

[25] Raymond of Aguilers, in Krey 127.

Prince Bohemund VI was not in Antioch when it was captured, so Baybars wrote a letter to him, addressing him not as Prince, but as Count, since he was Lord of Antioch no longer. In the letter Baybars first described the havoc he had caused in Tripoli, at which Bohemund had been present, recounting how everyone — men, women, and children — had either been killed or taken as slaves, and everything in the city pillaged or destroyed while Baldwin stood "like a man overcome by a mortal disaster."[26]

In graphic detail Baybars described his victory at Antioch and "the utter catastrophe that ha[d] befallen [Bohemund]." The sultan clearly enjoyed gloating over his success and the devastation he had caused. "Had you been there," he wrote to Bohemund, "you would have seen your knights prostrate beneath the horses' hooves, your houses stormed by pillagers and looters... your women sold four at a time. You would have seen the crosses in your churches smashed.... You would have seen your Muslim enemy... cutting the throats of monks, priests and deacons upon the altars.... You would have seen fire running through your palaces, your dead burned." And on and on he went, adding one nightmare after the other until, at the end, Baybars wrote, "Since no survivor has come forward to tell you what happened, we have informed you of it, and since no one is in a position to give you the good news that you have saved your life at the loss of everything else, we bring you the tidings in a personal message."

The exhausted and frightened Franks went to Baybars to request a truce, which he granted for one year. The tenacity with which the Franks continued to hold on is awe-inspiring. Yet the atmosphere of doom that was hanging over the last vestiges of the Latin East was palpable.

Louis IX's Second Crusade

The desire to undertake another crusade to recover Jerusalem had never left Louis IX. He announced his decision in 1267 and, in the presence of his barons and advisors, took the cross along with his three sons. Most of his barons spoke against another crusade. France was at peace and in excellent condition internally, owing to reforms Louis had instituted, and they believed it was the king's duty to remain. Even the faithful Joinville refused to go, saying that he was needed more at home than abroad and would do his people a great dis-service were he to die on a crusade. Louis was adamant, however, and most of his nobility were in the event willing to follow him. To Joinville it was "a great sin on the part of those who advised the king to go, seeing that he was physi-

---

[26] This and the following quotations are from Ibn 'abd Az-Zahir, "Baybar's Letter to Bohemund VI," in Gabrieli 310–12.

cally so weak that he could neither bear to be drawn in a coach, nor to ride."[27]

The timing for a new crusade seemed propitious. In 1266 the French king's brother, Charles of Anjou, had become King of Sicily, holding his kingdom as the pope's vassal. Until then the papal crusades against the Hohenstaufens had for nearly fifty years diverted manpower, money, and attention that might have gone to the Holy Land to crusading in Italy. In 1266 the resolution of that long, expensive conflict made a crusade to the East seem a good possibility.

Charles of Anjou was not much in favor of his brother's crusade. Charles had set his sights on the reconquest of Constantinople and the expansion of his kingdom from Sicily to the eastern Mediterranean. In this he was following in the footsteps of Frederick II, who, though unsuccessful, had hoped to carve out a Mediterranean empire. However, Charles knew that his plan would have to wait and that he had to follow his brother to the East.

Both the King of Aragon and the King of England, Henry III, had committed themselves to join the crusade, so in the beginning it was not exclusively a French undertaking. Henry was too old to travel, and the English forces were led by his son and successor, the future Edward I.

This crusade, like Louis's first one, was well organized and well financed. The king arranged to hire ships from Genoa and Marseilles to transport his men and planned to depart from Aigues-Mortes, as he done before, in the early summer of 1270.

The oddity about this crusade is that almost no one was privy to the destination the king had decided upon. The logical place to rendezvous with the other ships joining Louis would have been Cyprus, or even Crete, before moving, as most people assumed, against Egypt once more. In this case the king chose to go to Sardinia to meet the other fleets, and in Sardinia he told them that the next destination was Tunisia, in North Africa. Although the evidence for his choice is circumstantial, the likely explanation is that the king was influenced by his brother Charles.

Charles had been having difficulties with the Muslim emir of Tunisia that were seriously impeding what had been a flourishing trade. So he had his reasons for wanting to attack Tunisia. Whether, as has been supposed, the king believed that Tunisia would be a good base from which to sail to Egypt, or whether he believed the rumor that the emir might convert to Christianity, or whether he went simply out of family loyalty, we will never know for certain. In any event, Louis's fleet sailed to North Africa, arriving on July 18, 1270.

The king was opposed to attacking the Muslims until his brother Charles

---

[27] Joinville 347.

arrived. His army made camp in a fort that had been built on the ruins of ancient Carthage and prepared to wait. The Muslims, for their part, stayed behind their walls and also waited. It was then that disaster struck. The heat at the height of the summer was oppressive and food supplies were low, and in the crowded, unsanitary conditions in which the crusaders lived, it was inevitable that disease would overcome them. Typhoid fever and several other diseases ran rampant through the camp, and thousands died. Among the early deaths was the king's son Jean, who had been born in the terrible last days of Damietta during Louis's first crusade.

A. The Death of Louis IX

King Louis, who had been weak and unwell when he started out, was among the first to be stricken by disease. As his death approached, Louis gave instructions to his son and successor, Philip III, about the proper ways to rule his kingdom. He received the sacraments and was placed, at his request, on a bed of ashes. On August 25, 1270, he died. Charles arrived in North Africa just hours after his brother's death. Since the new King Philip was also ill, Charles took command of the armies. Illness had also overcome many Muslims, so neither side was eager to fight. In the end, Charles made a truce with the emir and was even given a sum of money as an indemnity against the costs of the expedition; his trading rights were restored as well.

King James I of Aragon had sailed from Spain in the fall of 1269 intending to join the crusade. His navy encountered a storm off the coast of Spain that wrecked so many ships that the majority of crusaders who survived turned back for home. The English reached North Africa only a day before Charles and the French were ready to depart for Sicily. The English prince had little choice except to join Charles.

A fierce storm blew up in the seas near Sicily, wrecking much of the Sicilian and French fleets. The English were so angry with Charles at the outcome of the crusade that the English chronicler Matthew Paris described the storm as "a divine vengeance."[28] According to Matthew Paris, the entire treasure Charles had taken from Tunis was lost.

King Philip, carrying with him the bodies of his father, his brother Jean, and many other nobles who had succumbed to disease, had to make a long overland march back to Paris. Louis was buried in the Church of Saint-Denis. "It is a pious duty," Joinville wrote, "and a fitting one, to weep for the death of this saintly prince, who ruled his kingdom and kept guard over it so righteously and loyally."[29] So great was the reputation of this "saintly prince" that it

---

[28] Matthew Paris, *English History*, vol. 3, 377.
[29] Joinville 349.

was only a few years later that the pope sent his representatives to Paris to inquire into the character, life, and miracles of the late king. In August 1298, Louis's body was disinterred and brought to a platform that had been specially built, where, in a moving ceremony, the king was canonized. His body was afterward returned to its eternal rest in Saint-Denis.

Baybars Continues On

Baybars had been reluctant to continue his attacks against the crusader fortresses until he learned the outcome of Louis's crusade and knew he had nothing to fear from a European army. In 1270, Baybars arranged for Assassins to murder Philip of Montfort, the Latins' most respected and strongest baron, a murder that effectively removed a major leader in the East. In the following year Baybars broke the truce with the Christians, and in February he captured the Templar castle of Chastel Blanc. Soon after he besieged the Krak des Chevaliers.

Krak was the most splendid example of the crusader kingdom's military fortresses, and to this day it is the best preserved of all the castles (see photo 4.3 in Chapter 4). It was built and rebuilt several times by the Hospitallers after they received what was once a small Arab fortress from Raymond II of Tripoli in 1142. So impregnable were its walls, which had been doubled in size and strength by the Hospitallers, so huge were its accommodations—as many as two thousand could be housed within the fortress—so well-supplied was it with water and provisions, so ideally located was it on a steep hill some twenty-three hundred feet (seven hundred meters) above the surrounding countryside that even Saladin had not dared to attack it.

When Baybars began his siege of Krak on March 3, 1271, only two hundred men remained in the fortress. Within weeks he had forced his way into the central courtyard. The garrison retreated to the keep, and, after Baybars assured them their lives would be spared, they surrendered on April 8. Baybars then wrote to the Master of the Hospitallers telling him of his victory: "These troops of mine are incapable of besieging any fort and leaving it able to resist them."[30] It was all sadly true for the Franks. Baybars went on to besiege 'Akkar, another Hospitaller castle, which he captured on May 1, and in early June he captured the Teutonic Knights' fortress of Starkenburg. The Latin Kingdom's inland defenses were now lost.

The English prince Edward had meanwhile resolved to carry on the crusade, and he sailed for Acre with a small fleet. He had too few men to engage in a war, and his few skirmishes accomplished nothing. With Edward's encouragement, a new truce was negotiated between Baybars and Acre, which was signed in 1272.

---

[30] Ibn al-Furat, in Gabrieli 317.

The most dramatic event of Edward's short stay in the East was the attempt made on his life by a Muslim who had gained Edward's confidence because he often carried friendly messages from the emir of Jaffa. Matthew Paris described how the assassin tried to stab the prince with the poisoned blade of a knife and how Edward managed to kill the Muslim with his own knife. Unfortunately Edward had handled the poisoned blade and was seriously ill as a consequence. In time, of course, he recovered and even prevented the Christians from taking revenge.[31]

Edward left some men in Acre, supported at his own expense, when he sailed for home in early September 1272. He was the last European prince to set foot in the Holy Land. When he reached England, he learned that his father had died and that he was King of England.

Among the people accompanying Prince Edward when he arrived in Acre in May 1271 had been the archdeacon of Liège, Teobaldo Visconti, who had come on a pilgrimage to the Holy Land. Teobaldo may also have been acting as papal legate in Acre. In any event, in the fall of 1271, Visconti was recalled to Italy because the College of Cardinals had elected him to the papacy, to fill the vacancy after an interregnum that had followed the death of Pope Clement IV in 1268.

The Papacy of Gregory X

For nearly three years the cardinals had been at loggerheads in Viterbo, where they were meeting to choose a new pope. The college was equally divided between French and Italian cardinals, and they could not, and would not, agree on a candidate. Finally, in total exasperation, the people of Viterbo rose up, tore the roof off the building where the cardinals sat, and refused to give them food until they elected a pope. Teobaldo Visconti was not a member of the college, nor was he, at the time of his election, a priest. When he went to Rome to be installed (in March 1272), he was first ordained and then consecrated pope. He took the name Gregory X.

A. A New Crusade Is Planned

As soon as he was elevated to the papal throne, Gregory called for a general church council to meet in Lyons in 1274. Gregory had three goals for the council: the reform of the church; the reunion of the Greek and Roman Churches; and, most important, the promulgation of a new crusade. He had, as he said, witnessed the terrible condition of the Holy Land and seen the horrors perpetrated on Christians living there. "The zeal of belief, the fervor of devotion, and the piety of compassion should arouse the hearts of the

---

[31] Matthew Paris, *English History*, vol. 3, 379.

faithful, so that all who rejoice in the Christian name are touched by pain within their hearts by the affront to their Redeemer, and rise up powerfully and conspicuously to the defense of the Holy Land and the assistance of God's cause."[32]

The pope assumed a heavy financial burden to support the crusade; he decreed that he and all his cardinals should donate a tenth of all their income for six years to help defray the costs. In addition, with the concurrence of the council, he ordered that all ecclesiastics, whatever their rank, contribute a tenth of their incomes for the same six years, to be paid in full "with no reduction whatever.... We wish that no privileges or indulgences assist anybody [to evade the tax]."[33]

Gregory left no loopholes. He required blasphemers to pay a financial penalty, collected either by the secular government or by the church, and threatened with excommunication anyone who tried to defraud the church. He also excommunicated those traders who were selling to the Saracens and who "transport to the Saracens the weapons and iron, wood for galleys and other sailing vessels, which they use to attack Christians... [W]e advise that they be punished with the loss of their own goods and become the slave of their captors." [34] And so it went, with tough-minded punishments for all infractions.

The pope also ordered a hollow trunk to be placed in certain churches, to be filled with alms collected from the faithful to aid the crusade, and that masses be sung in public for the remission of sins, one day each week.

Finally, in the most important decree, the pope granted "to all who undergo the labour of crossing over in aid of the Holy Land in their own persons and expenses, full forgiveness of the sins for which they are truly contrite in heart, and which they have confessed orally, and we promise them, as a reward for the just, an increase in eternal salvation."[35]

He sent preachers to the furthest corners of Christendom, even to Iceland and Finland; some historians claim that his preachers went as far as Labrador. Nonetheless, despite Gregory's determination, his energy, and his enormous efforts to promote the crusade, it came to nothing.

In retrospect we know that the long period of great armed conflicts between crusaders and Muslims in the Holy Land had ended after Louis IX's death. The sainted king's last attempt—his last hope—to rescue Jerusalem had been shattered before it began. Although the restoration of Jerusalem

---

[32] "The Decrees of the Second Council of Lyons on the Crusade, 1274," in Norman Housley, trans. and ed., *Documents on the Later Crusades, 1274–1580* (New York: St. Martin's Press, 1996) 16.
[33] Housley 17–18.
[34] Housley 19.
[35] Housley 20.

remained dear to the heart of the papacy, the "zeal of belief" and the "piety of compassion" that Gregory hoped would rouse Europeans for another crusade had demonstrably waned in the last decades of the thirteenth century. The question is why that should have happened.

Before addressing the reasons for this about-face, we will turn, briefly, to the two other areas that have a claim to be considered under the heading of crusading, the wars on the northeastern borders of Europe and the wars in Spain.

CHAPTER NINE

The New Frontiers of Crusading and the Last Years in the East

Concurrent with the crusades in the East, and lasting even longer, other armed conflicts were being waged within Europe — in the lands north-east of the German kingdom, in the Baltic region, and in Spain. Although they differ significantly in origin and intent from the crusades to the Holy Land, some contemporary historians are now calling these wars crusades. They are therefore included here, with the caveat that the understanding of how these wars relate to crusading as it has been traditionally understood is part of an ongoing debate among historians. Nevertheless, these are important wars to consider, and this historian's perspective on them will be clear from the following discussion.

The Northern Crusades

While St. Bernard of Clairvaux was preaching the Second Crusade in Germany (in 1147), he was approached, as we have seen (Chapter 5, p. 152), by some German nobles who asked that their war against the pagan Slavic people known as the Wends, who lived east of the Elbe River, be sanctioned as a crusade and accorded the same privileges as those given to crusaders to the Holy Land. This St. Bernard did. The wars that ensued are known as the Northern, or Baltic, Crusades.

The German drive to the east began with Charlemagne's subjugation of the Saxons in the late eighth century and continued intermittently until the changes that transformed Europe in the twelfth and thirteenth centuries accelerated German expansion and made it both possible and necessary. The population growth throughout Europe that impelled people to seek new lands for cultivation, the new methods for farming that increased productivity, new technologies like the heavy plow that enabled men to work the heavy northern soil, the development of industry and trade and the rise of towns—all these were the impetus for the eastward colonization.

The immense areas of uncultivated land, the forests to be cleared, and the marshes to be drained enticed nobles and peasants alike to settle the lands east of the Elbe and surrounding the Baltic. The peasants were offered many inducements to move, and they went in large numbers to the sparsely settled and mostly untamed land.

The early colonization was not religiously motivated, nor was it motivated by a desire to eradicate the native population. The Germans were driven primarily by land hunger and desire for economic gain. Once settled they needed to defend their lands from pagan raids and plundering. The new ingredient added to this mix came in the form of the papal blessing for the Wendish Crusade.

In St. Bernard's letter stating his intention for the Wends, he wrote that it was for "the complete wiping out or, at any rate, the conversion of these peoples, they [the German nobles and knights] have put on the cross, the sign of our salvation; and we, by virtue of our authority, promised them the same spiritual privileges as those enjoy who set out towards Jerusalem."[1] By all accounts the war was brutal and bloody.

The Wendish Crusade raised the issue of the use of force for conversion, and among many churchmen it was deplored. A group within the Church defended the traditional Christian view that conversion should be peaceful, brought about through preaching and prayer, not fighting. Despite such objections, from the mid-twelfth century on, the Christianization, by force when necessary—and it often was—of the Slavs and the Balts went hand-in-hand with the German eastward expansion.

In 1171 Pope Alexander III issued a papal bull giving the Germans fighting the pagans along the northeastern frontier many of the same privileges as those given to crusaders to the Holy Land. The remission of sins he granted for a one-year period. Although the pope urged the Germans "to love mercy, justice, and judgment; to hold back from pillaging and evil works," he also urged them "to spread the Christian religion with a strong arm, that you will be able to snatch the victory from your enemies."[2]

For settlers the situation along the frontiers was hazardous, and to help them Pope Innocent III, in 1198, authorized the Livonian Crusade against the pagan Livs in the Baltic region. In 1230, Pope Gregory XI authorized the

---

[1] "Letter of St. Bernard of Clairvaux, 1147," in Allen and Amt 268.
[2] "Bull of Pope Alexander III, 1171," in Allen and Amt 269–70.

Prussian Crusade. In fact crusades, so-called, were continuous in the north during the thirteenth century.

In the context of crusading, the most relevant aspect of the German expansion is the history of the third great military order, the Teutonic Knights. The Knights were invited north by the King of Hungary (in 1211), who wanted their help in defending his borders from the Turks. The king expelled them after only a few years, probably because they were, from his point of view, too successful. In any event, it was a temporary setback.

The Teutonic Knights in the Holy Land had been favored by the Emperor Frederick II, and he was more than generous to them in northern Europe. In return for their help in securing Prussia for his empire, Frederick granted the Knights the governance of Prussia, "as if it were an ancient imperial right, freely and unencumbered."[3]

As strong and wealthy as the Knights became, they still needed additional manpower to subdue the Prussians. The soldiers who came north were often given crusading privileges, although the wars they fought were not necessarily, or even usually, crusades formally proclaimed by the papacy. In 1245, Pope Gregory IX gave the Teutonic Knights the unusual authority to award crusading privileges to the men who fought alongside them, without having to have recourse to the pope at all. By the end of the century, the Knights were firmly established in Prussia.

The northern wars elicited the papacy's interest because the popes were eager to Christianize the Slavs and bring them into the orbit of the Roman Church before they could be converted by missionaries from the Eastern Orthodox Church coming west from Russia. The colonists brought with them the Roman Church and an ecclesiastical organization that, though strongly resisted by the Slavs, eventually was firmly planted in the eastern lands. In this way papal ambitions, the ideology of holy war, and the German expansion all converged in the north.

By the mid-fourteenth century, aided greatly by the Teutonic Knights, the Germans had added some two-thirds more territory to their kingdom than they had had two hundred years earlier. The Elbe was no longer the eastern border; the boundary had become the Vistula River, and in the Baltic area German control went up to the Gulf of Finland. The expansion was helped significantly by the generous use of crusading privileges to further this conquest. These wars were a curious anomaly. They belong as much, and actually more, to the history of German expansion and colonization east of the Elbe River than they do to the religious impulse of crusading.

---

[3] "Imperial Confirmation of the Gift of Land," in Allen and Amt 282–83.

The Spanish Crusades

The motivation for the Christian wars in Spain, the so-called Spanish Crusades, was different from that for the German wars and had a different character.

The Muslims invaded Spain as part of their initial conquest of the Mediterranean world, which had begun in the seventh century. By 708 their conquests had reached as far west as Tunisia; in 711 they entered the Spanish peninsula; and by 715 they had wrested nearly all of Spain from the Christian Visigoths. Only a small strip of land along the mountainous northern Atlantic coast and the Pyrenees remained in Christian hands. In 732 Charlemagne's ancestor Charles Martel successfully stopped the Muslim advance into France and pushed the Muslims back into Spain. In 778 Charlemagne crossed the Pyrenees to expand his own growing empire and fought several battles against the Muslims. The most famous was actually his one major defeat—the battle for Saragosa, immortalized in *The Song of Roland*. Charlemagne was usually successful, however, and before he left Spain, he had established a Frankish frontier along the Pyrenees to the border of Barcelona, known as the Spanish March. From the few tiny Christian settlements in that area the *Reconquista*—the wars to recover for Christian Spain the lands taken by the Muslims—would continue for eight hundred years.

Medieval Spain was a singularly diverse and fragmented country, and the story of the wars against the Muslims is complicated considerably by the endless civil warfare between the emerging Christian kingdoms. The strongest and most successful of the fledgling Christian kingdoms by the mid-eleventh century were Aragon; Léon-Castile, which was two kingdoms joined together; and Portugal.

In the early years of the Muslim presence in Spain, there was considerable fighting between the Arab settlers and the Berbers. That changed with the arrival in 755 of Abd al-Rahman, a young and talented refugee from Damascus whose family had been killed when the Abbasids wrested the caliphate from the Umayyads in 750. Al-Rahman's achievements in Spain ushered in the great age of Muslim influence in the Iberian peninsula. Al-Rahman made Córdoba the capital city of an emirate in the southern part of Spain known as al-Andalus that united the Arabs and the Berbers, and in the tenth century, his descendant transformed the emirate into a caliphate that dominated Spain and the western Mediterranean.

In the early eleventh century, however, the caliphate was weakened by internal fighting, and the unity gave way to the rule of several small *taifas*, or parts of the caliphate. This lack of Muslim unity gave the Christian kingdoms their opportunity to begin to push the Muslims out of the areas closest to them. During the last half of the century the Muslims were driven out of a third of their northern lands, and in 1085, they lost their important center at Toledo.

Map 9.1 Spain and Portugal, 1150–1250.

The papacy without doubt kept a watchful eye on the course of events in Spain. Pope Gregory VII was quick to point out to the French barons who were going off to aid the Spanish Christians in 1073 that "the kingdom of Spain...though long inhabited by pagans...belongs of right to no mortal, but solely to the Apostolic See."[4] Gregory's claim to overlordship of a future Christian Spain did not result in a formal crusade. Whether the Christian wars against the Muslims before the end of the eleventh century, that is before the First Crusade, can be characterized as precursors to crusading in the Holy Land seems highly dubious. The territorial ambitions of the Spanish kings were always uppermost, and fighting between the Christian rulers was regularly interposed between their aggressive wars against the Muslims.

Over time the Spanish wars began to take on a religious cast, owing in part to the spread of monastic orders, especially the Cistercians, and the growth in Spain of military orders. The Templars and Hospitallers both founded houses in Spain in the first half of the twelfth century, and these were soon followed by native orders. The two earliest and most outstanding were the Knights of Calatrava and the Knights of Santiago. The latter had assumed the protection of pilgrims who were coming in ever growing numbers to worship at the shrine of Santiago de Compostela.

The story of St. James, one of the twelve apostles—his coming to Spain to preach, his return to Jerusalem, where he was martyred by King Herod, and his body's return to Spain—is shrouded in myth and miracle. The story continues that following his death at Herod's hand and his burial in Judaea, his bones were disinterred by his followers and placed on a ship for Spain, where his body was buried. After having been forgotten for centuries, the saint's body was miraculously recovered, and the place where his bones had been found was named Santiago in his honor. In the ninth century, St. James was credited with having inspired the Christians to victory in the battle of Clavijo against the Muslims. He was from then on known as St. James, Slayer of Moors, and his cult spread.

By the eleventh century, pilgrims from all over Europe visited Santiago and returned with the sea shell that indicated they had successfully made the long journey. Since the pilgrims passed through southern France to reach Spain, the French Cluniac monks undertook to build beautiful pilgrimage churches all along the route and to keep the road to Santiago in good repair. Santiago, along with Jerusalem and Rome, became one of the three greatest pilgrimage destinations. The saint was Spain's own, and the cult of the Slayer of Moors added another layer to the religious aspect of the Spanish fight to recover lands from the Muslims.

---

4   Gregory VII, "Letter to the Barons of France," in Emerton 6.

After the King of Castile had conquered Toledo in 1085, the Muslims in al-Andalus asked for help from the Almoravids, a group of powerful and fundamentalist Muslim Berbers who had taken over North Africa and installed themselves in Morocco, with their capital at Marrakesh. In a brief time they succeeded in uniting al-Andalus and restraining the Christians from making further advances. However, their desire to reform the local Spanish Muslims caused them to be heartily disliked. In Morocco, they were losing ground to another fanatic Muslim group, the Almohads, who had conquered North Africa as far as Egypt and established their own emirate in Marrakesh. The Almohads soon seized control of Muslim Spain from the Almoravids and established their capital in Seville. In 1195 they inflicted a stunning defeat on Alfonso VIII of Castile at the Battle of Alarcos, which Alfonso was determined to avenge.[5]

Two years after the Battle of Alarcos, Innocent III was elected to the papacy. Throughout the twelfth century, until Innocent's pontificate, the wars in Spain were primarily a Spanish affair, with only occasional interventions from the outside. The first intervention occurred at the siege of Lisbon in 1147, undertaken by King Afonso I of Portugal with the help of the crusaders en route to the Holy Land. The siege succeeded because the crusaders were willing to help the king in exchange for the opportunity to despoil Lisbon if they captured the city. Once Lisbon was taken, the crusaders continued on to their destination in the East. The only relevance the incident has to crusading is the fact that it was the one successful operation concurrent with the Second Crusade in which crusaders were involved.

Almost immediately after his election to the papacy, Innocent turned his attention to the situation in Spain and took a great interest in the Spanish wars. The role he played in furthering the Christian cause is a blend of Innocent's ideology of crusading and his broad conception of papal power.

Innocent's first concern was to secure peace among the Christian rulers, since it was imperative that their fighting end if they were ever to unite against the Muslims. A tenuous peace had been agreed between Portugal and Castile before Innocent became pope, and he exerted every effort to see that it was kept. Although Castile and Léon had been united in the mid-eleventh century, by the mid-twelfth century, they had split apart again, and from then on relations between them were extremely hostile. The two kings had finally arranged a peace treaty, which was secured by the marriage between Alfonso IX, the king of Léon, and Berenguela, the daughter of Alfonso VIII of Castile.

However, the marriage was not legal according to canon law because the

---

[5] For a history of the turbulent events in and the culture of Muslim Spain, see, especially, Maria Rosa Menocal, *Ornament of the World* (Boston & New York: Little, Brown and Company, 2002).

two were cousins, and therefore their consanguinity forbade it. Innocent insisted that the two should be divorced, but neither king would allow it. The pope used all the weapons in his armory to persuade them to dissolve the marriage—interdict, excommunication—until finally, in 1204, the King of Castile yielded to the pope's demands. By then Berenguela had given birth to four children, all of whom the pope declared illegitimate.

The quarrel between Léon and Castile began again over the question of Berenguela's dowry, which included several well-fortified castles, which each king wished to keep. At last, in 1209, peace was restored. The kings agreed that Berenguela's eldest son, Fernando, would succeed to the throne of Léon at his father's death and that the castles would be given to him. The young prince was subsequently legitimized, not by Innocent, but by his successor, Pope Honorius III.

Finally Alfonso of Castile and Innocent could turn their attention to the coming war against the Muslims. Alfonso prepared to lead his army into battle in the week following Pentecost, in May 1212. Innocent organized an elaborate event in Rome to ask for God's help in the coming battle and to pray for victory. It was essentially a day-long mass and a penitential offering. Three separate processions, one of women, two of men, marched barefoot across Rome, accompanied by the sound of church bells pealing throughout the city, and converged in the square in front of the Basilica of St. John. They remained silent until the pope and his cardinals arrived bearing the relic of the True Cross. Innocent then preached a sermon to the large assembly, after which the processionals, the women first, went to the Church of Santa Croce, where the sacrament of the Eucharist was celebrated.

Innocent demanded that all the Roman citizens participate to dramatize his view that crusading should involve the entire Christian community, not only those who took the cross. In the course of his papacy, Innocent found several ways to involve all Christendom in the crusades: he lifted the earlier restrictions on participants that had kept the less able-bodied from going on the crusades; he permitted the redemption of crusader vows for payment and allowed those who redeemed their vows to keep their crusading privileges; he removed the right of wives to keep their husbands from joining the crusades, and he offered partial indulgences to those who gave financial support to the crusades. The practice of public prayer and rituals to intercede on behalf of a crusade was begun by Pope Gregory VIII following Saladin's victories, but, as in so much else that he did, Innocent took the practice to its furthest extreme in the procession he held for Spain.

In the late summer of 1212, later than originally intended, armies from Castile, Aragon, and Navarre, led by King Alfonso, engaged the Muslims at the

Battle of Las Navas de Tolosa, at an important pass leading into southern Spain. Innocent had allowed certain French prelates to offer remission of sins to those Frenchmen willing to fight alongside the Spanish, and a contingent of French knights had gone to join the Spanish. For reasons that are unclear, they did not remain to fight.

Las Navas de Tolosa was a splendid victory for the Spanish forces and was the decisive battle in the Christian offensive against the Muslims. In his report to Pope Innocent, Alphonso undoubtedly exaggerated the numbers of Muslims in their army and the numbers killed. "On their side there fell in the battle," Alfonso wrote, "100,000 armed men, perhaps more.... Of the army of the Lord—a fact...scarcely to be believed, unless it be thought a miracle—only some twenty or thirty in our whole host fell.... We ordered all this to be set down in writing for you, most holy father, earnestly offering all the thanks we can for the aid of all Christendom."[6]

The victory opened the way for the Christian conquest of al-Andalus. At the end of the thirteenth century only Granada remained under Muslim control. Although the *Reconquista* was not completed until 1492, the destruction of the Almohad army at Las Navas de Tolosa determined the eventual outcome of the Spanish wars. Even though the Muslim presence in Spain was diminished over the centuries, much of its rich cultural and artistic legacy endures to this day.

That the Christians in Spain absorbed the rhetoric of crusading to the East is certainly true. And it is also true that in certain circumstances the popes offered privileges to the Spanish normally accorded to those going to the Holy Land. Whether the Spanish wars can be considered part of a widespread European Christian offensive against Islam, as some historians claim,[7] or whether, as this author believes, the Spanish wars were wars of conquest given a spiritual underpinning in the atmosphere of the religious wars to the East, remains for now an unsettled issue. In the view of this historian, both the Northern and Spanish wars were offensive wars driven first and foremost by the desire for land and are tangential to the history of crusading.

During the thirteenth century, these wars, and the papacy's wars in Italy as well, were censured, primarily because they were viewed as detrimental to the Holy Land. This was only one among many criticisms of crusading that were becoming increasingly prevalent.

---

[6] Alfonso VIII, "Report on Las Navas de Tolosa," in Allen and Amt 313.
[7] See especially Joseph F. O'Callaghan, *Reconquest and Crusade in Medieval Spain* (Philadelphia: U of Pennsylvania P, 2003).

The Critics of Crusading

"Of all the desires of our heart," Innocent had written in his letter calling for the Fourth Lateran Council to meet in 1214, "we long chiefly for two, namely that we may work successfully to recover the Holy Land and to reform the Universal Church."[8] Yet, although the Holy Land was uppermost in his mind, Innocent was chiefly responsible for extending the crusades to include all those he believed were enemies of the Christian commonwealth and detrimental to the Church's well-being: the Slavs and the Muslims in Spain, heretics, the papacy's political enemies in Italy, and, reluctantly, even Constantinople.

It was in response to these innovations that criticisms of crusading began to be raised, slowly at first but more insistently as the thirteenth century progressed.

Throughout the twelfth century hostility toward crusading, to the extent it may have existed, was submerged under the passion for saving the Holy Land. At the close of the century, however, on the eve of the Third Crusade, one cleric, Roger Niger, expressed strong doubts about the validity of crusading.[9]

He questioned going to the East when the West was in grave danger from heresy, particularly from the Albigensian heretics. He also believed that the un-Christian character of the Christians living in the Holy Land and their dissolute conduct did not warrant help. William of Tyre had already deplored his countrymen's way of life, although their behavior was for him mainly a great sadness. Soon Jacques de Vitry would also inveigh against the Christians in Palestine. But it was Niger who strongly believed that they had, in effect, made their beds and should be left to lie in them. He also was well aware that what he had written would not dissuade anyone from going on the coming crusade.

In the early thirteenth century the crusade against the Albigensians, not surprisingly, elicited a storm of hostility in southern France.[10] The troubadours, who carried their songs across Europe, were enraged by the destruction caused by the crusading armies in the Languedoc, and their poems became more and more anti-clerical and anti-papal as their beloved countryside was despoiled and taken over by nobles and the king from the north.

The fact that money and manpower were diverted from the Holy Land to fight the popes' wars was to many people unacceptable, as were the amounts of money exacted and the means the papacy used to exact it.

The papacy was always in need of funds—to support the good works carried out by the Church, to fund the various crusades, and to maintain a grow-

---

8   "Letter of Convocation," in Baldwin 293.
9   George B. Flahiff, "*Deus Non Vult*: A Critic of the Third Crusade," *Medieval Studies* 9 (1947): 162–88.
10 Two significant books that take up the problem of criticism in detail are Palmer Throop, *Criticism of the Crusade: A Study of Public Opinion and Crusade Propaganda* (Amsterdam: Swets & Zeitlinger, 1940) and Elizabeth Sidbury, *Criticism of Crusading, 1095–1274* (Oxford: Clarendon Press, 1985).

ing bureaucracy in Rome. The pope collected rents and payments in kind from the lands the Church owned in Italy, lands in other countries that had been gifted to the Church, and bishoprics, monasteries, and parish churches across Europe. It has been estimated that by 1300 one-third of the landed wealth in Europe was held by the church.

The pope also received money from the benefices, or church offices, he gave out, and this practice eventually included virtually everyone, at all levels, appointed to work for the church. In some cases lay rulers who owed their kingdoms to the pope, such as Charles of Anjou, paid a regular tribute to the papacy.

Yet even with all these sources of revenue and with gifts made by the wealthy, the papacy was chronically short of funds. So at the end of the twelfth century, the papacy began imposing taxes, primarily on the clergy. Lay rulers also imposed taxes for crusading, beginning with the Saladin tithe used to support the Third Crusade. More and more taxes were demanded of the clergy in the course of the thirteenth century, the income mainly designated for the pope's Italian wars and the crusades in the north, as well as some for the Holy Land. Artful means were found to increase income, such as the redemption of crusader vows for money, which Innocent III had permitted and which became widely used.

The fiscal policies of the papacy came under severe censure. Matthew Paris (1200–1259), the most celebrated English chronicler in the thirteenth century and a renowned manuscript illuminator, was a monk in the famed monastery of St. Albans, which was a center of hostility toward the Roman See. Matthew was bitterly antagonistic to the papacy and to the Mendicant Orders and their—in his view—crass attempts to raise funds for crusading. "We know that the pope has enjoined on the Preacher and the Minorite brethren [Franciscans] to attend the dying, to question them carefully, and urgently persuade them to make their wills for the benefit, and to the succour of the Holy Land, and to take on them the cross, so that if they recover from their illness, those brethren may cheat them out of their substance; or if they die so much may be extorted out of their executors."[11]

Matthew went on to deplore the selling of church offices, even to non-clerics, and how the pope sent "false and disguised legates...armed with great power" to collect money by any means at all, and how "every kind of avarice, usury, simony, and robbery...reign in the court [the papal court], so that it is with justice said of it: 'To satisfy its avarice the whole world does not suffice.' "[12] He was here writing about papal fund-raising in the mid-thirteenth century.

---

[11] Matthew Paris, vol. 3, 48.
[12] Matthew Paris, vol. 3, 49.

By the pontificate of Gregory X (1271–1276), the criticisms had become sufficiently persistent and outspoken that in an attempt to understand and presumably to answer them, Gregory invited four churchmen to write reports analyzing public opinion, to be presented at the Council of Lyon in 1274. Collectively they offer a picture of the general concerns about crusading, as well as the clerics' own views about how next to proceed. All four reports, or memoirs, as they were called, spoke of the abuses and scandals in the European churches with regard to collecting taxes. The subtext was the papacy's responsibility for the abuses.

William of Tourney, a Franciscan friar, was the most outspoken critic of the abuses perpetrated by the church and royal governments when collecting taxes, including from the poor, to support a crusade. The extortionist taxes imposed on the churches and abbeys had led, in his view, to the increasing hostility of the clergy to crusading.

The solutions to the crisis depended on the writer's background and, as in the case of Bruno, Bishop of Olmütz, the location of his see. According to the German bishop the real enemy was not in the East but in northeastern Europe, along the borders with the Slavs and other pagans. He advocated a crusade to the north, not to the Holy Land.

Oddly enough an equally forceful opponent of another crusade to the East was a Dominican monk named William of Tripoli, who lived in Acre. He was the strongest advocate for peaceful conversion of the Muslims, and in this he represented a growing belief that conversion of the infidel should come through peaceful missionary work, not by the sword. He therefore believed that the Muslims should not be attacked again. William also believed that Islam's days were, in any event, numbered, because they were about to be eradicated by the Mongols.

Of the four reporters at the council, Humbert of the Romans gave the most detailed testimony regarding the popular opinion responsible for the apathy and hostility toward crusading.

"There are some of these critics who say that it is not in accordance with the Christian religion to shed blood in this way, even that of wicked infidels.... There are others who say that although one ought not to spare Saracen blood one must, however, be sparing of Christian blood and deaths.... There are others who say that when our men go overseas to fight the Saracens the conditions of war are much worse for our side, for we are very few in comparison to their great numbers."[13]

Conversion of the Muslims had never been a goal of the crusaders. On the

---

[13] This and the following quotation are from Humbert of Romans, "On Criticisms of Crusading," in Allen and Amt 369–70.

contrary, except in individual cases, the crusaders had little time to convert the infidel, and even less interest in it. When the idea of peaceful conversion was brought up at the Council of Lyons, the corollary that came to the fore was the usefulness of force. Humbert reported the question that bedeviled many people: "What is the point of this attack on the Saracens? For they are not roused to conversion by it but rather are stirred up against the Christian faith. When we are victorious and have killed them, moreover, we send them to hell, which seems to be against the law of charity."[14]

Finally, after enumerating several other criticisms, Humbert came to the all-important question that confronted the Church: Why "God has allowed and is still allowing [the misfortunes] to happen to the Christians engaged in this business... if this kind of proceeding had been pleasing to him?"

Humbert was at pains to show that the critics were in error, and he remained staunchly in favor of a new crusade. Like the pope, Humbert was a passionate believer in holy warfare and the salvation that would come to those who took the cross to recover the Holy Land.

Still the fundamental question remained. What had gone wrong? Why had God allowed the failures in the Holy Land to happen and then to persist? Although couched in different words, the answer given to explain all the Christian losses—Edessa and the failure of the Second Crusade—was basically what Pope Gregory VIII had written after the fall of Jerusalem: "Far from allowing ourselves to be cast down, or to be divided, we ought to be persuaded that these reverses are only to be attributed to the anger of God, against the multitude of our sins.... We ought not then to attribute our disasters to the injustice of the judge who chastises, but rather to the iniquity of the people who have sinned."[15]

The Jews offered a different explanation. According to the great Jewish theologian and philosopher Nahmanides, reflecting on the situation in the Holy Land soon after the mid-thirteenth century, the answer lay in the biblical promise to the children of Israel. As the Israeli scholar who summarized Nahmanides's texts wrote, the reason for the Christian failures was that "no nation can hold the land for long since it is divinely destined for the Jewish people. Even its desolation is pre-ordained for it prevents others from taking possession. The land awaits the coming of the Jews."[16]

How widespread the ideas and criticisms were, and what influence they may have had, is difficult to assess. Much research remains to be done before the amount and kind of popular resistance to crusading can be established

---

[14] Humbert of Romans 368.
[15] "Papal Bull of Gregory VIII, 1187," in Allen and Amt 164.
[16] Joshua Prawer, *The Latin Kingdom* 247–48.

with certainty. Nevertheless, the resentment against papal taxation and against the papacy's use of crusade ideology and crusader privileges to fight its enemies and the general perception that the papacy was misusing its power all seem to have permeated the consciousness of a public unwilling to respond to the crusade preached by Pope Gregory X. The sense of urgency that had spurred on the early crusaders had, at least for the time being, dissipated.

Europe at the End of the Thirteenth Century

The changed aspect of Europe by the close of the thirteenth century surely contributed to the malaise into which crusading had descended. The nearly two hundred years since the preaching of the First Crusade were formative centuries, during which the physical world and the mental outlook in Europe were transformed.

Life on the land had improved considerably with new farming methods and the increased amount of arable land under cultivation. When crops were abundant, many peasants were able to sell their surplus in the markets for money, and the money enabled some of them to translate the goods and services owed to their overlords into money payments. It gave them a freedom from servitude unknown at the turn of the millennium. With greater productivity and the growth in population, people were free to move into towns, where there were new opportunities for workers. The mason, the glassmaker, the fuller, the weaver and dyer—all these and more found ready employment. As the cities grew, so did the need for bakers, butchers, cooks, and candlestick makers.

Although Europe remained a predominantly rural society, towns that were small and insignificant at the end of the eleventh century soon became large and flourishing centers of industry and trade. Paris, for example, once a tiny, uninviting town, grew to at least thirty thousand people, large by the standards of the thirteenth century; Florence, Milan, and Venice, among others, all had populations upwards of fifty thousand people. Trade with the East brought spices and silks and many new goods into the European markets, and raw materials, some manufactured goods, and money flowed from Europe to the East and the Baltic. In the markets the money changer who had to deal with the many coinages that were being exchanged for goods was a ubiquitous figure. The world was knit together as it had not been since the Romans ruled the Mediterranean.

The administration of the cities became complex, and the demand for scribes, tax collectors, judges, and notaries grew. The increased need for literacy stimulated the spread of education, and by the twelfth century, universities began to take shape. New professions became essential in this expanding environment, and there was professional training for doctors, lawyers, teachers, philosophers, and translators. From the translation centers in Spain and

Sicily, a new world of learning entered the universities: the writings of Aristotle especially brought a new way of approaching knowledge and understanding the universe—a knowable universe, rather than an unknown and frightening one.

The two hundred years between 1100 and 1300 witnessed the growth of royal power in France and England, and with this development came royal courts, and taxes, and large bureaucracies to carry out the work of government. Although it is premature to speak of nations in the sense that we understand them, there was a growth of—for want of a better phrase—a national sentiment in both countries, a sense of allegiance to a secular government. Paris and London became capital cities, and Paris became the undisputed center of art and learning.

This was the great age of the Gothic cathedral. The perfect symbol for the age, the undisputed masterpiece, is the cathedral at Chartres, built to glorify God and the Virgin Mary. On the royal portal are the sculptural representations of the seven liberal arts, each associated with the men who were known as the founders of the field—among them Aristotle for logic and dialectic, Cicero for rhetoric, Euclid for geometry, and Pythagoras for music—now considered worthy to be accorded a place in the Christian universe.

This was the world that St. Francis embraced and to which he brought a new vision. The story of St. Francis preaching to the birds is a lovely invention that expresses a deep truth. To Francis all creatures were God's children and all nature was God's handiwork; the forests held no terrors for Francis, nor did the battlefield at Damietta. The message Francis conveyed was that the world was a safe place, to be embraced joyfully. It was a more secular world, the world of the late thirteenth century, and men's attentions were engaged with new pursuits and diverted from the Holy Land.

The crusade to the Holy Land was paramount in Pope Gregory X's plans when he called the Council of 1274, but two other important items were on his agenda: the reunion of the Eastern Orthodox Church with Rome and a claim put forward by Mary of Antioch to the throne of the kingdom of Jerusalem.

The Papacy, Byzantium, and Charles of Anjou

Gregory was convinced that he needed Byzantine help if the Holy Land was to be restored. However, Charles of Anjou was determined to have a Mediterranean empire, and to him that meant first and foremost the conquest of Constantinople. To that end he had made elaborate preparations. Charles acquired Corfu and some of the coast of Epirus, and he arranged marriages for his children in order to gain alliances and promises of aid. He married his daughter Beatrice to the son of the last Latin emperor, Baldwin II, which gave Charles a claim, however remote, to the late, lamented Latin Empire. By 1268 he was ready to invade Constantinople. He was held back the first time because he had to join Louis IX on his crusade, and he was prevented a second time, in 1270, when his fleet was destroyed off the coast of Sicily on his return from Tunis. None of these delays dissuaded him from pursuing his dream, and he continued making his plans while the Council of Lyons was meeting. So to compound his difficulties the pope was forced to deal with the ambitions of his own vassal, Charles of Anjou.

The Byzantine Emperor Michael VIII was willing to aid the pope, even agreeing to the union of the churches, hoping that the pope would dissuade Charles of Anjou from invading the Greek empire. Gregory begged Charles to postpone the invasion, and his plea was briefly successful.

In June 1274, the Byzantine emperor's envoys arrived at Lyon; a bilingual mass was celebrated, and the reunion of the churches was announced in July. The rapprochement was welcomed with great rejoicing by the Roman Church. There was, however, a large impediment to implementing the new agreement; the Eastern Orthodox prelates were vehemently opposed to union. Understanding that it was politically expedient, they went along, temporarily, in a very halfhearted fashion until they had an excuse to rescind the agreement in 1281.

Mary of Antioch came to the council with a legitimate claim to the throne of Jerusalem, a position held by Hugh III, king of Cyprus. Hugh's claim was also legitimate, although his relationship to the ruling family was further removed than Mary's. Gregory did not restore Mary's claim, but he did permit her to sell her title to Charles of Anjou for an enormous sum. The agreement giving Charles legal possession of the kingdom was not actually finalized until 1277.

Charles's intended invasion of Constantinople had been postponed by Gregory X. Gregory died in 1276, and the next popes all died early in their pontificates. In 1281 the cardinals elected a Frenchman, Pope Martin IV, who chose to support Charles and his allies rather than Byzantium. By 1281 Charles had negotiated a treaty with Venice that gave him a large fleet for the invasion. With the pope's blessing this time, Charles again prepared to attack Constantinople. The Greeks immediately rescinded the reunion of the churches, and the pope excommunicated the emperor.

Charles gathered his forces at Messina, but before he could sail to the East, he was faced with an insurrection in Sicily that ultimately caused his ruin.

The Sicilian Vespers

As vespers were about to begin in a church in Palermo on Easter Monday, March 30, 1282, mobs of Sicilians, who had a deep-seated hatred for Charles and his extortionate, heavy-handed rule, rose up and began killing all the French on the island. The immediate provocation was an insult given by a

Frenchman to a Sicilian woman. Her infuriated husband stabbed him to death and the uprising began. However, it is certain that the uprising had been carefully planned by Charles's enemies.

What made the revolt so successful was the intervention of King Peter II of Aragon, who maintained the Hohenstaufen claim to the Sicilian throne through his marriage to the daughter of Frederick II's son Manfred. Peter had been solicited as an ally by the Byzantine emperor Michael VIII, who gave financial support to the rebels and who had the support of the Genoese as well. At the end of August 1282, Peter and his army arrived in Sicily, and on September 2 he entered Palermo, where he was formally offered the crown. Charles was forced to evacuate his remaining troops and retreat to the Italian mainland.

The Sicilian revolt saved Byzantium, but the emperor never received the thanks from his countrymen that were his due. His wish to reunite the churches and his willingness to work with the papacy were bitterly opposed by the Greeks. When Michael died in December 1282, in a small town in Thrace, the Orthodox Church refused to give him a Christian burial, and in death his body was condemned to permanent exile from the capital he had saved.

Pope Martin IV stood by his French allies. He proclaimed a crusade against Sicily, excommunicated Peter of Aragon, and then declared a crusade against Aragon itself. Since Martin considered Aragon to be a papal fief, he offered the crown to the French king's son. The ensuing wars between the French and the Aragonese dragged on until 1302, when the French army was defeated by an onset of the plague as they landed in Sicily. In the negotiations that followed, the Angevins formally relinquished Sicily to the Aragonese, although they retained the crown of Naples. The settlement only served to increase the tensions between Sicily and Naples. The papal crusade against Aragon, so nakedly political, was very damaging to the papacy's reputation, which was already suffering and would soon suffer even more.

The Last Years of the Latin Kingdom
In the years after Gregory X's hope for a crusade failed to materialize, the Latin Kingdom, already in tatters, was seriously neglected by the West.

The one possible opportunity to give some real help to the Holy Land had arisen during the Council of Lyons in 1274. A Mongol mission had come to ask the pope for an alliance against the Mamluks. For the Christians, now on the verge of losing all their lands in the East, and for the Mongols of Persia threatened by the Muslim advances, the time seemed perfect for a joint venture against their common enemy. The Mongols had been negotiating with Christian princes, on and off, during much of the thirteenth century, but only Louis IX and Edward I of England seemed to have understood the advantage that might come from such an alliance. Sadly, it was not to happen, and it is easy with hindsight to regard the reluctance to join with the Mongols as a grievous error.

Fortunately for the crusader kingdom, Baybars had died in 1277, and the Franks were temporarily spared a Mamluk invasion until the succession to the sultanate was sorted out. Nevertheless, the Latin Kingdom was in dire straits. When Charles of Anjou had purchased his title to Jerusalem from Mary of Antioch in 1277, he sent a small army commanded by Roger of San Severino to establish his rule in the Holy Land. The Angevin cause was supported by Acre, but Tyre remained loyal to King Hugh of Cyprus.

So two new opposing factions were added to the continuing hostility between the Venetians and Genoese and the rivalry between the military orders. No matter how desperate their situation, nothing deterred the Franks from their internal fighting. Even the brief reprieve following Baybar's death was of no avail.

Moreover, the kingdom was in wretched financial condition. The Franks had depended for much of their own resources on the trade that passed through their ports en route from the Far East to the Mediterranean. That route was disrupted by the Mongol invaders in northern Syria and Iraq, who diverted the trade to ports on the Black Sea. As early as 1261 the Master of the Templars in the Holy Land had written to the Templar treasurer in England explaining the desperate need for funds in the wake of the Mongol successes. Unless help was forthcoming, he wrote, "we will be forced to default completely in respect of the defense of the Holy Land.... For times are so bad in these regions at the moment that it is not possible to borrow money either against interest or against pledges, and this not only because of the difficult [financial] situation, but also because there are no Genoese or other merchants in Acre." He was even ready to offer crosses, chalices, and other religious items the order owned as surety for loans. He was prescient in his prediction of the future "because we are totally at a loss as to how we ought to react in the face of scourges, tribulations, difficulties and pressures such as have never been seen or heard before."[17] There was much worse to come.

After Baybars's death in 1277, his two young sons, in rapid succession, were granted the sultanate, and each one, in rapid succession, had it taken from him by the emir Qalawun, who established himself as sultan in 1280. He had several competitors, however, and one of them appealed to the Mongols for help to oust Qalawun. The Mongols invaded Syria in 1281. Quite surprisingly, given the overwhelming size of the Mongol army, Qalawun defeated the Mongols at the Battle of Homs, forcing them to withdraw from Syria. Before Homs, Qalawun

---

[17] Thomas Berard, Master of the Temple, "Letter to Amadeus of Morestello, Treasurer of the Temple," in Barber and Bate 103.

renewed the truce Baybars had made with the Franks, but he had no intention of keeping it once the Mongol army was destroyed. After his victory Qalawun was relentless in his attacks on the remaining Frankish castles and cities.

The only potential support the Latins in Palestine could reasonably hope for was from Cyprus, whose king, Hugh III, had been crowned King of Jerusalem (albeit in Tyre) in 1269. It was Hugh's claim that Mary had come to the Council of Lyon to protest, unsuccessfully, as we have seen. But Acre was not in favor of Hugh, and soon after his coronation, Hugh returned to Cyprus. In 1283, he came once more to Tyre, believing he would be better received in the kingdom after Charles of Anjou's troops had left, but he was still unable to win over Acre. His troops gave up after four months and went home. Hugh stayed on, dogged by bad luck. One of his sons died in Tyre, and in early March of 1284 Hugh died there also. His eldest son succeeded to the throne of Cyprus, but he died after only a year on the throne. He was followed by his brother, Henry II, who was accepted as King of Jerusalem and crowned in Tyre in 1286.

In late April 1285, Qalawun successfully attacked the last fortress still held by the Hospitallers, a heavily fortified castle that guarded the northern frontier of the county of Tripoli. Despite such a serious loss, Henry II's coronation was celebrated the following year in Acre with sumptuous banquets, tournaments, plays, and diverse entertainments. After two weeks of partying, Henry went home to Cyprus.

One by one the Mamluks seized the Franks' remaining fortresses and cities. They took Latakia in 1287, and two years later they besieged and captured Tripoli. There were few survivors. "When the killing and looting were over," a Muslim historian reported, "the city, on the Sultan's orders, was demolished and razed to the ground." Women and children, led by a few Frankish men, had taken refuge on a small island separated from the mainland by the harbor. The Muslims swam out to the island, massacred all the men and captured the women and children. When the historian went to see what had happened he, "found it [the island] heaped with putrefying corpses; it was impossible to land there because of the stench."[18]

Tripoli might have fallen no matter what the Franks did, but the shameful fact is that it was barely defended. The Genoese and Venetian navies both defected, and the walls were easily breached. Until Tripoli fell, the Franks seemed unwilling to recognize just how perilous their situation was. They also seem to have deluded themselves into thinking the Muslims would not attack Acre because the city played such an important role in trade for the Muslims as well as the Christians and because it still had a treaty with Qalawun.

---

[18] Abu L-Fida, in Gabrieli 342.

When the Franks appealed for aid from the West, the response was worse than nothing. Some Venetian and Aragonese galleys came to Acre in August 1290, with men who were ostensibly crusaders but who had no experience, no real commitment to the Frankish cause, and no discipline at all. Muslim merchants who regularly gathered in Acre to sell their goods came and went without problems until the new Italian crusaders attacked a Muslim peasant, which led to rioting and fighting in the streets. It was exactly the pretext that Qalawun needed to break the truce.

However, before he could complete his preparations for the attack on Acre, Qalawun died in Egypt in December 1290. His eldest son, whom Qalawun had appointed his successor, had predeceased his father under somewhat mysterious circumstances. The sultanate went to his second son, Khalil, a tyrannical, brutal man who was also an excellent, courageous commander in the field.

Khalil sent to Syria to request additional men and especially siege engines. The Muslim who wrote the Arabic source describing the siege of Acre participated in the march that brought to Acre a great catapult in possession of the ruler of Hamat. It was called the Victorius and was so enormous that "a hundred wagons were needed to transport it. [It was dismantled and the pieces] distributed through the army.... The Sultan ordered all other fortresses to send catapults and siege-engines to Acre, and in this way a great number of large and small artillery concentrated under its walls, more than had ever been assembled in one place."[19]

The Franks finally set aside their grudges and animosities and came together to defend their city. Only the Genoese left, after making their own treaty with the sultan. When the Mamluks began their march to Acre in March 1291, many women and children were taken to safety on Cyprus. On April 6 the Muslims began their siege. They vastly outnumbered the Franks. In one Latin report the writer claimed that the Muslims had six hundred thousand men, surely an exaggeration, but it makes the point about the overwhelming odds the Franks faced. For the first weeks the Latins were able to receive supplies from Cyprus, and on May 4, the King of Cyprus arrived with reinforcements. They were too few and too late. Even within Acre's great defensive walls and towers, the Franks were too weak to hold out for long, although they fought valiantly to the bitter end.

The End of Hope: The Fall of Acre
On May 16 the Mamluks broke through the outer walls, and two days later they broke through the inner walls into the city. The fighting continued until

---

[19] Abu L-Fida, in Gabrieli 344–45.

9.1 The final seige of Acre, 1291. Note, among other details, the heads being pushed under the water.

a little past the middle of June, when "the most noble and glorious city of Acre, the flower, chief and pride of all the cities of the East, was taken."[20]

For the Muslims there was a special reason to celebrate the fall of Acre. "It is marvelous to observe that Almighty God permitted the Muslims to conquer Acre on the same day and at the same hour as that on which the Franks had taken it [a hundred years before]." At that time the Franks had "promised to spare the lives of the Muslims and then treacherously killed them.... The Sultan gave his word to the Franks and then slaughtered them as the Franks had done to the Muslims. Thus Almighty God was revenged on their descendants."[21]

---

[20] Ludolph von Suchem, "Description of the Holy Land," in Allen and Amt
[21] Abu L-Muhasin, in Gabrieli 349.

A number of the women and children still in Acre managed to escape to Cyprus, but the great part of the population was either slain or sold into slavery. The women and girls, unless ransomed, were killed or taken captive and kept as domestic slaves.

It was now only a matter of time before the remaining Frankish cities and castles fell. Tyre, Sidon, Beirut, Tortosa, and the last Templar castles all capitulated by the end of the summer. Only the small island of Ruad, opposite Tortosa, was held by the Templars until 1303. It was a poor place, in any event, and had no water supply.

The crown of the kingdom now passed to Cyprus. Although prosperous, Cyprus had difficulty absorbing the huge influx of refugees from the mainland, which included members of the military orders, other religious personages, nobles, and the poor and widowed. The refugee women on Cyprus and their descendants for the next hundred years, it is told, lived out their lives in black dresses as a sign of mourning for the loss of Acre.

The Question of Blame

A. The Templars Under Attack
In the West, the question of who should be held accountable for the disaster inevitably and promptly came to the fore. The major blame fell on the military orders, who were already in disrepute. For decades they had been criticized for their rivalry, which was so detrimental to unity in the Holy Land, for their immense wealth, for the separate treaties each order had made with sultans, and for their spiritual laxity. After the fall of Acre they were an easy target. It was proposed that the Hospitallers and Templars be reorganized into a single order. As one can readily imagine, this idea was strenuously resisted by both orders.

The proposal for unification had first been raised at the Council of Lyon in 1274 and been set aside. After the loss of Acre, Jacques de Molay, who had become Grand Master of the Templars in late 1292 or soon after, responded to the revival of the plan in a letter to Pope Clement V. He began by saying that the criticisms made of the military orders by the previous pope, Nicholas IV (1288–1292), were used as a way of deflecting criticism away from the papacy, "because the Romans and other nations were complaining loudly that effective help for the defence of that land had not been sent by him."[22] So the papacy came in for its share of blame, although the greater part fell on the military orders.

---

[22] James of Molay, "Reply to Pope Clement V," in Barber and Bate. This and the following quotations are from 235–38.

Jacques de Molay used every clever argument he could muster to explain the drawbacks of union, starting with his conviction "that it would not be honorable to unite such ancient Orders that have achieved such positive results in the Holy Land and elsewhere, since it is to be feared that the opposite of what they have achieved so far may occur, as innovation rarely or never fails to produce grave dangers." He had the temerity to argue that if the orders remained separate their rivalry would be a good thing for the Holy Land, since "the rivalry has always brought glory and advantages to the Christians."

The potential union of the orders would soon become irrelevant. In the closing years of the thirteenth and the opening years of the fourteenth century, a turn of events came about that shook the foundations of papal power, dramatically changed the relationship between the papacy and the secular rulers, and sealed the fate of the Templars. The turning point was the fight between Pope Boniface VIII and King Philip IV of France, which began in 1296.

B. The Fight Between King Philip IV and Pope Boniface VIII

Boniface VIII was elected to the papacy at the end of December 1294. The new pope was not a man who inspired affection. He was a cardinal descended from an illustrious Roman noble family; he was smart, experienced, well trained for the papal office, tough-minded, and obdurate. The first phase of the fight between Philip IV (1285–1314) and the new pope was over the issue of the monarchy's right to tax the clergy without the clergy obtaining papal consent. Since France was at war with England and the military expenses were enormous, Philip IV wanted a share of the churches' wealth. Boniface forbade this royal taxation and threatened excommunication if it was carried out. In response Philip forbade money and valuables from leaving France. This first stage concluded with a defeat for Boniface and a momentary renewal of the friendship between the papacy and the Capetians. But Philip was not finished.

Although the overt reason for the renewed fight was the king's jurisdiction in legal matters over the clergy in France, the even more basic issue, the underlying issue, was the secular government's fight against the papal claims to universal sovereignty. In 1302, Boniface VIII issued the bull *Unam Sanctam*, which is the most explicit statement of papal supremacy from the medieval period—and the last of its kind. "For, the truth bearing witness, the spiritual power has to institute the earthly power and to judge it if it has not been good. So is verified the prophecy of Jeremias [1.10] concerning the church and the power of the church, 'Lo, I have set thee this day over the nations and over kingdoms' etc."[23]

---

[23] Pope Boniface VIII, "*Unam Sanctam*," in Tierney 189.

Philip's reply was a physical attack on the pope. Aided by some Roman nobles hostile to Boniface, a small contingent of Philip's men went to the pope's residence in Anagni in early September 1303, captured Boniface, and brought him to Paris to stand trial. Philip's lawyers had drawn up a lengthy list of charges against Boniface, many of them extremely humiliating, such as sodomy, simony and heresy, along with anything else to do with corruption and sin they could include. Boniface died in 1303 before the trial could proceed, although his death did not stop Philip, who insisted that the pope be tried posthumously.

In 1305 a Frenchman, Clement V (1305–1314), was elected to the papacy. His task was unenviable. Philip did not wait long to put pressure on the new pope to eliminate the Templars. Although much has been written about Philip's motives, they remain hazy. He seems to have believed, or wished to believe, the accusations that the Templars profaned Christ, worshipped idols, committed unnatural sexual acts—that the Templars were, in sum, as Philip wrote in his order for the arrest of all the Templars in France, "a pernicious example of evil and a universal scandal."[24]

Philip had another, more pressing motive for his actions. He was in debt to the Templars, was unable to pay them back, and wanted to confiscate their land and considerable wealth in France. He had already expelled the Jews from France in 1306 and commandeered their money and property, which lends weight to the argument that he coveted the Templars' wealth as well.[25] Philip's next move was a major challenge to papal supremacy.

C. The Arrest of the Templars in France

Philip made his plans in secret. On his command, during the night of September 14, 1307, the Templars in France were arrested, brought before an inquisitor, and tortured to ascertain the truth of the charges. "Despite the fact that some may be guilty and others innocent... it is fitting that if there are any innocent ones among them these should be tested in the furnace like gold and cleared by the due process of judicial examination." According to the depositions recorded later that year, only four Templars denied the charges.[26] Even the Grand Master Jacques de Molay confessed, although he would later retract his testimony. Those who remained unrepentant were either sentenced to severe terms of imprisonment or burnt at the stake; those who recanted were allowed to go free, although no longer to live as Templars.

---

[24] This and the following quote is from Philip IV of France, "Order for the arrests (14 September 1307)," in Barber and Bate 244–47.

[25] Philip recalled the Jews in 1315, and they were expelled once more in 1332.

[26] Barber, Malcolm, *The New Knighthood: A History of the Order of the Temple* (Cambridge: Cambridge UP, 1994) 310–12.

9.2 The burning of the Templars.

To gain control of the investigative process, Clement set up a papal commission to hear the testimony of several Templars, including Jacques de Molay. In late 1307, Clement called for a council to meet at Vienne in 1311 to review the allegations and the depositions. He also ordered the arrest of all the Templars outside France.

The problem Clement faced was that Philip was determined to bring Boniface to a posthumous trial and make public the long list of terrible accusations his lawyers had drawn up. To prevent that, the pope finally acceded to Philip's demand to dissolve the Knights Templar. In March 1312, Clement issued a bull in which he formally suppressed the order. Two years later, Jacques de Molay, despite having recanted his original confession, was burnt at the stake.

The Hospitallers had also been castigated for the fall of the Holy Land, but less so than the Templars, and in fact they did well for themselves. In 1307, with the help of the Genoese navy, they began an assault on the Byzantine island of Rhodes, which they conquered and on which they built a strikingly beautiful, well fortified castle. In September 1307, Clement confirmed their possession of the island in a papal bull. The order benefited considerably from the suppression of the Templars. In May 1312, Clement transferred the Templar goods and properties, excluding those in Spain and Portugal, to the Hospitallers.

From 1307 until 1378 the popes resided in Avignon. Although the city was not technically French—the popes bought it from the Kingdom of Naples—the seat of papal authority was in French-speaking territory, which was reason enough to suppose royal influence on the papacy. The Avignonese popes were not necessarily under the thumb of the French monarchy, and many were good popes, but the absence from Rome further tarnished the papacy's already shopworn reputation.

What Next?

The decades following the loss of the Holy Land were a time for regrouping, for considering what should be done, and for posing alternative solutions, rather than making concrete plans for a new crusade, although there were some of those as well. The principal activity in the first half of the fourteenth century took the form of a new literature: tracts, pamphlets, and propaganda pieces urging various approaches to the problems posed by the fall of Acre and crusading generally.

For some, a new crusade was the only possible response. Soon after Clement V came to the papal throne, the Master of the Hospitallers, at the pope's request, wrote a memorandum in which he urged a new crusade and recommended exactly how it should be organized and how funds should be raised to support it. Not incidentally he also counseled the pope not to do anything to harm or hinder the military orders. At the same time, Clement asked for a report from the Grand Master of the Temple, Jacques de Molay—before his downfall. Some people had suggested a small, preliminary movement, a *passagium particulare*, as it is known, with limited objectives, either instead of, or to precede, a large international crusade, known as a *passagium generale*. De Molay was among those who favored "mounting a large, all-embracing expedition to destroy the infidels and to restore the blood-spattered Holy Land of Christ."[27]

Philip IV was committed to the idea of a large-scale crusade, and he was convinced that his victories over the papacy invested him with the leadership of Christendom and any new crusade to the East. In this he was supported and

[27] "The Report of James of Molay," in Barber and Bate 107.

encouraged by a great lawyer at his court, Pierre Dubois, who wrote a document for the king in which he offered solutions to all the possible problems arising from a new crusade. He had many ideas, some highly impractical, such as taking the papacy's lands in Italy and thus downgrading the popes' role in Christendom, let alone in crusading. He believed that the leadership belonged by right to the French crown, and that once victory was assured, a French king should rule the East from Egypt.

In addition to espousing a crusade, Dubois laid out a program for the education of children, both boys and girls, starting at age five, who would afterward be sent to the Holy Land, or to other places where they might be needed. As part of their education he emphasized the study of Greek and Arabic, so that they would be equipped to preach to the Greeks and Muslims.[28] He went so far as to suggest that young Christian women be married to Saracens and then work to convert their husbands.

For other writers, the way to proceed was by converting the Muslims through prayer and preaching, by realizing the missionary dreams of St. Francis and St. Dominic.

The seminal work on conversion in the fourteenth century was written by a remarkable Spanish scholar, philosopher, poet, mathematician, and linguist, Raymond Lull (1232–1316). After an extremely productive life as a teacher and writer—he produced more than two hundred and fifty works—and an active life in the world, he had a religious conversion and joined the tertiary order of the Franciscans. He went on his first, solitary mission to the Muslims in Tunis in 1285—and was expelled. He undertook two more missions to North Africa; during the third mission he was stoned, and he died soon after from his wounds.

Lull had bought a Muslim slave to teach him Arabic, and in the work he wrote on the recovery of the Holy Land, he counseled establishing four monasteries, one each for the teaching of Arabic, Greek, Hebrew, and the Mongol language. The men brought together to learn the languages would then go forth to preach. They should be willing, Lull wrote, "to die on behalf of that most benign Son of God, our Lord Jesus Christ, who did not fear to suffer death for them."[29]

Although Lull advocated missionary activity, he also described the formation of a new order of knights, which would threaten the Muslims with war if they failed to convert by peaceful argument.

Lull was instrumental in persuading Clement V to create chairs in Arabic and Hebrew at the major European universities and at the papal court. His

---

[28] Pierre Dubois, "The Recovery of the Holy Land," in Allen and Amt 366–68.
[29] Raymond Lull, *De Fine*, in Allen and Amt 371–72.

insistence on the value of learning languages in time led to a new under-standing of the Muslim world.

Over a century earlier the abbot of a Cluniac monastery, Peter the Venerable, made a trip to Spain, where he seized on the idea of translating several Arabic works into Latin. Among these was the Quran, which for the first time became available for study in western Europe. He considered Islam a heresy, and his purpose was to know the religion in order to refute it. His translations had less immediate influence than he had hoped, and it was not until the fourteenth century that the ideal of peaceful conversion and the need to study the languages of the non-Christian world came together.

Although the crusade Philip IV desired did not come to pass, the tradition of crusading was still strong in France, and other plans for crusades originated in the French court. The one crusade that appeared to have the promise of actually getting under way was initiated in 1330 by the French king, Philip VI, who hoped to emulate the sainted Louis IX. Considerable and serious problems stood in his way, however.

France and England had fought a war from 1294 to 1297 over disputed terri-tory in Gascony, in southwestern France. To seal the treaty that was signed in 1313, Philip IV's daughter Isabelle was married to the future King Edward II of England. For both the French and English this was not a marriage made in heaven.

A. Philip VI of France and the Aborted Crusade

None of Philip IV's three sons lived to reign for long. When the last of his sons died in 1328, leaving no male heir, the succession passed to Philip IV's nephew, Philip VI Valois (1328–1350). His succession was not wholeheartedly wel-comed by the French nobility, which weakened his position and made him vulnerable to the claims to the French throne put forward by King Edward II (1307–1327). Edward's wife's claim to the throne theoretically superseded that of Philip VI. So the real possibility of war again between France and England was in the background as Philip planned his crusade.

He encountered enormous difficulties when he began raising funds to outfit an army and build a navy to transport men and supplies to the East. Philip and the reigning pope, John XXII (1316–1334), negotiated for several years before reaching formal agreements about how the money would be collected and distributed, how much would come from the Church, how much from Philip and his subjects. There were objections from all quarters to the excessive taxes. In addition, an anti-crusade faction existed at the French court, its ranks increased as a result of the financial exactions required by the king and the real fear of war with England.

The participation of Isabelle's son Edward III (1327–1377), who had become king in England, was a prime consideration if the crusade was to succeed. The enmity between France and England was like a tinderbox, always ready to burst into flame, and neither Philip nor Edward was willing to leave his kingdom without the other. Although the two kings managed temporarily to come to terms, there remained, with good reason, an atmosphere of mutual distrust, heightened by the fact that France and England had each taken sides in the war in Scotland over the Scottish succession to the throne.

By 1336 Philip had assembled a large fleet in the harbor at Marseilles, but instead of sailing for the East, Philip diverted his fleet into the English Channel. Although Philip claimed that he was only going to defend his interests in Scotland, Edward III was certain that Philip planned to invade England and that he had never intended to use his fleet to go on the crusade. Whatever the truth of the matter, the damage was done. Pope Benedict XII canceled the crusade. It was the last *passagium generale* to restore the Holy Land that was ever attempted from Europe.

The Kingdom of Cyprus and Peter I's Crusade

Meanwhile, events in the East had not been at a standstill. The important Latin bastion in the Mediterranean after the fall of Acre was the Kingdom of Cyprus. When the Venetians and Genoese were forced out of the coastal cities, Cyprus inherited some of their Mediterranean trade; Famagusta, the island's main city, had already become a wealthy trading center, and with the increased Mediterranean trade it became even richer. Overall the island was prosperous and beautiful. The King of Cyprus, Henry II (1285–1324), fearing that the Mamluk Sultan, having had such a total victory on the mainland, would next move against Cyprus, led a preemptive strike on Alexandria in 1292. Although the attack failed, it so angered the sultan that he considered building a huge fleet to attack Cyprus.

Cyprus was spared because the Egyptians were diverted by the Mongol advance into northern Syria, which began in 1299. There followed years of warfare between the Mongols and Mamluks, which did not end until 1323. Not long afterward the Persian Mongol Empire started to fall apart, succumbing to its own internal power struggles.

Cypriots had a long tradition of crusading. Throughout the thirteenth century, they had participated in the crusades to the Holy Land, and the island served as the meeting place and supply depot for crusading armies coming from Europe. Following the cancellation of Philip VI's crusade, the locus for crusading shifted to Cyprus, but the island did not have the manpower to launch a general crusade without significant help and support from the European mainland.

The last Cypriot king to attempt a large international crusade was Peter I (1359–1369). In the fall of 1362, Peter began a whirlwind tour of Europe to recruit support for his crusade. En route he stopped briefly on Rhodes, where he was assured of the Hospitallers' support. In Venice he negotiated for a much-needed fleet; from there he visited the northern Italian towns, and then went to Paris to win over the French king. In the early spring of 1363, he visited the papal court at Avignon, where Pope Urban V proclaimed the new crusade. Peter made a grand sweep through much of France and Germany and sailed to England to meet with King Edward III. Wherever he went he was welcomed with great ceremony and assured of the help he needed.

Ever since King Richard the Lionheart had counseled attacking Egypt first and then moving on to rescue Jerusalem, the crusades in the thirteenth century had all attempted to conquer Egypt. Peter's plan was to attack Alexandria, although until the last minute his exact destination was kept secret.

In early October 1365, his fleet assembled near Rhodes and sailed for Alexandria. The city was wealthy and well fortified, and it was captured only because the crusaders exploited an undefended gap in the walls to force their way in to the city. Alexandria was sacked and looted beyond repair. Everything that could be taken was grabbed by the soldiers, and what could not be moved was burned to the ground. Those residents who were unable to flee were massacred, the animals that had carried the loot out of the city were killed and their bodies were burned. The wreckage left behind was incalculable.

Victory and Loss: The End of Crusades to the East

When the sack was ended, the crusaders immediately prepared to depart. The chancellor of Cyprus, a participant who wrote a report of the crusade, described King Peter's despair when he realized the troops were leaving after their victory. "In tears the king piously implored knights of every rank to stay with him, but they refused.... He showed clearly how God's honour, the good of Christendom, and the acquisition of the city of Jerusalem, [all] hung on the retention of Alexandria.... What more is there to say? Their hearts were hardened and they were overwhelmed by wickedness. The grief-stricken king and the [papal] legate, who was almost dying of anguish, were overcome by the wicked. They decided on withdrawal."[30]

After some raids on the Syrian coast, Peter came to Europe once more to win allies and to rekindle the crusade, but this time with no success. Peter returned to Cyprus from his disappointing European trip in late fall of 1368. He learned that in his absence his wife had committed adultery, and he became angry with the barons in his court when they did not take his side

---

[30] Philip of Mézières, "Account of the Alexandria Crusade," in Housley 87–88.

against the queen and her lover. The barons for their part were angered at all the manpower and money they had spent on the king's expensive and ineffectual wars. Peter became disillusioned, unpredictable, and vengeful, so much so that his behavior provoked a group of his nobles and knights, including his own brother, to swear to kill him. At the end of January 1369, Peter was murdered. Each man involved took a turn stabbing the king: a sad and dreadful end for a man who had won the respect of Christendom and had been wholeheartedly devoted to a crusade to the Holy Land. In his commitment to the Latin Kingdom, he had no successor.

During Peter's lifetime, he had negotiated with the sultan's representatives for a treaty, an option the papacy favored, but before it could be concluded, the Venetians had rushed to the sultan's court to make a separate peace. The Venetians gave out the erroneous news that Peter had made peace with Egypt, so fearful were they that the Cypriots' continued enmity with Egypt would ruin their trading privileges. The aftermath of Peter's crusade demonstrated all too clearly how far the various interests in Europe had moved away from the crusading ideal, and how much economic self-interest would prevail in the Mediterranean.

Many events conspired against a new crusade to the Holy Land. Papal supremacy over Christendom, for good or ill, had been weakened by the attack on Pope Boniface VIII, the trial of the Templars, and the prolonged papal residence in Avignon.

Great writers, such as Dante (1265–1321), and philosophers, such as Marsiglio of Padua (ca. 1275–1343), directly challenged the supremacy of the papacy. To Dante, who believed in the unity of Christendom, the ruler should not be the pope but the Holy Roman Emperor, and in his treatise "De Monarchia" he argued that the temporal power came from God directly, not from the pope, and was therefore independent of the papacy.

Marsiglio of Padua wrote even more strongly about the separation of the state from the church. In his most famous and influential work, the *Defensor Pacis*, written in 1324, he was also severely critical of Pope John XXII, whom he accused of misusing funds to wage war against Christians and heretics. "And, what is horrible to hear, this bishop declares that such action is just as pleasing in God's sight as is fighting the heathen oversees." After graphically describing all the horrendous acts committed by the men who obeyed the pope's command to fight his enemies, Marsiglio wrote, "Such are the purposes for which this bishop wastes the ecclesiastical temporal goods that devout believers have put aside for the aid and support of Gospel ministers and the hapless poor."[31] These were not solitary voices. All during the fourteenth

---

[31] Marsiglio of Padua, "*Defensor Pacis*," in Allen and Amt 375–77.

century and into the early fifteenth century, the papacy's assertion of its supreme power over secular rulers was under attack. With the new theories favoring the growing power of secular states, the papacy's once exclusive right to call a crusade was undermined.

The fourteenth was a century of hard times. All over Europe there were regional wars: renewed papal wars in Italy, wars in Sweden, wars fought by Poles and Danes against the Germans, civil wars in the Holy Roman Empire, and constant border wars. In 1337 the Hundred Years War between France and England began. Although it was fought on and off rather than continuously, it did not end until 1453 and caused great economic, social, and political damage to both countries.

In 1315 extraordinary rains began, which brought on a succession of crop failures in Europe. The effects of the famines that resulted were devastating. People suffered from malnutrition or simply starved; whole industries, such as the wine trade, failed; food prices soared; animals died by the thousands; and the suffering led to rioting and unrest. Finally, there was the onset of the plague. The Black Death arrived in Italy in 1347, spread rapidly throughout the continent and recurred in waves for decades. The plague did not fall equally on all parts of Europe, but the conservative estimate is that one-third of the total population died from the dread disease. It was an unimaginable disaster.

Among the many changes that resulted from the decimation of the population, the one that impinged on warfare in general and the now-remote possibility of enlisting a crusading army, was the significant loss of manpower. This led to the increasing use of mercenary soldiers, who were recruited for a limited time and, since they were a financial burden, were discharged as quickly as possible.

Thus the times were hardly auspicious for raising an army or funds to salvage the Holy Land. The desire to restore the Holy Land was not completely lacking in the next centuries, but the will was wanting. Meanwhile, a new enemy had appeared, the Ottoman Turks, who threatened Europe itself. Before the fourteenth century was over, a new era in the warfare between the Christian West and the Muslim world had begun.

Part III. Suggestions for Further Reading

Amitai-Preiss, Reuven. *Mongols and Mamluks: The Mamluk-Illkhanid War, 1260–1281*. Cambridge: Cambridge UP, 1995.
Atiya, Aziz S. *Crusade, Commerce and Culture*. Bloomington: U of Indiana P, 1962.

———. *The Crusade in the Later Middle Ages*. London: Methuen & Co., 1938.

Christiansen, Eric. *The Northern Crusades*. London: Penguin Books, 1997.

Edbury, Peter W. *The Kingdom of Cyprus and the Crusades, 1191–1374*. Cambridge: Cambridge UP, 1991.

Flahiff, George B. " 'Deus Non Vult:' A Critic of the Third Crusade." *Medieval Studies* 9 (1947):162-88.

Folda, Jaroslav. *Crusader Art in the Holy Land: From the Third Crusade to the Fall of Acre, 1187–1291*. Cambridge: Cambridge UP, 2005.

Housley, Norman. *The Avignon Papacy and the Crusades, 1305–1378*. Oxford: Clarendon Press, 1986.

———. *The Italian Crusades*. Oxford: Clarendon Press, 1982.

———. *The Later Crusades, 1274–1580*. Oxford: Oxford UP, 1992.

Jackson, Gabriel. *The Making of Medieval Spain*. New York: Harcourt Brace Jovanovich, 1972.

Jackson, Peter. *The Mongols and the West, 1221–1410*. Edinburgh: Pearson Education, 2005.

Lower, Michael. *The Barons' Crusade*. Philadelphia: U of Pennsylvania P, 2005.

Menocal, Maria Rosa. *Ornament of the World*. Boston: Little, Brown and Company, 2002.

Morgan, David. *The Mongols*. 2nd ed. Malden, MA: Blackwell Publishing, 2007

Moore, John C. *Pope Innocent III (1160/61–1216)*. Leiden, Neth.: E.J. Brill, 2003.

———, ed. *Pope Innocent and His World*. Aldershot, Hampshire, UK: Ashgate Publishing, 1999.

Nowell, Charles E. "The Historical Prester John." *Speculum* 28.3 (July 1953): 435–45.

O'Callaghan, Joseph F. *Reconquest and Crusade in Medieval Spain*. Philadelphia: U of Pennsylvania P, 2003.

Pegg, Mark. *A Most Holy War: The Albigensian Crusade and the Battle for Christendom*. Oxford and New York: Oxford UP, 2008.

Phillips, Jonathan. *The Fourth Crusade and the Sack of Constantinople*. New York: Viking Penguin, 2004.

Powell, James M. *Anatomy of a Crusade, 1213–1221*. Philadelphia: U of Pennsylvania P, 1986. (This book is on the Fifth Crusade.)

———. *The Crusades, the Kingdom of Sicily, and the Mediterranean*. Aldershot, Hampshire, UK: Ashgate Publishing, 2007.

Purcell, Maureen. *Papal Crusading Policy, 1244–1291*. Leiden, Neth.: E.J. Brill, 1975.

Queller, Donald, and Thomas Madden. *The Fourth Crusade: The Sack of Constantinople*. 2nd ed. Philadelphia: U of Pennsylvania P, 1997.

Raedts, Peter. "The Children's Crusade of 1212." *Journal of Medieval History* 3 (1977): 279–323.

Runciman, Steven. *The Sicilian Vespers*. Cambridge: Cambridge UP, 1958.

Sidberry, Elizabeth. *Criticism of Crusading, 1095–1274*. Oxford: Clarendon Press, 1985.

Strayer, Joseph. *The Albigensian Crusades*. New York: Dial Press, 1971.

Throop, Palmer A. *Criticism of the Crusade: A Study of Public Opinion and Crusade Propaganda*. Amsterdam: Swets & Zeitlingen, 1940.

Epilogue

The End of the Dream

The new era seeped slowly into the European consciousness. The change had begun in the years following the Mongol conquest of the Seljuk Turks in Anatolia during the 1240s. Seljuk power had quickly disintegrated, and several small emirates emerged from the ruins of the Seljuk Empire.

The most successful emirate was ruled by Osman, who gave his name to the Ottoman dynasty. He and his successors conquered the other emirates and, in the early fourteenth century, having set their sights on the Greek Empire, began their conquest of Byzantine territory in Anatolia.

A. Byzantium in the Fourteenth Century

The Byzantine Empire by 1300 was totally down on its luck. Constantinople had never recovered from the destruction and poverty caused by the Crusade of 1204 and the subsequent decades of misrule under the Latins. Although the Emperor Michael VIII's clever political maneuvering in the last half of the thirteenth century had saved the empire from the ambitions of Charles of Anjou, he had paid dearly to accomplish it, and Constantinople was destitute. The empire had scarcely any navy left and had neither the financial resources nor the manpower to undertake an effective defense against a determined aggressor. To add to the difficulties, Constantinople had become the battlefield on which the Genoese and Venetians fought for control of trade in and out of the Aegean and the Black Sea.

In the course of the fourteenth century, Constantinople's problems became even more desperate. The Black Death descended on the city in 1347, and more than 50 per cent of the population succumbed to the disease. The city was torn apart by internal dissensions followed by a breakdown of central authority and civil wars. And two strong powers threatened Constantinople's borders: the Serbs in the Balkans and the Ottoman Turks in Asia Minor.

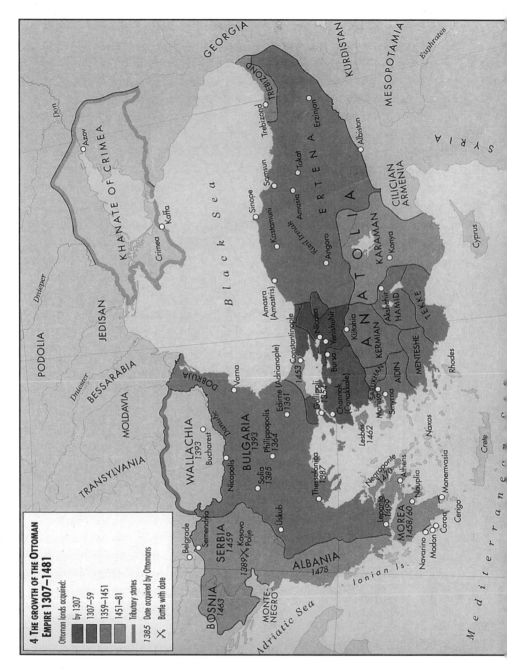

Map 10.1 The Growth of the Ottoman Empire, 1307–1481.

To gain an ally in the civil war that had broken out in 1341, one of the contenders for the imperial throne, John of Cantacuzenus, first called on aid from the Serbian ruler, Stephen Dusan. When John consolidated his power in Constantinople, Stephen withdrew his support, probably preferring to attack Constantinople. John turned next to the Ottoman Turks.

B. The Ottoman Turks on the Move

In return for their help in the ongoing civil war, John permitted the Ottomans access to Europe. In 1348 they crossed the Straits of the Dardanelles; by 1354 they were in Gallipoli; by 1361 they had taken most of Thrace and established their capital in Adrianople. Before the end of the century, the Turks had conquered the Serbs and reduced the Bulgarians to a vassal state in the growing Ottoman Empire. It was principally Constantinople that was now held by the Greeks and only its seemingly impregnable city walls still saved it.

During John of Cantacuzenus's reign he had traveled to the West to implore the Latins for aid, but the issue of the reunion of the churches once again was a major stumbling block, and only sporadic and useless aid was forthcoming. Basically nothing was done to save the Byzantine Empire.

The West finally woke up to the seriousness of the Ottoman threat when the Turks advanced into the Danube region. The Hungarian king, Sigismund, sent an ambassador in 1395 to the court of the French king Charles VI to beg for help against the Turks. Europe at last responded. In the summer of 1396 a great force was assembled from France, Germany, Burgundy, and eastern Europe, which joined with the Hungarian army to try to halt the Turks. They had some minor victories as they marched south of the Danube, until they reached Nicopolis, a heavily fortified city overlooking the Danube.

C. The Battle of Nicopolis

The French, led by the duke of Burgundy, insisted on having the honor of being the first to attack, although the Hungarians had experience fighting the Turks. The French knights easily defeated the Turkish cavalry in their first charge, but they found their way up the hill to the city strewn with wooden stakes. They dismounted to pull them up and were attacked by Turkish archers. Thousands of men were killed.

The duke of Burgundy surrendered early in the fighting, and a little later the Hungarian king fled and was taken by ship to Constantinople. When his men saw that the king had gone, they, too, fled. Many tried to swim to the ships in the harbor nearby. A German participant who described the scene wrote that, "Of those who could not cross the water and reach the vessels, a

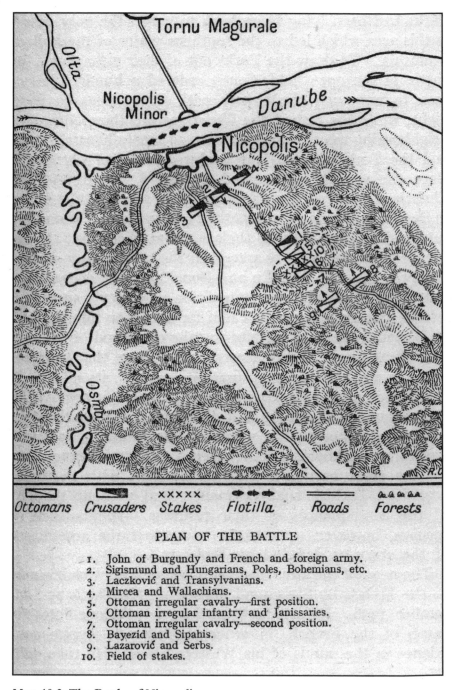

Map 10.2 The Battle of Nicopolis.

portion were killed; but the larger number were made prisoners."[1] The Duke of Burgundy was among them, as well as countless lords, horsemen, and foot soldiers.

This appalling disaster at Nicopolis is often called a crusade. In reality the battle at Nicopolis is like the Roman god Janus, the god of beginnings and endings, who faced both the past and the future. The battle marked the beginning of centuries of warfare against an enemy determined to conquer Europe. The response in the Latin West to the Ottoman Turks differentiated the so-called later crusades from all those that had preceded them. Until the Turks were finally defeated outside the walls of Vienna in 1683, Europe was on the defensive against them.

The rhetoric of crusading did not disappear; indeed it is still with us. But after Nicopolis, the rhetoric was used to inspire men to save Europe from the Ottoman Turks. The era of the armed pilgrimage to reclaim Jerusalem was over.

D. The Fall of Constantinople

The sad coda to the history we have been following was the fall of Constantinople to the Turks on May 29, 1453. Although the defenders tried valiantly to save the city, they were at the mercy of a stronger foe and had no reserves to replace the men who fell in battle. When Sultan Mehmed II entered the city, expecting to see its beauty, its buildings elaborately adorned, and its great churches filled with treasure, he saw instead "what a large number had been killed, and the ruin of the buildings, and the wholesale ruin and destruction of the city, [and] he was filled with compassion.... Tears fell from his eyes as he groaned deeply and passionately: 'What a city we have given over to plunder and destruction.' "[2]

The mortification in Europe over the failure to do anything to save the great city was felt most acutely by the pope, Pius II (1458–1464), who struggled in vain to win support for a crusade to relieve Constantinople. At a council he called in 1459 to enlist aid, he said, "We came full of hope and we grieve to find it vain. We are ashamed that Christians are so indifferent.... The Turks do not hesitate to die for their most vile faith, but we cannot incur the least expense nor endure the smallest hardship for the sake of Christ's Gospel."[3] Nonetheless, the pope was somehow convinced that a new crusade would soon be under way, and he intended to join it. In 1464, on his way to Ancona, where he planned to sail for the East, Pius died. He had been spared the knowledge that he had called for a crusade and nobody came.

---

[1] Johann Schiltberger, "The Bondage and Travels of Johann Schiltberger," in Allen and Amt 398–99.
[2] Kritovoulos, "On the Fall of Constantinople," in Allen and Amt 404–405.
[3] "The Commentaries of Pius II, Books II and III," trans. F. A. Gragg, in Allen and Amt 410–11.

The Holy City in the Fourteenth Century

The greatest sadness for Latin Christians was that the Church of the Holy Sepulchre was lost to them. The loss was especially hard to bear because after 1291, with one small exception, their most precious church and all the other churches and holy places in the Holy Land were in the care of the Eastern Christians. The Latins regarded them as heretics and schismatics, and despised them.

Soon after Jerusalem fell, a group of three Franciscans was given permission by the sultan in Cairo to live in the Church of the Holy Sepulchre and guard Christ's tomb. After Acre fell, the pope sent envoys to the sultan to ask that he allow more Franciscans to return to Jerusalem. Through the intermediary of the King and Queen of Sicily (and the lavish expenditure of their money) an agreement was reached.

Pope Clement VI issued a bull in November 1343 announcing the conclusion of successful negotiations, according to which Franciscans would be permitted to live continuously in the Church of the Holy Sepulchre and officiate at the liturgies in the church. The queen was permitted to build a monastery on Mount Zion for twelve friars and the three laymen who would look after them. The Franciscan residence in the Holy Land was thus officially sanctioned. Over time, other holy sites were purchased for the Franciscans to care for, including the Church of the Nativity in Bethlehem, and their presence was assured in perpetuity.

Still the Pilgrims Come

Christian pilgrims continued to visit Jerusalem in large numbers during the fourteenth century. Since many pilgrims wrote wonderfully graphic accounts, we know a good deal about the hardships of their travel, the expense, the precautions they had to take to survive in the Islamic world, the sights, sounds, and smells of the places they visited.

The great majority of pilgrims sailed in Venetian galleys and went in groups for safety and companionship. On board ship they were crammed into small, miserable spaces with sometimes more than five hundred other travelers, as well as animals of all sizes. The damp, putrid quarters bred mice, rats, and lice; many passengers became ill; and they all had to deal with the thievery of the galley slaves and with boredom. The discomfort was relieved on more than one occasion by shipwrecks. These voyages were not for the faint of heart.

Once they reached the Muslim shores, the Christians were obliged to hire guides and interpreters, pay tributes and taxes of various sorts and, most of all, pay to prevent being attacked and robbed by Bedouin tribesmen who roamed the hills and the roads, waiting to prey on the Christian travelers.

A Franciscan friar who visited Jerusalem in 1346 described his terror when he was taken prisoner and brought before the emir of Jerusalem. His interpreter explained that the friar had no money to pay the tribute the sultan required. "Because of these words, the amir [sic] had our interpreter beaten on the spot. When I saw him so beaten, I expected to have my own share along with him, and in the greatest fear I stood in the corner among those accursed men who held me; and I thought within myself that I was going to die."[4] In any event, he was given the money for the tribute from the Franciscan friars living on Mount Zion and was freed.

The pilgrims who wished to enter the Church of the Holy Sepulchre had to pay a fee to the Muslim guards who unlocked the door, let them inside, and then locked them in, ordinarily for a full day and night. Even the three friars assigned to live in the church had to pay to enter. Twice a year, on the holiest days, the Muslims let all the Christians in the city into the church without charge. On those special days there were shops in the church, as if it were a market in a European town. "On Palm Sunday and on Holy Easter all go there, each Christian group to its own priest, and each priest celebrates for his own people in his own tongue.... The Latins, namely the Friars Minor, celebrate at the altar of Mary Magdalen, which belongs to us, the Latin Christians."[5]

Some pilgrims, like tourists everywhere, were badly behaved, and some even carved their initials and their coats of arms on the pillars inside the Church of the Holy Sepulchre.

For most pilgrims, however, the experience had a religious intensity that was genuinely moving and inspiring. Even though, as a renowned author of a pilgrimage text wrote, "No one should think visiting the places to be a light task; there is the intense heat of the sun, the walking from place to place, kneeling and prostration; above all there is the strain that everyone puts on himself in striving with all of his might to rouse himself to earnest piety and comprehension of what is shown to him of the holy places."[6]

All the hardships were worth the moment when the pilgrims had their first sight of the Holy Land. As they approached the shore on one of the pilgrim ships, everyone began to sing the *Te Deum*. "I have never heard so sweet and joyous a song," a pilgrim wrote, "for there were many voices, and their dissonance made as it were sweet music and harmony.... Meanwhile some bowed their faces to the deck and prayed, looking toward the Holy land; others wept for joy while they sang, and so all sang a new song before the throne of God, and the earth and sea rang with their voices."[7]

---

4   Niccolo Poggibonsi, "A Voyage Beyond the Seas," in Peters, *Jerusalem* 434–35.
5   Poggibonsi, in Peters, *Jerusalem*, 441.
6   Felix Fabri, "The Book of the Wanderings," trans. A. Stewart, Palestine Pilgrims' Text Society, vol. 1, 1893 (New York: AMS Press, 1971) 299.
7   Fabri 208–09.

Jewish pilgrimage to the Holy Land also continued. Since many Jews who came from Spain or Egypt and North Africa, for example, were accustomed to living in Muslim lands and the Muslims were accustomed to them and friendly, the Jews had less to fear when they traveled.

The Jews came to stand where historic events took place: the Western Wall, the Mount where Abraham was called upon to sacrifice Isaac, the site where the walls of Jericho had once stood, and the graves of the patriarchs and the prophets whose lives are sacred in Jewish tradition. Most of all, the Jews came to pray for the restoration of their temple and the land that God had promised to Abraham.

Early in the thirteenth century a number of Jews migrated to the Holy Land from France and Spain, and smaller groups came from Germany and Italy. In the next century, the pattern of Jewish settlement changed; the important center of Jewish life and religious study was established at Safed, and many diaspora Jews settled in cities in the Galilee. The migration from Europe would continue for centuries, and the history of Jewish pilgrimage was subsumed in the larger history of Jewish immigration and settlement in the Holy Land.

For Muslim pilgrims, of course, the whole Islamic world was one community — the *Dar al-Islam*, the "Abode of Islam" — and from one end of this world to the other Muslims could travel freely, assured of protection and help along their way. By far the best known Muslim traveler in the fourteenth century was Ibn Battuta, who was born in Morocco in 1304, studied law, and at the age of twenty-one set out to make his first *hajj* to Mecca and Medina. Altogether he made four pilgrimages to Mecca and toured the places that were customary for a Muslim to visit: Egypt, Palestine (including Jerusalem to pray on the Temple Mount in the third holiest city in Islam), Syria, Persia, Muslim Spain, and North Africa.

What makes him such an extraordinary traveler was that in his lifetime he crossed the length and breadth of the *Dar al-Islam*. He sailed down the coasts of west and east Africa; he sailed the Persian Gulf, and crossed the Arabian Desert with a camel caravan to reach Mecca; he went to India, where he lived and worked in Delhi for eight years, and traveled through southern India. He worked in the Maldives and went by ship to Burma, Ceylon, and the southern coast of China. He traveled through Asia Minor and toured the Black Sea coast; he crossed the Sahara Desert with a camel caravan to visit the Sudan.

Ibn Battuta was an acute observer, and the sights, sounds, and smells of the worlds he described are so alive they jump off the page.[8] Wherever he went he found fellow Muslims and familiar Islamic institutions: traders and merchants,

---

[8] Ibn Battuta, *The Travels of Ibn Battuta, A.D. 1325–1354*, trans. H.A.R. Gibb, 2 vols. (Cambridge: Cambridge UP, 1958).

ship captains and sailors, craftsmen, bazaars, always a mosque, and often a school—in sum a whole Muslim community, all part of a world he knew and understood.

His experience was a sharp contrast to the Christian experience. Christian pilgrims knew themselves to be in a hostile world—not unwilling to give them entrance, but never welcoming. "All who come on pilgrimage to it [the Church of the Holy Sepulchre]," Ibn Battuta wrote, "are liable to a stipulated tax to the Muslims and various humiliations, which they suffer very unwillingly."[9]

It has been estimated that Ibn Battuta traveled between 73,000 and 78,000 miles (between 116,800 and 124,800 kilometers). Nearly all of it was in the Islamic world. His travels are thus a paradigm of the changed landscape of the fourteenth century. Christian Europe had retreated from the eastern Mediterranean; only Cyprus and Rhodes remained to the Latins, and both would fall to Islam in the fifteenth century. The last bastion of Christendom in the East, the Byzantine Empire, was being dismantled by the Turks a half century before they captured Constantinople in 1453.

What Is the Legacy of the Crusades?

Until the middle of the twentieth century, historians believed that the crusades were responsible for opening the Mediterranean for trade with the East. We now know that Italian merchants were crossing the Mediterranean to Alexandria, Damietta, Constantinople, and the port of Antioch long before the First Crusade. The Venetians and Genoese were actually reluctant to support the First Crusade because they worried that the warfare would impede their trade. As we know, events proved them wrong.

In the mid-thirteenth century, the Silk Road to China was opened to Europeans. The security of the several roads that made up the overland route to China was made possible by the Mongols—a strange and wonderful byproduct of the crusading era and of the relations, however uneasy, between the Mongols and the Latins. Despite the physical hardships of the journey, traders and Christian missionaries were able to travel the Silk Road, protected all along the route by the Mongols. Before the Silk Road was opened, Italian merchants were forced to wait in the eastern Mediterranean port cities for the luxury goods, the jewels, and the spices to be brought to them by Eastern merchants. Then, for a century, they could travel the route themselves and, without intermediaries, make a handsome profit.

The goods imported into Europe increased the desire for silk, linen, and cotton, for carpets from Persia, jewels from India, paper from China, dyestuffs, and for hundreds of herbs and spices. The new products expanded the

---

[9] Ibn Battuta, vol. 1, 80.

numbers and size of the European markets, and enormous profits were made by the Italian merchants who, in addition to their near monopoly on the trade, grew rich from shipbuilding and carrying crusaders and pilgrims to the eastern Mediterranean.

Although the economic changes that benefited Europe were, in quantity and kind, greater than what had come before the crusades, it is no longer possible to attribute the beginning of these changes to the crusades.

In 1368 the Chinese successfully rebelled against their Mongol overlords, and the Mongol Empire began to disintegrate. At the same time, the Tartar commander Tamerlane, from his capital in Samarkand, was threatening to make good on his intention to conquer the world. During his lifetime Tamerlane blocked foreign travel on the Silk Road to the East. By the time he died in 1405, Samarkand, once the heart of the Silk Road, where traders and merchants gathered to exchange their goods — the city known as the Athens of Asia — was destroyed. The Silk Route was no longer passable, and the Chinese had closed their doors to Westerners.

A small number of missionaries were intrepid enough, and strong enough in their faith, to venture East while the Silk Road was open. Their faith is admirable. Whether they went to convert the Mongols or whether they went hoping for martyrdom is difficult at this remove to know. For a short time a mission led by the Franciscan John of Monte Corvino had some success. He arrived at the court of the Great Khan at the end of the thirteenth century and labored in the vineyards of the Lord for twelve years alone; his only help came from an Italian merchant. He established a Catholic mission and was made an archbishop early in the fourteenth century. After he died, two other Franciscans, in turn, were sent to continue his work. When the Chinese began their rebellion against the Mongols, they killed the last Catholic bishop and in 1369 expelled the Christians from Peking. Christian missionaries did not return until the end of the sixteenth century.

Although the traders and missionaries were gone from the Far East, removed as if they had never come, their travels and reports had a profound effect on the European understanding of the world. By the close of the fourteenth century Europeans were well aware of the vast and exotic world beyond the eastern Mediterranean seaboard. The closing of the overland routes to China and the loss of the eastern Mediterranean ports led to the quest for new paths to the East. The future would belong to the great navigators who sought to find a sea route around Africa to India and China.

Little of the great learning and culture of the Islamic world entered Europe through the Latin Kingdom. It came instead through the translation centers in Spain and in Sicily, where Muslims, Christians, and Jews sat side-by-side to translate the Greek and Roman works from classical antiquity that had been preserved in the Muslim world. By this same route the important Islamic philosophical, scientific, and medical works entered the West. As these works became better known and valued in the thirteenth and later centuries, the genius of the classical and Islamic worlds expanded the intellectual world of western Europe. We are the inheritors of this richness. This incredible harvest, however, did not come from the Latins in Syria-Palestine.

The Story Continues

There is about the crusades something marvelous, something dreadful, and something fantastical. All the stories of courage, military glory, and feats of daring; of martyrs, saints, and their relics; of chivalry and the grand gesture, of larger than life heroes engaged people's imaginations from the start of the crusades.

In addition to the many chronicles written during the crusades, which were widely circulated in Europe, the crusades became a popular subject for songs, romances, and plays, and the stories of the crusades were quickly absorbed into the culture of the Western world.

A favorite, enduring invention, written in the early fourteenth century, was the selection of Nine Worthies, nine people, grouped in threes, chosen to represent the greatest examples for all time of perfect chivalry. They were drawn from the pagan classical world, from the Old Testament, and from among the outstanding Christian heroes. King Arthur, Charlemagne, and Godfrey of Bouillon make up the Christian triad. The Nine Worthies quickly became a popular theme for literature and plays, and they were depicted over and over in sculpture and drawings for centuries—even showing up on a set of silver spoons in the late sixteenth century. Godfrey was fixed in the European imagination as the perfect knight of the crusading era. (See Color Plate 8.)

Over the centuries the ways in which the crusades were perceived underwent many changes. The crusades suffered by association with the negative view of the Middle Ages that began with the revival and veneration of classical antiquity during the Renaissance in the fourteenth and fifteenth centuries. The negativism was reinforced by the anti-Catholic attitudes that flourished during the Reformation, and later during the eighteenth-century Enlightenment, when everything connected to the Roman Church was considered to have been tainted with dogmatism, repression, and ignorance.

Two new movements in the nineteenth century brought about a revival of enthusiasm for the crusades. The nineteenth century was the age of Romanticism in music, art, literature, and history. The Romantics had a passion for history, and they found in the Middle Ages more than enough colorful material to satisfy their desire to breathe new life into that long ago past.

Sir Walter Scott was one of the most influential novelists of the Romantic Age and his novels, principally *Ivanhoe* and *The Talisman*, assured the crusades their permanent place in Romantic literature. In his introduction to *The Talisman*, Scott described how he chose to write about the time "at which the warlike character of Richard I, wild and generous, a pattern of chivalry with all its extravagant virtues, and its no less absurd errors, was opposed to that of Saladin, in which the Christian and English monarch showed all the cruelty and violence of an Eastern sultan, and Saladin, on the other hand, displayed the deep policy and prudence of an English sovereign." Scott's depiction of one of the great heroic eras in European history was so compelling, so beautifully written, and so persuasive that his books—and his prejudices—have left an indelible impression.

The nineteenth century was also the age of nationalism, the rise of a national self-awareness and sensibility that affected all nations, established or newly emerging. In their search for the roots of national identity, historians turned back to the crusades and adopted as national heroes the great crusading heroes. The French had several in their past: the French leaders of the First Crusade, Philip II, and Louis IX, and a host of families whose ancestry could be traced to the crusades. The crusades were woven into the fabric of French national history, as they were into the histories of most European states.

In 1853 the English Parliament, having decided to overlook Richard the Lionheart's French genealogy and his preference for France, honored him as their national hero by placing a bronze equestrian statue of Richard outside the British Houses of Parliament, formerly the Palace of Westminster. Germany had Frederick Barbarossa; Belgium, as it attained nationhood, adopted Godfrey of Bouillon.

So nations discovered in their pasts the most chivalrous, the bravest, the grandest—and the most romantic—of people and times. In this way the crusades entered into what is called the "nationalist discourse," which simply means that they were no longer viewed—as previously they had been—as an international movement, but were segregated into separate national histories. On the whole, into the early twentieth century, historians reflected the romantic picture painted in Sir Walter Scott's novels, and they kept alive the legendary figure of Saladin as Scott portrayed him and the exotic world he represented.

Until the nineteenth century, Arab historians did not view the crusades as a distinct phenomenon with its own special character. To the Muslims writing about the two centuries of warfare with the Franks, the invasions were not singled out as special or unusual. The infidels from the West were simply one among many invaders—the Seljuk Turks, the Mongols, the Ottomans—yet another player in the continuous warfare in the East. There was no recognition that the crusaders—that term was never used in the writings of medieval Islamic historians—were engaged in a holy war. The Franks came, eventually they were defeated, and they left. In the long history of the Middle East, the Frankish success was short-lived.

It is a curious irony that the awakening of serious Muslim interest in the crusades derived from the same European writers whose works were so influential in the West. In Syria, where French cultural influence was strong, the French historians were read in French; other European works were translated into Arabic by Arab scholars learned in the European languages. The development of history as an academic discipline, combined with a new interest in reading the medieval sources themselves, led to a desire to assess the crusading era and understand what it meant in the context of Islamic history.

The great change in the Muslim attitude toward the crusades, and the one we live with to this day, also has its roots in the nineteenth century. The century was the age of imperialism. With an amazing certitude in the rightness of their conquests and the arrogance of believing they were the bearers of a higher form of culture, civilization, and religion, the British, followed closely by the French, and ultimately by the Belgians, set out to win dominion over the world. Even earlier, the Spanish and Portuguese were imperialists, but here the direction of imperialism into the Middle East is our concern.

The Russians actually led the way in the Middle East in the late eighteenth century. In 1769, and more decisively in 1783, the Russians defeated the Turks in the Crimea and won control of the Black Sea. The other powers quickly advanced against the Ottomans. Napoleon's expedition to Egypt in 1798 was short-lived, but his temporary success (he was defeated by the British) and the Russian permanent success were early indications that Ottoman power was weakening. Before the First World War, the French captured Algeria and Tunis. Although the British had never annexed Egypt formally as a colony, control of Cairo and especially the Suez Canal, vital to assure the British their route to India, meant that Egypt was *de facto* if not *de jure* part of the British Empire.

The seminal event in modern Muslim history was the dismemberment of the Ottoman Empire following the Turkish defeat in the First World War and the political decision to divide the Ottoman lands among the great European powers. The exceptions were Iran and what was left to Turkey.

European colonialism, the subjection of much of the Islamic world in the Middle East to the Western nations, began to be compared by Muslims to that time in the crusading era when Christian forces from Europe overran the Middle East and brought Muslims under the yoke of foreign invaders. In the fight to eject the colonial powers in the Middle East, the imagery of the crusades in all its negative aspects became a powerful tool. In their histories, and in the political rhetoric used by politicians and leaders to win their independence, the Muslims found in the crusades terrible examples of the

Christian threat to the Islamic world—and of their own heroes and their own past victories.

Not surprisingly it is Saladin who emerged as the hero of the renewed *jihad* against the Christians. After the founding of the state of Israel in 1948, Saladin was accorded special prominence for his impressive and definitive victory over the Christians at the Battle of Hattin and his capture of Jerusalem. He became the prototype of an Arab nationalist. Saddam Hussein, for example, had himself portrayed with pictures of Saladin in many media, showing himself alongside the hero of the *jihad* to strengthen his own role as a leader of Arab nationalism. By coincidence Saddam Hussein was born in Tikrit, the same town where Saladin was born. In Damascus there is an enormous group sculpture that has an equestrian statue of Saladin as the centerpiece; behind him are two defeated crusaders, King Guy of Jerusalem and Reynaud de Châtillon.[10] Saladin is not without his critics today, as he was during the crusading era, but overall he has emerged in the Arab world as the *jihad*ist to be emulated above all others.

In the post–9/11 world, Muslim extremists continue to interpret the crusades as the prime example of Western imperialism and the putative desire of the Western powers, the United States now included, to eradicate Islam.

I stress most emphatically that we should not believe that this position is held by all Muslims, because it assuredly is not. But, it is a position expressed by fundamentalist Muslims and extremists. The historian Carole Hillenbrand has cited A.S. Ahmed, a contemporary Islamic writer living in the West, whose lucid summary of the current state of affairs I quote here: "The memory of the Crusades lingers in the Middle East and colors Muslim perceptions of Europe. It is the memory of an aggressive, backward and religiously fanatic Europe. This historical memory would be reinforced in the nineteenth and twentieth centuries as imperial Europeans once again arrived to subjugate and colonize territories in the Middle East. Unfortunately this legacy of bitterness is overlooked by most Europeans when thinking of the Crusades."[11]

Contemporary Western historians assessing the role of the crusades from the perspective of European history do not ordinarily burden them with a rhetorical political agenda. Not that we lack our own prejudices. Writing the history of the encounters between the West and the societies of Islam is, sadly, weighed down with prejudices and misunderstanding.

According to the historian Norman Daniel, the legacy we have inherited from the crusades is a dark one; it is the image of the "terrible Turk" that was

---

[10] There is a photograph of the sculpture in Carole Hillenbrand, *The Crusades: Islamic Perspectives* (Chicago: Fitzroy Dearborn Press, 1999) 596–98.

[11] A.S. Ahmed, in Hillenbrand 590.

imprinted on the European mind beginning with the First Crusade, when Pope Urban II called the Turks "a race so despised, base, and the instrument of demons" and again "a race utterly alienated from God." The pope described how the Turks defiled and destroyed the altars and churches and committed cruelties so inhuman that they were almost beyond imaging. The Turks were the enemies of a pure Christian society and must be eliminated. They were never called Muslims, but rather Turks, Arabs, Saracens, and infidels, names that refused to recognize the legitimacy of Islam. Throughout the crusading era and beyond, this negative image of the Muslim was deeply ingrained.

Norman Daniel has called this hostile image the "medieval canon." "We are entitled to say that this canon [of ideas] was formed during the twelfth and thirteenth centuries and the earlier part of the fourteenth…. By the middle of the fourteenth century it was firmly established in Europe; and it was to continue into the future so powerfully as to affect many generations, even up to the present day."[12]

Other historians, who take a more positive view of the relations between the West and the Islamic societies in the Middle East, remind us that during the medieval centuries, including the crusading era, Christians and Muslims did business together and lived side-by-side in the East, in Spain, and in Sicily. Positive feelings and influence as well as enmity derived from these interactions.

Many historians recognize that the Muslim influence on Western culture in the Middle Ages was a major fertilizing agent in the development of European culture. European civilization, so backward in 1100 compared to the intellectually sophisticated world of Islam, was enriched in important ways by Islamic culture during the twelfth and thirteenth centuries.

The renaissance of learning that began in Europe in the twelfth century had two main roots: the revival of classical Roman learning that, for the most part, had lain dormant since the collapse of the Roman Empire, and the knowledge of the classical Greek world that had all but disappeared in the West. The Greek language itself was unknown in 1100, and the great works of Greek science, philosophy, and literature were literally a closed book. It was to the Arabic world that the West owed the revival of the Greek texts.

What made Arabic culture so extraordinary in the medieval period was that the Arabs valued and preserved the heritage of the civilizations they conquered or met through trade. Wherever they went, the Muslims adapted into their culture the best in the native cultures they encountered. The Arabs thus discovered in the Middle East the major Greek works: the medical, mathematical, and scientific texts; the philosophical works, Aristotle especially. To these

---

12 Norman Daniel, *Islam and the West: The Making of an Image* (Edinburgh: The University Press, 1980) 275.

treatises the Arab scholars added their own interpretations and ideas, and the texts, when translated into Hebrew and Latin and transmitted to Europe, stimulated the growth of European culture. The flowering of European culture that began in the twelfth century was the consequence, as Steven Runciman believed, of "the long sequence of interaction and fusion between Orient and Occident out of which our civilization has grown."[13]

The contrary position is held by Bernard Lewis, a gifted historian of the Muslim world. He views the relationship between Europe and Islam as confrontational, and that from first to last the history of Islam and western Europe can be told in terms of attacks and counterattacks, of *jihads* and crusades. "Indeed," Professor Lewis wrote, "the whole complex process of European expansion and empire in the last five centuries has its roots in the clash of Islam and Christendom." He called Europe and Islam "intimate enemies, whose continuing conflict derived a special virulence from their shared origins and common aims."[14] The crusades are understood as the counterattack following the Muslim expansion in the seventh and early eight centuries. The victory of Islam over the crusaders was the Muslim counterattack, and so it has gone, and so, in Professor Lewis's analysis, it will continue unless there are some radical shifts we cannot predict.

The eminent Egyptian historian Aziz Atiya, whose many books on the crusades have influenced western historiography, has placed the crusades in a longer perspective. The crusades, he wrote, "are important phases in the story of mankind in general and in the history of the Eastern Question.... The conflict of East and West goes far back into antiquity."[15] He begins the story with the war between the Greeks and Persians in the fifth century BCE, the first struggle between the East and the West and the moment in Greek history when the Hellenes defined the superiority of their culture over that of the East.

The Greeks established the spiritual and geographical boundary between the Orient and the West, and the Persian wars were the Greek solution to the Eastern Question, as Atiya has framed it. The Romans followed with their solution, the Byzantine Greeks with theirs, and then the crusades, which were yet another chapter — what Atiya has called the Frankish Solution to the Eastern Question.

Many crusade historians are currently wrestling with different kinds of questions. One group, whose most persuasive member is Jonathan Riley-Smith, is called pluralists. They take the position that all wars that were called by

---

[13] Runciman, vol. 3, 480.

[14] Bernard Lewis, *Islam and the West* (Oxford: Oxford UP, 1993) 17. See also Lewis' book, *What Went Wrong? Western Impact and the Middle Eastern Response* (Oxford: Oxford UP, 2002).

[15] Aziz Atiya, *Crusade, Commerce, and Culture* (Bloomington: U of Indiana P, 1962) 13.

a pope to fight against the enemies of the Church and Christendom were legitimate crusades. Both the geography and the time frame of crusading are, in this view, considerably extended. The geographical boundary, as we have discussed, includes the Northern Crusades, the wars against the Muslims in Spain, wars against heretics, and the political wars against the pope's Christian enemies in Europe. The ending date for the crusades varies considerably. Riley-Smith would carry the history to the end of the eighteenth century; his chosen date is marked by the Hospitallers' surrender of Malta to Napoleon in June 1798.[16]

The other major group is called traditionalists. They take the position that the goal of Jerusalem at the time of the First Crusade defined crusading for all time. Only those movements that were launched by the papacy to recover or preserve the Holy Land for Christendom should rightly be considered crusades.

There is still one more group, called generalists (for want, one presumes, of a better term), who place the crusades under the umbrella of holy war and study the crusades as the manifestation of a war, or series of wars, fought in the name of God and sanctified by God.

The arguments among these three groups and their offspring will undoubtedly go on for decades. The benefit is the wealth of research that is being done, which is exponentially expanding our knowledge about the crusades.

The one persistent legacy we have inherited from the crusades, the one idea that has permeated Western consciousness ever since, is, I believe, the ideology of the holy war. The idea was formulated by the reforming popes in the last half of the eleventh century, but it came to fruition at the time of the First Crusade. "In our time," the chronicler wrote, "God has instituted a holy manner of warfare." The many miracles recorded during the crusades—the finding of the Holy Lance, the visions, the multiplying of the crusade armies, the victories against formidable odds—were proof that God was guiding the soldiers fighting under the banner of Christ. The armed pilgrims who went East were indeed God's warriors.

We live today with the ideology of the Christian holy war just as Muslims live with the ideology of the *jihad*. The crusades, if there is a lesson lodged in the story—and I believe there is—should teach us to be very wary of how we use violence in the name of God or Allah.

Sir Steven Runciman's magnificent three-volume *History of the Crusades* was revered as the high-water mark of crusade scholarship for decades after he published it in 1951–1953. Current research is to some extent supplanting his work with newer ideas. Yet, it seems to me, that his final words on the

---

[16] Jonathan Riley-Smith, *The Crusades: A History*, 2nd ed. (New Haven, CT: Yale UP, 2005) 296.

crusades have resonance for us all, perhaps more so today than when he wrote them. Since the lands along the Syrian–Palestinian coast of the Mediterranean Sea continue to be among the most troubled places on the face of the Earth, we would do well to remember what he wrote: "The triumphs of the crusades were triumphs of faith. But faith without wisdom is a dangerous thing…. There was so much courage and so little honor, so much devotion and so little understanding."[17]

Suggestions for Further Reading

Daniel, Norman. *Islam and the West: The Making of an Image*. Edinburgh: The University Press, 1960.
Dawson, Christopher. *Mission to Asia*. 1955. Toronto: U of Toronto P, 1980.
Kedar, Benjamin Z. *Crusade and Mission*. Princeton: Princeton UP, 1984.
Lewis, Bernard. *The Muslim Discovery of Europe*. New York and London: W. W. Norton & Co., 1982.
Southern, Richard W. *Western Views of Islam in the Middle Ages*. Cambridge: Harvard UP, 1962.

---

[17] Runciman, vol. 3, 480.

Appendices

Chronology of the Crusades

1095	November 27	Pope Urban II preaches the First Crusade.
1096		Massacre of Jews in the Rhineland.
1096	July–August	Peter the Hermit and the Peoples' Crusade reach Constantinople.
1096	October	The Peoples' Crusade is destroyed by the Turks.
1096	November	The crusading armies arrive at Constantinople.
1097	June	The Siege of Nicaea
1097	October	The Siege of Antioch begins.
1098	June	The crusaders capture Antioch.
1099	July 15	Jerusalem is captured by the crusaders; First Crusade ends.
1099	July 22	Godfrey of Bouillon is elected Advocate of the Holy Sepulchre
1100		Godfrey of Bouillon dies.
1100	December	Baldwin of Boulogne is crowned first King of Jerusalem.
1101	March–September	The Crusade of 1101; defeat by the Turks
1118	April 2	Baldwin I dies.
1118	April 14	Baldwin II (count of Edessa) is crowned King of Jerusalem.
1119	June	The Field of Blood; Roger of Antioch is killed and the Franks defeated.
1124	July	Tyre is captured by the Franks.

1131	August 21	Baldwin II dies.
1131	September 14	King Fulk of Anjou and Melisende are crowned King and Queen of the Latin Kingdom.
1143	November 10	King Fulk dies.
1143	December 25	Melisende and her son Baldwin III are crowned Jointly.
1144	December 24–26	Edessa falls to Zengi.
1145	December	Pope Eugenius III proclaims the Second Crusade.
1146	March	St. Bernard preaches the Second Crusade at Vézelay.
1147	July–September	The German Crusade against the Wends
1147	September–October	Emperor Conrad III and King Louis VII of France arrive in the East.
1147	October	Lisbon falls to the Portuguese with the help of crusaders.
1148	July 24–28	The crusaders withdraw from Damascus; Second Crusade ends in failure.
1151–52		Baldwin III breaks with Melisende; rules alone.
1153	August	The Franks capture Ascalon.
1163		Baldwin III dies; Amalric, Baldwin's brother, becomes king.
1169		Saladin becomes vizier of Egypt.
1171	September	Saladin becomes caliph in Egypt.
1174		Nur-ad-Din dies.
1174	July 11	Amalric dies.
1174	July 15	Baldwin IV (the "leper king") is crowned.
1174		Saladin takes control of Damascus.
1175		Saladin begins his advance toward Latin Kingdom.
1180		Truce between Saladin and Baldwin IV
1181		Reynaud de Châtillon attacks Muslim caravan; truce is broken.
1186		Baldwin IV dies.
1186		Baldwin V becomes king of Jerusalem.

1186		Queen Sybilla and King Guy de Lusignan are crowned.
1187	July 4	Battle of Hattin; Christian forces annihilated by Saladin.
1187	October 2	Saladin captures Jerusalem.
1187	October 29	Pope Gregory VIII proclaims the Third Crusade.
1187–1189		Saladin captures most Latin states, Tyre excepted.
1188–1189		Henry II of England; Philip II of France; and Emperor Frederick I (Barbarossa) take the cross.
1189	May	Frederick I leads his army overland to the East.
1190		Richard I and Philip II leave for crusade.
1190	June 10	Frederick I dies; the German Crusade effectively ends.
1191	April 20	Philip II arrives at Acre.
1191	June	Richard I captures Cyprus; sails to Acre.
1191	July 12	Acre surrenders to Richard and Philip; becomes capital of Latin Kingdom.
1192	September 2	Richard and Saladin sign Treaty of Jaffa; Third Crusade ends,
1192		Guy de Lusignan dies; Isabella I marries Conrad of Montferrat, who briefly rules as king, until his death.
1192–1197		Henry of Champagne becomes king by marriage to Queen Isabella I.
1197		Henry of Champagne dies; Isabella I marries Aimery de Lusignan and they rule jointly.
1198		Innocent III elected to the papacy; proclaims the Fourth Crusade.
1200		al-Adil (Saladin's brother) becomes sultan of Egypt and Syria
1202–1204		The Fourth Crusade

1202		Crusaders capture Zara.
1204		Crusaders capture and sack Constantinople; Latin Empire of Constantinople established; Count Baldwin of Flanders becomes the first Latin emperor.
1205		Isabella I and Aimery die.
1209–1229		The Albigensian Crusade
1210–1212		Queen Mary and King John of Brienne rule the Latin Kingdom.
1212–1225		Mary dies; John of Brienne rules alone.
1212		The Children's Crusade
1212	July 17	Christian victory over Muslims in Spain at Las Navas de Tolosa.
1213		Innocent III proclaims the Fifth Crusade.
1215		Innocent presides over the Fourth Lateran Council.
1217		The Fifth Crusade
1217		Crusaders arrive in Palestine.
1218		Siege of Damietta
1219	November	Crusaders capture Damietta.
1221		Crusaders defeated at Mansurah and retreat from Egypt; Fifth Crusade ends.
1225		Frederick II marries Isabella II, heiress to the throne of Jerusalem; claims kingship.
1228	February	Frederick leaves for the East.
1229	February	Frederick regains Jerusalem by treaty with al-Kamil.
1229	April	Peace of Paris ends the Albigensian Crusade.
1239–1241		Crusade of Thibault of Champagne and Richard of Cornwall
1239		Papacy proclaims crusade against Frederick II
1241		Mongols invade Poland and Hungary
1244	July–August 23	Jerusalem falls to the Khwarismians
1245	October	Battle of La Forbie

1248		The Sixth Crusade, the first under-taken by Louis IX of France, begins
1249	June 5	Crusaders capture Damietta
1250	April	The Crusaders surrender to the Egyptians and the Sixth Crusade ends.
1250		Mamluks take power in Egypt
1254		Louis IX returns to France after his stay in Palestine
1256		Mongols destroy the Assassins' stronghold
1258		Mongols sack Baghdad
1260	September 3	Battle of Ain Jalut between Mongols and Mamluks
1260		Baybars seizes the sultanate in Egypt
1261		The Byzantine Greeks seize Constantinople and the Latin Empire of Constantinople is ended
1261	August 15	Emperor Michael VIII crowned in Constantinople
1263		Baybars advances on the Latin Kingdom, captures coastal cities and fortresses
1267		Louis IX takes the cross a second time
1268		Baybars captures Antioch
1270	July	Louis IX and the French crusaders leave France and sail to Tunisia
1270	August 25	Louis IX dies in Tunisia
1271		Edward of England reaches Acre; Gregory X becomes pope
1272		Edward returns to England
1274		Gregory X presides over the Council of Lyons.
1276		Gregory X dies
1277		Charles of Anjou purchases the crown of Jerusalem
1277	July	Baybars dies
1279		Qalawun seizes Mamluk throne
1281		Mamluks defeat Mongols at Battle of Homs
1282	March	The Sicilian Vespers begin

1284	March	Hugh III dies
1285		John I (Hugh III's son) succeeds to the throne of Jerusalem
1286		Henry II of Cyprus crowned King of Jerusalem following death of John I
1289		Mamluks capture Tripoli
1290		Qalawun dies; his son al-Kamil becomes sultan
1291	May 18	Mamluks capture Acre
1291	August	The last Frankish strongholds are taken by the Mamluks; the Latin Kingdom is ended.
1303		Boniface VIII dies in France; Clement V becomes pope
1306		Hospitallers begin invasion of Rhodes
1307	October	Philip IV arrests the Templars in France
1310		Hospitallers win control of Rhodes
1312		Clement orders the Knights Templar suppressed
1313		Philip IV of France and Edward II of England take the cross
1349		The Mongol dynasty in Iran is ended
1354		Ottomans occupy Gallipoli
1358		Peter I becomes king in Cyprus
1365		Crusade of Peter I; Peter invades and successfully captures Alexandria; he holds it briefly and his crusade ends in failure
1369		Ottomans capture Adrianople; Byzantine emperor appeals to the West for aid
1371		Ottomans take over much of Bulgaria and Serbia
1394		Crusade of Nicopolis proclaimed
1396	September 25	Crusaders defeated at the Battle of Nicopolis
1453	May 30	Constantinople falls to the ottoman Turks

Lists of Rulers

Rulers in the Latin Kingdom of Jerusalem

1099–1100	Godfrey of Bouillon, advocate of the Church of the Holy Sepulchre
1100–1118	Baldwin I of Boulogne
1118–1131	Baldwin II of Edessa
1131–1152	Melisende (daughter of Baldwin II), queen and regent
1131–1143	Fulk of Anjou, by marriage to Melisende
1152–1163	Baldwin III (son of Baldwin II)
1163–1174	Amalric (son of Baldwin III)
1174–1186	Baldwin IV, the "leper king" (son of Amalric)
1186	Baldwin V (son of Sybilla; nephew of Baldwin IV)
1186–1190	Sybilla (sister of Baldwin IV)
1186–1192	Guy de Lusignan, by marriage to Sybilla
1190–1205	Isabella I (daughter of Amalric)
1192	Isabella I marries Conrad of Montferrat, who is assassinated in the same year.
1192–1197	Henry of Champagne, by marriage to Isabella
1197–1205	Aimery de Lusignan, by marriage to Isabella; also ruler of Cyprus
1205	Death of Isabella I and Aimery
1205–1210	Jerusalem governed by regencies.
1210–1212	Mary (daughter of Queen Isabella I) and John of Brienne, by marriage to Mary
1210–1225	John of Brienne rules alone after Mary's death.
1225–1228	Isabella II, also known as Yolande (daughter of John of Brienne and Mary)
1225–1243	Emperor Frederick II claims throne of Jerusalem through marriage to Isabella II.
1243–1254	Conrad (son of Frederick II and Isabella II)
1254–1268	Conradin (grandson of Frederick II)
1268–1284	Hugh III, king of Cyprus, becomes King of Jerusalem
1277	Charles of Anjou purchases claim to kingship.
1284–1285	John I, king of Cyprus and Jerusalem
1285–1291	Henry II, king of Jerusalem and Cyprus

Latin Rulers of Cyprus (descendants of the Lusignan family)

1191	King Richard I of England conquers Cyprus
1192–1194	Guy de Lusignan
1194–1205	Aimery de Lusignan (1197–1205, also King of Jerusalem)
1205–1218	Hugh I
1218–1253	Henry I
1253–1267	Hugh II
1267–1284	Hugh III (1269–1284, also King of Jerusalem)
1284–1285	John I (also King of Jerusalem)
1285–1324	Henry II (1286–1291, also King of Jerusalem)
1324–1359	Hugh IV
1359–1369	Peter I
1369–1382	Peter II
1382–1398	James I

Byzantine Emperors during the Crusading Era

1081–1118	Alexius I Comnenus
1118–1143	John II Comnenus
1143–1180	Manuel I Comnenus
1180–1183	Alexius II Comnenus
1183–1185	Andronicus I Comnenus
1185–1195	Isaac II Angelus
1195–1203	Alexius III Angelus
1203–1204	Isaac II Angelus and Alexius IV
1204	Alexius Murzuphlus
1261–1282	Michael VIII Palaeologus
1282–1328	Andronicus II Palaeologus
1328–1341	Andronicus III Palaeologus
1341–1391	John V Palaelogus
1347–1354	John VI Cantacuzenus
1390	John VII Palaeologus

Latin Emperors of Constantinople

1204–1205	Baldwin I of Flanders
1206–1216	Henry of Hainault
1217	Peter of Courtenay

1217–1219   Yolanda (daughter of Peter)
1221–1228   Robert of Courtenay
1228–1261   Baldwin II (1231–1237, John of Brienne, co-ruler)

The Major Muslim Rulers

1127–1146   Zengi
1146–1174   Nur al-Din
1174–1193   Saladin
1193–1200   Civil war in Muslim provinces
1200–1218   al-Adil (Saladin's brother), sultan of Egypt and Syria
1218–1238   al-Kamil, sultan in Egypt
1238–1260   Civil wars resume; short, contested sultanates
1260–1277   Baybars seizes sultanate in Egypt; Mamluk period begins
1279–1290   Qalawan seizes Mamluk throne
1290–1293   al-Khalil (son of Qalawan)

List of Credits

Black and white images

1.1 Photograph of Jerusalem.

1.2 Pilgrims to Jerusalem and Santiago. Twelfth-century sculpture on the tympanum of the Church of St. Lazare at Autun, France. Photo after Grivot and Zarnecki, *Gislebertus, Sculptor of Autun*, pl. R.

2.1 Peter the Hermit riding his donkey. From an illuminated manuscript, ca. 1270. Bibliothèque nationale de France, Paris. Arsenal Bible, MS. 3139 f. 176v.

2.2 Crusader embraced by his wife. Twelfth-century sculpture from the cloister of the priory of Belval in Lorraine, France. Conway Library, The Courtauld Institute of Art, London.

2.3 "Monstrous Races of the World." A twelfth-century crusader © British Library Board. All rights reserved. HRLEY.2799 f243r.

2.4 Muslim soldier with his heavy sword. Freer Gallery of Art, Smithsonian Institution, Washington, DC. Purchase F1953.91.

2.5 Knight kneeling in prayer. © British Library Board. All rights reserved. Royal.2.A.XXII f220.

3.1 Siege scene with mangonel. Pierpont Morgan Library, New York. MS M.638, f.12r.

3.2 The siege of Nicaea. Bibliothèque nationale de France, Paris. MS. Fr. 2630 f. 22v.

3.3 The siege of Antioch. Bibliothèque nationale de France, Paris. MS. Fr. 9084, f. 53r.

3.4 Pilgrims praying at the Holy Sepulchre. Biblioteca Medicea Laurenziana, Florence. MS. Upon concession from the Ministry for Cultural Assets and Activities. Plu.LXI.10, *History of Outremer*, Fol. 89v, Bk. 9, Ch. 1.

4.1 The coronation of Baldwin I. Biblioteca Medicea Laurenziana, Florence. Upon concession from the Ministry for Cultural Assets and Activities. MS. Plu.LXI.10, *History of Outremer*, Fol. 994, Bk. 10, Ch. 1.

4.2 Pilgrim being attacked. Courtesy of akg-images. MS. Fr. 823.

4.3 Krak des Chevaliers. Courtesy of Sonia Halliday Photographs/Jane Taylor. SY25-8-15 JT.

5.1 Guardians of the Holy Sepulchre. Sculpture from the tympanum of Strasbourg cathedral. Fondation de l'Œuvre Notre-Dame, Strasbourg, France.

6.1 Crusader canteen. Thirteenth-century canteen, made in Syria. Freer Gallery of Art, Smithsonian Institution, Washington, DC. Purchase F1941.10.

6.2 The coronation of Baldwin III. Bibliothèque nationale de France, Paris. MS. Fr. 2824 f. 102v.

6.3 Patriarch of Antioch exposed on the citadel by Reynaud de Châtillon. Bibliothèque nationale de France, Paris. MS. Fr. 9084, f. 232v.

6.4 The Battle of Hattin. Saladin seizes the True Cross. With the permission of the Master and Fellows of Corpus Christi College, Cambridge. CCC MS 26, f. 140r.

6.5 Saladin ravaging the Holy Land. © British Library Board. All rights reserved. MS.Y.T.12 f161.

7.1 The siege of Acre, 1190. © British Library Board. All rights reserved. ADD.15268 f101v.

7.2 Philip and Richard receive the keys to Acre, 1191. Illustration in *Grandes Chroniques de France* (fourteenth century). Bibliothèque nationale de France, Paris. MS. Fr. 2813, f. 238v.

7.3 The siege of Constantinople, 1204. An illustration from Geoffrey de Villehardouin's *Chronicle of the Fourth Crusade*. Bodleian Library, University of Oxford. MS. Laud. Misc. 587, fol. 1.

7.4 The torture of the heretics. Bibliothèque nationale de France, Paris. MS. Latin 9187, f. 29v.

8.1 Depiction of the Mongols as cannibalistic savages. Illustration by Matthew Paris, from his *Chronica Majora* (ca. 1255). With the permission of the Master and Fellows of Corpus Christi College, Cambridge. CCC MS 16 f. 167r.

8.2 Blanche of Castile instructing her son, Louis IX. Pierpont Morgan Library, New York. Gift; J.P. Morgan (1867–1943); 1924. MS M.240, fol. 8r.

9.1 The fall of Acre, 1291. Bibliothèque nationale de France, Paris. MS. Fr. 2825, f. 361v.

9.2 The burning of the Templars. ©British Library Board. All rights reserved. Royal.20.C.VII f44v.

Color Plates

1 Map of Jerusalem. Twelfth-century map of Crusader Jerusalem and sur-rounding holy sites. Koninklijke Bibliotheek, The National Library of the Netherlands, The Hague. MS. 76 F5, fol. 1r.

2 Playing chess at Shaizar. Bibliothèque municipale, Lyon, France. MS 828 fol. 160v.

3 Page from the Melisende Psalter (ca. 1131–1143) depicting Christ's entry into Jerusalem. © British Library Board. All rights reserved. Egerton 1139, f. 5v.

4 Thirteenth-century decorated terra-cotta tile with roundels of Richard and Saladin. From Chertsey Abbey, Surrey. © British Library Board. All rights reserved/ The Bridgeman Art Library.

5   Women fleeing from mounted Muslim soldiers. © British Library
    Board. All rights reserved. ADD.27376 f45.

6   Saint Louis setting out on Crusade. Bibliotheca Medicea Laurenziana,
    Florence. MS Plu.LXI.10, f.336v.

7   Mamluk warriors in training. © British Library Board. All rights
    reserved. Add 18866, fol. 140.

8   The Nine Worthies. From a late-fourteenth-century manuscript show-
    ing Godfrey de Bouillon as one of the three Christian "worthies."
    Bibliothèque nationale de France, Paris. MS. Fr. 12559, f. 125v.

9   Charles and the Spectacle. Bibliothèque nationale de France, Paris. MS.
    Fr. 2813 f. 473v.

Maps

1.1   Islamic World, ca. 800. From Barbara H. Rosenwein, *A Short History of the
      Middle Ages,* 2nd ed. (Peterborough, ON: Broadview Press, 2004) 103.

1.2   Christianity and Islam on the eve of the First Crusade, 1096. G.S.P.
      Freeman-Grenville, *Historical Atlas of the Middle East* (New York: Simon
      and Schuster, 1993) 47.

2.1   Crusaders' routes to Constantinople. From Thomas Asbridge, *The First
      Crusade: A New History* (Oxford: Oxford UP, 2004) 90.

4.1   The Crusader States, ca. 1140. From Barbara H. Rosenwein, *A Short
      History of the Middle Ages*, 2nd ed. (Peterborough, ON: Broadview Press,
      2004) 184.

4.2   Jerusalem in the twelfth century under crusader occupation. From
      Angus Konstam, *Historical Atlas of the Crusades* (New York: Checkmark
      Books, 2002) 72. Rights secured through the Copyright Clearance
      Center.

5.1   The Near East during the Second Crusade, 1146–1148. From Kenneth
      M. Setton, ed., *A History of the Crusades*, vol. I (Philadelphia: U of
      Pennsylvania P, 1969) opposite p. 506. Reprinted by permission of the U
      of Wisconsin P.

7.1 The sack of Constantinople by the Fourth Crusade, 1204. From Angus Konstam, *Historical Atlas of the Crusades* (New York: Checkmark Books, 2002) 160. Rights secured through the Copyright Clearance Center.

7.2 The Fifth Crusade, 1218–1221. From Kenneth M. Setton, ed., *A History of the Crusades,* vol. II (Philadelphia: U of Pennsylvania P, 1969) 486. Reprinted by permission of the U of Wisconsin P.

8.1 The Mongol Empire, ca. 1260–1350. From Barbara H. Rosenwein, *A Short History of the Middle Ages*, 2nd ed. (Peterborough, ON: Broadview Press, 2004) 252.

9.1 Spain and Portugal, 1150–1250. From Kenneth M. Setton, ed., *A History of the Crusades,* vol. III (Philadelphia: U of Pennsylvania P, 1975). On second page following p. 434. Reprinted by permission of the U of Wisconsin P.

10.1 The Growth of the Ottoman Empire, 1307–1481. From Patrick K. O'Brien, ed., *Atlas of World History* (Oxford UP, 1999) 97.

10.2 The Battle of Nicopolis. From Aziz Suryal Atiya, *The Crusade of Nicopolis* (London: Methuen & Co., 1934) 83.

A Selected Bibliography of the Crusades

Narrative Histories

There is an outpouring of research now being done on the crusades. From among the many fine general histories, I recommend the following:

France, John. *The Crusades and the Expansion of Catholic Christendom*. London and New York: Routledge, 2005.

Hillenbrand, Carole. *The Crusades: Islamic Perspectives*. Chicago: Fitzroy Dearborn Publishers, 1999. As the title indicates, this is from the Islamic point of view; it is therefore unusually valuable.

Madden, Thomas F. *The New Concise History of the Crusades*. Lanham, MD: Rowman & Littlefield Publishers, 2005.

Mayer, Hans Eberhard. *The Crusades*. Trans. John Gillingham. Oxford: Oxford UP, 1972. Although not recent, this remains an important work with a distinctive point of view.

Riley-Smith, Jonathan. *The Crusades: A History*, 2nd ed. New Haven and London: Yale UP, 2005. Riley-Smith is the preeminent crusades historian of his generation, and his history is a detailed and important study.

Runciman, Steven. *A History of the Crusades*. 3 vols. Cambridge: Cambridge UP, 1951–55. New York: Harper & Row, 1964–67. A masterpiece of scholarly writing, with a pro-Byzantine perspective.

Setton, Kenneth M., general ed. *A History of the Crusades*. 2nd ed., 6 vols. Madison: U of Wisconsin P, 1969–1989. An encyclopedic study of all aspects of the crusades.

Tyerman, Christopher. *God's War: A New History of the Crusades*. Cambridge: Belknap Press of Harvard UP, 2006.

On a specialized subject covering the whole period

Mitchell, Piers D. *Medicine in the Crusades: Warfare, Wounds and the Medieval Surgeon*. Cambridge and New York: Cambridge UP, 2004.

Collected Essays by Outstanding Scholars

Bull, Marcus, and Norman Housley, eds. *The Experience of Crusading*, vol. 1. Cambridge: Cambridge UP, 2003.

Edbury, Peter, and Jonathan Phillips, eds. *The Experience of Crusading*, vol. 2. Cambridge: Cambridge UP, 2003.

Kedar, Benjamin Z, ed. *Franks, Muslims and Oriental Christians in the Levant*. Aldershot, Hampshire, UK: Ashgate Publishing, 2006.

Madden, Thomas F., ed. *The Crusades*. Oxford: Blackwell Publishers, 2002.

———, ed. *Crusades. The Illustrated History*. London: Duncan Baird Publishers, 2004; Ann Arbor: U of Michigan P, 2005.

Riley-Smith, Jonathan, ed. *The Oxford History of the Crusades*. Oxford: Oxford UP, 1999.

Riley-Smith, Jonathan, ed. *The Oxford Illustrated History of the Crusades*. Oxford: Oxford UP, 2000.

Saunders, John J. *Aspects of the Crusades*. 2nd ed. Christchurch, NZ: U of Canterbury P, 1962.

Internet Sources

The single best and most reliable Internet source for medieval documents in translation, including the documents on the crusades, is www.fordham.edu/halsall/sbook.html (International Medieval Sourcebook).

For military history, see www.deremilitari.org, the website of De Re Militari: The Society for Medieval Military History.

For the military orders, the ORB Online Encyclopedia contains a wealth of information. It can be accessed at www.the-orb.net/encyclop/religion/monastic/milindex.html.

Primary Sources in Translation

The most valuable and interesting books to read are the original sources. Fine English translations are easily available. The following have been cited in the text:

Collected Sources (most of these cover several centuries of crusading history)

Allen, S.J., and Emilie Amt. *The Crusades: A Reader*. Peterborough, ON: Broadview Press, 2003.

Baldwin, Marshall W. *Christianity through the Thirteenth Century*. New York: Harper & Row, 1970.

Barber, Malcolm, and Keith Bate, trans. and annotated. *The Templars: Selected Sources*. Manchester and New York: Manchester UP, 2002.

Brundage, James A. *The Crusades: A Documentary Survey*. Milwaukee: Marquette UP, 1962.

Falkner, R.P. *Translations and Reprints from the Original Sources of European History*. New York: AMS Press, 1971.

Gabrieli, Francesco. *Arab Historians of the Crusades*. Berkeley and Los Angeles: U of California P, 1969.

Henderson, Ernest F., ed. and trans. *Select Historical Documents of the Middle Ages*. London: George Bell & Sons, 1896.

Housley, Norman, ed. and trans. *Documents on the Later Crusades, 1274–1580*. New York: St. Martin's Press, 1996.

Kobler, Franz, ed. *A Treasury of Jewish Letters*, vol. 1. Philadelphia: The Jewish Publication Society of America, 1953.

Krey, August C. *The First Crusade: The Accounts of Eyewitnesses and Participants*. 1921. Gloucester, MA: Peter Smith, 1958.

Munro, Dana C., ed. and trans. *Urban and the Crusaders*. 1895. New York: AMS, 1971.

Peters, Edward, ed. *Christian Society and the Crusades, 1198–1229*. Trans. John J. Gavigan. Philadelphia: U of Pennsylvania P, 1971.

———, ed. *The First Crusade: The Chronicle of Fulcher of Chartres and Other Source Materials*. 2nd ed. Philadelphia: U of Pennsylvania P, 1998.

Peters, F.E. *Jerusalem*. Princeton, NJ: Princeton UP, 1985.

Rosenwein, Barbara, ed. *Reading the Middle Ages*. Peterborough, ON: Broadview Press, 2006.

Setton, Kenneth M., and Henry R. Winckler. *Great Problems in European Civilization*. 2nd ed. Englewood Cliffs, NJ: Prentice-Hall, 1966.

Tierney, Brian. *The Crisis of State and State, 1050–1300*. Englewood Cliffs, NJ: Prentice-Hall, 1964.

Individual Primary Sources

Abbot Daniel. *Pilgrimage in the Holy Land*. Trans. C.W. Wilson. London: Palestine Pilgrims' Text Society, vol. 4, 1895. New York: AMS Press, rpt., 1971.

Anonymous Pilgrims. *Anonymous Pilgrims I–VIII (Eleventh and Twelfth Centuries)*. Trans. A. Stewart. London: Palestine Pilgrims' Text Society, 1894. New York: AMS Press, 1971.

Comnena, Anna. *The Alexiad*. Trans. E.R.A. Sewter. London: Penguin Books, 1960.

Jean de Joinville. "The Life of Saint Louis," in *Chronicles of the Crusades*. Trans. M.R.B. Shaw. London: Penguin Books, 1963.

Geoffrey de Villehardouin. "The Conquest of Constantinople," in *Chronicles of the Crusades*. Trans. M.R.B. Shaw. London: Penguin Books, 1963.

Jacques de Vitry. *History of Jerusalem*. Trans. A. Stewart. London: Palestine Pilgrims' Text Society, vol. 11, 1896. New York: AMS Press, 1971.

Eidelberg, Shlomo, ed. and trans. *The Jews and the Crusaders: The Hebrew Chronicles of the First and Second Crusades.* Madison: U of Wisconsin P, 1977.

Felix Fabri. *The Book of the Wanderings of Felix Fabri.* Trans. A. Stewart. 2 vols. London: Palestine Pilgrims' Text Society, vols. 7–10, 1893. New York: AMS Press, 1971.

Fulcher of Chartres. *A History of the Expedition to Jerusalem, 1095–1127.* Trans. Frances Rita Ryan. New York: W.W. Norton & Co., 1973.

———. *Chronicle of the First Crusade.* Trans. Martha E. McGinty. Philadelphia: U of Pennsylvania P, 1941.

Rodulfus Glaber, *The Five Books of Histories.* Trans. John France and Paul Reynolds. Oxford: Clarendon Press, 1989.

Hill, Rosalind, ed. and trans. *Gesta Francorum: The Deeds of the Franks and the Other Pilgrims to Jerusalem.* Oxford: Clarendon Press, 1962.

Ibn al-Qalansi. *The Damascus Chronicle of the Crusades.* Ed. and trans. HA.R. Gibb. London: Luzac & Co., 1967.

Ibn Battuta, *The Travels of Ibn Battuta, 1325–1354.* 2 vols. Trans. H.A.R. Gibb. Cambridge: Cambridge UP, 1958–1962.

Usamah Ibn-Munqidh, *Memoirs of an Arab-Syrian Gentleman.* Trans. Philip K. Hitti. 1927. Beirut: Khayats, 1964.

John of Wurzburg. *Description of the Holy Land.* Trans. Aubrey Stewart. London: Palestine Pilgrims' Text Society, vol. 5, 1896. New York: AMS Press, 1971.

Levine, Robert, trans. *Gesta Dei per Francos: The Deeds of God through the Franks.* Woodbridge, UK: The Boydell Press, 1997.

Liudprand of Cremona. *The Embassy to Constantinople and Other Writings.* Ed. John J. Norwich. Trans. F.A. Wright. London: J. M. Dent; Rutland, VT: Charles E. Tuttle Co., 1993.

Nasir-I-Khusrau. *Diary of a Journey through Syria and Palestine.* Trans. and annotated G. Le Strange. London: Palestine Pilgrims' Text Society, vol. 4, 1893. New York: AMS Press, 1971.

Odo of Deuil. *De Profectione Ludovici VII in Orientam.* Ed. and trans. Virginia G. Berry. New York: Columbia UP, 1948.

Oliver of Paderborn, *The Capture of Damietta.* Trans. John J. Gavigan. Philadelphia: U of Pennsylvania P, 1948.

Otto of Freising and his continuator, Rahewin. *The Deeds of Frederick Barbarossa.* Trans. Charles C. Mierow. 1953. Toronto: U of Toronto P, 1994.

Matthew Paris. *English History*, vols. 2–3. Trans. Rev. J. A. Giles. London: Henry G. Bohn, 1953–54.

———. *The Illustrated Chronicles of Matthew Paris.* Ed. and trans. Richard Vaughan. Cambridge: Alan Sutton Publishing, 1993.

Pope Gregory VII. *Correspondence: Selected Letters from the Registrum.* Ed. and trans. Ephraim Emerton. New York: Columbia UP, 1969.

Robert of Clari. *The Conquest of Constantinople.* Trans. Edgar Holmes McNeal. 1936. New York: Columbia UP, 1969.

Saewulf. *Pilgrimage to Jerusalem and the Holy Land.* Trans. bishop of Clifton. London: Palestine Pilgrims' Text Society, vol. 4, 1896. New York: AMS Press, 1971.

St. Bernard of Clairvaux. *In Praise of the New Knighthood.* Trans. Conrad Greenia. Kalamazoo, MI: Cistercian Fathers Series 19, 1977.

Theodorich. *Description of the Holy Places.* Trans. Aubrey Stewart. London: Palestine Pilgrims' Text Society, vol. 5, 1896. New York: AMS Press, 1971.

William of Tyre. *A History of Deeds Done Beyond the Sea.* 2 vols. Trans. and annotated E.A. Babcock and A.C. Krey. New York: Columbia UP, 1943.

Index